THE GLOBAL HISTORY OF ORGANIC FARMING

The Global History
of Organic Farming

GREGORY A. BARTON

OXFORD
UNIVERSITY PRESS

OXFORD
UNIVERSITY PRESS

Great Clarendon Street, Oxford, OX2 6DP,
United Kingdom

Oxford University Press is a department of the University of Oxford.
It furthers the University's objective of excellence in research, scholarship,
and education by publishing worldwide. Oxford is a registered trade mark of
Oxford University Press in the UK and in certain other countries

First Edition published in 2018

Impression: 1

Published in the United States of America by Oxford University Press
198 Madison Avenue, New York, NY 10016, United States of America

British Library Cataloguing in Publication Data
Data available

Library of Congress Control Number: 2017954533

ISBN 978–0–19–964253–3

Printed in Great Britain by
Clays Ltd, St Ives plc

In memory of my Grandfather, James Gentry Russel,
Oregon farmer and gentleman

Acknowledgments

This book owes a great deal to many individuals and institutions, without whose support the story of organic farming as told in this book would be impossible. I worked on this project while employed as a permanent Research Fellow at The Australian National University, and as Professor of History at my current employers, Western Sydney University and the University of Johannesburg. The Australian Research Council generously provided a grant that took me to archives around the globe. Dr. Frederik Kruger, one of the leading lights in the history of ecological research from the 1980s to the present, generously read this draft and offered innumerable constructive comments. Dr. Adam Lucas, historian of science at the University of Wollongong, helpfully read the early chapters. Michael Bennett kindly read numerous chapters. An initial paper on the topic benefited from a seminar run by Dr. Brett Bennett and Anthony Hopkins in the School of Humanities and Communication Arts at Western Sydney University. Dr. Tatshushi Fujihara, from Kyoto University, kindly scanned and forwarded vital documents on the history of organic farming in Japan, including sections of his own work. Toshi Asakura-Ward translated these documents from Japanese into English and without his work, funded by Western Sydney University, the story of the organic farming movement in Japan would not have been made available to the English-speaking world. My mentor, Harold Perkin, now deceased, continued to inspire with his example of understanding global history through the analysis of social history. The *Journal of Agricultural History, Itinerario* and Palgrave Macmillan have generously allowed me to reprint sections of two articles and a book chapter, respectively. I have benefited from discussions with the historian John Paull and from the organic farmer Steve Solomon in Tasmania who runs an extensive online archive, the Soil and Health Library.

My greatest debt is owed, however, to the Matthaei family, who carefully preserved the archives of Albert Howard, and his first and second wives, Gabrielle and Louise. Long thought lost, these newly found papers form a core middle section of this work. The family has kindly allowed me free reign to use this material where the evidence has led, and never intimated any restrictions on my conclusions. I am grateful to them for their generosity. St. John's College, University of Cambridge, has also kindly accepted the offer of the archival collection from the Matthaei family so that future generations will be able to access the papers. And, finally, I must mention my mother, Ina Mae Barton (née Russell), who used her considerable genealogical skills to hunt down and find the extended relatives of Louise Howard that led to this discovery. She also transcribed the considerable correspondence of Gabrielle Howard. The limitations of this work—which on a topic so vast, will prove to be many—are my responsibility alone.

Table of Contents

1. Roots of the Organic Challenge   1

2. The Cultural Soil of Organic Farming   20

3. Albert Howard and the World as Shropshire   49

4. The Howards in India   62

5. The Search for Pre-Modern Wisdom   80

6. The Compost Wars   94

7. To the Empire and Beyond   118

8. The Globalization of Organic Farming   156

9. The 1980s to the Present   184

10. Organic Farming and the Challenge of Globalization   197

Bibliography   205
Index   223

1

Roots of the Organic Challenge

Almost a hundred years ago the predecessors of the organic farming movement threw down the gauntlet and challenged modern agriculture and, in particular, the doctrine of progress that informed it, with its emphasis on bigger as better, machines as improvement, and chemicals as fit products for fertilizers, pesticides, and food. Organic farming can be defined as a system of agriculture that relies on ecological processes to minimalize or eliminate the need for chemical fertilizers and pesticides in the production of crops. Organic farming is a protocol, a system based on philosophical assumptions about how nature works. It is a thoughtful and a self-conscious practice. It is also a cultural movement and at times engages the Christian tradition of stewardship and the domination of humans over nature. It is allied with sustainable agriculture in the past (because it drew inspiration from the past), but it is a relatively new movement in human history, born out of a reaction to the perceived failures of industrial agriculture. We should not conflate organic farming with sustainable agriculture, which is a term coined in the 1980s to broaden the appeal of organic farming to include other approaches that did not carry the same political opposition. Sustainable agriculture is more of a goal than a process.[1] Political opposition to organic farming abounded because in many ways it challenged modernity itself, and the enlightenment doctrine of progress that the future will always improve. Organic farming turned the gaze of millions of people, institutions, and governments backwards to look at the past as a source of guidance and wisdom. It changed how farmers over large swaths of the earth treat soil, and the crops grown on the soil. It changed how birds feed on crops, and the quality of water that drains into our streams, rivers, and oceans. It changed our consumer habits, and in many ways our ethics, demanding that we think about how our food is grown and the effect our daily habits have on nature.

This book is a critical appreciation of the history of the organic farming challenge. It covers the beginning of the movement in the early and mid-twentieth century up to nearly contemporary times when the organic farming movement transformed

---

[1] See a discussion of the introduction of the term "sustainable agriculture" by J. Patrick Madden in *The Early Years: the LISA, SARE, and ACE Programs*. Available online at: https://www.google.com.au/url?sa=t&rct=j&q=&esrc=s&source=web&cd=2&ved=0ahUKEwi7svyg9Z3UAhXDUZQKHRDSBYEQFggsMAE&url=http%3A%2F%2Fwww.sare.org%2Fcontent%2Fdownload%2F50101%2F661407%2FThe_Early_Years_(Madden).pdf%3Finlinedownload%3D1&usg=AFQjCNF3zBQStYFZNsvtjDCB2mOS4lcklw [accessed June 2, 2017].

from a cluster of outsider organizations and achieved mainstream acceptance in the 1980–90s. It focuses particularly on the towering personalities of Albert Howard (the preeminent figure in the founding of organic farming) and his second wife Louise. Following the trail of newly discovered archives this book unveils Louise as a pivotal—and entirely overlooked—champion of the environmental movement, a movement that she profoundly impacted in the decades following the Second World War. This book opens new trails for investigation that are only touched upon here: the fascinating story of how small circles of civic minded individuals can launch global change; how movements fermenting in isolation or in abeyance spring suddenly onto the public landscape; and, not least, the unsung role of women in science, reminding us that much of the past is undiscovered, and may still bring forth, in the immortal words of Chaucer: "new corn from old fields."

The organic farming movement changed the world. It is a bewilderingly complex and surprising story, chock full of contradictions that sprouted and thrived from barren soil, fertilized by unlikely impulses and personalities. Organic farming is likely to continue to challenge the smug assumption that science is incorruptible by vested interests and industrialization and that humans have the knowledge to ignore natural processes with impunity. This book in turn excavates the myths that sustain the ethical and spiritual appeal of organic farming. It seeks not to advocate or deconstruct, but to explain and understand. It also focuses on the highlights of a movement whose roots are legion and almost impossibly tangled, and whose influence is vast.

The organic farming movement arose in a witch's brew of disparate elements—stirred together to create a potent movement that has affected land use and consumer habits in almost every part of the globe. Formerly unallied forces came together in the early and mid-twentieth century to produce a new movement dedicated to the restoration of soil fertility, human health, and nature itself. As shown in this book, organic farming constituted the core of a middle stage of the environmental movement, tying together the threads of the earlier conservation movement with the modern environmental movement of the 1960s and 70s. It is not possible to identify any single intellectual cause of organic farming. Instead its roots reveal a tangled skein of interacting forces. We can however trace a broad outline of these ideas and, more particularly, how these ideas shaped the actions of individuals, social movements, and legislation. We can even identify the main founder of organic farming, Albert Howard, though it is possible to ascribe too much to a single person or even to a set of organizations. The main trunk of its growth occurred in Britain and its imperial outposts in Asia, Africa, and North America, with offshoots and allied impulses in Europe, Japan, and most parts of the globe, until by the twenty-first century the organic farming movement has touched every region on earth.

A cluster of ideas came together in the 1920s–30s that shaped the origin of organic farming. The utilitarian impulse of the global conservation movement is one element; rural romanticism another. Likewise, the tradition of yeoman independence in England, the British settlement colonies, and the orientalist hunt for hidden wisdom in the East that would restore lost traditional values also all played a role. The advance of science provided further understanding of the ecology of the soil in the late nineteenth and early twentieth century. Further, a society weary from the horrors of a mechanized war from 1915–18 yearned to return to a simpler rural life and desired to find space for personal and spiritual healing. Fascism, with its emphasis on the vital link between culture and the soil also played no small part, as did many Christian, and sometimes Hindu, and Buddhist followers. By 1980 the movement had gained traction with, and public acceptance from, the very corporate, government, and democratic institutions its followers had often railed against. Advocates hailed from both the left and the right of the political spectrum, attracting the support of green activists, neo-traditionalists, socialists, capitalists, and even British royals, such as Prince Charles. Born as a marriage between science and romanticism, it remained in abeyance in the mid-twentieth century and gained acceptance and popularity as a transplant into a materialistic consumer market in the latter decades of the twentieth century. It remains to be seen if, in the twenty-first century, organic farming will thrive as a potted plant in its new corporate and bureaucratic plot, or lose the vital ecological and spiritual principles that inspired its founding.

AGRICULTURE BEFORE THE INDUSTRIAL AGE

Agriculture is the cultivation of fields. The word "agriculture" is the conjunction of two Latin words, *ager* (field) and *colere* (cultivate), and suggests human skill, culture, and industry. In the contemporary age it also connotes scientific expertise, yet still retains overtones of religious feeling and national vitality. Agriculture embraces both crops and livestock; the biblical tale of Cain and Abel offering sacrifices of grain and meat illustrates how human history intertwined both plants and animals in agricultural practice and in myth. Agricultural history shades into the misty past and grew out of hunting and gathering into the domestication of animals and the planting of grains, roots, and other plants. It is only in the great river systems in Euro-Asia where we may detect the rise of agriculture, where shards of pottery and traces of civilization thousands of years before the Christian era reveal their secrets.

Humans, before industrial agriculture, did not always practice sustainable agriculture—that is agriculture practiced in a manner that did not deplete the soil and enabled more or less permanent cultivation. The flooding of the Nile River valley is a perfect example of farming in a sustainable fashion without design or intent. The Nile floods from the seasonal inundation flowing north from the tropical rains in north-east Africa that make their way to the sea through the longest river on earth breaching the banks in its lower reaches and spreading and depositing a fine layer of silt rich in nutrients, microorganisms, and minerals. Egyptian peasants did not aerate the soil, nor did they apply fertilizer and dung, or rotate crops to raise the fertility. Thus, the common error that before the industrial age almost all farmers practiced sustainable agriculture—or organic farming by default—cannot be maintained.[2]

Ancient farmers—except in a number of river systems—practiced slash and burn, or if they had no shortage of land, simply moved from plot to plot, in search of fresh soil fertility (an approach practiced by both nomad and pastoral settlers). In the early modern era, most of the land surface of the world still exhibited exactly this type of agriculture, with many European, Asian, Middle Eastern, and African farmers practicing intensive farming. Letting the ground lay fallow and applying manure to ploughed land enabled continued cultivation.[3] Yet even these approaches do not all fall under "sustainable" practices because they did not always maintain soil fertility over long periods, for a number of reasons. In central Asia, for instance, grazing cleared tree cover. Then farmland appeared, and finally invasions by Mongols and others decimated many populations, leaving the soil depleted of nutrients, unsuitable for crops, and open to erosion. In some cases, continued deforestation reduced rainfall, making agriculture difficult or impossible.[4]

In India, the farmer, though higher than the untouchables, toiled under the warrior and priestly caste. Indians burned dried cattle dung for fuel leaving few nutrients returned to the land. Because villagers did not compost human waste and return it to the fields, British imperial officials noticed a ring of verdant growth around villages where villagers deposited sewage. Before industrial fertilizers farmers in India survived by planting varieties of wheat and other crops that flourished with low nutrients. Some may consider this a variant of sustainable farming, but one cannot describe it as organic.

In Greece and Rome free citizens cultivated their own fields, rented to tenants, hired labor, or owned slaves to work the soil for them. As wealth collected at the top of Roman society, absentee landlords and sheep farming replaced many of the productive small farms, a process hastened by imports of cheap grain and other vegetable and fruit products. Virgil's *Georgics* present a romantic yearning for the lost culture of farming; an early echo of a similar process that took place in the age of industrial farming 1900 years later. In short, "ancient" farming techniques did not always equate to sustainable farming practice.

[2] Robert C. Allen explains how these sustainable practices were used by elites to sustain a stable state structure in "Agriculture and the Origins of the State in Ancient Egypt," *Explorations in Economic History* 34/2 (1997): 135–54. Christian Isendahl and Michael E. Smith argue that, unlike cities in Euro-Asia the Mayas and Aztecs practices a sustainable agriculture within low density urban areas. See "Sustainable Agrarian Urbanism: The Low Density Cites of the Mayas and Aztecs," *Cities* 31 (2013): 132–43. For an excellent account of the history of "sustainability" as a concept see Paule Warde, "The Invention of Sustainability," *Modern Intellectual History* 8/1 (2011): 153–70.
[3] Peter M. Jones argued that the rise of the knowledge economy in the latter part of the eighteenth century broadly influenced agricultural changes in this period. See *Agricultural enlightenment: knowledge, technology, and nature, 1750–1840* (Oxford, 2016).
[4] For a good summary of the scientific and historical literature on how human activity in Central Asia has led to deforestation see N. Kharin, *Vegetation Degradation in Central Asia Under the Impact of Human Activities,* (Dordrecht, 2011). See especially Chapters One and Two; Robert Costanza, Lisa Graumlich, and William L. Steffen, *Sustainability or Collapse?: An Integrated History and Future of People on Earth,* (Cambridge Mass., 2007).

THE AGRICULTURAL REVOLUTION

The low countries of Europe—England, Flanders, and Germany among others—experienced an agricultural revolution in the eighteenth century that the Industrial Revolution only hastened; a spectrum of improvement in output that has continued to the present day.[5] But even this revolution has deeper roots. The Cistercian order proved innovative not only in the spiritual realm, but in the agricultural as well, reducing land that lay fallow by planting legumes to fix nitrogen in the soil. They utilized roots and fodder crops that increased animal stocks and, in return, produced more manure that farmers then returned to the soil. Meanwhile, the Dutch practiced poldering—draining tidal flatlands and enclosing the former seabed into farmland. Not scientists, but farmers launched these improvements.[6]

In the seventeenth century English farmers improved agricultural productivity through marling and manures. Marl is a sedimentary rock composed of fine grains high in calcium carbonate from the breakdown of shells. Enclosure also raised productivity. The latter displaced many small cottagers and farmers who had traditional relationships to the landed elite and created a surplus labor pool that migrated to the cities. When an aristocrat paid out the small farmer for enclosure the farmer did not have sufficient funds to buy more land. He usually spent the money quickly and swiftly fell in status from a small semi-independent cottager or farmer with rights to the commons to a farm laborer paid lowly wages. Often he migrated, with his family, to the towns.

The botanist John Ray toured the southeast coast of Scotland and observed that farmers rarely allowed exhausted soils to lay fallow, but manured the farms with seaweed, an example of incomplete attempts to sustain fertility. Elsewhere in the British Isles, particularly England, turnips as a winter crop added nitrogen, and clover broke up and aerated the hardened soil pan. John Houghton, an apothecary and English fellow of the Royal Society, wrote one of the first treatises on agriculture which correctly outlined the role of nitrogen. In a *Collections on Husbandry and Trade* (1691) he wrote that,

> Some in Essex have their fallow after turnips, which feed their sheep in winter, by which means the turnips are scooped, and so made capable to hold dews and rain water, which, by corrupting, imbibes the nitre of the air, and when the shell breaks it runs about and fertilizes. By feeding the sheep, the land is dunged as if it had been folded; and those turnips, though few or none be carried off for human use, are a very excellent improvement, nay, some reckon it so, though they only plough the turnips in without feeding.[7]

---

[5] Frank Uekötter traces the history of the environmental movement in Germany against the backdrop of rapid modernization in *The Greenest Nation? A New History of German Environmentalism* (Cambridge Mass., 2014).

[6] B. H. Slicher van Bath, *The Agrarian History of Western Europe, A. D. 500–1850*, trans. Olive Ordish (London, 1963), 178.

[7] As quoted in W. R. Park, "The Progress of Agriculture," *The Farmer's Magazine*, 32 (1867): 142.

Yeomen, who usually rented their farms from large landowners or owned their land outright, drove improvements. They often read widely and highly prized books and tracts recommending agricultural reform. Other factors played a role in the agricultural revolution as well. The rise in urban population and the demand for foodstuffs in the seventeenth century created a profitable market and a steady incentive for higher food outputs. Since serfdom proved impossible to maintain after the Black Death, farmers intensified effort to save on labor costs. In addition, the Glorious Revolution established absolute property rights for landlords, eliminating most feudal obligations.[8] The new cash economy prized contract over traditional feudal obligations. Thus, while yeomen farmers lacked the wealth of the lords to whom they often paid rent, they nonetheless remained largely independent and responsible for their own production and profit, which in turn increased the incentive for creativity and gave rise to an entrepreneurial farm culture in England.[9]

These developments stand in direct contrast to France and Imperial Russia where feudal landlords profited from the serfs and sharecroppers who bore the brunt of agricultural labor throughout the eighteenth century. While the Junkers in eastern Prussia, as well as the Amish, showed advances in productivity, England led the way.[10] England's scientific revolution and advances in education, credit, and the rise of prices during the Napoleonic Wars radically raised Scottish productivity as well. The Corn Laws of 1815 kept prices higher even as food imports into Britain resumed after the war.

Amateurs and entrepreneurial farmers drove agricultural innovation, not scientists. Farmers in the nineteenth century widely recognized this fact and may have even influenced scientists like Albert Howard, who saw like many farmers a disconnect between the abstract and airy formulations of the Royal Society and applications in the field. "What has science done for agriculture?" a Highland agricultural journal asked, with some justification, in 1842; practical farmers, the author noted, lacked confidence in science because almost no men of science initiated innovations in farm technology.[11] While true in 1844, particularly regarding farm implements, and true also of the effect of the early Industrial Revolution, scientists soon inserted themselves into agriculture in a revolutionary way, and the advances of the second Industrial Revolution in chemistry especially altered agriculture almost beyond recognition in the next century. Hydraulics, physics, genetics, botany, and chemistry played a leading role.[12]

[8] Adam Lucas discusses how in some parts of England and Scotland lords managed to maintain feudal obligations long after this, even into the early twentieth century in some parts of the West Country. See *Wind, Water, Work: Ancient Medieval Milling Technology* (Leiden, 2011), 59.

[9] Daniel E. Vasey, *An Ecological History of Agriculture: 10,000 BC–AD 10,000* (Ames, Iowa, 1992), 220.

[10] Ibid., 222.

[11] *Highland Agricultural Society, Transactions*, (March, 1842) in J. Loudon, *Encyclopedia of Agriculture Edition* (5th Edition), (London, 1844), 1, 295.

[12] Fred W. Kohlmeyer and Floyd L. Herum, "Science and Engineering in Agriculture: A Historical Perspective," *Technology and Culture*, 2/4 (Autumn, 1961): 372.

Sir Humphry Davy preceded the famed Justus von Liebig in the analysis of the chemical composition of soil by three decades, publishing in 1815 a series of lectures delivered—beginning in 1792—to the Board of Agriculture. He approached the problems of soil fertility as a chemist, analyzing the types of soils and determining the chemical elements that allowed crops to flourish. He told the story of how famed botanist Joseph Banks put into his hands a soil sample from Lincolnshire, "remarkable for sterility." He then added lime, which "converted the sulphate [of iron] into manure," producing a soil capable of growing abundant crops. The appeal of his work as a scientist grew exponentially with these lectures. He argued that plants themselves contained the clues for what nutrients must be put into the soil. This he ascertained by burning the plant and then examining the constituent parts of the ash.[13] Healthy soil had a balance of constituent parts derived from different strata of soil types that nature by happenstance "intimately blended together." To improve soils artificially, "the farmer cannot do better than imitate the processes of nature" by adding the missing elements.[14]

Farmers desperately desired to add needed nutrients to infertile soil. Sir Humphry Davy's *Elements of Agricultural Chemistry* placed him as the "supreme chemical authority" in Britain and the United States for a generation and launched a scientific approach to farming problems that would define the future.[15] Davy spoke poetically of the mysteries of nature and the limitation of human knowledge. In fact, he exhibited every sign of believing in a form of vitalism—a spiritual force that lay behind physical phenomenon—very similar to the concepts that organic farming activists later advocated. Davy helped launch the scientific investigation of agricultural problems that would soon provoke an anti-science and anti-specialist reaction, even as he also proclaimed the limits of science.

> Every discovery opens a new field for investigation of facts, [and] shows us the imperfection of our theories. It has justly been said, that the greater the circle of light, the greater the boundary of darkness by which it is surrounded.[16]

Historians of agriculture credit the German scientist Justus von Liebig, the founder of organic chemistry, with the radical changes in agriculture that led to the mass use of fertilizer and industrial farming. His contemporaries, such as the naturalist Alexander von Humboldt, held him in high prestige, and for good reason. Farmers generated the largest economic activity in every part of the world and the use of nitrogen fertilizers that Liebig advocated raised crop production and thus materially reduced the threat of famine.[17]

Liebig predicted that scientists would one day produce organic compounds like sugar and morphine from non-living entities. He thus argued against artificially dividing living and non-living processes into discrete polar opposites. He argued in

---

[13] Bath, The *Agrarian History of Western Europe*, 157.   [14] Ibid., 182.
[15] See Wyndham D. Miles, "Sir Humphrey Davie, the Prince of Agricultural Chemists," *Chymia*, 7 (1961): 126.
[16] Humphry Davy and John Davy, "Consolations in Travel—Dialogue V—The Chemical Philosopher," *The Collected Works of Sir Humphry Davy*, 9, (1840): 362.
[17] John D. Post, *The last great subsistence crisis in the Western World* (Baltimore, 1977).

his 1840 masterpiece, *Organic Chemistry in its Application to Agriculture and Physiology*, that chemistry could and should revolutionize agriculture. Farmers mistakenly assumed that humus produced healthy plants when it played no such role—a position organic farmers held in anathema less than a century after he penned his book. Liebig argued that plant production required only the minimum of all its needed nutrients, and thus the key to higher productivity lay in eliminating the deficiencies of the soil, not in overloading the soil with more nutrients by volume. The followers of Liebig analyzed the ash of plants for inorganic substances, such as iron, sulfur, calcium, sodium, phosphorus, and potassium. They then applied to the soil a solution containing these elements in the proportion to the deficiencies detected in the analyses in the belief that the plants would then absorb these elements through their roots.[18]

In England the Rothamsted Experimental Station, founded in 1843, advanced this new cause of "scientific husbandry." Its progenitor and financier, John Bennet Lawes, promoted superphosphates as well as Peruvian guano and nitrate of soda as fertilizers. *The Farmer's Magazine, Rural Affairs*, and the *Quarterly Journal of Agriculture* spread knowledge of new chemical fertilizers throughout Great Britain and its empire.[19] Other agricultural research stations soon followed. While private funds founded Rothamsted research station, government funds in Saxony funded the new Mockern research station in 1852, with other German states following suit. The United States launched the first agricultural research station in Connecticut in 1876, soon followed by many others with the land grant system of agricultural universities.[20]

The perennial shortage of animal manure inspired Lawes to launch experiments that increased crop production. His work led him to patent a new process that broke down phosphate rock with sulfuric acid (often called oil of vitriol in the nineteenth century), an acid that acted as a corrosive on metals. Mining operations produced sulfuric acid from the oxidation of iron sulfide. Putting these two ingredients together amounted to an inexpensive form of fertilizer. Together with another amateur scientist, Joseph Henry Gilbert (who took on the management of the Rothamsted research station), Lawes introduced the widespread use of superphosphates into agriculture.

The nineteenth century also saw wider use of pesticides. Since ancient times farmers used Sulfur (known as brimstone in the Old Testament) to protect crops. Formed from the burning of petroleum products, it is one of the most abundant elements in the world and easily mined in Sicily. Dusting with sulfur protected against many fungi, including fungi that killed grape vines.[21] In 1807 a Swiss

---

[18] Justus von Liebig, *Chemistry in its Application to Agriculture and Physiology* (Cambridge, 1842).

[19] For a history of the manufacture and use of superphosphates, see William H. Waggaman, *Phosphoric Acid, Phosphates, and Phosphatic Fertilizers* (New York, 1952); Gilbert H. Collings, *Commercial Fertilizers: Their Sources and Use* (Philadelphia, 1934); United States Department of Agriculture (USDA) and Tennessee Valley Authority (TVA), *Superphosphate: Its History, Chemistry, and Manufacture* (Washington, D.C., 1964). John Bennet Lawes is discussed in E. John Russell, *A History of Agricultural Science in Great Britain: 1620–1954* (London, 1966), 91–5.

[20] Vasey, *An Ecological History of Agriculture*, 224.

[21] E. C. Large, *The Advance of the Fungi* (New York, 1962), 44–53.

citizen residing in France, Isaac-Benedict Prevost, discovered that copper salts acted as a fungicide on wheat by destroying fungal spores.[22] Farmers sprayed sulfur, copper, arsenic, and then nicotine to protect crops up until the First World War. In 1921 farmers began to use coal tar, first introduced as a pesticide against aphids and moths. After World War Two, farmers applied a wide variety of organophosphates to crops, DDT and benzene hexachloride the most notorious. Over the last 60 years the variety of pest-specific pesticides proliferated, growing in effectiveness and chemical complexity.[23]

THE LAW OF RETURN

Widely discussed in the nineteenth century, and adopted later by romantic farming literature and the organic farming movement, the "law of return" launched the widespread application of fertilizers on the land. Most of these fertilizers were "natural" in the early period, which is clearly seen in the history of guano. Ironically, the move toward chemical fertilizers in the nineteenth century did not represent an intentional rejection of natural processes for revitalizing the soil. On the contrary, the perceived need to return to the soil the nutrients harvested fueled the artificial fertilization industry. The need to save labor costs in the storage, handling, and dispersal of fertilizer also led farmers to adapt farming practices to an industry that offered, or claimed to offer, a solution to soil infertility.

Until the 1870s in Britain and the United States, many agricultural theorists and entrepreneurs offered plans for recycling waste based on modern, ecological ideas of recycling. Farmers in the mid-nineteenth century used the word "cycle," "circulation," or "round of creation" to denote the return of nutrients to the soil. Many argued that their nation stood to lose its agricultural base if it did not mend its ways. By the 1850s, large urban areas presented city planners with the serious problem of waste disposal, and proposals abounded for recycling "night soil" (human excreta), along with animal waste. In 1893, the Consulting Chemist to the Royal Agricultural Society in England proposed to raise Indian agricultural production by composting, using street sweepings, household refuse, and also human waste.[24] Agricultural chemist to the Government of India, John W. Leather suggested that,

> There is, perhaps, no more important subject in relation to agriculture than the proper disposal of night-soil and other town refuse, for it may be said, without exaggeration, that nearly one-half of the plant food extracted by food-crops from soil is contained in the materials which are included under these two heads. It follows, therefore, that

[22] Vasey, *An Ecological History of Agriculture*, 227.
[23] Robin Cowan, "Pest Control," *The Oxford Encyclopedia of Economic History*, ed. Joel Mokyr (Oxford, 2005), 44.
[24] F. K. Jackson and Y. D. Wad, "The Sanitary Disposal and Agricultural Utilisation of Habitation Wastes by the Indore Process," *Institute of Plant Industry Indore, Central India* 1 (1934), 3. Reprinted from *The Indian Medical Gazeteer*, LXIX/2, (February, 1934). See also J. A. Voelcker, *Report: Improvement of Indian Agriculture*, (London, 1893).

on their proper disposal and return to the soil, depends the addition of a large proportion of the food necessary for the crops.[25]

Though "poudrette" (processed human dung) had some commercial success, proposals for collecting and distributing human waste to distant fields proved so financially impractical that municipalities and companies rarely used the process. Further, the introduction of fertilizer in concentrated form by fertilizer companies made poudrette even more impractical. Guano—the accumulated dung of seabirds—provided a handy fertilizer in concentrated form, and importing companies offered in guano a natural product that proved easier to store, ship, and spread over the fields.[26]

Due to its limited supply guano had a short run. When the price of guano skyrocketed commercial suppliers introduced "superphosphates." Guano had prepared farmers to expect concentrated fertilizer, and the new "superphosphates" more than met that expectation. "Super" referred to the higher concentration achieved when sulfuric acid broke down the phosphate rock and removed impurities. The same process also worked on bones. Phosphate entrepreneurs made outrageous claims about phosphates, but the ease and convenience of superphosphates and other chemicals won over the majority of farmers in Britain and the United States. During the Liebig era simple chemical analysis attacked the problem of plant nutrition and, according to Howard and other proponents of organic agriculture, soil lost biological complexity and interaction. By 1900, such conventional fertilizers as ashes and manure, though not forgotten, became obsolete.[27]

[25] As quoted in Jackson and Wad, "Sanitary Disposal and Agricultural Utilisation," 3.

[26] John Claudius Loudon, *An Encyclopaedia of Agriculture* (London, 1825), quoted in *American Farmer* 9 (1827–28): 9; NA, "Guano," *Plough, Loom and Anvil: An American Farmer's Magazine*, ed. J. A. Nash and M. P. Parish, 10 (1857–58): 9; See also John Hannam, *The Economy of Waste Manures: A Treatise on the Nature and Use of Neglected Fertilizers* (London, 1844); Cuthbert W. Johnson, *On Fertilizers* (London, 1839).

[27] F. M. L. Thompson discusses the end of the "closed circuit system" in Britain in "The Second Agricultural Revolution, 1815–1880," *Economic History Review* 21 (April, 1968): 64. For a contemporary discussion of the agricultural uses of manure derived from the stable, see Nyle C. Brady, *The Nature and Properties of Soil* (New York, 1974), 537–40. Guano had been known as a fertilizer long before its commercial application. See Anted & Francois Frezier, *A Voyage to the South-Sea, and Along the Coasts of Chile and Peru, in the Years 1712, 1713, and 1714* (London, 1717); Jorge Juan and Antonia de Ulloa, *A Voyage to South America* (New York, 1748/1978). Leached ashes contained 28–30 percent lime, along with other useful properties. See Gilbert H. Collings, *Commercial Fertilizers: Their Sources and Use* (Philadelphia, 1938), 234. With the loss of soil fertility farmers depended increasingly on fertilizers, natural or chemical. See Avery O. Craven, *Soil Exhaustion as a Factor in the Agricultural History of Virginia and Maryland, 1606–1860* (Urbana, 1926). A number of works explored the potential of various methods of fertilizing. See Samuel W. Johnson, *Essays on Peat, Muck and Commercial Manures* (Hartford: 1859); Edmund Ruffin, *An Essay on Calcareous Manures* (1832; reprint, Cambridge, 1961); Charles L. Bartlett, *Guano: A Treatise on the History, Economy as a Manure and Modes of Applying Peruvian Guano* (Boston, 1860). A history of the importation of guano into Great Britain can be found in George Evelyn Hutchinson, "The Biogeochemistry of Vertebrate Excretion," *Bulletin of the American Museum of Natural History* 96 (1950): 42; Holmer J. Wheeler, *Manures and Fertilizers* (New York, 1914), 75–6. A number of entrepreneurs and writers sold British farmers on guano, including John H. Sheppard, who wrote *A Practical Treatise on the Use of Peruvian and Ichaboe African Guano: Cheapest Manure in the World* (London, 1844) and *Anonymous Hints to Farmers on the Nature, Purchase and Application of Peruvian, Bolivian, and African Guano* (London, 1845). See also Anthony Gibbs and Sons, *Peruvian and Bolivian Guano: Its Nature, Properties, and*

The triumph of the new scientific husbandry came at the expense of traditional folk methods of farming. In Britain around 1870, the importation of cheap food-stuffs from abroad forced farmers to raise yields dramatically or fail. Calamitous weather in the last quarter of the nineteenth century also worsened the plight of the small landholder. Beginning in 1878 and continuing to the late 1890s, bad weather lowered agricultural productivity to such an extent that many small traditional farms could not remain competitive. Initiated by the Board of Agriculture in 1882, the new farmers' co-operatives promoted further homogenization of technique. The introduction of the internal combustion engine made manure increasingly scarce as a fertilizer. Humus, though not discarded completely, became secondary to chemical fertilization.

The final break with traditional farming methods came after 1896 when high death duties led to a massive transfer of wealth.[28] Though the attempt to overpower the old, landed elite succeeded, these measures merely transferred land into the hands of large businessmen-farmers and corporations, destroying the traditional tenant-landlord relationships that—though much attenuated—still facilitated agricultural methods that employed manure, mixed farming, and labor-intensive composting. As late as 1937 the Duke of Portland complained: "Large estates... have been and are still being broken up, and the houses attached to them sold to individuals, most of whom have little or no connection to the land."[29]

Against this background of retrenchment, many thinkers, artists, and traditional farmers resisted alienation from the land. The Romantic Movement, through its various incarnations as a literary, intellectual, and political phenomenon, proved deeply ecological in outlook, and protested the presumptions of the Liebig era with various degrees of specificity. In 1860 Henry David Thoreau argued that the succession of forest trees involved a natural method that farmers could not neglect without losing the health of the soil and the plants that grew in it. He insisted on the need to "consult with Nature," arguing that otherwise land would become worthless scrub. In *Man and Nature* (1864) George Perkins Marsh argued for a similar distinction between the "natural" and the "unnatural" in planting forests. The botanist Eugene Hilgard, in *Soils* (1906), argued for a "permanent agricul-ture," whereby farmers could maintain soil fertility indefinitely. In 1906, he intro-duced the wider public to the conflict between chemical analyses alone ("mineral dope fertilizers") and a more ecological approach to the soil for both forest and agriculture. Empire forestry (popularized in the *The Jungle Book* by Rudyard Kipling) preached a new gospel of ecology, in which a web of life linked all plants and soil fertility required the return of nutrients to the soil.[30]

Results (London, 1843). The word "guano" came to mean fertilizers in general, as with "guanos" in John Collis Nesbit, *History and Properties of the Different Varieties of Natural Guanos* (London, 1859).

[28] Harold Perkin, *The Rise of Professional Society: England Since 1880* (London, 1989), 251–8.
[29] As quoted in Ibid., 252.
[30] See Henry Thoreau, "The Succession of Forest Trees" as quoted in Donald Worster, *Nature's Economy: A History of Ecological ideas*, (Cambridge, 1994), 68, 69; George Perkins Marsh, *Man and Nature, Or, Physical Geography as Modified by Human Action* (Seattle, 2003), 199–222; Eugene W. Hilgard, *Soils: Their Formation, Properties, Composition, and Relations to Climate and Plant Growth in*

Industrial farming spread throughout the world as a result of the international trade in fertilizers. Just as the Industrial Revolution in Britain spread to north-western Europe, and the United States, so too did the British, French, Portuguese Spanish, and Belgian Empires increasingly import chemical fertilizers. Competition for new agricultural markets in a globalized world required the adoption of new machinery, the creation of larger farms, and the widespread use of chemical fertilizers.

ECOLOGY AND HOLISM

As the growing population in the cities felt dislocated by industrial conditions and longed for a return to nature, so too did many in Britain—where the Industrial Revolution began—feel a romantic nostalgia for mixed farming and the communal conditions of a lost countryside. Professional scientists and amateurs fused science and romanticism to forge a new philosophy of holism from the 1920s to the present. Reacting against industrial farming, advocates of a "back to the land" ethic launched a battle against malnutrition and soil infertility. Individuals seeking a move toward healing and wholeness expressed themselves in poetry, painting, and literature in Britain, its colonies, and former colonies, and across Europe.

Though Ernst Haeckel only coined the term in 1866, ecology is a concept with deep historical roots. It is an idea that emphasized wholeness and connectedness and runs as a strand throughout the western tradition, interwoven with and often at odds with another tradition, that of philosophical realism—the idea that matter exists independently of our subjective mind. Milton beautifully laid out the concept in *Paradise Lost* (1667) where he depicted the sapphire earth, "hanging in a pendant down" and connected in a golden chain to heaven. Milton gave poetic expression to the Christian idea of the Great Chain of Being, the title of a 1936 book by A. O. Lovejoy. This idea of the interconnection of particular manifestations in the world held a dominant place in western thought until the end of the eighteenth century.[31]

The advance of science aided in the secularization of these ideas in the nineteenth century. Through the testing of hypotheses, humans ascertain in the changing material world around us the permanent laws of nature that govern existence. This teleological scheme lay behind the classification of all species and the cataloging and systematization of nature. While the idea of the Great Chain of Being faded in the nineteenth century, it made a partial comeback with the growth of ecology.

the Humid and Arid Regions (New York, 1906). See also a review of Hilgard's book, which highlights his disagreement with simplistic chemical analysis: Franklin H. King, "Review of Soils, by Eugene W. Hilgard," *Science* 24 (January, 1906): 681–4. See Rudyard Kipling, "In the Rukh," *The Jungle Book*, ed. W. W. Robinson, (Oxford, 1987) 371.

[31] Though Milton was a philosophical realist, he also mixed elements of romanticism and rationalism together. Rationalism is often contrasted to romanticism: the idea that the world is transparent to human reason and that there are simple, fundamental laws which determine behavior in the social and natural worlds. This contrast is clearly laid out by M. H. Abrams *The Mirror and the Lamp: Romantic Theory and the Critical Tradition* (Oxford, 1953). I owe this suggestion to private correspondence with the historian of science Adam Lucas, at Wollongong University.

Ideas, contrary to the assertion of Lovejoy, are subject to an almost infinite variation, digression, and shading. No attempt is here made to assert that ecology *merely* reflects a secularized version of the Great Chain of Being. Lovejoy envisioned this Great Chain of Being as strictly hierarchical, while ecological metaphors are more egalitarian. Rather, we can see that the organic farming movement picked up and applied Christian ideas of connectedness and ecological thought. Ecology became a scientific inquiry that focused on the relationship between living things and their environment. It studied interactions that often cut against the study of species as a separate and discreet unit. It took into account the entire life history of a plant with other plants, animals, microorganisms, soil, and climate and has evolved to become a central focus of earth science and biodiversity.

Holism also escapes easy definition. As a movement it is downstream from romanticism, and then vitalism. Vitalism asserted that a force or principle lay behind physical phenomena, distinct from material processes. Holism runs parallel to this idea. It preceded and informed the organic farming movement. Like vitalism, holism offered a scientific philosophy that sought to escape from a purely mechanistic view of nature, aiming to explore the operation of scientific laws while still affirming an Aristotelian immanence, or "soul," in the operations of physics and biology. Holism attempted to "re-enchant" a scientific enterprise that left humans in a cold and meaningless universe. It has led to an emphasis on the interconnectedness of nature, often summed up as "the whole is greater than the sum of its parts." This concept easily overlapped with the notion that spirituality infused the material world of nature.[32]

Holism shared with ecology the examination of the total environment. It functioned, however, less as a strict scientific system and more as a philosophy and even as a religious conception. It had cultural antecedents in prose and poetry, and influenced like-minded individuals who attempted to reform society at many levels. Advocates of holism maintained that humans should view the entire phenomenon of our environment and our place within it as a whole, without the overspecialization and breakdown into individual and discrete entities arising from a purely mechanical philosophy. The reduction of biology to chemistry stood out as a prime example of simplistic reductionism that holism attempted to redress. It stood in opposition to a Cartesian philosophy that posited a radical break between human spirit and the material world.

Holism had religious as well as cultural and philosophical roots. Advocates of the doctrine of divine immanence saw the material world as porous to the spiritual, claiming that the divine presence impregnated all life forms. Much as a stained-glass window channeled light through particular colors of glass, so too the divine presence flowed into and throughout nature. The doctrine of immanence fed into the transcendentalist movement. God saturated nature with the divine presence, and thus created nature and humans as good, the "once born" and not in need of

---

[32] A good summary of holism, particularly as developed on continental Europe, can be found in Anne Harrington, *Reenchanted Science: Holism in German Culture from Wilhelm II to Hitler* (Princeton, 1996), xvi–xvii.

redemption from an original state. Ralph Waldo Emerson and Henry David Thoreau, both transcendentalist writers, long remained favorites of those who advocated holism. The American transcendentalist movement branched off from the Romantic Movement in Britain and on the European continent in the late eighteenth and early nineteenth century. It absorbed—and mistakenly interpreted— Hindu ideas of the sacredness of all life, influencing in turn, Hinduism itself as it evolved under British rule in the Victorian age. Walt Whitman turned the transcendentalist impulse that privileged innate and intuited knowledge about ourselves and the world around us toward egalitarian and political ideas that celebrated the American Republic. The advocates of holism in the early part of the twentieth century grew from the fertile soil of transcendentalism and, mixed with the new science of ecology, enunciated a world view that attempted to meld human knowledge into a single, coherent understanding of everything—the whole—as a single guiding idea.

General Jan Smuts, an Afrikaner war hero from the Boer War, and later prime minister of South Africa, coined and popularized the term "holism." One of the best-known advocates of holism, Smuts wrote an unpublished biography, *Walt Whitman: A Study in the Evolution of Personality* that contained many of the ideas for his 1926 book *Holism and Evolution.*[33] The idea that smaller units progressed into larger structures fit with his political ideas of the Union of South Africa, the British Commonwealth, as well as his support for the League of Nations. But Smuts decisively impacted philosophical debates. He argued that analysis lost effectiveness if based on individual particulars without comprehending the whole. This idea had been a cardinal rule of medicinal practice since Hippocrates who made the same argument in ancient Greece. A few decades later advocates of holism soon found a home for their ideas in the organic farming movement.

DESICCATION THEORY

Desiccation theory influenced millions of people who in turn changed much of the land surface of the earth. It played a role in three distinct areas of environmental development: forestry conservation, organic farming, and development initiatives. Desiccation theory is founded on the belief that trees and other vegetative cover recycle water back into the atmosphere—when it rains, trees break the fall of the raindrops and preserve topsoil from washing away. Trees then absorb the moisture acting as great pumps that evaporate water back into the air where clouds form and return water to the earth again in precipitation. Trees both cool the temperature when hot and warm the groundcover when the weather is cold. Desiccation theory held that deforestation caused desiccation by allowing water to run quickly into streams and rivers—often causing flooding in times of high rainfall. Without the recycling of water deserts advanced and topsoil drained into the sea.

---

[33] J. C. Smuts, *Holism and Evolution* (Cape Town, 1987).

Desiccation theory was the ruling theory of environmental history, providing the imaginative stir to action, the eschatological warning of Armageddon, and the justification to seek authority to set aside existing forests, to plant new ones, and to terraform the landscape for the protection of the climate. It is this theory that also led to the first efforts to launch the conservation movement on a global scale. Because of this fear of desiccation, in addition to other concerns of resource exhaustion and ecology, British imperialists launched the worldwide conservation movement, considered by most environmental historians as the first stage in the modern environmental movement. By the early decades of the twentieth century, fifty separate forest departments managed large tracts of the earth—approximately 8 percent of the land surface of the world.[34]

Environmentalist thought before the 1960s revolved around forests and their preservation for a number of reasons, not all of them limited to the economic obsession with timber supply or the governmental quest for revenue.[35] Parallel with these concerns, climate theory explained how forest lands affected rainfall, water flow, soil preservation, and thus a variety of flora and fauna. Climate theory gave forestry a very modern patina of ecological concern—though neither the term "ecology" nor "environmentalism" had been used before 1900. Thus, environmental activists in the late nineteenth and early twentieth centuries raised the question of public land use as the premier question of the day.

Settlers and farmers in the eighteenth and nineteenth century expanded into the grasslands in the United States and Russia. Settlers moved west, as the young Republic expanded toward the Pacific, and South and East into the Steppes as Russians exploited the vast grasslands that supported grazing, wheat, and other crops.[36] Vasilii Dokuchaev, considered the founder of modern soil classification, addressed the vexing problem of drought in the Steppes, and raised the question in the 1890s of whether the problems arose from agricultural practice itself. The temperate grasslands in north-western China, Central Asia, the Russian Empire, North America, Argentina, South Africa, Australia, and New Zealand shared many similar challenges.[37] In Russia, as elsewhere, the hot dry winds that accompanied dust bowl conditions wreaked so much damage that the observers compared the damage from deforestation to the Mongols.[38] Dokuchaev argued that the loss of

---

[34] Gregory A. Barton, "Sir Albert Howard and the Forestry Roots of the Organic Farming Movement," *Agriculture History*, 75/2 (Spring, 2001): 168–87. William Beinart discusses the South African context for desiccation concerns in *The Rise of Conservation in South Africa: Settlers, Livestock and the Environment 1770–1950* (Oxford, 2003), 64, 77, 102, 111, 369.

[35] An example of this can be found in the journal *Forest and Conservation History*, founded in 1957, which broadened beyond forest issues in the 1980s. It merged with *The Journal of Environmental History*. See also Michael Williams, "The Relations of Environmental History and Historical Geography," *Journal of Historical Geography* 20 (January, 1994): 3.

[36] The Russian experience of peasants expanding on the Steppes is told by David Moon, *The Russian Peasantry: The World the Peasants Made* (London and New York, 1999), 254–62.

[37] David Moon, "The Environmental History of the Russian Steppes: Vasilii Dokuchaev and the Harvest Failure of 1891," *Transactions of the Royal Historical Society* 15 (2005): 156.

[38] Ibid., 162. Stalin adopted some of the ideas expressed by Dokuchaev for shelter belts and other conservation methods. For a full exposition of Dokuchaev's work see David Moon, *The Plough that Broke the Steppes: Agriculture and Environment on Russia's Grasslands, 1700–1914* (Oxford, 2013).

vegetation, particularly on the banks of rivers and streams, accelerated the run off
of water. Excessive plowing, along with deforestation, had thus lowered water
tables and depleted the Steppes of moisture needed to sustain crops.[39]

The dependence upon chemical fertilizers alarmed some agriculturalists who,
along with foresters, became increasingly skeptical of simplistic chemical analyses of
plants that ignored both their complexity and their interrelationship with the
larger biological community. Forestry investigations advocated the importance
of fertile soil for disease-resistant trees. This had major implications for agriculture. A review in the *Forest Quarterly* of a bulletin of the U.S. Bureau of Soils
observed that,

> many foresters, if not all, have long known…that the physical conditions of the
> soil…are of infinitely more importance in wood production than the chemical
> composition.[40]

What worked for the forest also worked for agriculture, the author concluded.
The organic farming movement arose in the context of this debate over soil fertility.
What approach, conservationists asked, would lead to more "permanent agriculture"
and not exhaust the soil?

Edward L. Nichols, president of the American Association for the Advancement
of Science addressed the question in 1909 at the association's Baltimore meeting.
Nichols explained that the forest stood as nature's model for soil fertility. If the
law of return operated fully in an unmolested forest, it would recycle nutrients
and guarantee fertility. While "forests may be renewed and the soil restored to its
maximum fertility," a similar law of return for agricultural land had, he argued,
yet to be discovered:

> The problem which is presently to confront the race is that of civilized existence
> without recourse to energy stored by the slow processes of nature. This problem must
> be definitely solved before the complete exhaustion of our inherited capital.[41]

The key questions that Nichols and other environmentalists posed incessantly
were: Can the farm model itself on the forest? Can we return nutrients fully
to the soil? If so, how? By chemical fertilizers? By other methods yet to be
discovered?

Though the conservation movement could not provide a ready-made solution
to the problem for agriculture, it nevertheless pointed the way. It did so in part
because conservation had already attacked and solved many problems of soil fertility
for the forests. Scientific forestry had implemented working plans that (1) replanted
after cutting and (2) forbade further cutting for decades in some cases, over 100 years
in others, so that nutrients might return to the soil through natural processes. But
while a national forest service could bank on the passage of time to address soil

[39] Ibid., 165.
[40] Milton Whitney and F. K. Cameron, "The Chemistry of Soil as Related to Crop Production,"
Forestry Quarterly 2 (1903): 30.
[41] Edward L. Nichols, "Science and the Practical Problems of the Future," *Science*, NS 29/731
(January 1, 1909): 2.

fertility, a farmer had to harvest yearly, without the luxury of letting the land return to nature and replenish itself. How could agriculture return fertility to the soil without relying increasingly on chemicals? To this question the organic farming movement offered an answer.[42]

Early advocates of organic farming shared the same concern over desertification.[43] Closely echoing forester's predictions, Howard warned that modern agricultural methods depleted the humus and would reduce India to a vast desert. He feared that if farmers destroyed the macrobiotic elements of the humus which acted as the glue of the soil, deserts would dominate. Like foresters, he looked to the Mediterranean countries to provide an example. He understood that in north-western Europe, where a temporary cover crop (grass or leys) and a large area of woodland forest stopped erosion, the danger was small. But in North America, Africa, Australia, New Zealand, and the countries around the Mediterranean, where deforestation "has been practiced and where almost uninterrupted cultivation has been the rule, large tracts of land once fertile have been almost completely destroyed."[44] In Persia "the soil was transformed into sand," and similar changes took place in Egypt "when the forests were devastated." Low rainfall did not create the deserts of North Africa and north-western India, he argued, but rather, ruined humus, making the soil impermeable and allowing a complete runoff.[45]

Stopping desertification had to include not just forestry, but organic farming to keep the soil permeable and healthy. The combination of forestry and organic farming would properly hold and drain the rain for the benefit of the soil, plants, climate, and man. A litany of historic lessons loomed in Howard's mind. Japan prudently safeguarded agriculture against soil erosion by planting trees on hills where heavy rains rendered the soil vulnerable. Forests thus protected the mainstay of the Japanese food supply. But China lost much arable land through deforestation and the flood of the Yellow River. Howard believed that India, with the advent of empire forestry, had only recently pulled back from the brink of environmental and agricultural disaster.[46]

Only organic farming, he concluded, could bring back fertility, health, and a vigorous national culture. Why organic farming? Because it replicated nature—the forest. Since all agriculture involved "deliberate intrusions into the natural cycle," and since these intrusions were essential for human culture, humans should skirt as closely as possible to the original model, rather than exploit the land and rape the soil

---

[42] The observation of organic methods of farming (without elucidating the principles behind the methods) were popularized by Franklin H. King, professor of agricultural physics at the University of Wisconsin, who traveled to China, Japan, and Korea to record his observations of "permanent agriculture" in Asia. See Franklin H. King, *Farmers of Forty Centuries* (Madison, 1911).

[43] Organic farmers drew on a rich history of desertification theory. For a good overview see Richard Grove, *Green Imperialism: Colonial Expansion, Tropical Island Edens and the Origins of Environmentalism, 1600–1860* (Cambridge, 1996). Diana K. Davis traces French colonial concerns on desertification in *Resurrecting the Granary of Rome: Environmental History and French Colonial Expansion in North Africa* (Athens, Ohio, 2007). See also Gregory A. Barton, *Empire Forestry and the Origins of Environmentalism* (Cambridge, 2002).

[44] Albert Howard, *Farming and Gardening for Health or Disease* (London, 1945), 90.

[45] Ibid., 96. [46] Ibid., 93.

of nutrients. He concluded that for any successful long-term use of the soil, and thus for the health of crops and humans, agriculture needed to replicate the forest.[47]

FORESTRY AND ORGANIC FARMING

While experimenting with Indore compost on a tea plantation, Howard happened to read an account of a botanist's work on conifers in Dorsetshire, England, where small applications of humus resulted in a faster and healthier growth of trees. The result confirmed his work on the tea plant, where Indore compost lessened insect attacks, and increased yield.[48] Further research led to the conclusion that living fungus threads (mycelia) absorbed nutrients from the humus and then invaded the roots of the plant, where the plant digested the fungus threads along with the nutrients that composed them. He concluded,

> It was this, the mycorrhizal association, which was the explanation of what had happened to the conifers and the tea shrubs [that had failed to thrive and were] both forest plants, a form of vegetation in which this association of root and fungus has been known for a long time.

It was this direct "method of feeding" that explained the spectacular results of the mycorrhizal experiments.[49] He concluded that modern crops live on an exhausted, thin, upper layer of soil. Trees act as deep pumps that pull dissolved mineral salts from the weathering rock below into a mineral stream up the vessels of their trunks and into their leaves. Farmers must imitate this and use compost to re-enact artificially the operations of nature and the mycorrhizal association. Humans must return nutrients to the soil—not in a chemical "mineral dope" with a few selected and indigestible minerals—but in the full natural range found in organic matter and the fungi that make it available to the plant, and thus to humans. For humans living outside the hunter-gatherer stage, compost was the farmer's only substitution for the forest.

Even the Indore method of compost was not enough, Howard declared. Along with the imperial conservationists, he proposed a marriage of forestry and farming, in which arable land would alternate over long periods from forest to farm and back to forest again. Afforestation would improve agricultural crops by allowing farmland to suckle at the breast of nature herself. This forest/farm rotation would not only restore the fertility of the soils, but would also provide timber and revenue. Future agricultural policies must adopt this rotation along with the broad use of compost.[50] Howard had much sympathy with the burgeoning field of forestry because forest management involved scientific specialists such as botanists and ecologists who worked with forest rangers to manage the whole "household of

---

[47] Ibid., 183.   [48] Howard, *Farming and Gardening*, 22–3.
[49] Ibid.   [50] Ibid., 186.

nature."[51] Howard's emphasis on a big picture of wholeness, even while specializing in plant disease and crop yields, opened the possibilities of popularizing his work in the future.

CONCLUSION

Organic farming merged romanticism, holism, ecology, science, and desiccation theory, and fitted within the larger environment movement that spanned from the nineteenth century to the present. It placed an emphasis on wholeness and change that have inverted or rejected the main thrust of philosophical assumptions underlying scientific rationalism realism and re-introduced into mainstream European culture elements of immanence and mysticism. The idea that the whole is greater than the sum of its parts is a mystical statement—an element of the magical that is often interwoven with environmental discourse. The whole may of course function differently than the sum of its parts, but it cannot be greater than its parts, any more than the effect can be greater than the cause, or the summation of causes. That does not mean the statement is not a useful analytical approach that solves the challenges humans face. It is certainly a conception that has shaped human cultures and values. It represents a marriage between two opposing strands of western thought, subjectivism, and scientific rationalism, which also draws inspiration from many world cultures and world religious faiths. Organic farming, following the development of ecological thought generally, brought these strands together and along with the larger environmental movement of which it is a part, holds the two conceptions in balance.

[51] Gregory A. Barton, "Sir Albert Howard and the Forestry Roots of the Organic Farming Movement," *Agriculture History*, 75: 2 (Spring, 2001): 168–87.

2

The Cultural Soil of Organic Farming

The globalization of the Industrial Revolution in the late nineteenth century set in train economic and social changes around the world. Along with higher agricultural productivity came improved transportation and lower prices. The increase in trade stimulated the burgeoning factories with their towering smokestacks, but also increased urbanization. In an effort to escape the pollution and overcrowded conditions of the growing cities the middle classes began migrating into newly created leafy suburbs on the outskirts of the world's major industrial cities. Globalization also changed politics, and the politics of rural areas. In the late nineteenth to mid-twentieth-century industrialization and a fall in agricultural income kindled agrarianism and the rise of peasant parties in Europe. As discussed shortly many farmers, writers, and politicians sought to restore the income and prestige, as well as the culture and political power, of rural areas.

The romantic backlash was also a response against the growing rationalization of the age, driven by international trade and the Industrial Revolution, and the accompanying social changes these brought.[1] They included a disparate set of political ideas that ranged across the political spectrum and no one person or school of thought fully exemplifies them.[2] As a general rule, capitalism, high finance, and Marxism, had become anathema to the English adherents of rural romanticism, because of their emphasis on a material universe and a strict adherence to utilitarian results. Both burgeoning socialism and capitalism were products of an increasingly urban society changing rapidly as the result of industrialization.

The movement to maintain the influence of the countryside and of farmers in particular, dominated political thought in England and the United States throughout most of the nineteenth century, and into the mid-twentieth century. Aspects of agrarianism, romantic farm literature, and its many variants on the continent of Europe—including biodynamics and German biological farming—all can be seen as building blocks that merged with the organic farming protocols pioneered by Albert Howard (discussed further in later chapters). The response to industrialism must be understood as both a cultural and a political philosophy. Socialist and leftist thinkers of all stripes also shared some agrarian ideals, however, those on the right of the political spectrum espoused the main arguments against the effects

---

[1] Gregory Barton traces both the rise of rationalization and its resistance, in *Informal Empire and the Rise of One World Culture* (Basingstoke, 2014). See especially pages 186–97.

[2] The Romantic Era as a term represents a wide sweep of disparate ideas and political positions, such as the views of the utopian Robert Owen (1771–1858); artists John Ruskin (1819–1900); churchman John Henry Newman (1801–90); and the philosopher Thomas Carlyle, (1795–1881).

of industrialism. Marxists welcomed industrialization as a step forward in the emancipation of the working class and many other socialists saw it as a means of improving the lot of the poor and downtrodden. Marxists also saw the peasantry as the lowest social order lingering in a primitive state that would soon wither away. Stalin expressed this contempt in its most extreme form by launching large collectivist enterprises designed in part to abolish rural values. Nor did capitalism treat agrarianism and its romantic variants any better. Corporations sought to buy out small land owners and rationalize rural life into a modern global economy. Consumerism and advertising all cut against indigenous and regional cultural icons and offered new, and, according to romanticists, false ideals of modern living. While Christian socialists and the Arts and Crafts movement can be classified as being to the left of the political spectrum, many of the ideas espoused on race and culture folded into later fascist movements. Therefore, the agrarian activists and visionaries who sought to reform industrial society and mitigate its ills tended to arise in the 1920s and 1930s from what today we would call the far right, espousing a vision that posited a strong central government to protect the common man from the ravages of both Marxist state capitalism and monopoly capitalism whilst simultaneously enshrining the natural connection between the soil, traditional culture, and ethnicity.

AGRARIANISM

Agrarianism has deep roots in Western civilization, and can be traced back to the late Roman period. In the modern era it survived as a political movement into the 1920s and 30s. Agrarian advocates argued that living on the land produced rugged and virtuous individuals and that corrupt elites in cities bought off the rootless and poor with food handouts and debased entertainments—the equivalent of the bread and circuses offered to appease the Roman populace. According to this view, the financier in the nineteenth and twentieth centuries ruled the mob through the mass media, while the capitalist factory owners and labor leaders debased national culture. Over and against an urban elite stood the farmer—the foundation of society, both with respect to its economy and the moral order. Rural life produced superior citizens that supported a healthy republic.[3]

Ancient history inspired modern agrarian advocates with numerous examples of how rural values reinvigorated the state. In ancient Greece clans held land collectively and assigned long-term rights that allowed enough support for each family. When population outstripped the available land, and when cities such as Athens provided a large market for agricultural goods, a new cash economy changed land tenure dramatically. The traditional power of the clan waned and peasants mortgaged the harvest of the farm to pay the creditors. The great magistrate and populist Solon in the sixth century BC attempted to break the chains of mortgaged debt with debt

---

[3] David B. Danbom, "Romantic Agrarianism in Twentieth-Century America," *Agricultural History*, 65/4 (Autumn, 1991): 1–12.

forgiveness, returning all rights to the farmer who owned the land. After his death when creditors managed to regain control of agricultural land for debt, the dictator Peisistratus again broke the mortgage obligations and returned land rights to farmers, thus remaining in power for his lifetime by gaining the undying loyalty of the peasantry.[4]

Livy, the ancient Roman historian, recounts the exploits of the farmer-general Cincinnatus who took up arms to lead Rome to victory in battle, only to return again to live a simple life on the land. He had two duties: to repel an outside invasion and to repress a democratic mob that threatened anarchy in the city. The Roman senate chose Cincinnatus as dictator because of the simple, incorruptible nature he possessed as an ideal farmer. He swiftly attacked the invaders and restored order. He then handed back his authority to the senate and retired to the fields, only to be called upon to save Rome again a few years later. After victory, he again retired to the fields. Because the incorruptible Cincinnatus willingly served, and willingly surrendered his authority, this vigorous and wise famer passed into legend as a model for the Republic. Livy saw farmers as a national resource: a reserve of manhood and humility, to be called upon in time of dire need.[5]

After Livy other Roman writers continued to promote the agrarian ideal. The poet Virgil, in the *Eclogues*, wrote romantic pastoral idylls that captured the virtue and simplicity of living close to the land. Hesiod and Cicero also echoed these sentiments, which suggests they were broadly infused throughout all levels of Roman society. Long after owner occupied farmers faded from the Italian peninsula, the ideal of agrarian virtue remained ingrained in the Roman elite, almost all of whom were either landowners or financiers. The ideal of Cincinnatus as an agrarian pillar of honest leadership and hardy manhood remained enshrined in classical literature however distant in reality.

In Britain in the early modern and modern period, large land owners privately controlled almost all land in Britain. William the Conqueror initiated new land tenure arrangements that largely abolished the smaller plots of land held freely by independent Anglo-Saxon farmers. He consolidated freely held land into larger holdings controlled by lay and ecclesiastical lords at the will of the king, and subsequently leased for multiple generations to smaller landowners and tenants. These tenants managed to accumulate sufficient wealth to claim the status of freedom in the late Middle Ages, making up the yeoman class of farmers around which subsequently arose a cultural tradition of rugged independence, reinforced by literature, poetry, and political tradition, including the traditions of ancient Greece and Rome.

---

[4] B. M. Lavelle "The Compleat Angler: Observations on the Rise of Peisistratos in Herodotos (1.59–64)" *The Classical Quarterly* 41/2 (1991): 317–24; Tom Dale and Vernon G. Carter, *Topsoil and Civilization* (Oklahoma, 1955), 91–107.

[5] This tale is told in the third book of Livy and takes place in the fourth century BC. See Livy, *The Early History of Rome, Books I–IV: The History of Rome from its Foundations*, trans. Aubrey De Selincourt (London, 2002); Jeremy Engels, "The Two Faces of Cincinnatus: A Rhetorical Theory of the State of Exception," *Advances in the History of Rhetoric* 17/1, (2014): 53; See also H. H. Scullard, *From the Gracchi to Nero: A History of Rome from 133 B.C. to A.D. 68* (London, 1963).

In America, Thomas Jefferson propounded an ardent agrarianism. He boldly asserted that hardy small farmers formed the core of a healthy democracy,

> Generally speaking the proportion which the aggregate of the other classes of citizens bears in any state to that of its husbandman, is the proportion of its unsound to its healthy parts, and is a good enough barometer whereby to measure its degree of corruption.[6]

In this he completely agreed with the physiocrats that property owning men lay the foundation for a free society. The physiocrats were French intellectuals who were the first to study political economy as a science. They had a significant influence on the course of the French Revolution, and their ideas still linger to this day.[7] They argued that all wealth ultimately derived from land. Work on the land produced national wealth, not the accumulation of wealth via trade as mercantilism asserted. Rather, human labor on the land produced wealth and cities were unnatural outgrowths, parasitic on productive labor.[8] This philosophy also emphasized *laisse-faire* ideals because private property safeguarded the individual's relationship to nature through ownership. Society was not based on a social contract, as Rousseau asserted, but on a natural order where men worked for their own self-interest, owned property, and lived off their own labor on their own farms. Elements of early environmental thought can be seen in the physiocrats' assertion that wealth had limits—the land can only produce so much, and humans can only work a certain amount. Wealth is not and cannot be an endless accumulation of worthless currency, but is a product by humans for humans within limits set by nature.

Jefferson differed from the physiocrats by promoting the allocation of land to every citizen. Indeed, he suggested that to vote citizens must own land and that the government should give at least eighty acres of land free to all adult males.[9] Society should attempt to redress the concentration of wealth at the top—by all efforts short of confiscation—to encourage small holdings and, where possible, to break up the large estates, thus broadening the base of ownership in the population. His travels to Europe shocked him. He had seen armies of paupers in Paris and elsewhere, an effluence from the rising manufacturing centers located in the major urban areas. This led him to conclude that the manufacturers are "the instruments by which the liberties of a country are generally overturned."[10] Along with this, he decried the malodorous effect of cities both on human health and healthy culture. All of these sentiments would find an echo in the organic farming movement in the twentieth century.

---

[6] Thomas Jefferson, *Notes On Virginia*, (New York, 1801), 243–5.

[7] Henry Higgs, *Physiocrats: Six Lectures on the French Economistes of the 18th Century*, (London, 1897), 7, 8. Higgs, writing at the end of the nineteenth century, correctly reminds us that the Mercantilists were not a school, nor an organized body of thought.

[8] Liana Vardi, *Physiocrats and the World of the Enlightenment* (Cambridge, 2013), 3.

[9] Patrick F. Quinn, "Agrarianism and the Jeffersonian Philosophy," *Review of Politics*, 2/1 (January, 1940): 87–104.

[10] Ibid., 100; Dumas Malone ed., *Correspondence Between Thomas Jefferson and Dupont de Nemours* (Boston and New York, 1930), 173.

Agrarianism fed into the Romantic Movement in the late eighteenth and early nineteenth century because both celebrated rural living. The Romantic Movement began as a rebellion against the objectification of human thought by the Enlightenment *philosophes*. It is generally understood to be an expressive movement revealed in philosophy, literature, poetry, painting, and architecture. Arthur Lovejoy points out the difficulty of defining this era. He saw the origins of the romantic era as an outgrowth of the seventeenth- and eighteenth-century literary and philosophical argument between the "ancients" and the "moderns." In this debate the partisans of the ancients claimed that the best poetry, science, and philosophical thought lay behind us: nature declined with time, and did not produce minds with as much vigor or clarity. The past guided us to wisdom. The moderns on the other hand began to discern that Europeans had broken through new barriers and taken science and culture to a new height and that the best still lay in the future. Progress was not only a possibility, but inevitable.[11]

The debate between the ancients and moderns did not entirely fade, however. Interest in classical life and culture expanded to include old European gods and pagan culture and a renewed interest in the Middle Ages. Thus, many in the romantic era viewed a cathedral as a reflection in stone of the great northern European forests, imperfect in line and form, but natural, majestic, and, like nature, magnificent. This interest in ancient tradition also evolved into an interest in the divine within nature—often taking on the form of pantheism. Romantic expression provided a counter-weight to rapid scientific endeavor and a rising professional class that promoted specialization as the essence of modern progress. Unlike the classical tradition, however, which emphasized clarity and beauty of form, Lovejoy traced in the romantic era a fascination with the Nordic and claimed the romantic era harbored an intuition about an inner unseen world of the infinite and the mystical.[12]

Individuals that scholars assign to the Romantic Era could also be highly religious or atheistic of radical political leanings or traditionalists. The central attribute that tied the movement together was a rejection of a mechanistic view of the universe, and a sense that humans had become alienated from nature—from the land, our own bodies, from how we should relate to each other, and in many cases, how we should relate to the Divine. Nostalgia for the Medieval Period formed a powerful strand in this movement, where humans expressed thought and art organically—that is, where culture grew and found expression naturally from human experience.

The Romantic Movement idealized the past because many felt unease with the societal changes effected by industrialization. Life under a feudal system, or the old governors of society was, as Harold Perkin has pointed out, vertical instead of horizontal.[13] People were not working class or bourgeoisie: they did not have

---

[11] On the doctrine of progress see J. B. Bury, *The Idea of Progress* (London, 1920), 5.

[12] Arthur O. Lovejoy, "The Meaning of Romanticism for the Historian of Ideas," *Journal of the History of Ideas*, 2/3 (June, 1941): 267–8.

[13] Harold Perkin, *The Origins of Modern English Society, 1780–1880* (London, 1969), 1, 3–5.

a class consciousness that found a semblance on a horizontal level, as with a working-class man in Birmingham who would share the concerns and self-identify of a working-class man in London. In contrast to the class-conscious factory worker, a yeoman farmer rented from a titled landowner and each belonged to that territory, with its memories, customs, and identity. A priest or a doctor served clients above and under his social station. Merchants and other permanent urban dwellers in the modern world offered a rootless alternative to the hierarchical rural order that had prevailed in previous generations.

Natural theology also highlighted agrarian ideals. Alongside a host of Protestant and Catholic divines in the eighteenth century, Gilbert White, an Anglican clergyman, proclaimed that all nature revealed the intimate personality of God. He meticulously drew out the ecological associations between plants and animals in his parish of Selbourne and saw a hierarchy of plant, animal, and Man. Though he did not use the word "ecology," White's ideas are considered by many to represent an early prototype of ecological and environmental thinking.[14] In Selborne, he told a series of anecdotes that revealed the hand of God in everything. The teleology of the natural world clearly proved the creative mind of God behind all he saw. White particularly drew out the mutual dependence between plants, insects, and animal life, and, on that basis alone, is often credited with laying the foundation for an early environmental ethic. English settlers abroad and British farmers at home often placed White's *Natural History of Selborne* (1789) beside the English Bible and *Pilgrim's Progress* (1678) on their shelves. His sense of the picturesque in a farming community and his deep love for village life became a classic source for romantic farm literature that began to flourish at the beginning of the twentieth century.[15]

Those in nineteenth-century Britain seeking a return to modes of lost traditional living rejected the cold utilitarianism of Jeremy Bentham that characterized the new industrial age. William Cobbett, while a social reformer and political radical, nonetheless wrote his famous classic, *Rural Rides* (1832), to chronicle a countryside rapidly changing from the Industrial Revolution. Along with Gilbert White's *The Natural History of Selborne*, Cobbett's work revealed a keen eye for pastoral beauty that served as a model for later agricultural writers. Later historians found it difficult to pin down Cobbett's class status: a perennial problem in classifying "yeomen" or small farmers. Cobbett saw himself as a farmer, but to most contemporaries he was a journalist and publisher.[16]

His politics also foreshadowed many of the same issues and inspired later romantic farm literature. Cobbett detested finance, bankers, "stock jobbers," and

---

[14] Donald Worster presents an "Imperial" and "Arcadian" strand of early environmental thought, and posits Gilbert White in the latter. See Donald Worster, *Nature's Economy: A History of Ecological Ideas* (Cambridge, 1985), 2, 76. For a critique of this position see Gregory Barton, *Empire Forestry and the Origin of Environmentalism* (Cambridge, 2002), 43, 44.

[15] Gilbert White, *The Natural History of Selborne* (Boston, 1975).

[16] To E. Halevy, he was middle class. See E. Halevy *History of the English People in the 19th Century* (vol. 3), trans. E. Watkin (London, 1961), 44. To E. P. Thompson he was upper class. See E. P. Thompson, *The Making of the English Working Class* (London, 1963), 206.

Jews, including all bureaucrats. He particularly detested London. When visiting farmers, he engaged in what he called the "rustic harangue" and found the conversation to be practical, wholesome, honest, and without pretense. His narrative in *Rural Rides* moved effortlessly from detailed natural description of lovely English countryside and charming homes buried in woodland, to rants against usury that impoverished the farmer tenants of the great landlords. Hence, he advocated a radical middle ground: an empowerment of the middling sort which involved the disparagement of the urban mob on the bottom of society and the domination of the great manufacturers, financiers, and the landed lords at the top. This polemic laid the foundation for a new sort of politics in the later nineteenth century that came to be seen as proto-fascist—the representation of the interests and the empowerment of the lower-middle and middle class to both rescue and prevent rootless urban poor, and to remove a parasitic elite that deformed society by enacting healthy agrarian norms.

An example of Cobbett's writing gives a foretaste of the romantic farm literature that inspired and recruited the early followers of organic farming and that effortlessly moved from the pastoral to the political and from the aesthetic to anti-Semitic,

> ...always so beautiful in forests and parks, are peculiarly beautiful in this lofty situation and with verdure so smooth as that of these chalky downs...and though we met with no gothic arches made of Scotch-fir, we saw something a great deal better; namely, about forty cows, the most beautiful that I ever saw, as to colour at least. They appear to be of the Galway-breed. They are called, in this country, Lord Caernarvon's breed. They have no horns, and their colour is a ground of white with black or red spots, these spots being from the size of a plate to that of a crown-piece; and some of them have no small spots. These cattle were lying down together in the space of about an acre of ground: they were in excellent condition, and so fine a sight of the kind I never saw...I could not help calculating how long it might be before some Jew would begin to fix his eye upon Highclere, and talk of putting out the present owner.[17]

Others followed in his political and aesthetic tastes, each in their own right, a forerunner of many of the ideals of organic farming. Poets like Wordsworth, philosophers such as Carlyle, and novelists like Disraeli painted a picture of lost rural life that suggested that health and healing from the industrial age required a return to values and tradition misplaced. On the Continent, Johann von Herder (1744–1803), a Lutheran pastor and philosopher of history advocated a deep and sentimental attachment to the soil, and the unique culture that humans rooted in a particular time and place produced.[18]

Farmers prospered in Britain during the Napoleonic Wars between 1803 and 1815. But after the collapse of the Continental System that enforced Napoleon's embargo on trade with Britain, cheap food stuffs, particularly grain, flooded the market. Prices fell precipitously. Responding to the suffering of farmers, parliament passed the Corn Laws in 1815 which stayed in place until 1846. While protecting

---

[17] William Cobbett, *Rural Rides* (vol. 1) (London, 1832), 7, 8.
[18] F. M. Barnard, *Herder's Social and Political Thought* (Oxford, 1965) is the best analysis on Herder's ideas about the *Volk*, organicism, and national characteristics.

farmers, the Corn Laws also inadvertently strengthened the political hand of manufacturers who cherished free trade over import duties. Political agitators financed by the manufacturing class roiled Britain with a campaign against the Corn Laws. This battle reflected a Britain swiftly transforming from an agricultural country into an industrial country that increasingly exported manufactured goods and imported agricultural products. The Corn Laws protected both small and large landowners from the fall in agricultural prices and the political arguments for the Corn Laws clearly drew on agrarian theory: namely, that Britain's wealth depended upon the prosperity of the farming classes. This class alone produced the food necessary to survive in times of war and peace. The Corn Laws also produced a better class of citizen. Later advocates of organic farming pointed to the abolition of the Corn Laws in 1846 and the rise of industrial farming as harbingers of a new phase of land exploitation that sought only profits with no regard for the long-term fertility of the soil or the culture and health of society.[19]

In Britain, the predominance of private ownership of land led to fewer owner-occupied farms, with large landowners renting farmland to tenants. Tenancy had a long and storied tradition in Britain, with the tenant, as well as the landowner, celebrated as part of the Yeoman tradition of farming. With the Reform Act of 1867 large landowners had an incentive to sell off individual farms or estates. This act extended the voting franchise, from around one million adult males to approximately seven million within a few years of its passage. This meant that large landlords who previously held political power by influencing the votes of their tenants became a smaller share of the electorate. Campaigns, persuasion, and propaganda, though certainly a part of elections before 1867, became far more important after this date with the expansion of the electorate. Landlords became far more willing to sell off portions of their estates to their tenants—or the entire estate when the conditions were right—because land ownership no longer guaranteed political domination. Though large estates still carried prestige, the traditional landlords had less political motivation to keep estates intact.

The percentage of land under the ownership of small- and medium-sized farmers seesawed in the latter part of the nineteenth century. For a brief period in the early 1870s agricultural prices rose and numerous tenants could afford to borrow the money needed to buy their own land. Then the agricultural depression that began in 1874, along with the increased importation of cheap food from the Americas, drove down ownership again—a process accelerated by adverse weather. Many farmers went bankrupt, abandoned farming, or gave the land back to the mortgage holder. This led in turn to a movement among larger landlords to liquidate many of the tenancies and farm the land themselves once more by concentrating land into large holdings. In 1900, the owner himself cultivated 13.5 percent of farmland in Britain and by 1950 the figure had risen to 37.5 percent.[20]

---

[19] Gregory Barton, *Lord Palmerston and the Empire of Trade* (London, 2012), 13–15.

[20] S. G. Sturmey, "Owner-Farming in England and Wales, 1900–1950," *Essays in Agrarian History: Reprints edited for the British Agricultural History Society* (vol. II), ed. E. E. Minchinton (Newton-Abbot, UK, 1968): 281–306.

Heavy death duties, which often required the heirs to sell the estate to pay the taxes, also played a role in breaking up large estates. Along with an increase in credit resources both tenants and farmer entrepreneurs had the opportunity to buy more land.[21] As ownership diversified, the increase in the total number of farmers provided a sizable demographic base for the organic farming movement that arose before, during, and after the Second World War. Between 1909 and 1927 owner-occupied farms increased dramatically, rising to 36 percent in 1927 and remaining stable into the 1950s. This increase of owner-occupied farms also played an important role in the rise of romantic farm literature, which in turn provided a successful audience for the ideas of Albert Howard.

There are a number of reasons why an increase in owner-occupied farms lay the groundwork for an organic farming movement. The owner occupied farmer did not live off rents. He felt a visceral attachment to the land that his own children would inherit. Associating the long-term viability of the farm with the well-being of his own family over generations, farmers displayed a passionate concern for soil fertility. Because the yeoman (whether an owner or a tenant) was a practitioner and not a specialist, he drew information where he could find it. His approach was not only financial, but also sentimental and cultural. All of this allowed the more literate among them to write romantic farming literature, and provided in addition a ready audience to buy the books, both in rural areas and to readers in suburban and heavily industrialized cities yearning to read about a simpler, more wholesome life.

In the United States during the 1930s the revival of the agrarian movement in the American South mirrored many of the same concerns of romantic farming enthusiasts in Britain. Southern Agrarianism found strong advocates amongst a group of southern historians, essayists, and novelists, including the Poet Laureate of the United States, Robert Penn Warren. Warren, and a group of eleven other writers produced in 1930 a classic tract of the movement titled *I'll Take My Stand: The South and the Agrarian Tradition*. This book advocated the distinctive features of the antebellum south as distinct from the rest of the country. These Southern Agrarians shared many of the identical values with British romantic farm enthusiasts, particularly the primacy of agrarian values over industrial values. Southern Agrarians were also a literary group, like their British counterparts, using essays and poetry to persuade their audiences. True to the tradition of southern literature, and echoing the same concerns as yeoman farmers in Britain, the Southern Agrarians emphasized the cultural centrality of rural homesteads.[22] While not proposing a modern secessionist movement, the Southern Agrarians argued against the south conforming to the modern "American Industrial ideal" or to the jingle of "The New South."

In a 1962 introduction to *I'll Take My Stand*, Louis Rubin summarized the key points of the twelve authors. He wrote that the South needed to return to tradition, and to reject "the Cult of Science" that was, not science at all, but merely "applied

---

[21] Ibid.

[22] Laura Barge, "Pastoral in Southern Poetry," *The Southern Literary Journal*, 26/1 (Fall, 1993): 30–41. See also Lewis P. Simpson, *The Dispossessed Garden: Pastoral and History in Southern Literature* (Athens, 1975).

sciences and...practical production." The authors argued that moderns "have more time in which to consume, and many more products to be consumed." But in return for this increase in products and the leisure to enjoy them, life had become meaningless, "brutal and hurried." In short there were products, but no "sense of vocation."[23] Modernism in the guise of the industrialist "superstate" would effectively mimic the Communist threat and the authors "expect in America at last much the same economic system as that imposed by violence upon Russia in 1917." All culture, particularly religion and art, decay under modern industrialism. But "nature industrialized" into cities, and artificial living, "is no longer nature" but the bastard child of nature.[24] Though no direct links are seen between Southern Agrarianism and the organic farming movement in the United States, the philosophical parallels are striking. Romantic farm literature in Britain, the United States, and early organic farming enthusiasts intuited a deep connection between labor and culture.

Though the essays of *I'll Take My Stand* advocated the rural farm as the cornerstone of the sectional revival of the South, none of the advocates actually got their hands dirty in agricultural work.[25] Unlike the British romantic farm enthusiasts they remained largely writers and academics (in contrast to the British romantic farm writers who found expression in actually farming the soil as landowners). This last fact highlights a difference with the organic farming movement in Britain. The advocates of Southern Agrarianism lacked contact with the soil. They had little idea of what to do with a compost pile—or the Indore method pioneered by Albert Howard. In the end, the Southern agrarian movement remained only a literary movement.

Agrarian ideals in Britain, Europe, and the United States all fed directly into romantic farm literature in the 1920s–30s, and formed the fertile soil from which organic farming protocols spread. Scholars have pointed out that Agrarianism in the twentieth century adapted its message to changing times. Rather than merely asserting the moral superiority of rural to urban life, agrarian partisans asserted that agriculture was economically vital to a nation's health, and closely interlinked with a healthy industrial base and with urban culture. This is particularly true during the period of the Great Depression, when the declining prices for farm goods in the 1930s led to mass poverty in rural areas. Yet moral arguments lingered, as one agricultural historian argued,

> Suffice it to say, the acceptance of urbanization by more and more farmers did not mean that they approved of city life. Farmers were, in fact, often critical of the moral, social and intellectual consequences of urban life and routine factory work.[26]

This mistrust came to be explicitly expressed by organic farming advocates.

---

[23] Ibid., xvii.   [24] Ibid., xviii.

[25] Lucinda H. Mackethan, "I'll take my Stand: The Relevance of the Agrarian Vision," *VQR* 56/4 (Autumn, 1980). Available online at: http://www.vqronline.org/essay/i%E2%80%99ll-take-my-stand-relevance-agrarian-vision [accessed January 24, 2017].

[26] Clifford B. Anderson, "The Metamorphosis of American Agrarian Idealism in the 1920's and 1930's" *Agricultural History* 35/4 (October, 1961): 187–8.

AGRICULTURE AND THE PROBLEM OF
HEALTH IN MODERN SOCIETY

While hundreds of authors throughout Europe and the English-speaking world published literary books on agricultural themes in the 1920s and 30s, only a small number of authors fed directly into the organic farming movement. Romantic farm literature exposed a mystical connection to the land and a deep sense that the traditional ways of farming produced a rich and spiritually satisfying culture. Some of these authors also promoted the idea that traditional farming methods produced healthier crops, although scientists and medical doctors introduced this idea to farmers. While their politics differed, many of the authors of romantic farm literature espoused the views of the far right and sported a robust appreciation of fascism in Italy and Germany, as will be seen in subsequent chapters. Most of these writers were British and echoed the same concerns for "blood and soil" prevalent in National Socialism in Germany, and cherished the new continental ideology that stressed the importance of peasant farming to national culture. While romantic farm literature should not be conflated with fascism, it should be seen as comfortable with both agrarian and fascist ideas.

Romantic farming literature often allied with health food fads driven by the perception that health had precipitously declined in the modern era. While it is often assumed that mortality decreased and life expectancy steadily increased during the Industrial Revolution, some medical historians suggest otherwise. If infant mortality under the age of five years is excised from the calculations of life expectancy, then individuals in the mid-Victorian period between 1850 and 1880 lived longer than those of the late Victorian era—and indeed, lived longer than the contemporary British population today. Then a change occurred. Height and life expectancy began to fall after 1880 and fell to its lowest point at the turn of the century. The year 1900 marks the nadir of this decline. From that point on height and life expectancy bounced back and slowly climbed higher over the course of the twentieth century. Interestingly, most discussions of increasing health in the twentieth century posit the baseline at 1900 and therefore miss the lower rates of mortality in the mid-Victorian period. This is significant because it has led scholars to lose sight of the remarkable gain and loss in the previous century. It also has obscured the deep suspicions harbored by the authors of romantic farm literature and advocates of organic farming that industrial methods of farming and food processing led to a serious degeneration of health.[27]

Most who enthusiastically endorsed Howard's organic protocols in the 1930s and 40s were born in the mid-to late Victorian period and lived through the period of mortality decline to 1900. Thus, they perceived a disparity between the health of their immediate forbears and that of their contemporaries. They also witnessed the steadily rapid increase in cancer and heart disease from 1880 onward—only partially

---

[27] See Paul Clayton and Judith Rowbotham, "An unsuitable and degraded diet? Part one: public health lessons from the mid-Victorian working class diet," *Journal of the Royal Society of Medicine*, 101 (2008): 282–9.

balanced by medical advances in other fields, such as antibiotics. This added relish, and alarm, to their warnings that the British population experienced a decline in health and vigor from industrial modernism.[28]

Various lifestyle changes may have accelerated falling mortality from 1880 to 1900. Paul Clayton and Judith Rowbotham assert that the mid-Victorians ate up to ten helpings a day of fresh and unprocessed fruits, vegetables, and meats, and that this diet radically changed with industrialized farming and food, particularly the importation of canned goods. Simultaneously, Victorians reduced physical work with industrial machines and mechanical transportation, while increasing the consumption of sugar.[29] Importation of cheap meat from the British Dominions, as well as Argentina and the United States, meant that while the working class had a rapid increase in protein consumption, they also had a rapid decline in fresh meat locally produced, and a decline also in variety. Refrigeration also led to an increase of canned meats, because the meat-packing houses, particularly in Chicago, used ammonia-cycle commercial refrigeration to ship meat from the farm or abattoirs into the processing plants with less loss. Herbal preparations of meat, often served with fruit and vegetables, likewise declined in the homes of the working class as the availability of cheap canned good, packed with sodium and premade sauces, increased. Refrigeration in the 1890s, on the one hand, increased the imports of meat, along with fruits and vegetables, but because of the time involved from harvest to dinner table, the food arrived with reduced vitamin content. Regular shipments of beef from Argentina and lamb from New Zealand and Australia eroded home markets for fresh meat. The manufacture of industrial cigarettes and the lower cost of alcohol also added to lifestyle changes that adversely affected health.[30]

The demand for canned foods, at first a novelty item for the upper classes, rose as the price of production fell. By the 1860s the working class began to indulge in canned foods primarily because it saved the need to go to markets daily for fresh produce. But the importation of canned goods skyrocketed when leading companies such as Heinz, Nestlé, and Underwood specialized in selling canned food cheaply to urban dwellers in the late nineteenth century. The variety expanded exponentially from meats and fruits, to pasta dishes like spaghetti and ravioli, to coq au vin, baked beans, and almost every item needed for the dinner table. Romantic farm

[28] Ibid.

[29] Ibid. Clayton and Rowbothom cite an array of literature, cookbooks, and housekeeping tracts to demonstrate the wider use of fresh food in the Mid-Victorian period. They also depend on the works of: J. Burnett, and D. Oddy, *The Origins and Devleopment of Food Policies in Europe* (Leicester, 1994); Y. Akiyama, *Feeding the Nation: Nutrition and Health in Britain before World War One* (London, 2008); and J. Benson and G. Shaw, eds. *The Evolution of Retail Systems c. 1800–1914* (Leicester, 1992).

[30] Thomas McKeown argued that working class diets improved in the mid-Victorian era, conferring greater resistance to infectious disease, and thus explains the longer life expectancy. See Thomas Mckeown, "Reasons for the Decline in Mortality in England and Wales in the Nineteenth Century" *Population Studies*, 16 (1962): 94–122. More recent scholarship has questioned aspects of this assertion, such as J. Colgrove, "The McKeown thesis: A Historical Controversy and its Enduring influence," *American Journal of Public Health* 92 (2002): 725–9. However, the evidence of a rise in life expectancy in the mid-Victorian period, and a fall between 1880 and 1900, is borne out by the evidence presented in J. Charlton and M. Murphy, eds., *The Health of Adult Britain 1841–1994* (vols. I and II) (London, 2004).

authors, and health activists who sounded the alarm in the 1920s and 1930s bemoaned the importation of canned meats, the mass production of sugared products and the modern diet after 1880 that—at least for the working class—emphasized canned fruit and vegetables. These changes in consumer habits, and the industrialization of farming and mass retailing, had a dramatic impact on the views of those who argued for reform.

This perceived decline in health accompanied other misgivings about the modern age. Increased mechanization ran parallel to the rise of mass culture and urbanization. Cheaper transportation undercut the market for cottage industries and local crafts. Competition with mass-produced goods shipped inexpensively reduced the market for small artisans producing high quality products. Fewer animals in rural and urban areas meant less manure available for fertilizing the soil. The use of the automobile for transportation, and the introduction of heavy trucks and tractors on farms, lowered the utility of animal power. Someone born in 1870 would see far fewer horses throughout their lifetime. Urban living, including large apartment blocks, meant fewer pets, particularly dogs. This furthered a sense of loss and disconnection to nature and to rural values. It meant humans increasingly lost the sense of connection with "nature" through animals. This sense of loss led to an increased awareness that modern society was moving away from a happier and healthier past, both physically and emotionally.[31]

By the 1920s most information available to the public came from mass-circulation newspapers, with two thirds of the British population reading on average one newspaper per day. The content had over the course of the century gone through a process of "Americanization," that took on an overtly partisan and sensational tone. Readers increasingly felt they observed the world as helpless spectators.[32] In the 1930s radio added to the top down feeding of mass information and aggravated the loss of local and peculiar cultural traits, resulting in cultural alienation, a feeling of displacement, and a loss of individual identity.[33] In this same period movie productions and neighborhood cinemas competed with local gatherings in pubs, churches, and local amateur sports teams. While mass media created a new

[31] For the connection between humans and nature, and the sense of well-being that flows from that connection, see F. S. Mayer, C. M. Frantz, E. Bruehlman-Senecal, and K. Dolliver, "Why is nature beneficial?: The role of connectedness to nature," *Environment and Behavior*, 41, (2009): 607–43. Some studies suggest that environmental action is connected to biophilia. See E. Kals, D. Schumacher and L. Montada, "Emotional affinity toward nature as a motivational basis to protect nature," *Environment and Behavior*, 31, (1999): 178–202; J. Vinning, M. S. Merrick, and E. A. Price, "The distinction between humans and nature: Human perceptions of connectedness to nature and elements of the natural and unnatural," *Human Ecology Review*, 15, (2008): 1–11; E. O. Wilson "Biophilia and the conservation ethic," *The biophilia hypothesis*, eds. S. Kellert and E. O. Wilson (Washington, D. C., 1993): 31–41.

[32] See Joel H. Wiener, *The Americanization of the British Press, 1830s–1914: Speed in the Age of Transatlantic Journalism* (London, 2011).

[33] Archer Spiral and L. Gleason, *History of Radio to 1926* (Washington D. C., 1938); Asa Briggs, *The History of Broadcasting in the United Kingdom* (Oxford, 1961). For an understanding of how radio disconnected creativity from the listening audience, see Ira Brodsky, "The History of Wireless: How Creative Minds Produced Technology for the Masses" (New York, 2008). Tim Crooks explore how radio became an extension of the journalism of newspapers. See Tim Crook, *International Radio Journalism: History, Theory and Practice* (London, 1998).

currency of narratives and vocabulary that reinforced national stereotypes, they also pushed aside local and rural knowledge. This had knock-on effects: playing sports locally developed increasingly into professional teams with citizens as mass spectators.[34] Alienation from organized religion and the increased pace of secularization added to the sense that modern society disconnected the individual from the local community. The "social gospel" that won adherents among clergy in mainstream Protestant churches echoed the collectivist ideas promoted by newspapers, movies, and radio from both the right and the left of the political spectrum.[35]

The global conservation movement pushed back against many of these developments, responding in part to the problems launched by industrialism and the sense of displacement in the modern age. First in the British Empire, and then spreading around the world, legislatures authorized massive set-asides of land to redress the balance between humans and our need to exploit nature. In Britain and other western societies where private land owners controlled most of the land, the movement to restore balance between human society and nature found expression in urban planning that promoted parks and boulevards lined with trees, and leafy suburbs. But the conservation movement—the first stage of modern environmentalism—must be considered only part of the response to the problems created by urbanization, industrialization, and mass consumerism. Many individuals saw that society needed to be radically re-ordered in order to get back to nature, even if it meant using artificial means to recreate a natural environment. They were determined to extend the ideals of the conservation movement from the forest to the farm, and, eventually, to the whole of society.

ROMANTIC FARM LITERATURE

Romantic farm literature prospered in the 1920s and onward as a direct result of the unease created by industrial agriculture and the new consumer age. One influential writer, Edgar J. Saxon, merged the values of agrarianism with the advocacy of health food. He himself was not a farmer, but owned and edited the *Healthy Life* magazine from 1920 (changing its name to *Health and life* in 1934), and published on a wide variety of topics that all involved agriculture and whole foods. Saxon like most of those writers in the 1920s and 30s who romanticized traditional farming methods, followed the ideas of foresters who promoted desiccation theory. He particularly admired the ideas of the founder of "The Men of the Trees," Richard St Barbe Baker, who promoted the idea, among many others, that deforestation led to a diminution of rainfall and that raping the earth drove the world "into desert."[36]

---

[34] For a history of how amateur sports differed substantially from professional, see *Amateurism in British sport: It matters not who won or lost*, eds. Dilwyn Porter and Stephen Wagg (London, 2008).

[35] Harold Perkin traces the shift in the late nineteenth century from the entrepreneurial ideal to the professional ideal, and from individualism to collectivism. See Harold Perkin, *The Rise of Professional Society: England since 1880* (London, 1989).

[36] Ibid., 30.

Saxon romanticized traditional farming methods and gave voice to a plethora of romantic farm writers. He founded "vitamin cafes" in Britain, and raged against the industrialization of modern life, including modern finance and fertilizer and chemical companies. He supported a wide range of alternative approaches to health, including nudism and social credit (to reduce stress over money), and, in the 1930s, he allied with the burgeoning organic farming movement.[37] Saxon was a forerunner of themes distinctly ecological, and wrote tirelessly against waste, pollution, and adulterated food.[38]

While Saxon strived to restore human health through natural living, he is also a representative example of how romantic notions of traditional life fueled and inspired opposition to the use of chemicals in agriculture. He noted how his grand-father grew wheat, ground it in his own windmill, baked his own bread in his own oven, and sold it in his own village shop. The shop boasted enormous randy-balls, black treacle, and soft brown sugar from a huge hogshead straight from the West Indian plantations, home cured bacon, tea from China, cloves and nutmeg from Malaya and the Spice Islands, and butter from his own dairy. His grandfather made wholesome bread because "it retained the living germ" with all of its nutrition— the same white bread that his forefathers had eaten in the Middle Ages and not, he pointed out, the denatured white bread sold in his own time.[39]

He learned as a young man a mystical sense of the health-giving life that is found only in nature. Working in an office firm, he escaped with a day off in 1897 and walked up the small hills to the River Dee. He suffered foot problems, and to ease the pain, at a waterfall he took off his boots and socks and "let my feet swing in the torrent." By the next morning he discovered that the rush of icy water cured his feet. He believed that energy in the moving water—unknown to science—had worked a "nature cure" to restore his cells and heal his feet.[40] Our break with nature interrupted the natural stream of life, and the natural healing properties of our bodies. The worst part of modern living—in addition to the lack of fresh air and natural sunlight on the skin—was "persistently to eat food that is not worth eating because it has been robbed through processing."[41]

Saxon admired Gerard Vernon Wallop, another prominent and influential writer and organizer who romanticized traditional agriculture. Today Wallop is most remembered for his book, *Alternative to Death* (1943) published under his title of the Earl of Portsmouth (later, Viscount Lymington).[42] Unlike Saxon, Wallop inherited a sizable estate which he actively farmed in Hampshire. In this book Wallop lamented the calamity of a falling birth rate, caused, he had no doubt, by "biological despair"—a despair that grew like a rank weed from the neglect of the soil, and the inevitable decay of human health that followed. Fertility would return

---

[37] Edgar J. Saxon, *A Sense of Wonder*, (London, ND). John Stewart Collis published a selection of Saxon's writing from this period in *A Sense of Wonder*. A biographer and novelist in the 1920s he also published *While Following the Plough* (London, 1946) and *Down to Earth* (London, 1947).

[38] John Stewart Collis, "Preface," *A Sense of Wonder*, 5, 6.

[39] Ibid., 7.   [40] Ibid., 15.

[41] Ibid., 22.   [42] Gerard Vernon Wallop, *Alternative to Death* (London, 1943).

to the human race again to rebuild a glorious civilization when and only when fertility returned to the soil.[43]

Wallop intuited a deep and vital connection between the production of meaningful culture and how much we cherish the earth, believing a proper relationship with the soil led to local craftsmanship and a vital national life. Soil fertility gave birth to "the condition of wholeness."[44]

> Farming is the greatest single factor in producing health for the individual, through food and clothing...Spiritual health, granted the foundation of physical wholeness, comes from the satisfaction of creative life, harmonious relationships and hope for the future [that is crafts, and peace]. To "bear and be borne" is the future.[45]

Modern elites, he believed, overspecialized and over-centralized our society. The masters of society have turned us into slaves, "herded together" in movie theatres where propaganda masquerades as art, boasting the "most degenerate aspects of life with Asiatic profusion." To escape from this "proletarian thralldom," he continued, we must decentralize, and allow the individual to flourish; we must rediscover rural values. To do that, he argued, it is essential that we raise our own food.[46]

In a hint about the root cause of World War One and Two—quite subversive given he published under wartime conditions in 1943—he echoed the liberal economist John Hobson in *Imperialism: A Study* (1902) who argued that harsh competitions for trade and industry changed the way livelihoods were gained and led inevitably to conflict between nations. Germany and Italy under fascism had partially succeeded in restoring rural values. In Germany however, the need for security against the Soviet Union and Britain required mass industrialization to compete, and this in turn hindered the return of labor to the land. For all these great powers, however, rural life remained the only theatre of healing, health, and international concord. Only decentralization, he concluded, could produce peace.[47]

In his autobiography Wallop retells the romantic appeal that traditional farming held for himself and his fellow travelers in 1920s and 30s Britain and Germany. In his chapter, "Kinship in Husbandry," he tells his story by sharing the vague and undefined roots of the romantic farming movement. He realized as he began to farm his own estate that "a complete rethinking of our problems" was necessary.[48]

> So what I want to try to do here is to describe what I might call a school of agricultural philosophers, perhaps I should say ecological thinkers, but no one word can describe the underlying thought and instincts which prompted us in very varying degrees, and gave us as many facets as a rose-cut stone. The underlying thing that brought us

[43] Ibid., 5–6. Wallop was also inspired by another romantic farm writer, H. J. Massingham, particularly his book *English Countryman: A Study of the English Tradition* (London, 1942). He also echoes Colonel Pollitts, *Britain can Feed Herself* (London, 1942) and Montague Fordham, *The Land and Life: A Survey of Problems of the Land* (London, 1942).
[44] Wallop, *Alternative to Death,* 161.   [45] Ibid., 161.
[46] Ibid., 122.   [47] Ibid., 125.
[48] Earl of Portsmouth, [Gerard Vernon Wallop] *A Knot of Roots: An Autobiography* (London, 1965).

together was a deep feeling that our headlong "progress" was destroying our minds and bodies in peace as well as war. The more we received a modern education the more spiritually illiterate we were becoming. The more we watched, be it sport, cinema and later television, the less we did. The more we hear the less we listened, the more we ate of preserved and processed food the less we truly digested.[49]

Wallop founded two groups to recreate traditional farming methods and rural culture arts and crafts: the English Mistery and the Kinship of Husbandry. Rolf Gardiner who later used his estate in Dorset to host conferences and cultural events that attracted members of both groups, joined him. After World War Two, Gardiner helped found the *Soil Association* and worked to popularize organic farming. Wallop writes that Gardiner spent his "whole life rooted half mystically in tilled fields and tall forests."[50] A forester, musician, farmer, and poet, he also created and led village folk-dances. One group, the Springhead Ring consisted of singers and youth workers on both sides of the North Sea, in Britain and Germany. His neighbors regarded his interests as light hearted and even foolish "whimsy."[51]

Gardner descended from a family of rural merchants. His father however was an Egyptologist and thus Rolf lived his earliest years near the University of Berlin and retained fond memories of Germany and German culture. As a boy his family then moved to the West Downs and he later attended St. John's College, Cambridge. There he studied medieval and modern languages. His prosperous family then had the means to purchase a small estate—a "land reclamation" farm in 1927 called Gore Farm—in Ashmore, Britain. Gardner's grandson, in an interview, remarked eighty years later that,

It was a broken-down landscape of scree and brambles, gorse and rabbits. With my great-uncle [the composer] Henry Balfour Gardiner, he established four million trees over the next 30 years. Initially, he employed up to 30 men who were glad to have the work in forestry when agriculture was so depressed in the Twenties.[52]

The family bought, five years later, another farm close by, named Springhead, Fontmell Magna, which to this day operates as a trust for sustainable living and rural culture. Gardiner's family also owned estates in Nyasaland, today Malawi, which Gardiner visited in 1947.[53]

Gardiner was a neo-traditionalist who witnessed the mass societies of Russia and the United States wrecking European Christendom, bringing down on the luckless citizens of Britain and Europe a new dark age. He answered this new threat with forestry and farming in order to create safe retreats—as the monasteries had done after

[49] Ibid., 77–8.   [50] Ibid., 81.   [51] Ibid., 80.
[52] Stephen Pritchard, "At home with the organic conductor," *The Guardian* (January 28, 2017). Available online at: http://www.theguardian.com/lifeandstyle/2007/jan/28/foodanddrink.features5 [accessed June 1, 2017].
[53] Andrew Best, "Introduction," in Henry Balfour Gardiner, *Water Springing from the Ground: An Anthology of the Writings of Rolf Gardiner* (Dorset, 1972): xi.

the fall of Rome. Each of us, he taught, should seek to be "an ameliorator of land" and to "create islands of example" to restart the upward climb of civilization again.[54]

True to the memories of his youth, he sponsored youth exchanges between England and Germany after World War One to foster understanding based on music, culture, and love of nature. War would be impossible, he believed, if only the two racial cousins knew and understood each other. Both sides had in common one central thing as Europeans—a love of the land and of the culture that rural life produced. This life connected man to the mystical home of his ancestors and inspired him with explosive spiritual energy. Europeans forged western civilization on the anvil of the gods and in the shadow of pagan altars. The "sacramental element of agriculture" pumped the life blood of the future.[55]

Gardiner associated with many rural reconstructionists who welcomed the rise of fascism in Europe as a defense against the expansion of communism. In the neo-traditional agriculturalists he hoped to find a vanguard that would lead the renewal of tradition against mass democracy and communism. The Wandervogel youth movement and the Bunde, so popular in Germany, were exactly the kind of organizations that Gardiner felt would renew England. He wrote a letter to Goebbels praising the work of the Bund, which Goebbels then had printed in German newspapers. As Britain slipped into war against Germany, this letter, and Goebbels response, tarred his public reputation with the British press as a crypto National Socialist—an accusation that during the course of the war and afterwards he denied. Many neo-traditionalists and early organic farmers shared his politics.[56] When Britain declared war on Germany on September 3, 1939, he wrote,

> The dreaded thing has come upon the world and the work for union, relevance and truth in the relations of kindred nations... has been savagely interrupted.

Gardiner remained a prominent figure in the early organic farming movement during and after the war, and a prominent figure in the Soil Association of Britain, established in 1945.[57]

Perhaps the most widely read writer who promoted healing through connection to the soil was William Beach Thomas. His books can be considered a twentieth-century counterpart to the romantic pastoral writing of Gilbert White's classic *History of Selbourne*. Beach appealed more to aesthetics than science. Like White, Beach chronicled a yeoman's England with detail and poetic description, mixing in an amateur's knowledge of land management. He promoted a commitment to the value of traditional knowledge and skills and examined the intricate web of interaction between plants, animals, and humans. He did not paint dark pictures of modernism. There is not much of a hint of the threat posed by cities or even pollution. Rather Thomas takes his readers into the picturesque world of the countryside and dwells on a series of lovely details.

---

[54] Ibid., xi, 1.   [55] Ibid., 10.   [56] Ibid., 137.   [57] Ibid., 110.

In *The Yeoman's England* (1934) Beach quoted the simple lines of a German balloonist who strayed by accident over England and how these lines perfectly sum up his view of the English countryside:

> We came to the most beautiful country I ever saw. It made me think of Grimm's Fairy Tales. The greenest fields imaginable and no fences, just hedges and an occasional stone wall...Most of the fields were pasture fields or seemed so. They were covered with this intensely green grass. There was never a frame house. The houses were of the softest red brick—I mean the colour—and all pretty, or I should say, picturesque, and never an inch wasted.[58]

This was the England that Beach wished to preserve. He did mix in a social vision however. He believed there existed a "town mind" that denied the "democracy of the land" and reigned in tyranny over the rural culture. It divided those who own, rent, and labor on the land, and kept them all silent with almost no say in national affairs. England must "restore gusto" and pride to all classes of farm workers by granting common control over the land—turning rural England into a type of giant commune.[59]

Romantic accounts of traditional farming methods in Britain were not, however confined to a literary movement, such as the Southern Agrarians in the United States. A wide number of scientists and amateurs mixed advocacy and science to advance the cause of more sustainable farming methods. One of these was George Stapledon, an ecologist and expert on grasslands. Gardiner, who incorporated him into his rural culture projects, called him "Stapes." He described him as a "birdlike man" with a great shock of grey hair that crowned an extraordinary and passionate mind. Gardiner credited him with revolutionizing the use of grass in farming by rediscovering ancient principles of land management. Even if Stapledon did not rediscover ancient principles, he did successfully breed new grass strains well suited for the pastures of Britain. Gardiner reminisced years later about how he would chauffeur Stapledon and his assistant around the countryside. On hot days Stapledon "would preach under a tree like Buddha or Socrates to the listening farmers."[60]

In *The Land: Now and To-morrow* (1935) Stapledon argued that bad management wasted two thirds of the landscape of Britain. Farmers underutilized large tracts of land on hillsides that could be used for grazing. With the proper use of grass agricultural populations could be doubled to provide jobs for the unemployed in the city and at the same time provide parklands and recreational space for the urban populations.[61] If the unconstrained growth of "ribbon development" of suburbs were not controlled then no countryside "in the real meaning of the word" would survive in the British Isles—except remote parts of Wales and Scotland. Sprawl, he preached, destroyed culture. Stapledon sought to keep the cities and the countryside distinct with little in-between. He envisioned concentric circles moving out from the cities from a city wall, then playgrounds, golf courses, and still further,

---

[58] In William Beach Thomas, *The Yeoman's England* (London, 1934), xv.   [59] Ibid.
[60] Gardiner, *Water Springing from the Ground*, 79–80.
[61] R. G. Stapledon, "The Green Hills," *Country Life* 79 (1936): 22–33.

cottages for getaways on weekends, with camping grounds and national parks interspersed throughout the agricultural areas. Suburbs were only a blight on the land. If "hybrid growth" was not stopped, it would "devour practically the whole land surface of Great Britain."[62]

Other writers in the same vein promoted the vision of an ideal countryside. H. J. Massingham dropped out of Oxford and became a journalist and poet and a widely read author of romantic farm literature. Like other advocates of rural life his work ran parallel to British Fascist economics—in this case supporting the ideas of Douglas and Social Credit advocated by the leader of the British Union of Fascists, Oswald Mosely. His work can be seen as a precursor to the organic farming movement, which he wholeheartedly joined when he came across the ideas of Albert Howard. His connection with the past acted as a bridge joining the ideas of Gilbert White and Cobbett with modern life. In *English Downland,* (1936) he surveyed the English chalk country, and like White, merged with a poet's eye of both geology and history, and envisioned an England of parks, fields, hedgerows, and woodlands.[63] In the *Wisdom of the Fields* (1945) Massingham unapologetically argued for agrarian values. Like Cobbet he agreed that the age of the machine did more than eliminate drudgery, "what it actually did was to eliminate skill and pride in work and so create a new drudgery of its own." The machine age also alienated humans from the past—from rural and spiritual values—leaving us without a sense of wholeness. Health for individuals as well as health for the surrounding culture lay in the restoration of craftsmanship, regionalism, and cultivation to the center of national life.[64]

BIODYNAMICS

In very small circles, biodynamics ran parallel to romantic farm literature and shared a mystical connection to nature. It had however no influence on the formation of the scientific protocols that underlie organic farming methods. The founder of biodynamics, Rudolf Steiner, and his immediate followers—particularly Ehrenfried Pfeiffer—did exert a pronounced cultural influence among a small subset of those who valued traditional farming methods. Albert Howard and the vast majority of organic farming activists rejected the ideas of Rudolf Steiner, considering him to be an occultist who took a thoroughly unscientific approach. One historian of the organic movement in Britain, Phillip Conford, rightly claimed that biodynamic farming practiced an "organic-plus" method—that is, its mystical adherents tended to apply the methods and protocols pioneered by the organic farming movement

[62] Stapledon, *The Land Now and To-morrow* (London, 1935).
[63] For his economic and political views see Harold J. Massingham, *Tree of Life* (London, 1941); Harold J. Massingham, *English Downland,* (London, 1936) 1. Dropping out of Oxford because of poor health Massingham became a journalist and best friends with a farmer. *English Downland* reads like a well written tour guide. It served the function of drawing the attention of city dwellers to the countryside. He later joined the Kinship in Husbandry.
[64] Harold J. Massingham, *Wisdom of the Fields* (London, 1945), 18, 34.

and then added mystical formulations into the mix. Steiner originally named his movement Anthroposophy, which in turn had grown out of the spiritualist teachings of Henry Steel Olcott and Helena Blavatsky, the founders of Theosophy.[65] The Theosophy movement claimed to have direct access to secret and hidden knowledge derived from ancient spiritual masters, which, when channeled through séance-like rituals, could reveal truths about the reality of the spiritual world that lies behind all nature. Steiner also revealed his doctrines to followers in a didactic fashion that resembled the revelations of a yogi to his followers. Conford concluded that Steiner's doctrines did not materially affect the growth of organic farming.[66]

Steiner grew up in the Austro-Hungarian Empire. His father served as gamekeeper on a large aristocratic estate—before working as a telegraphist with the South-Austrian railway—and the stories his father told him may have inspired his dream of living close to nature.[67] Dabbling in philosophy and literary criticism he came to the attention of Annie Besant, president and leader of the Theosophy Society. A few years later she appointed him to lead the movement in Germany. He then broke away to form the Anthroposophical Society in 1923 which shared many of the same characteristics as Theosophy. He also came to fame as the founder of the Waldorf School that had many imitators around the world.[68]

What cannot be denied, however, is that while Steiner's ideas had little influence on the development of organic farming, and while his ideas are rarely fully applied by farmers (for very practical reasons), he did catch the imagination of a number of romantic farm enthusiasts with a bent for mysticism. Steiner never used the term "biodynamic"—those who attended his lectures popularized the phrase. Organic farmers today often use the term to describe organic farming protocols with a number of mystic elements added into the mix.[69] As with Theosophy, Steiner's approach to agriculture has been described by his adherents as a spiritual science that merged the esoteric world of metaphysics with advances in empirical science. But Steiner never trained or practiced as a scientist. Before he adopted the teachings of Theosophy, Steiner considered himself a philosopher and literary critic with a particular specialization in the writings of Goethe. He firmly convinced his followers however that he successfully merged spiritual questions with a rigorous scientific mentality.[70]

Steiner's fame in agriculture comes from a series of lectures given in 1924 to a group of farmers in Koberwitz, Westphalia (at the time part of Germany and after 1945, in Wroclaw, Poland), at the invitation of Count Keyserlingk, scion of an old noble family and himself a farmer. Even though he shared an impulse against the

---

[65] Holger Kirchmann, "Biological Dynamic Farming—An Occult Form of Alternative Agriculture?" *Journal of Agricultural and Environmental Ethics* 7/2 (1994): 173.
[66] Philip Conford, *The Origins of the Organic Movement* (Edinburgh, 2001): 80.
[67] Holger Kirchmann, "Biological Dynamic Farming—An Occult Form of Alternative Agriculture?" *Journal of Agricultural and Environmental Ethics* 7/2 (1994): 184.
[68] Rudolph Steiner, *The Education of the Child: Lectures on Education* (London, 1927).
[69] John Paull, "Attending the First Organic Agriculture Course: Rudolf Steiner's Agricultural Course at Koberwitz, 1924," *European Journal of Social Sciences*, 21/1 (2011): 65.
[70] Robert A. McDermott, "Rudolf Steiner and Anthroposophy," *Modern Esoteric Spirituality*, eds. Antoine Faivre and Jacob Needleman (New York, 1992): 288.

use of chemicals in agriculture, his lectures were anything but scientific, and he admits that the lectures were "about agriculture from an Anthroposophical point of view" and sprang from "spiritual impulses."[71] His lectures were esoteric and given in a series of "hints, which he asked, for the present, should not be spoken of outside this circle."[72] Of those attending the conference less than a third can be identified as farmers or agricultural workers. The rest were largely middle class and professional, seeking guidance on spiritual matters.[73] The following reveals the extent to which the core of his teaching relied upon mystical protocols. These protocols were not drawn from peasant traditions, or even mythical tradition rooted in local European history, but are given as a revelation to his followers.

> So if we want to work with chamomile, as we did with yarrow, we must pick its beautiful, delicate, white and yellow flower heads and treat them just like we did the yarrow umbels; but we must stuff them into cattle intestines rather than in a bladder... In this case, since we want to be worked on by a vitality that is as closely related to the earthly element as possible, we need to take these precious little sausages... and again let them spend the entire winter underground. They should be placed not too deeply in soils that is as rich as possible in humus. We should also try to choose a spot that will remain covered with snow for a long time, and where this snow will be shone upon by the Sun as much as possible, so that the cosmic-astral influences will work down into the soil where the sausages are buried. Then, when spring comes, dig up the sausages and store them or add their contents to your manure... You will find that your manure... has the ability to enliven the soil so that plant growth is extraordinarily stimulated. Above all, you will get healthier plants—really much healthier plants—if you fertilize this way... To our modern way of thinking, this all sounds quite insane. I am well aware of that.[74]

Steiner believed that the quality of agricultural products had declined, and that due to low nutrition food would soon be unfit for human consumption. The answer to this problem lay in abjuring chemical fertilizers and pesticides, and viewing the farm as a single living organism. Farmers restore nutrition by tapping into cosmic forces that permeate the universe. Herbal preparations added to manure pull these cosmic forces from the universe and channel them into the soil.[75] This clearly deviates from both industrial and organic agricultural thinking that postulated the need to return nutrients to the soil. To close a system off and view the farm as an organism would only work when crops are not harvested and consumed outside the perimeters of the farm. Otherwise, harvesting and selling the produce outside the farm slowly reduced the nutrient level of the soil and required inputs—either artificial or natural composts with material brought in from outside. A biodynamic farm would therefore at best only work for crops that thrive in low nutrient soil, such as grapes. Most other produce would lower the soil fertility on the farm. Neither did his prescriptions address environmental concerns. Steiner ignored the

[71] Paull, "Steiner," 316.   [72] Ibid., 10.   [73] Ibid., 67.

[74] As quoted in Philip Conford, *Origins*, 65. Kirchmann also gives an excellent analysis of the herbal compounds and methods of handling them as laid out by Steiner. See Kirchmann, *Biological Dynamic Farming*, 175–84.

[75] Ibid., 174.

problem of the loss of ammonia from soil when using animal manures and the nitrate leaching from agricultural soils into groundwater after manuring. Nor did he advocate the use of township waste to recirculate plant nutrients. Rather he aimed to restore agriculture through "cosmic and terrestrial forces."[76]

While his prescriptions were scientifically untenable his course of lectures found ready adherents motivated by a desire to recapture pre-industrial culture and re-enchant modern life.[77] That his herbal remedies for soil infertility had little actual base in folk tradition, and far more in common with the nineteenth-century movement of homeopathy and Theosophy, did not deter his listeners. Steiner's "biodynamic" methods rapidly spread to small groups of adherents around the world, and were occasionally absorbed by a subset of romantic farm writers. While Steiner died in 1925, his advocates continued to promote magical herbal formulas placed in manure. Steiner's herbal preparations and rituals seamlessly folded into organic farming practices that spread in the 1930s and afterward. Steiner himself contributed nothing to the scientific and practical success of organic farming protocols.[78]

The historian must be alert to highly vocal and organized activists who project an exaggerated influence onto the historical record. Certainly, the biodynamic movement has had cultural influence among a subset of organic farmers, and the number of its adherents is still increasing. But because it lacked innovation in scientific methods and protocols it merely added esoteric rites to a protocol laid out by the founder of the movement, Albert Howard. In addition, the term biodynamic is often used by farmers who do not practice a closed system with no outside inputs, such as envisioned by Steiner, for good reason. His method of not adding material to the land from outside the farm can succeed only for crops that have low nutrient requirements. The Rothamsted research station maintains to this day a control strip of wheat that still produces a yield—though low—without any fertilizers added since the year 1843.[79] But a closed system that harvested high nutrient crops yearly would soon exhaust the soil, with or without mystic rites, and, for this reason, few farmers could afford to strictly practice Steiner's method.[80] To those inclined towards Steiner's mysticism, the protocols of Albert Howard proved of vital importance, because the Howard protocols worked, and did indeed restore soil fertility, and thus almost all practitioners of biodynamic agriculture that do not include low nutrient crops rely upon Howard's classic methods as the base of operations for the farm.

---

[76] Ibid., 175.

[77] An article that critiques Steiner's ideas in light of mainstream science is Linda Chalker-Scott, "The Science Behind Biodynamic Preparations: A Literature Review," *HortTechnology* 23/6 (2013).

[78] Conford, *Origins*, 78.

[79] "Broadbalk Winter Wheat Experiment," e-RA: the electronic Rothamsted Archive. Available online at: http://www.era.rothamsted.ac.uk/index.php?area=home&page=index&dataset=4 [accessed August 18, 2017].

[80] See also Linda Chalker-Scott, "The Myth of Biodynamic Agriculture" (2004). Available online at: https://puyallup.wsu.edu/wp-content/uploads/sites/403/2015/03/biodynamic-agriculture.pdf [accessed May 30, 2017].

Howard, on the other hand, did not inspire the same romantic response as Steiner. This can be seen in the example of the Earl of Portsmouth who, though he adopted Albert Howard's method of organic farming, found Howard's work too cold and scientific for his taste. He wrote, rather condescendingly,

> Albert Howard had done famous work in India on agricultural stations where practical experience had turned him into a fanatic convert to compost and non-chemical manures. Good as he was, he was too one-sided to be wholly practical; for the same reason it was easier to find him liveable than lovable or to be taken into intimate friendship, but I learned much from him.[81]

Following Steiner's death in 1925 his followers spread his teaching throughout the European and colonial world in small pockets, particularly in Germany. Overseas his teaching followed the same path where Theosophy flourished, largely in the British imperial world, North America, and then in parts of continental Europe.

Another factor that helped fold Steiner's mystic ideas into the mindset of some followers of traditional farming methods is Steiner's political position. His ideas proved compatible with the fascism that appealed in the 1930s on the continent and in the British world. Steiner derived his brand of Social Darwinism from Ernst Haeckel (who coined the term "ecology") on race, *volk*, and politics.[82] Steiner equated reincarnation as racial progress with Aryans at the top of the pyramid. He taught that Aryans descended from the race that founded the lost continent of Atlantis, and that a war between the wandering races of whites and non-whites would one day settle the mastery of the earth.[83] Like many organic farming enthusiasts, he distrusted democracy. He saw it as utterly materialistic and devoid of spiritual sensitivies, a position in which the United States and the godless Soviet Union were prime examples, followed by the failing Weimar Republic.[84] Steiner's followers cannot be politically classified today in the same camp. But the early advocates of Steinerism, like many advocates of organic farming, fitted comfortably within the politics of European fascism and nativist nationalism.[85]

One of the most influential propagandanizers of Steiner's ideas was Ehrenfried Pfeiffer. Though his followers refer to him as a scientist, he had no scientific training, and followed in the footsteps of his mother and father in anthroposophist philosophy. He founded at Dornach a laboratory to experiment with crystallization methods of copper chloride, and from reading the pattern of the crystals claimed to predict

---

[81] Portsmouth, *A Knot of Roots*, 86.

[82] See Ansgar Martin, *Rassismus und Geschlichtsmetaphysik: Esoterischer Darwinismus und Freiheitsphilosophie bei Rudolf Steiner* (Frankfurt, 2012).

[83] Rudolf Steiner, *Die geistigen Hintergründe des Ersten Weltkrieges*, (Berlin, 1921): 38. See also Rudolf Steiner, *Ueber die Wanderungen der Rassen* (Berlin, 1904).

[84] For an excellent review of Martin, *Rassismus and Geschlichtmetaphysik*, see Peter Staudenmaier, "Review of *Rassismus und Geschechtsmetaphyik* by Ansgar Martins," Waldorfblog (December 22, 2012). Available online at: https://waldorfblog.wordpress.com/2012/12/22/staudenmaier-rezension/ [accessed August 18, 2017].

[85] See "Der ursprüngliche politische Kontext der Waldorf-Bewegung" (March 1, 2011). Available online at: https://blog.psiram.com/2011/03/anthroposophie-dreigliederung-und-demokratie/ [accessed June 1, 2017].

early cancers in patients. For this achievement, Hahnemann Medical College in Philadelphia, a homeopathic institution, awarded an honorary doctorate.[86] A 1939 article in *Time* magazine, picturesquely described his discovery,

> One cold winter day 14 years ago, while young Dr. Ehrenfried Pfeiffer was pondering cancer problems in Basel, Switzerland, he noticed a cup of steaming hot coffee and one of tea resting side by side on a window sill. The steam from both cups condensed on the cold window pane, but the crystals of the frost patterns were very different. Dr. Pfeiffer had a hunch that the blood of cancer victims and the blood of healthy persons might perhaps form crystals as different as those of coffee and tea. After trying some 23 substances, he hit on copper chloride as blood's best crystallizing agent. Last week Dr. Pfeiffer and his colleague, Dr. George Miley of Philadelphia's Hahnemann Medical College, described their new test for the presence of early cancer.
>
> A drop of blood is taken from the finger tip of a cancer suspect. The blood is dissolved in a small amount of lukewarm sterile water, mixed with copper chloride and spread on a glass microscope slide to crystallize. Healthy blood forms a green crystal pattern which, under a microscope, looks like a delicate, fan-shaped palm leaf. But in cancerous blood some unknown chemical forms a pattern of scattered, double-wing bow ties. In 1,000 trials on known cancer victims, said Drs. Pfeiffer and Miley, the copper test was 80% accurate.[87]

No subsequent scientific work confirmed his findings. Pfeiffer's book *Bio-Dynamic Farming and Gardening* did much to publicize Steiner's ideas in the English-speaking world, published in 1938 and reprinted many times, translated into French, Italian, Dutch, and German. Pfeiffer's book reveals that he did as much for organic farming as he did for biodynamics, by basically advancing the organic protocols of Howard—often without attribution—and then adding the mysticism of Steiner. This method of organic-plus proved enduring among biodynamic followers.[88] He carefully laid out Howard's method of composting, mixing air and water into vegetable matter and animal manures, and then added the "plant preparations" to "induce the right kind of fermentation."[89] Perhaps wishing to introduce his audience gently into the mysticism of Steiner, he remained coy about the magic preparations. Instead of referring openly to the herbs and cosmic forces that animal parts like the cow horn attracted, he stated that he and his associates ran experiments in the "chemical-biological research laboratory at the Goetheanum" (a Steiner institute) to scientifically test the mystical preparations that, he claimed, proved scientifically effective.[90]

---

[86] Naomi Rogers, *An Alternative Path: The Making and Remaking of Hahnemann Medical College and Hospital of Philadelphia*, (New Brunswick, 1998), 200.

[87] (Untitled), *Time*, 34/13, (September 25, 1939): 38.

[88] Holger Kirchmann, "Biological dynamic farming–an occult form of alternative agriculture?" *Journal of Agricultural and Environmental Ethics*, 7/2 (1994): 173–87.

[89] Ehrenfried Pfeiffer, *Bio-Dynamic Farming and Gardening: Soil Fertility, Renewal and Preservation*, trans. F. Heckel (New York, 1938), 38–52. The herbal composting formulas were labelled by Steiner, formulas # 500, 501, 502, 503, 504, 505, 506, 507.

[90] Ibid.

On the European continent biodynamic agriculture is often conflated with organic farming. This is particularly true of the period from the 1930s to the end of the Second World War. Biodynamic farming has remained a small part of European agriculture. Because most practitioners of biodynamic farming also practiced organic techniques that did not originate with Steiner, it is difficult to entirely separate out the strands of organic farming from biodynamic methods in Europe. This is clearly seen in Germany in the 1930s where Richard Walther Darre and other high-level officials of the National Socialist government supported organic methods, often while attempting to eschew the occultism of biodynamic farming and to instead instate sustainable traditional farming.[91] Organic farming methods—because so often mixed with Steiner's occultism—were stifled in this period, and never became more than a marginal part of agricultural production. Not until after 1980 did the global organic farming movement gain institutional support or make significant inroads in Europe.

GERMAN BIOLOGICAL FARMING

In Germany agricultural romanticism produced a decidedly nationalistic message. The birth of a single German nation from a multitude of small states kindled artistic and philosophical ideals that labored to produce national unity.[92] The *Lebensreform* (Life Reform) movement exemplified this. It arose in the late nineteenth century as German national consciousness fully developed and loosely influenced congeries of overlapping groups and individuals that advocated variants of alternative ideas and lifestyles: youth movements (*wander Vogel*), vegetarianism, nudism, pantheism, mystic nationalism, anti-Semitism, racism as well as the revival of crafts, ruralism, and *Volkish* ideas. Alternative agricultural practices and ideas took its place as a tenet of *Lebensreform*—called biological farming—and slowly absorbed global organic farming protocols. Today organic farming and biological farming, now largely stripped of its national focus, are used interchangeably on the continent.

A hospital chaplain and Prussian parliamentarian, Eduard Baltzer, pioneered the *Lebensreform* movement in the 1870s. He stridently criticized agricultural methods, including traditional mixed farming. He feared the specter of famine and the political instability that followed. Because grains sustained a greater human population per acre than animals, he advocated the radical idea that farmers should neither raise animals for food nor use them as beasts of burden on the farm. All citizens should be vegetarian. More animals meant less grain for people and a national

---

[91] See Anna Bramwell, *Blood and Soil: Walter Darre and Hitler's "Green Party"* (Bourne End, 1985). A balanced approach can be found in Peter Staudenmaier, "Organic Farming in Nazi Germany: The Politics of Biodynamic Agriculture, 1933–1945," *Environmental History* 18 (April, 2013): 383–411.

[92] Thomas Nipperdey, *Réflexions sur l'histoire allemande, traduit de l'allemand par Claude Orsoni*, (Paris, Gallimard, March 24, 1992), 156–73.

threat to Germany. Since artificial fertilizers stimulated crop production, Baltzer urged readers to fully embrace the chemical industry.[93]

Many other voices blossomed from the cultural soil of *Lebensreform*. Maximilian Klein, a vegetarian activist, promoted both artificial fertilizers and night soil from urban wastes. Along with Eugene Simon, a French agricultural scientist, he highly praised Chinese methods of returning excrement to the soil.[94] Another vegetarian enthusiast, Karl Untermöhlen, settled in Heimgarten—a life reform colony—and preached against artificial fertilizers. Instead he advocated a new formula—powdered stone—invented by Julius Hensl, for fertilizing the soil. The "Stone Meal manure of Hensel" rejuvenated crops, and he personally testified that his fruit trees grew free from the damage of frost, insects, and disease. With fertilizers, including animal manures "fibers are relaxed, their sap is checked, [and] diseases develop," but with Hensel's formula "the trees become strong and hardened."[95]

Julius Hensl invented Stone Meal by grinding stones he found in his garden. He claimed that this technique created bread from stones and unlocked the "inexhaustible nutritive forces...stored up in the rocks, the air and the water," thus raising agricultural production, solving unemployment, and liberating men to "attain true happiness by discovering the sources whence all early blessing flow and put an end to self-seeking and greed."[96] He argued that the closer the mountains to the farm, the better the match between people and the soil and a guarantee of German soil for German nutrition. One follower of Hensel wrote that,

> Ground stone fertilizer does not come from overseas
> From Jews, from abroad it does not come here
> It comes to me and you from mountains
> Truly: it comes to us from side to side
> We warn, we warn the farmer
> From terrible enemies who lie in wait.[97]

One scholar of biological farming on the Continent, Corinna Treiterl, remarks that after the 1880s,

> "Natural" came in their hands to refer not to social structures and habits but to the geographical sources and physiological effects of ground stone on German bodies. In their quest to reform fertilizer habits, in short, life reformers also began to articulate a pro-ecological perspective that embedded Germans in nature and pinned their survival on Germans feeding themselves from and within their own natural environment. Given its origins in the mountains rather than manure, of course, ground stone fertilizer was in the nineteenth-century sense of the word merely a special type of artificial

---

[93] Corinna Treitel, "Artificial or Biological? Nature, Fertilizer and the German Origins of Organic Agriculture," *New Perspectives on the History of Life Sciences and Agriculture*, eds. Denise Phillips and Sharon Kingsland (Geneva, 2015): 183–4.

[94] Treitel, "Artificial or Biological?" 189. Eugene Simon's work, *La Cité chinoise* (Paris, 1891) became a classic. Justus von Liebig was also interested on how Chinese peasants recycled wastes. See Justus von Liebig, *Chemische Briefe*, (Leipzig and Heidelberg, 1878), 452.

[95] Julius Hensl, *Bread from Stones: A New and Rational System of Land Fertilization and Physical Regeneration*, anonymous trans. (Unknown, 1894), 45.

[96] Ibid., 12.   [97] Heinrich Bauernfeind, as quoted in Treitel, "Artificial or Biological?," 193.

fertilizer. Nonetheless, its special claims to Germaness, healthfulness, and naturalness would prove highly appealing for decades to come.[98]

At the start of the First World War, the alarms about the need for nutritional self-sufficiency took on new urgency. By 1913 importers supplied one third of Germany's wheat supply from overseas.[99] Importers also shipped in fertilizers, with Germany the largest customer in the world of nitrates from Chile. During the economic crisis under the Weimar Republic, politicians and industry representatives called for the domestic production of even more synthetic fertilizers. But as farmers dramatically increased the application of chemicals in the 1920s, crop yields fell along with soil fertility. This cycle of fertilizer overuse and soil depletion intensified the popularity of natural farming methods.[100]

Slowly in the 1930s–40s ecological ideas of organic farming were absorbed from Britain. The *Lebensreform* movement turned against artificial fertilizers and by the 1930s mimicked most of the practices of composting popular in the organic farming movement in the Anglo world. Rather than using the term "organic farming," those pursuing sustainable farming methods used the term *biologisch*, or "biological farming," which on the continent, even today is the preferred term for organic farming. Biological farming however connotes less a precise protocol for the organic method and signals instead life found in the soil that should be cultivated in a sustainable fashion.[101] Another difference with organic farming in the Anglo world regards the characteristics of the advocates and followers of biological farming: very few moved to rural areas and adopted organic farming protocols or consumer habits.[102] With some exceptions, it remained an urban romanticism. By the 1930s during the National Socialist era biological farming had dropped the democratic ideals of Baltzer. Nor was the *Lebensreform* an organic movement per se, but rather like romantic farm literature in Britain, provided a cultural milieu attractive to later organic farming enthusiasts.[103]

CONCLUSION

The Continental antecedents for organic farming reveal a number of points of agreement with organic farming in Britain, the British Empire, and North America: a sense that trade must be fair; that it must protect the farmer's livelihood; that rural areas and simple farm life preserve not only simplicity but also beauty and spirituality; that wholesome living, wholesome food, and the health of the individual are connected; and that the very life of the soil, the forests, and the ecosystem are

[98] Ibid., 194.   [99] Ibid.   [100] Ibid., 195.   [101] Ibid., 185.
[102] Judith Baumgartner, *Ernährungsreform- Antwort auf Industrialisierung und Ernährungswandel— Ernährungsreform als Teil der Lebensreformbewegung am Beispiel der Siedlung und des Unternehmens Eden seit 1893* (Frankfurt, 1992). See especially the final chapter, "Gesunde Ernährung."
[103] The journal *Bebauet die Erde* (Cultivate the Soil), became the main clearing house for ideas within the *Lebensreform* movement. Walter Rudolph founded the journal in 1925. See issue in 1928 and 1933 for organic standards. They started the "biologisches Werterzeugnis" (biological premium product) branding, one of the first anywhere in the world. It closed in 1943.

intertwined in a way that means no "consumer" is unconnected to the greater web of life. A fuller survey could be done in Asia, and Japan will be treated in a later chapter, but Asia also has its own counterpart of these same ideals: for instance, Confucius denigrated trade and considered the merchant class as inferior to the farmer. In India, Ghandi, influenced more by the West and romantic farming literature, advocated for simple peasant crafts and a rural economy. Until Ghandi, the priestly and warrior class, and below them, the untouchables, gained and maintained supremacy over the farmer, meaning that India, a vast rural nation, had exhibited the least romanticism for the peasant anywhere in the world. Gandhi popularized farming and the revival of ancient crafts, himself under the influence of the organic movement.[104] But while more work can always be done tracing cultural antecedents to organic farming in every part of the world, the British, imperial, European, and North American antecedents have been highlighted because they constitute the major theatre of action in which organic farming first took root, before spreading around the world into a global phenomenon.

[104] L. A. Maverick, "Chinese Influences upon the Physiocrats," *Economic History*, 3 (February, 1938): 54–67.

3

Albert Howard and the World
as Shropshire

Albert Howard, along with his first wife, Gabrielle, and his second wife, Louise, played a central role in the rise of organic farming around the world. Most historians regard him as the founder of organic farming. The discovery of his archives, kept safe by the family of Louise Howard and used here for the first time, add weight to this assumption. The new archive also throws light on the remarkable teamwork of Albert, Gabrielle, and Louise. Gabrielle emerges as the love of Albert's life. They worked side by side in a team in which Gabrielle's accomplishment is substantial and she played a significant supporting role. Yet the creative mind was Albert's own, and the drive for knowledge and the prodigious amounts of published output, as well as the daring to stand against bureaucracy and accepted modes of thinking, demonstrate the extent of his own unique genius.

Louise, his second wife, emerges as a dynamic organizer after Gabrielle's early death from cancer. Faithfully advocating Albert's work, particularly after his death, she served as the organizational hub for his key ideas, and launched newsletters, organizations, and conferences, as well as engaging in extensive letter writing, positioning herself as a single-handed representative of the organic farming movement during the late 1940s through the 1950s. But she also did more to further the organic cause. It would be useful to think of the organic farming movement as a middle stage between the conservation movement and the modern environmental movement. In this period, Louise Howard's ideas, her drive, and her connections created a clearinghouse of ideas, a web of influence and information flows that positions Louise Howard as one of the most important personages, along with Albert Howard, in the environmental movement from the late nineteenth century to the present. Louise Howard's work in the 1940s and 1950s presages almost every idea and issue of environmental concern that we associate with the most modern stage of the environmental movement after 1970 and she played the single most important role in this period in terms of transmitting earlier ideas and knowledge to a new generation. The accomplishments of Albert, Gabrielle, and Louise described in this volume are a new history, and do not simply add detail to what we already know. Their work helps us to understand how and why in a globalized world, environmental values have become more popular than even democracy itself. They are giants of an overlooked period of environmental consciousness that explain much about ourselves in a global world: why we believe what we believe about nature, food, and health, and why hundreds of millions of individuals—turning gradually to billions—have accepted the ideas and values the Howards promoted through the channel of organic farming and environmentalism.

Howard was born December 8, 1873 at Cottage Farm in Bishop's Castle, a small town in the southern marches of Shropshire county.[1] His father bred cattle and the young Albert Howard grew up with a romantic attachment to folkways. He held in high esteem the Saxon practice of mixed farming, in which no single crop predominated, and where vegetables, fruits, and animals were raised on the same plot of land. Throughout the county the Normans built forts and churches and the Elizabethans, Georgians and Victorians each added further architectural layers. Bishop's Castle was still a largely untouched market town in Howard's youth, blending modern architecture with old. Howard often roamed in the adjacent countryside where patches of stately oak and beech still survived and in spring bluebells, wood anemone, and primrose carpeted the woodland floor.

The countryside around Howard inspired his idea of an ideal farm. Standing on the prominent ridge of the Wrekin (a hill 34 miles north-east of Bishop's Castle) Howard could trace the hedges and woodlands that etched a patchwork of green and yellow. This bucolic scene presented a balance of farmland and forest that Howard later championed as the ideal balance between forest and agriculture, and not just in Shropshire: he later imagined a vision of organic farming that would transform the world into the same image. The world he envisioned would look very much like Shropshire—a sentiment also shared by his countrymen A. E. Housman and J. R. R. Tolkien.

In the 1600s local glassmakers began burning the forests that clothed the Wrekin. They burned the wood for charcoal to provide the fuel for heating furnaces and the ash to produce potash. By the late nineteenth century, while still an idyllic region of fields and woodlands, the iron industry had scarred the landscape. Howard, along with the poet Housman and the novelist Tolkien, felt saddened by the transition to a mixed industrial and agricultural landscape in Shropshire. Tolkien had enjoyed long walks in the West Midlands region of England, which encompassed Gloucestershire, Shropshire, Warwickshire, Herefordshire, and Staffordshire. These walks served as a model for the description of the shire in *The Hobbit* and *Lord of the Rings*.[2] Housman, born in nearby Worcestershire, also found inspiration in the region, "by brooks too broad for leaping," as he wrote in "A Shropshire Lad."[3]

---

[1] Albert lived at the Cottage farm, close to Bishop's Castle, until eleven years of age. Albert's father rented the property from the Garnet-Botfield family. His father then moved to a new farm on an elevated limestone escarpment called Wenlock Edge, north of Bishop's Castle, which boasted both farmland and woodlands. Albert's brother William Henry worked the farm until 1896 when the Meddens family took over the lease. I owe this information to Trevor Chalkely, and Pat and Chris Robinson of the Albert Howard Society, Bishop's Castle.

[2] See Tom Shippey, "Tolkien and the West Midlands: The Roots of Romance," in *Lembas Extra 1995* (Leiden, 1995); NA., "J. R. R. Tolkein in Staffordshire." Available online at: http://www.staffordshiregreatwar.com/wp-content/uploads/2014/10/Tolkien-Trail-Booklet1.pdf [accessed August 18, 2017].

[3] A. E. Housman, "A Shropshire Lad," *Collected Poems of A. E. Housman*, ed. Michael Irwin, (London, 1999).

The revival of romanticism that arose in the 1890s cast its spell on all three: Tolkien, Houseman, and Howard. Howard like Housman held a view of nature that revived more than an earlier Wordsworthian view of nature where man found peace and spiritual meaning in the contemplation of beauty. For both Houseman and Howard, (although less so for Tolkien), scientific understanding informed their view of nature in Shropshire—a bucolic home for humans but also a nature— to use Tennyson's phrase—"bloody in tooth and claw." Nature offered both Housman and Howard an open book they could explore and exploit but not abuse. Thus, this Darwinian nature offered beauty and meaning but also danger. Play by the rules of Mother Nature and abide in peace. Break the rules and pay the ultimate price: sickness and death and the collapse of civilization.

Albert Howard's father, Richard Howard, ran a farm of 550 acres.[4] While Howard fondly recalled bringing food and drink to the farm laborers during harvest season—a fact repeated by his biographer and second wife, Louise Howard— this should not lead to the impression that Howard grew up in a poor family.[5] Rather during the 1870s and 1890s, "the cottage farm" that Howard grew up on could support—outside of periods of severe agricultural depression—a yeoman's lifestyle that included abundance of food at home, decent clothing, respectability, and enough income to pay the fees of a local public school—that is, a privately owned school and not a free education dependent on county rates. The family also had, according to the 1881 census, four farm servants, one house servant, a nurse maid, and five separate farm laborers who may have lived off the main property.

Albert grew up in the company of his parents and many siblings—he was the eighth of ten children. Curiously, Howard never mentions his mother or his brothers or sisters in any of his writings.[6] When Albert's father died in 1893 he left behind a considerable sum of £8,154 to his oldest son, William Henry Howard, and Richard Jones, a farmer who was possibly a husband of one of Albert's sisters. Albert inherited only memories of the farm but his future depended entirely on his own efforts.[7]

Howard's mother, Anne, died November 7, 1892, when he was 18 and still attending school.[8] He only briefly mentioned his father when discussing the start of the agricultural depression of 1879. This is odd because Howard wrote autobiographical notes on his life in a number of his books and his reminisces of working with seasonal laborers paint a romantic and positive picture of his family farm. Nor did his second wife, Louise, who also wrote his biography, mention Howard's

---

[4] Louise Howard, "Biography Sheet" File 1947: *Matthaei Family Archive*, Birmingham, UK.

[5] Rodney George Edrich (February 25, 2015). Private Correspondence. Edrich is an historian at Wrekin College.

[6] Albert had six older brothers and sisters, William Henry, Richard, Mary Ann, Catherine, Ada, Agnes, and John who died the year Albert was born. He had two younger brothers, Thomas and William Kilvert. Pat and Chris Robinson, along with Trevor Chalkley, of the Albert Howard Society of Bishop's Castle, kindly provided details on Richard Howard's property, and biographical data about the family. The information above was drawn from census material.

[7] Ibid.

[8] Albert's older brother Richard moved with his parents in approximately 1890 to Shipton and died the same year as his mother, 14 July, 1892 at 24 years of age. Ibid.

family in more than the mere passing reference to the name of his father and mother. No scraps of letters or other documents from his boyhood remain, or have been allowed to remain, in the extensive archive of his life and work that Louise collected.[9]

Louise recounts how Albert described to her how his family treated seasonal farm laborers.

> Sir Albert's boyhood on his father's farm has already been mentioned; on the relations between employers and employed, he had good recollections. It was his business, as the farmer's son, to carry round the food and drink given in those days to the workers in the field; he described to me once the extraordinary care which was bestowed on carrying out this duty; there was an art in varying what was offered, especially for the hot work of hay-making, and home-brewed cider, beer, small beer, tea, etc., were all provided in turn, at the farm's discretion, whose reputation rose and fell with the skill he showed in providing for his workers what was so necessary for their comfort. On this point the standing of his own family was particularly good as excellent generous employers. I have every reason to say that these fine recollections, gathered from the last years of the best period of nineteenth-century farming in England, were of profound influence throughout Sir Albert's life.[10]

Much later in life in 1947, a year before he died, Howard recounts how mixed farming had been the rule of his childhood, and that farmers used "good old fashioned muck"—that is, manure to fertilize the land. He recounts that "one day I saw a curious grey powder being applied to a crop of swedes [potatoes]." The men spreading the fertilizer told him it was "monkey muck" because it had such an evil smell. Later he learned that instead of monkey dung the bags were "from sulphuric acid and bones in a factory," manufactured by the same company that had founded Rothamsted Experimental Station—the agricultural research station that later symbolized everything he spent his career and life work opposing.[11]

While Howard had sunny memories of farm life, the omission of personal details in his writing may point to a lonely childhood focused on work and even perhaps a severe and regimented home life. In adulthood he revealed little religious sentiment. The letters of Gabrielle, his first wife, mention only once attending an Anglican church in India. But this absence of color and detail from his lost years of boyhood must be balanced by the fact that Howard's father willingly paid his fees for tuition at nearby Wellington College—40 guineas per annum for boarders over 12 years of age. Prior to sending him off to Wellington College, he must have provided Albert with enough quiet space at home to become an exemplary student.[12]

Howard began attending Wellington College in 1888 at the age of fifteen. John Bayley, a local businessman and educational reformer, founded and managed the school. Located above the market town of Wellington, it had a commanding view

---

[9] Ibid.   [10] Louise E. Howard, *Sir Albert Howard in India* (Emmaus, 1954), 235.
[11] Albert Howard, "The Nitrogen Problem," *Organic Farming* (January–September, 1947): 12. Found in File 1947: *Matthaei Family Archive*, Birmingham, UK.
[12] Wellington College was later renamed Wrekin College in 1920. Albert was a pupil there between 1888 and 1893.

of the Wrekin. The popular school enjoyed a growing reputation, and so Bayley indulged the luxury of charging a year's tuition in advance. Howard enrolled in a small class—the whole school contained no more than sixty-five to seventy students when he graduated in 1893 at the age of twenty.

The unique qualities and ideas of John Bayley that are echoed in Howard's own life suggest he may have influenced Howard in a number of ways. Bayley despised academic degrees. He also took umbrage at professional pride. He himself earned no degrees and he hired teachers who he believed could teach, not those who necessarily had proper credentials. He dressed always in "a morning coat with striped trousers, a grey waistcoat, a white slip under it, a low collar and a grey tie with a fine tiepin, spats, highly polished boots," and carried a cane, always with him, that he did not hesitate to use on errant boys. When hiring teachers, he never checked references, but hired the candidates by their interview performance. He valued knowledge highly, and personal skills. For him, the main point of college training was "to culminate in the polished gentleman."[13]

His boys worked hard. Up at the morning bell at 7:00 a.m., they ate a hurried breakfast at 8:00 consisting of "slabs and scarpe"—that is, thick toast and butter, with coffee from a single oversized urn.[14] Then they took a twenty minute walk in the morning. Lessons were from 9:14 to 12:30 p.m.; dinner at 1:00 p.m., when they were allowed meat or fish with vegetables; more lessons from 2:30 to 4:45, followed by tea and then "prep" for 90 minutes with masters; supper at 8:00, and then bedtime with lights out and complete silence by 9:30.

There were few distractions from work. After church, wearing Eton collars and dark jackets with mortarboards, they were fed cake on Sunday afternoon. During half holidays, the boys played games on Wednesday and Saturday, providing some relief from the grueling school schedule. In winter they played association football and in summer, cricket. Sometimes the masters allowed a special treat off the school grounds, where,

> In bad weather, or merely as a change, the whole school trailed in crocodile though the town to the Forest Glen or to the top of the Wrekin.[15]

An old boy who had attained the rank of general visited sometime after the First World War. He remarked, "I must say they taught me well, but it was hard work."[16] This hard work produced results. In the words of an early college historian, "The really remarkable thing is the great success achieved by so many of these early old boys in so many walks of life, successes out of all proportion to the numbers in the school."[17] This included renowned chemists, such as Dr. A. E. Everest whose research specialized in the study of natural dyes for use as food additives. In addition to a wide variety of professionals, and military men, the school produced a high court judge, generals and air marshals, and of course, at least one eminent agricultural scientist, Albert Howard. Sadly, all records prior to 1921 are

---

[13] Benjamin Johnson, *Wrekin College, 1880–1964: A Brief History* (Shrewsbury, 1965), 8.
[14] Ibid., 12.   [15] Ibid., 33.   [16] Ibid.   [17] Ibid.

missing—probably because Bayley himself took the records with him, or destroyed them, when he sold the school.[18]

From here Howard went to the Royal College of Science (RCS) in South Kensington, London, in 1893. The RCS specialized in training science teachers who—in return for their paid tuition and a stipend of a guinea a week—were expected upon graduation to teach science for a number of years in public and private grammar schools. The RCS specialized in botany, biology, and agriculture and boasted T. H. Huxley as Dean from 1881 to 1885. As with Wellington College, no record of Howard's years at the RCS survive. He did however fulfill the mission of the RCS. After taking his degree, and gaining his PhD from Cambridge University, he taught for a number of years at Harrison College in Barbados before moving into a research position.

The RCS faced the Imperial Institute, which Howard almost certainly visited. The design of the Imperial Institute and its function made its placement next to the RCS apt because it too focused on science—in this case, science and industry in the British Empire. The building itself stood as a symbol of empire—much like the building in which Howard would one day produce his pioneering research: the Agricultural Research Institute at Pusa, Bihar, India. Both boasted architecture on a monumental scale with touches of Indo-Anglo design, and both mirrored the impressive scientific accomplishments that the architects assumed would assure the progress and security of the empire. The Imperial Institute particularly encouraged the development of science and the natural resources of the empire. It boasted the inspiring motto, "Strength and Honor are her Clothing." It is survived now only by the Queen's Tower which rose in the center of the building.[19]

H. G. Wells, who attended the RCS concurrently with Howard, gives some idea of the atmosphere of the school in his autobiographical novel, *Love and Mr. Lewisham*, describing how the hallways buzzed with the excitement of the students, who exulted in the esteemed place in society that the school conferred. In this novel the young man, Mr. Lewisham, understood the chances of getting in had been stacked against him. The Science and Art Department offered the "Kensington thing" with free tuition and a stipend. The generosity of the scholarships was intended to attract students who would turn into science teachers—a rare commodity—and therefore many students applied. Few were chosen. For Lewisham/Wells, and undoubtedly Howard, his life chances changed dramatically when he received in the post a "marvelous blue document from the Education Department" with his acceptance letter. He would be paid to go to lectures and achieve his ambitions in life, all while living in London.

> Among the names that swam before his eyes was Huxley—Huxley
> and then Lockyer! What a chance to get! Is it any wonder that for
> three memorable years the Career prevailed with him?

---

[18] Ibid.; A. E. Everest and A. G. Perkin, *The Natural Organic Colouring Matters* (London 1918), 9.
[19] "Imperial College," Royal Institute of British Architects. Available at: https://web.archive.org/web/20121002170023/http://www.architecture.com/LibraryDrawingsAndPhotographs/Albertopolis/TheStoryOf/ImperialCollege/ImperialInstitute.aspx [accessed August 18, 2017].

Not all the students were on scholarship, however. H. G. Wells described, in this autobiographical portrait, how Lewisham walked down Exhibition Road and through a gate of wrought iron to see the hallways crowded with students, "the paying students" who were the best dressed, even on this first day of class in black coats and silk hats, or tweed suits. By contrast, other students, like himself, were "raw, shabby, discordant, grotesquely ill dressed, and awestricken."[20]

One can guess that Howard may have been in the tweed suit category—a serious scholar certainly—but without the finery of the paying students. Yet, neither was he a working-class boy with the socialist consciousness of Lewisham/Wells. An egalitarian establishment, the school also had women students, who were expected to take off their hats (and this often meant taking out the hat pins) and assume a work-like professional attitude alongside the boys and young men. Interestingly this gender equality also may have influenced Howard. He later married a woman scientist and worked side by side with his wife in the work that would define his mission in life.

If Howard was unlikely to have assumed the bohemian and working-class rebelliousness of Lewisham, his home life in London, if such it could be called, would have been equally impoverished. H. G. Wells describes a character that he imagined to be from the upper-middle class "sitting in a convenient study with a writing table, book-shelves, and a shaded lamp" while he himself used for a desk a chest of drawers, his feet wrapped in linen to keep warm. Howard, a farm boy and yeoman's son escaped much of the class consciousness of either the upper or lower class, having a past tied to the land situated somewhere midway between the landowning aristocracy and the life of farm laborers. He would have taken his place in between, what the social historian Harold Perkin described as "middling." This middling range, swiftly disappearing in the nineteenth century, typically kept relations of a vertical as opposed to a horizontal nature—looking up or down from their station in life, from landowner and clergy down to household, factory and farm workers as opposed to a horizontal class consciousness. Howard's life certainly showed little resentment on that score. A few statements show that he exhibited pride in the gentry that rented small landholdings as did his father.[21] In a remarkable contrast to H. G. Well's story, however, where Mr. Lewisham stumbled into a love interest that ruined his brilliant career, Howard found, after graduation from RCS, a perfect match in love that complemented his work and materially advanced his scientific research.

But whether Howard felt conscious of class status or not, others certainly did, if H. G. Well's description is accurate. Wells describes how Lewisham sought a job teaching, just before he completed his degree, at a number of employment agencies. After he left one interview, the agent and another youth discussed his prospects; the youth meditating the polished handle of his cane walking stick,

> "A bounder of that kind can't have a particularly nice time," he said, "anyhow, if he does get into a decent school, he must get tremendously cut by all the decent men…"

[20] H. G. Wells, *Love and Mr. Lewisham* (1900). Available online at: http://www.telelib.com/authors/W/WellsHerbertGeorge/prose/lewisham/lewisham008.html [accessed August 18, 2017].
[21] Harold J. Perkin, *The Origins of Modern English Society, 1780–1880* (London, 1969), 37, 47–51.

[The agent answered] "He's a new type. This South Kensington place and the poly-technics are turning his kind out by the hundred."[22]

It is not clear if Albert Howard felt a similar sting personally, or whether Wells exaggerated the negative reputation of RCS. However, neither Howard nor his biographer and second wife Louise give any details of Albert's time here, merely mentioning in passing Albert's tenure at RCS. If Howard had a mark against him on the issue of class, it was largely settled when, after graduating from the RCS, he won a scholarship, a "sizar," to St. John's College Cambridge.

At Cambridge University, Howard studied under Marshall Ward, a man with a catholic intellect that made him a fit successor to his own mentor, T. H. Huxley, the popularizer of Charles Darwin. Cambridge opened new and exciting opportunities for Howard to show off his quick mind and many talents. Ward took a liking to Howard: like Howard he had grown up in the respectable lower-middle class. Ward had also graduated from one of the amalgamated precursors of the RCS—the Science and Art Department—under the leadership of Huxley. We have little information on how Howard interacted with Ward, but we know that he attended lectures and worked with Ward in the laboratory and in tutorials. Albert and his biographer wife Louise stated that Ward inspired Howard by his ideas and by his disciplined approach to work.

Ward built on and advanced the pioneer field of plant pathology and furthered understanding of the causal link between microbes and plant disease. This link is taken as general knowledge today. Only a few decades before Howard studied under Ward, however, the French scientist Heinrich Anton de Bary proved that parasitic fungus caused potato rot—a monumental discovery given the dramatic and tragic potato famines that afflicted Ireland and the millions of deaths that fol-lowed.[23] Ward met and studied with De Bary in his laboratory at the University of Strasbourg. He then returned to Britain with high hopes of launching his own investigations. His opportunity came when the Colonial Office appointed Ward as Government Cryptogamist in Ceylon to fight coffee blight. This plant disease had left coffee plantations in ruins and led to mass bankruptcies among growers. He wrote to his mother that many planters wander about the barren plantations "in a moody and despondent way that speaks of disappointed hopes: misplaced talent and wretched despair."[24] Planters hoped Ward would produce a chemical spray to solve the problem quickly. However, his experiments discovered that plant disease could spread through aerial spores. While this breakthrough led over time to improved farming techniques, he did not devise an effective new pesticide.[25]

Despite this, Ward's suggestions had a practical approach that clearly appealed to Howard. Ward argued that coffee plants should be manured to provide a healthier

[22] "Imperial College," British History Online, see ref. 32. Available online at: http://www.british-history.ac.uk/survey-london/vol38/pp233-247#anchorn34 [accessed August 18, 2017]; H. G. Wells, *An Experiment in Autobiography* (Philadelphia and New York, 1934), 159–229.

[23] Peter G. Ayres, *Harry Marshal Ward and the Fungal Thread of Death* (St. Paul, MN, 2005), 6.

[24] Ibid., 1.

[25] It was left to another scientist to invent the world's first pesticide. In 1885 Pierre Alexis Millardet invented the "Bordeaux Mixture" to fight a mildew that destroyed grape vines as well as potato blight.

growth that would in turn help them resist disease. He suggested that the coffee plant needed to grow in cohabitation with other plants, as it did in its indigenous environment in Ethiopia. The coffee blight *H. vastatrix* also originated in Ethiopia but the coffee plant did not, in its indigenous environment, suffer the same devastating consequences. Ward concluded that farmers therefore needed to replicate the original growing conditions of the plant to restore its health. This could happen by either mixing crops or interspersing the coffee plants with natural vegetation, which provided barriers to the spores of the coffee rust.[26] All of these prescriptions foreshadow Albert Howard's future work.

After a stint at the Royal Indian Engineering College at Cooper's Hill, (that prepared students for imperial service in India) Ward became, at the age of forty-one, Chair of Botany at Cambridge University. Here he met Howard, as an undergraduate.[27] Ward's further experiments continued to pioneer the idea of symbiosis between plants, fungi, and other bacteria, proving that "micro-organisms...invaded the root via the root hairs."[28] Ward's ideas launched mycorrhizal science and played a particularly big role in Howard's work and that of the organic farming movement. He also taught another famous student, F. F. Blackman, who, working with Gabrielle Matthaei as his assistant, advanced the knowledge of plant photosynthesis.[29] Gabrielle and Albert eventually married.

Howard graduated in 1896 with honors in botany at St. John's College and a Diploma of Agriculture in 1897. In 1899 he gained a position as lecturer in agricultural science at Harrison College in Barbados and thus fulfilled his duty to RCS to teach science upon completion of his terminal degree. Harrison College had become in the nineteenth century the most prestigious boys' grammar school in the West Indies. But the lag time between graduation from Cambridge and the remote location of the school suggests that Howard found difficulty obtaining employment in Britain, notwithstanding his Cambridge PhD. After the fulfillment of his term of service he found another position more suitable for his accomplishments and interests: Mycologist and Agricultural Lecturer at the Imperial Department of Agriculture for the West Indies. Here, working on the origins of plant disease (specializing in arrowroot) he officially began his research career and his dream of working in an agricultural research station.[30]

By the end of the nineteenth century the Caribbean was known as the slum of the empire. The sugar plantations saw declining fortunes after the British abolished slavery in the 1830s. Aggravating this, the price of sugar continued to fall due to competition with other producers both in the Caribbean and Latin America. In order to stimulate the sugar industry and to diversify the agricultural economy with new crop

[26] Ibid., 10, 18. See also Marshall Ward, *Preliminary Report on the Enquiry into the Coffee-Leaf Disease in Supplement to the Ceylon Observer* (Colombo, Ceylon, 1880); Marshall Ward, "Coffee Leaf Disease: Second Report," Ceylon Sessional Paper 50 (Colombo, Ceylon, 1880).

[27] Ayres, *Thread of Death,* 111.   [28] Ibid., 137.

[29] F. F. Blackman and G. L. C. Matthaei, "Experimental researches on vegetable assimilation and respiration. IV. A quantitative study of carbon-dioxide assimilation and leaf temperature in natural illumination," *Proceedings of the Royal Society,* B76 (1905): 402–60.

[30] Louise Howard, *Albert Howard in India,* 20.

varieties, the Colonial Office encouraged agricultural research in the botanical gardens—modeled on Kew—and also a number of church-sponsored gardens that missionaries built around their stations. In 1896, a year before Howard earned his Diploma of Agriculture from Cambridge, the Crown appointed the West Indian Royal Commission to address the continuing economic slump. The commission recommended that botanical stations be improved and extended to launch an empire-wide Imperial Department of Agriculture. Jumpstarted with generous funding, Howard benefited from this expansion of tropical Departments of Agriculture. It is in this new department that Howard gained his first research position, in Barbados.[31]

His new post offered him a laboratory to research fungal disease with a special emphasis on sugar cane. But a broader mandate gave him the work of delivering lectures to schoolmasters to spur them to take up the study of nature and better utilize school gardens in the Windward and Leeward Islands. This latter responsibility pushed him out of the role of a "laboratory hermit" where he learned "more and more about less and less." It spurred him to understand the whole process of raising crops from the beginning stage to harvest—and then to market. His remit expanded to include cacao, limes, oranges, bananas, sugar cane, arrowroot, ground nuts, and nutmegs. Decades later he reminisced that he had made the Caribbean his laboratory. By doing so he swiftly saw the limitations of his specialist approach and saw the need for a method that addressed the bigger picture of plant disease. Though he had not developed his organic philosophy at this stage, he did detect that he needed more than a laboratory. He needed land, he needed to raise crops himself, and he needed to drop the specialist jargon that obscured rather than illuminated problems. But this only led to more frustrations as he found that by spending most of his time in the laboratory he "could not take my own advice before offering it to other people." He felt that a chasm existed between the specialist and the farmer, one that he became convinced would have to close in order to solve the economic problems that farmers faced.[32]

After Albert Howard returned from the Caribbean in 1902 he spent two and a half years as a botanist at the South Eastern Agricultural College (known colloquially as Wye College), at Wye in Kent, sixty miles to the east of London. As an agricultural college within London University, the college maintained an active research program. Howard joined the staff at Wye just as its famed founder, Alfred Daniel Hall, left to take on the directorship of the Rothamsted research station. Howard picked up and continued the work begun by Hall. In a number of ways Hall and the experiments that he started fitted perfectly with Howard's personality and interests. The two men resembled each other in many ways. Hall insisted that all the science teachers and researchers should learn to apply their works the field, thus breaking the distance between the laboratory and the farm.[33] He eschewed

[31] NA "Agricultural Development in the West Indies," *Nature*, 105, (May 13, 1920): 344. The Imperial Department of Agriculture in Barbados, including its books and papers, was transferred in 1921 to Trinidad. In 1922 the Imperial Department of Agriculture and the West Indian Agricultural College merged to form the Imperial College of Tropical Agriculture.

[32] Albert Howard, *The Soil and Health: A Study of Organic Agriculture* (London, 1947), 1–2.

[33] E. J. Russell, "Alfred Daniel Hall, 1864–1942," *Obituary Notices of Fellows of the Royal Society*, 4 (1942–44): 233.

jargon and attempted to communicate agricultural science to lay people, including the general public and school children. When Howard arrived, he took over from Hall the ongoing experiments on hops. This gave Howard a head start in what would become his life work—researching how plant health and vitality offered the best means of resisting disease. Ironically, though Hall and Howard shared many personality traits that railed against scientific formalism, Hall moved on to head the institution—the Rothamsted research station—that in a few decades gained Howard's animosity as a symbol of everything he opposed.[34]

In the short period he spent at Wye, Howard earned the respect of local farmers by introducing a radical improvement in the management of hop farms. Howard had advised Kentish famers that they would be more successful growing hops if the young male would fertilize the female plant, which produced the cones used for brewing beer. Farmers feared that male hops would make the hops coarse and so farming tradition kept the male hops out of the gardens and the farms. Hops varied in crop yields dramatically, and the health of the female hops plant which produced the fruit was critical, particularly given the availability of cheap imports. For his actual contribution to hop growing he advocated not merely vegetative proliferation of hop plants, but also planting young male hops among them so that they would reproduce sexually, and naturally, to fight disease. This new natural method proved highly successful.[35]

Wye College also provided an ideal location for the future development of Howards work. Kent county produced 60 percent of Britain's hop crop—and hops required constant manuring. Dung proved superior but expensive. Phosphate and potash proved useful when not overused, but only raised yields in the initial usage. Often a mix of chemical fertilizer and dung worked best, and the best dung came from mixed farms. All this Howard in his short time at Wye College quickly assimilated. Cultural factors also influenced Howard's future work. Hop gardens imported large amounts of laborers from London during the picking season. On his father's farm in Shropshire and also in Kent, farmers often produced their own coinage with fanciful designs due to a shortage of small coins by which to pay the laborers. The regenerative effect of farm work on poor city youth from London impressed Howard and he saw firsthand how agricultural labor refreshed the spirits and restored physical health. This experience may also have led to an appreciation of the connection between currency reform, financial policy, and agriculture—a key platform in British and European fascist movements. Later Howard would lacerate British elites on the evil practice of usury in Britain and in India.[36]

On November 4, 1905 in the Bombay Cathedral, Albert Howard married a remarkable women with an extensive scientific background—Gabrielle Matthaei.

[34] Ibid., 235.
[35] NA. *Kentish Express* (June 25, 1910). See also NA. *Kentish Gazette and Canterbury News* (June 25, 1910) and "Canterbury Farmers' club and East Kent Chamber of Agriculture," *Kentish Observer* (June 16, 1910).
[36] Years later at the Canterbury Farmer's Club, June 25, 1910, a member of staff at Wye College spoke of their disappointment when Howard, after such a short time with them at Wye, gained his appointment to India. Staff at Wye were indignant that he would not continue to develop his promising work on hops, and instead opted for India. See NA. *Kentish Express* (June 25, 1910).

In doing so he married into a family with strong German ties. The most detailed information on her family comes from the unpublished autobiography of the brother of Gabrielle and Louise—Ernst Matthaei. We learn that Gabrielle's father emigrated from Gotha, in present day central Germany, to England in 1863. He worked at the firm of a Messrs. Bieber (also German), which imported goods from Brazil. Gabrielle's father reached a high management position, though not a managing director, and laid the financial groundwork for the family as solidly middle class—what today we would describe as upper-middle class.[37] He married on the Continent a woman of French Swiss extraction whose parents came to England in 1840. They bore four children: Ernst, Marie, Gabrielle, and Louise. Ernst considered that his "race is certainly mixed" and though culturally English, the family had strong sympathies with the Continent, and with Germany in particular. The mother played piano, sometimes professionally, and passionately loved music. Marie spent most of her time in Germany and returned to England only just before the outbreak of the Second World War. All were passionate about learning. Gabrielle and Louise turned to higher education: Gabrielle was an early pioneer of women in science, winning a fellowship at Newnham College, Cambridge—a woman's only college established in 1871. After graduation she worked with F. F. Blackman, a pioneer researcher of plant respiration and transpiration. Louise also attended Newnham College, winning a scholarship, and took a first-class honors degree in the Classical Tripos and then became a lecturer in classics at Newnham, publishing a book on Greek tragedy. Ernst became a school teacher, spending the largest portion of his career in Egypt under the British administration.[38]

These accomplishments however did not come easily. The premature death of the father interrupted a life of relative luxury. The family had lived in the Boltons, in the Royal Borough of Kensington and Chelsea—an area that boasted large homes and private communal gardens. They also had a taste for "objects d'art" and this continued even though the family faced straitened circumstances, headed by a widow who began giving piano lessons to raise money. Even so, they still had the ability to spend an extended amount of time on the Continent—at one time spending ten months in Germany to attend school to perfect the German language, before returning to a comfortable home at Clifton Hill at Blackheath, near Hampstead.[39]

Their neighbors at Blackheath included Edward Onslow Ford and his family. Ford was a famous Victorian sculptor known for his personal charm. His family had close ties with the Matthaei family. His works expressed a sense of playful pathos that blended classical and imperial themes while capturing intimate and personal feeling. He is best known for his statue of General Gordon riding on a camel exhibited in the Royal Academy in 1896. He also produced the statue of the Prime Minister Gladstone, now in the Liberal Club, in London, and the Queen Victoria

[37] Ernst Matthaei, "Autobiography, 1." *Matthaei Family Archive*, Birmingham, UK.
[38] Ibid., 2, 3, 7.   [39] Ibid., 8, 11.

memorial in Manchester. He gifted the Matthaei family a small bronze statuette of Gabrielle. She was considered by all to be a remarkably beautiful child.[40]

Another close Blackheath neighbor was Sir William Reynolds-Stephens, born in Detroit and an eminent British painter and sculptor, also with strong ties to Germany, famous for his decorative memorials. The Matthaei family continued to summer abroad in Germany, Switzerland, and northern Brittany.[41] As with many before the First World War, ties to the Continent were closer. This connection between Germany and Gabrielle had small but detectable influences on Howard and his turn away from a formal science and towards a romantic view of the material world as Gabrielle and Howard embarked on their life work, in India.

In Gabrielle, Albert found a mate where love and work blended. As a scientist Gabrielle threw herself into her work at Albert's side, co-authoring with him and publishing on her own. Though she never intimated that Albert's ideas were anything but his own, her own engagement in every step of his development in India justifies the view that she partnered and supported him not only as an assistant and co-worker, but also in his creative development. In a twist of fate, after her untimely death, Albert married her sister Louise, who became a timeless crusader of Albert's ideas and life mission.

---

[40] Ibid., 27, 28.   [41] Ibid., 23.

4

The Howards in India

In the nineteenth century conservationists in the British Empire sponsored legislation that changed land use policy over a large section of the planet. The global
conservation movement arose in India when the governor general, Lord Dalhousie,
issued the groundbreaking Forest Charter in 1855, which declared "wasteland" as
Crown lands that would henceforth be managed by foresters to protect timber
supplies, "the household of nature," and the climate, with a particular concern
for preserving rainfall and protecting soil from erosion. These principles and the
British Indian model of organizing forest departments spread to other parts of the
Empire, then to the United States, and, to a lesser extent, back to Britain itself.
Inspired by, and informed heavily by developments in Britain, this new model of
land management created a new approach to nature that matured into the first
stage of the global environmental movement.[1]

Organic farming arose in India because a unique culture of independence
evolved in British Indian institutions. This greater scope of action in turn allowed
a scientist like Albert Howard to have more freedom in his investigations than
he would at home in Britain.[2] The Viceroy of India, Lord Curzon, in particular
attempted to create a space for science, free from the oversight of institutions in
London. Curzon had this precisely in mind when he the created the Board of
Scientific Advice (BSA) in 1902 and, later, the Imperial Agricultural Research
Institute (IARI).[3] Inaugurating the IARI, Curzon compared the new scientific ini-
tiative to the conservation of Indian heritage:

> The stone which I am to lay at Pusa in two days' time, will, I hope, be the foundation-
> stone not only of a fabric worthy of its object, but also of a policy of agricultural
> development henceforward to be pursued systematically, in good years and bad years
> alike, by the Government of India; so that a time may one day arrive when people will
> say that India is looking after her greatest living industry as well, let us say, as she is
> now looking after her greatest inherited treasure, viz. her ancient monuments.[4]

[1] Gregory A. Barton, *Empire Forestry and the Origins of the Environmental Movement* (Cambridge, 2002).

[2] Deepar Kumar suggests that British scientists in Indian institutions sought to create a culture of independence and autonomy. See Deepar Kumar, "Reconstituting India: Disunity in the Science and Technology for Development Discourse, 1900–1947," *Osiris*, (2nd series) 15; Roy Macleod, ed., *Nature and Empire: Science and the Colonial Enterprise* (Chicago, 2000): 243.

[3] Ibid. See also Roy Macleod "Scientific Advice for British India: Imperial Perceptions and Administrative Goals, 1898–1923," *Modern Asian Studies* 9/3 (1975): 343–84.

[4] Thomas Raleigh ed., *Lord Curzon in India: Being a Selection from his Speeches as Viceroy & Governor-General of India, 1898–1905* (London, 1906), 214.

British India had a long tradition of officials expressing concern about returning nutrients to the soil to improve agriculture. Allan Octavian Hume, known chiefly as the founder of the Indian National Congress, had argued for the use of manure to return nutrients to agricultural land, and advocated forest plantations to produce fuel that would in turn replace the burning of manure for cooking. He also opposed the use of land as collateral for usurious loans by rapacious moneylenders.[5] Lord Mayo (Richard Bourke), Viceroy of India from 1869–72, argued similarly, and made a point of asserting that while Indians had much to learn from the British, the imperial masters of India had much to learn from them.[6] Augustus Voelcker, a British chemist born in Germany, surveyed Indian agriculture and also suggested saving manure for soil fertility by planting forest plantations that would provide fuel for the domestic household. He particularly advocated that the Indian government merge scientific research with "native requirements" to advance India's vast agriculture.[7]

Sweeping aside objections, Curzon founded an all-India Department of Agriculture. Once proposed to the British cabinet in 1903, the project moved forward swiftly. Mr. Phipps, a Chicago millionaire and Curzon's father in law, donated £30,000. Pusa was (and still is) a small village, close to the Ganges River on the broad swath of alluvial soil between the Himalayas and the elevated central plains of India. The location of the IARI also came to bear his name, "Phipps" and "USA" turned into "Pusa."[8] India consisted of provinces with widely varying climate zones and agricultural conditions, and the argument against an India-wide department rested on the claim that research and experimental stations should be sponsored only by provinces. In this way, projects would be funded by and focused on the special conditions of the province hosting the experimental station. Curzon preemptively rejected pleas from scientists to fund regional and highly specialized research stations sensitive to the peculiar climatic and soil needs of each province and substituted instead a grand vision for a new imperial temple of science to support a unified India. He established Pusa to reflect the status of a central postgraduate research hub of agricultural science for the whole of the Indian Empire, similar in function to the Imperial Forest School at Dehra Dun. After Lord Curzon established the Agricultural Research Institute at Pusa in 1905, it was renamed in a few years the IARI. When the Indian Department of Agriculture hired Albert Howard, it did

[5] Allan Octavian Hume, *Agricultural Reform in India* (London: 1897). Edward Moulton, "The Contributions of Allan O. Hume to the Scientific Advancement of Indian Ornithology" in *Petronia: Fifty Years of Post-Independence Ornithology in India*, eds. J. C. Daniel and G. W. Ugra (New Delhi, 2003): 295–317.

[6] W. W. Hunter, *The Life of the Earl of Mayo: Fourth Viceroy of India* (London, 1875), 317.

[7] John Augustus Voelcker, *Report on the Improvement of Indian Agriculture* (London, 1893), 24, 27. I must disagree with Macleod who states that the concept of "colonial science" owes its origin to historians of science in the last three decades. See Roy Macleod, "Introduction" *Nature and Empire: Science and the Colonial Enterprise*, ed. Roy Macleod (Chicago, 2000): 7.

[8] F. G. Sly, "The Departments of Agriculture in India," *Agricultural Journal of India* (Calcutta, 1906), 1–4; Louise E. Howard, *Sir Albert Howard in India* (London, 1953), 13–15.

so with the expectation that his work could materially benefit the Indian people and strengthen the economic underpinnings of the Indian Empire.[9]

The IARI represented the power, and it was hoped, the future of the Raj. The building boasted a central dome with four adjunct domes, each topped again by a second-tier open dome in the Indo-Saracenic style. These overlooked massive Roman wings fronted by two marching rows of neo-classical columns. It fitted in well with the new empire style favored by Curzon. This new temple of science symbolized an imperial synthesis where modern Europe met ancient India. Curzon predicted that,

> an enormous future lies before Agricultural research, experiment, administration, and education in India. This large central institution, with proper officers and scientists would turn a seed into "a mighty tree."[10]

Thus, Pusa would formulate solutions to agricultural problems that threatened to undermine British imperial power on the subcontinent. Curzon saw the station as a blend of east and west, a "unity of European science and native art," in the words of one scholar's description of Saracenic architecture.[11] Curzon personally oversaw the architectural plans for the Agricultural Research Institute. Interestingly his notes in the margin of the plans questioned the soundness of the design against earthquake, which proved to be a prescient foreboding. The prospectus of the new institute, published in 1906, anticipated an agricultural chemist, a mycologist, an entomologist, an agriculturalist, and an economic botanist.[12]

As the Economic Botanist for the IARI at Pusa, Howard considered himself a respected member of the mainstream scientific community. At the time of his arrival in India he had not formed any definite theories regarding "wholeness" that would separate him irrevocably from many of his professional colleagues. But his work at the IARI at Pusa, built near the banks of the Ganges river in Bihar, would force his views to take flight from what he considered the iron cage of scientific specialty and would reinforce in the mind of his many followers around the British Empire a distinction between a trustworthy and objective imperial science and a capitalist science beholden to vested interest.

Howard also arrived in India at a fortuitous moment. His suspicions of overspecialization had hardened into obstinate clarity. Howard despised governmental technocrats who fortified learned reports with scientific jargon. He wanted to see scientific investigations cross specialties and draw on a broad array of community experiences and common sense. This decompartmentalized approach dovetailed perfectly with what Curzon, had in mind.

[9] Ibid., 24. For a general discussion of Lord Curzon's philosophy of administration and his opposition to bureaucratic lethargy, see John Bowles, *The Imperial Achievement: The Rise and Transformation of the British Empire* (Boston, 1975), 313–15.

[10] Curzon to St. John Brodrick, Secretary of State for India (January 12, 1905), India Office, [Mss. Eur.F. 25–6].

[11] On colonial architecture see Thomas R. Metcalf, "Architecture and the Representation of Empire: India, 1860–1910," *Representations*, 6 (Spring, 1984): 56.

[12] *The Prospectus of the Agricultural Research Institute and College, Pusa*, (Calcutta: Superintendent Government Printing, 1906), 2.

Under the new Viceroy, Lord Minto, Albert Howard arrived in late 1904 to take up the duties in 1905 of Economic Botanist, charged with researching plant diseases and raising the yield of staple crop varieties (particularly of the most important crop grown on the subcontinent, wheat). His earlier work did not inevitably steer him to his later conclusions in India.[13] In fact, when Howard arrived in India he held a far more mainstream view of the use of chemicals to enhance agricultural productivity, and had little aversion to the use of chemical pesticides. Howard did not unpack his ideas about the "Law of Return" from his luggage when he arrived at Pusa from England.[14]

Albert Howard's entrepreneurial energy brought him into the limelight before he arrived. While still in England he sent a list of typed questions to the Directors of Agriculture of every province in India to enquire about the challenges each director faced in their respective provinces. He asked that the directors provide a description of the varieties of wheat grown in their province and a physical sample of each to be sent to him in England, so he could quickly ascertain the characteristics of the wheat varieties used across India and write a paper that detailed the research challenges that lay ahead of India as a whole. The directors gladly complied. After writing his report, he sent it directly to the Inspector General of Agriculture, F. G. Sly, who, as Gabrielle wrote her mother,

> was exceedingly pleased with the paper. [He] put all his clerks on to typewrite it and in 24 hours had a copy in the hands of every member of the board. Smart work wasn't it.[15]

Howard arrived in India December 25, 1904. He presented his pre-circulated paper at Pusa only three weeks later, on January 25, 1905.[16] Based on this remarkable summary of wheat in India, one year later the Inspector General Sly asked him to write, within a six-month deadline, "a summary of all the work and literature of Indian wheat up to date. It will be big business."[17] So it proved, for it launched him immediately into high profile work among agricultural staff in India. The Inspector General sent Howard the books he had on the topic to help and the book was published in 1909, titled *Wheat in India*.[18] Howard was also put on an India-wide Agricultural Education committee responsible for the syllabus of Botanical courses launched in the Provincial colleges, which were only just forming.[19] In a very short period of time, he had made an auspicious start.

---

[13] Albert Howard, "Fertilization and Cross Fertilization of the Hop," *The Hop and its Constituents: A Monograph on the Hop Plant*, ed., Alfred C. Chapman, (London, 1905), 17–29.

[14] The Law of Return refers to the necessity of recycling nutrients that agriculture takes from the soil back to the earth. Both traditional agriculturalists and agriculturalists who relied on chemical fertilizers struggled with the challenge to maintain the necessary nutrients for plants. Barton, "Sir Albert Howard," 178.

[15] Gabrielle Howard, File Letters: *Matthaei Family Archive*, Birmingham, UK, 290.

[16] Gabrielle Howard, Letters, 259. See also F. G. Sly, "The Department of Agriculture in India," *Agricultural Journal of India*, 1 (1906): 3.

[17] Gabrielle Howard, Letters, 291.

[18] Albert Howard and Gabrielle Howard, *Wheat in India: Its Production, Varieties and Improvement* (Calcutta, 1909).

[19] Gabrielle Howard, Letters, 291.

Howard also sidestepped an early controversy. Gabrielle mentioned in a letter to her mother that Harold Maxwell-Lefroy, an Imperial Entomologist appointed in 1903 to survey and classify Indian insects, quarreled with the head of Pusa, Bernard Coventry. On Albert's ship to India, Lefroy shared these concerns with him and attempted to gain Howard's sympathy to side against what he considered the unfair policies of Coventry.[20] Albert, however, held back his judgment and would not sign a petition circulated by Lefroy. Gabrielle writes that,

> Mr. Lefroy is still grumbling [about it] and is rather cross with Bert that he will not join him in his grievances. It seems a bit doubtful whether he will ever settle down. I am so glad Bert has not yet mixed up in it.[21]

Lefroy, though a prickly character, established a respectable career in India and eventually returned to Britain to take up the post of Professor of Entomology at Imperial College London. He also established a successful pest control company that is still operating today.[22]

While Albert Howard's professional life ran at break-neck speed, the domestic affairs of setting up a home in Pusa went slower. Gabrielle was shocked at "what a primitive place Pusa is."[23] The agricultural laborers sent to them were "a rabble" and she hoped she could choose a few good staff from them: "Here we are in a really primitive Indian state in spite of a certain amount of European furniture, which has been imported."[24]

Neither she nor Albert considered the social life at Pusa particularly appetizing. The staff had "quarts of talk ... and sentimentality in torrents," but little immediate action. She found the Indians were difficult to deal with, "composed mainly of knaves and fools."[25] Ice lemon squashes, as on the trip to India, kept life tolerable.[26] Albert smoked occasional cigars and enjoyed his whiskey and port, which also helped.[27] The lack of cultural outlets, however, frustrated Gabrielle. Servants were untrained in Western standards. A number of small inconveniences irritated her. For instance, the local hairdresser had moved away three months earlier and Gabrielle found to her chagrin that she had to wash her own hair.[28] She quickly developed a firm belief in Indian incompetence. In one instance, she described how, traveling with six servants on a trip to north-west India, she and Albert looked out of the train and saw railway staff attempting,

> to stick the railway labels on our boxes with pins. It seems they had no paste. So they tried to nail the labels on with pins and a hammer. As that would not succeed, they picked up a half-eaten mango and smeared the juice on the labels hoping it would stick.[29]

---

[20] Imperial Agricultural Research Institute, *Scientific Reports* (London, 1906. Republished, 2013) 21–2.

[21] Gabrielle Howard, Letters, 259.

[22] Some of his works include H. Maxwell-Lefroy, *Indian Insect Life: A Manual of the Insects of the Plains (Tropical India)* (Calcutta, 1909); H. Maxwell-Lefroy, *List of Names Used in India for Common Insects* (Pusa, 1910).

[23] Gabrielle Howard, Letters, 83.   [24] Ibid., 88.   [25] Ibid., 30.   [26] Ibid., 91.

[27] Ibid., 138.   [28] Ibid., 93.   [29] Ibid., 107, 108.

As a result, their boxes did not arrive on time. She did, however, come to value quite a number of Indian servants who she genuinely admired.

She showed in these letters very little interest in Indian culture. "The museums here are bad, practically nothing in them but a few examples of native industries."[30] Visiting Bhutan, she was appalled at the peasants she encountered, and exhibited no sense of romanticism about peasant culture. One morning, planning to meet some guides and workers for a day's outing she noted that "our room was invaded by a horde of Bhutani women and men. You never saw such a set of absolute ruffians."[31] Gabrielle was a highly educated and cultivated middle-class woman who had high personal standards, and it is not surprising that life in a remote research station struck her as roughing it. The difficult life led the IARI to pay high salaries and provide large and spacious cottages to compensate for the remote location and the scarcity of services. Nor is it surprising that she found many Indians to be difficult to work with: her response to Indian life and culture is to be expected in a crowded, overpopulated, and largely impoverished colony—a scene very far removed from the gracious, wealthy, and sophisticated life she knew in the suburbs of London.

Other social stresses abounded. Albert's second wife, Louise, admitted, tellingly, that the Howard's spent little time in social engagements. In a remote research station where British staff had only each other for amusement, the Howard's self-imposed isolation had not "added to their popularity" at the Pusa station.[32] They did not fit well into the social scene and kept largely to themselves, happy in their marriage and in their own absorbing work. Gabrielle confessed to her mother an abject horror at spending unnecessary time with her colleagues and their families.

> There is a spasmodic effort to make this a social place. They are starting a club which they are most anxious to make a success but Bert and I secretly trust it will die. To meet the same people day after day just to talk is too much of a good thing besides there are so many things we want to do.[33]

The constant round of dinners and dances depressed them. She added that "We have just heard that it is proposed to give a dance tomorrow night. Our spirits are rather low in consequence."[34]

There were compensations, however. In addition to the satisfaction of their scientific work and the many publications that flowed from their pens, they were very much in love and enjoyed a happy domestic life. Recognition cascaded in from the outside. Only eight years after their arrival in India, first Gabrielle, and then a year later Albert, received awards from the highest levels of British government. In 1913 Gabrielle received, quite unexpectedly, the Kaiser-i-Hind award. Queen Victoria inaugurated the Kaiser-i-Hind in 1900 to honor pubic service in India. While to modern ears the award sounds German, the word "Kaiser" in the title is a cognate of the Latin "Caesar" derived from Hindi, and literally refers to "Emperor of India." She won the highest of the three grades—gold—a distinction also shared by Mohandas Gandhi a year later, when he still enthusiastically supported the

---

[30] Ibid., 105.   [31] Ibid., 146.
[32] Louise E. Howard, *Albert Howard in India and Earth's Green Carpet* (Cambridge, 2012), 28.
[33] Gabrielle Howard, Letters, 305.   [34] Ibid., 308.

British Empire. While unconnected to Germany, the award nonetheless reminded the family of their warm relations with all things German. Albert wrote to Gabrielle's mother that, due to the family's German background, Gabrielle was "really intoxicated with joy"—to such an extent, he could see "the Frau shining through the thin British varnish."[35] A letter from Gabrielle's mother to her daughter Marie reveal the enthusiasm felt in the family,

> Dearest Marie…I have the most astounding piece of news for you. Gabbie [Gabrielle] has a gold medal…there was the usual list of New Year's honours and at the end Indian Honours—6 men and then came Gabbie's name. The King has been pleased to grant the Kaiser-i-Hind gold medal…I can't think why Bert did not have it but suppose if he had, all the other Pusa men would have had to have it.[36]

Gabrielle's mother mused that while such awards are rarely given to a woman, a Mrs. Emmanuel had previously been awarded one for distinguished service fighting the plague. "I believe Gabbie…has saved the life of someone and never told me."[37]

She was partially correct. While Gabrielle had not saved a life, her work as a volunteer fit the conditions of the award. Gabrielle explained in a letter to her mother that,

> They are generally given to doctors for good work on plague, or malaria investigations and to collectors for famine relief work, quite senior men. Sir Robert Carlyle said he was going to try to get recognition for the five years unpaid work I did—we were both fearfully pleased and Bert immediately took me to the stores and bought me a gold bracelet—large gold—set with opals.[38]

One year later, in 1914, Albert Howard received an even greater distinction. Gabrielle revealed the moment in her letters. They were sitting in their office when a cable came in. Albert Howard disliked cables and they did not expect anything out of the ordinary.[39] She writes,

> …when we were sitting in the office talking to the overseer a telegraph was brought in addressed to Bert by title so I only thought it was a demand for seed or papers or something. When Bert said in a funny voice, "oh it seems I have been made a C. I. E.!"[40]

The C. I. E. stood for Companion of the Indian Empire, the most junior grade of the Most Eminent Order of the India Empire, a chivalrous order founded in 1878 by Queen Victoria.[41] They were both "tremendously pleased" and Gabrielle noted to her mother that except for the head of the department, Mr. Coventry, Albert

---

[35] Ibid., 72 (this is a note from Albert Howard to Gabrielle's mother in the same collection).
[36] Ibid., 46.   [37] Ibid., 48, 49.   [38] Ibid., 52.
[39] Ibid., 66.   [40] Ibid., 67.
[41] NA., "Supplement," *The London Gazette* (June 19, 1914). Available online at: https://www.the-gazette.co.uk/London/issue/28842/supplement/4879 [accessed May 31, 2017]. Albert Howard was knighted in 1934. The C. I. E. that Howard received did not confer knighthood. The C. I. E. is an award in the Order of the Indian Empire, third grade. The higher two grades of Knight Commander (KCIE) and Knight Grand Commander (GCIE) do confer knighthood. I owe this explanation to Dr. Karen Fox, Research Fellow with the Australian Dictionary of Biography at the Australian National University.

had the highest decoration in the department. She does not mention her share of that work as a scientist and this reveals clearly that she saw Albert as the sole progenitor of his own accomplishments and herself, as the two awards make clear, as a faithful and selfless partner in his work. She also noted with satisfaction that "it is a much greater compliment to get it now early in his career than on retirement." She was ecstatic that they had both been recognized for their labors. She teased her mother that she must now address her letters to "A. Howard Esqr. C. I. E." But there was a serious side to her suggestions. She noted that people in India with knighthoods acted horribly when their letters were misaddressed: "Bert hasn't had time to develop this yet" she remarked, and added, "He will be so angry with me when he reads this!!"[42]

Other distinctions came to both. Gabrielle continued to break gender barriers. She was asked by the Lieutenant General to attend the 1911 Durbar at Government House in Delhi. "I was the only woman" she remarked, to attend the ceremonies at Government House.[43] Albert Howard was also a recipient of a Silver Medal of the Royal Society of Arts in 1920.[44] In 1923, Gabrielle Howard was elected President of the Section of Agriculture and Chairman of the Joint Sections of Botany and Agriculture, a sub-group of the Indian Science Congress. Then, in 1926, Albert was elected President of the thirteenth session of the entire Indian Science Congress. Later, in 1930, Albert Howard was awarded the Barclay Memorial Medal of the Royal Asiatic Society of Bengal.[45]

After eighteen years in India, Albert Howard had not yet developed the protocols for organic farming. When Gabrielle labored to write the Presidential address for her new appointment in 1923, she admitted that "we can't think of a really first class subject." This is highly revealing. At this stage, neither held a passion for organic farming. If the two of them (indicated by how she used the word "we" to describe their lack of appropriate ideas for the address) were writing a speech of this nature two decades later, they would have known exactly what to write—it would have been a campaign for organic farming.[46] Interestingly, the letters—up to this point—mention nothing about composting, or even an early interest in returning nutrients to the soil out of the ordinary understanding of the importance of soil fertility—save one intriguing reference: "We have just been out for a cycle ride with Captain Keyes to see some potatoes—under a special manure."[47] Whether this special manure stimulated any interest in later research we never learn. But one thing is clear: they were both highly distinguished in their fields, and no radical departure had yet taken place that would distinguish them as founders of organic farming. Thus, to understand the radical nature of Howard's organic farming protocols, and how they departed from conventional thinking, we need to understand the ideas of Albert Howard at this mid-point of his career before he developed distinct ideas about what came to be known as the Indore method.

[42] Gabrielle Howard, Letters, 69, 70.   [43] Ibid., 77.
[44] Louise Howard, *Sir Albert Howard in India*, 33.   [45] Ibid.
[46] Gabrielle Howard, Letters, 76.   [47] Ibid., 11.

HOWARD BEFORE ORGANIC FARMING

Howard's work on a committee investigating the problem of reducing plant disease and insect pests through fumigation illustrates this early stage in the development of his ideas. At a conference in 1919 Thomas Bainbrigge Fletcher, a brilliant amateur scholar appointed to Pusa as Second Imperial Entomologist in India, assailed the lax laws throughout the British Empire that "until about a year ago" had left India as "a free dumping-ground for the plant-breeding pests of the whole world."[48] Anyone, he argued, was at liberty to bring in fruit, ornamental plants, sugarcanes, and other plants with "any insects that happened to be living on them." Insects and plant diseases had thus spread widely. While a parasite may have lived for "innumerable thousands of generations" in its own country with little harm due to natural predators, the change of climate and conditions that this biological laissez faire offered to parasites and predators, including animals, led many to go on a rampage.[49] For instance the West Indies and Guiana had been ravaged by a sugarcane weevil from Antigua (*Sphenophorus sacchari*), India had a sugarcane beetle from Java (*Holaniara pecsen*); and the aphis species from Ceylon and England feasted on young coconut trees and apples.[50] While the Indian Government had tried in the past to prevent these problems through legislation, it had been to little avail. At last, however a project had been initiated on the advice of a qualified committee: the restriction of importation to a few ports and effective fumigation of plant material in fumigation devices that soaked the plants in hydrocyanic acid gas at the point of entry.[51] A committee, Howard boasted, had been appointed to meet at his own research station at Pusa in November 1919 at the order of the Agricultural Department and the Inspector General of Agriculture to oversee implementation.[52]

Albert Howard served on this committee and approved its mission. There is no record that he held any reservations. This heavy reliance on artificial chemicals to fumigate select fruits, vegetables, and other plant materials was applied at the seven ports allowed to import plant material by sea. Land routes were exempt on the assumption that ancient roadways had already normalized botanical—and thus pest and disease—exchange between neighbors. Further, the Government of India was strongly urged to consult "foreign Governments and Native states" with seaports in India to implement similar restrictions.[53] Howard's work on this committee indicated that his later aversion to chemical pesticides was not imported into India with him from England.

---

[48] T. Bainbrigge Fletcher, "Note on Plant Imports into India," *Proceedings of the Third Entomological Meeting 1052- held at Pusa 3–15th February 1919* (Calcutta, 1921), 1052.

[49] Ibid., 1052.   [50] Ibid., 1053.

[51] In response, in 1906 the Government directed that cotton-seed imported from the new world be fumigated with carbon bi-sulfide at the port of entry. Ibid., 1055.

[52] The committee members were: Messrs. B. Coventry (Inspector-General of Agriculture), E. J. Butler (Imperial Mycologist), A. Howard (Imperial Economic Botanist), T. Brainbregge Fletcher (Imperial Entomologist), A. T. Gage (Director, Botanical Survey), R. F. L. Whitty (Customs Department, Bombay), and R. D. Anstead (Planting Expert, South India). See Ibid., 1054.

[53] Ibid., 1054.

As will be shown shortly, Howard also had the main outline of his ideas for organic farming in place at Pusa before he developed his now famous "Indore" compost method, which lies at the core of his ideas for organic farming. These markers of his progress are important because they indicate that his ideas developed in the milieu created by the IARI at Pusa, and that he then tested and then further developed these ideas at the research station at Indore. Since Albert Howard would later rail against the use of pesticides, chemicals, and artificial methods of agriculture, his early views only highlight the transformative effects that the IARI at Pusa had on Howard.

Albert Howard did not stand out from his colleagues as a unique advocate of mixed farming techniques, nor as a scientist that romanticized traditional agriculture. Others at the IARI did espouse romantic notions, as did D. Clouston, the director of the IARI, who oversaw the team of specialists that included Howard.[54] In a report on Indian agriculture, Clouston used language similar to romantic farming literature published in England, and appealed to the same popular sentiments that Howard promoted later in books aimed at a popular audience. He praised an "Eternal India...whom to know well is to love." The Indian peasants, he wrote, possessed "patience, [a] high standard of honesty and rustic charm" while "the common feature is the hamlet and the village, and it is in rural life that both in the past and present India has found her most distinct medium of self-expression."[55] Written in 1925 his language on rural India is almost identical in tone and sentiments to the romantic farm literature that lavished praise on the peasants of Europe and on Anglo-Saxon farming methods. Clouston described the Indian village as largely self-contained, with peasants living a simple and happy life, free from capitalistic usury where even "finance [was provided] by country traders who were found mostly in the large villages and small towns." In these Indian villages the railway, the steamship, and the construction of the Suez Canal later ruined "Arcadian economic conditions." Good intentions had bad effects, where "the extension of peace and security by the growth of British power effected great changes in our time."[56] Clearly, to Clouston, if Merry England had been lost to modernity, so too had Merry India.

The bacteriologist C. M. Hutchinson, also at Pusa, worked on the nitrifying organisms in the soil, and ways to encourage their activity.[57] He experimented with ways of "supplying such organism to soils in which they are deficient, or...adopting methods of agricultural practice which would allow the fullest development of those already naturally present."[58] In one annual report, he suggested that the "biological factor on soil fertility" is of "prime importance in agricultural practice." This included the biological availability of plant nutrition found in the soil, and above all, those biological factors "concerned in the decomposition of organic matter in Indian cultivated soils," and how that related to manuring, the

---

[54] Clouston was Agricultural Advisor to the Government of Indian and Director of the Agricultural Research Institute, Pusa.

[55] S. R. Christophers, *Souvenir: The Indian Empire* (Calcutta, 1927), 142.   [56] Ibid., 142.

[57] Ibid., 48–9.   [58] Ibid., 50.

evolution of soils, and plowing.[59] This research gets tantalizingly close to Howard's later breakthrough on compost at Indore, and in fact makes it clear that, though his early colleagues have not been discussed in the historical accounts of organic farming, Howard's narrative of organic farming arose from interaction with a web of imperial scientists working on similar problems.

Howard began his work at the IARI by completing a botanical survey of the varieties of wheat in India.[60] His India-wide investigations had as their main objective the improved resistance to disease and better hybridization of wheat. But his work also focused on fruit, fibers, oil seeds, barley, opium, and cassava varieties, as well as tobacco, tea, and an abiding interest in tree diseases that affected Indian forests.[61] He also advised the Kashmir Durbar on hop cultivation, while advising too on the development of the fruit industry at Quetta, in Baluchistan, where he also ran field research.[62] On leave back in England he worked on rust-resistant wheat, and the opportunities for the importation of Indian wheat and tobacco. He wanted Indian and Kashmir products to "enter the market of the world as a competitor with California."[63] He was proud that his newly discovered wheat varieties were in demand in Hungary, the United States, and Australia.[64] He also visited agricultural stations in Ceylon and revisited stations of interest in England.[65] His constant touring of the Indian Empire, his scientific publications, and his praise from superiors tell us that he was not a maverick working outside established scientific networks in India. Bernard Coventry, the Inspector General of Agriculture in India, and his supervisor, offered exceptional praise for Howard and his achievements at Pusa.[66]

In Howard's first major publication, *The Wheat of India*, co-written with Gabrielle, we see how early in his career—well before he arrived at the Indore research station—he absorbed assumptions about the need to return nutrients to the soil and to learn from the Indian farmers themselves. He framed his investigation by noting, in a similar manner to empire foresters, that India required the "application of Western Scientific methods to the local conditions," in order to improve Indian farming "on its own lines." He traveled personally over the ancient "alluvial plain" that lay south of the Himalayas, stretching from Bombay to Bengal, and rapturously

[59] Ibid., 52.

[60] Albert Howard, and Gabrielle Howard, *Report of the Agricultural Research Institute and College, Pusa (including report of the imperial cotton specialist) 1907–09* (Calcutta, 1910), 6. For the book that emerged from their survey of Indian wheat varieties see Howard, *Wheat in India* (1909). The Howards published a condensed version of the book the same year in the *Memoirs of the Department of Agriculture in India*. See Albert Howard and Gabrielle Howard, "The Varietal Characters of Indian Wheats," *Memoirs of the Department of Agriculture in India* (Calcutta, 1909): 1–66.

[61] Ibid., 35.

[62] Howard could often cut in half the time required to test new varieties by growing a crop in Pusa and then planting the seeds in Quetta, or vice versa, without waiting for a new year seasonal change. See E. Fairlie Watson, "The Lessons of the East," *Organic Gardening Magazine*, 13/8 (September, 1948).

[63] *Report of the Agricultural Research Institute and College, Pusa (including report of the imperial cotton specialist) 1910–11*, (Calcutta; Superintendent Government Printing, 1912), 6.

[64] Ibid., 13.

[65] *Report of the Agricultural Research Institute, 1907–09*, 32.

[66] *Report of the Agricultural Research Institute, and College, Pusa (including report of the imperial cotton specialist) 1909–10*, (Calcutta; Superintendent Government Printing, 1911), 2.

described the soil of northern India, from the fringes of the central plateau, to the rice swamps of Bengal, which had "only recently recovered from the sea."[67] His extensive survey of wheat variety in India included a close reading of regional farm experiments that had taken place in most of the Indian Empire. This breadth of research gave him food for thought. The voluminous literature on Indian agriculture that he read for this survey provided key concepts that formed the nucleus of his thinking well before the Indore experiments that followed. Rather than artificial fertilizer, the return of nutrients to the soil in the form of manure and plant products lay at the core of his future ideas on compost. His book, *The Wheat of India*, shows that experimentation with manure by other imperial science officers was already widespread at experimental farms throughout India.

Pusa was not the best location to grow wheat and to test for successful varieties that would resist orange, black, and yellow rust.[68] But Albert and Gabrielle Howard put this disadvantage to good use by testing varieties quickly through a process of elimination—they reasoned that if they and their colleagues could make any one variety thrive in the inhospitable soil at Pusa, it would do well resisting the three rust infections. A long series of publications by Albert and Gabrielle Howard documented this early progress. India was known internationally for its low-quality grains. The Howards proved that higher grain quality could be grown for an international market in India, and be rust resistant as well, raising the domestic production. By the late 1920s, wheats named Pusa 4, 12, 52, 54, and 100 were widely cultivated in India. Ironically, these early strains provided the first steps of a green revolution in the 1960s in India that would combine improved crop varieties with massive increases in chemical fertilizers and pesticides.[69]

By the 1920s, the Howards had gained international attention and praise for their work on wheat. The scientific community and the press both recognized in effusive terms this unique husband wife team. In *The Times Trade and Engineering Supplement* an unnamed author provided a careful analysis of the impact that the Howards had in India, Britain, and around the world, particularly looking at the new strain, "Pusa 12,"

> Seldom in the sphere of practical economic investigation has there been a more fruitful collaboration between husband and wife than that of Mr. Albert Howard, for many years Imperial Economic Botanist at the Agricultural Research Institute, Pusa, and Mrs. Howard, Second Imperial Botanist…After the IARI focused the work of the botanical section on wheat, remarkable progress has been made. The results are of great interest to Britain, because this country is by far the best customer for surplus Indian wheat.[70]

[67] Howard, *Wheat in India*, 9. Many took such a romantic view of the India soil. See George Watt, "Conditions of Wheat Growing in India," *Journal of the Royal Agricultural Society of England*, 24 (1888): 26.

[68] Such as *Puccinia iriticina, Graminis,* and *Glumarum.*

[69] Albert Howard and Gabrielle Howard, "The Improvement of Indian Wheat: A brief summary of the investigations carried out at Pusa from 1905 to 1924 including an account of the new Pusa hybrids," *Agricultural Research Institute: Bulletin* 171 (Calcutta, 1928): i, ii, 2, 4, 24.

[70] Anonymous, "Indian Wheat," *The Times Trade and Engineering Supplement* (May 5, 1928).

The author notes that imports in the last few years into Britain from India increased from 176,000 tons to 300,000 tons. The Howards had proved that high-grade wheats could be produced for the Indian and world economy, "of the same class as the best of those exported from North America." India could soon, he argued, take its place as the new Canada in exports. The new varieties not only raised the quality, they also replaced a wide variety of mixed wheats in India of bewildering diversity and produced "pure varieties" that have "high yielding power, rust-resistant, good standing power" and boast a visibly red chaff that helped the farmer observe impurities in any crop that suffered from genetic drift. The Howards had more than "revolutionized the production of Indian wheat," they had also increased wheat output in other countries like Argentina—where Pusa 12 proved to be high yield and adaptable. The Howard's special varieties of hard wheats also won awards in Australia and Britain. In terms of bread-making—a key factor in economic value—they are "as good as any wheat produced in the world."[71]

Other innovations followed. Before Howard had formulated his Indore compost process, he had already concluded that new growth accelerated by nitrogen fertilizers did not produce a healthier plant. He also observed that it was time to pay attention to the "quality as well as on the yield of wheat."[72] He noticed that continuous application of saltpeter, a nitrogen-heavy mineral used as a fertilizer, injured the tilth and the humus of the soil, and resulted in "a gradually diminishing yield compared with the animal nitrogenous manures." He also discovered that results from plowing a crop back into the soil as a green manure was "not very encouraging."[73] Significantly, he saw that old plant refuse gave a higher yield than fresh refuse. These conclusions led him to the first steps of solving a unique problem: designing a "compost pile" with bacteria that broke down refuse composed largely of plant material, with a relatively small amount of manure, which in turn could then be spread over the soil.

Between 1905 and 1923, while working at Pusa, Albert and Gabrielle published together or separately 93 reports, articles, or books on agriculture in India.[74] The Howards, from the start, energetically tackled a number of sequential problems: advising Bihar wheat farmers on the flax dodder plague; classifying wheat, tobacco, linseed, gram, fibers, and other crops; and developing tobacco strains that proved more resistant to disease. They developed a method of "green manuring," along with special drainage techniques and deep plowing, which delivered more nutrients to the plant and thus improved health and productivity. South Africa, Australia, and other parts of the British Empire copied the technique Howard developed for soil aeration, and his success with tobacco gained recognition in the British parliament. In agricultural circles at least, he had begun to make a name for himself.[75]

---

[71] Ibid.　　[72] Howard, *Wheat in India*, 52.　　[73] Ibid., 58.

[74] The early efforts of Gabrielle and Albert Howard focused on wheat. Gabrielle remarks that "Our wheats are however doing splendidly all over and the people are very pleased with them. They are sure to spread." Gabrielle Howard, Letters, 166.

[75] Lord Henry Cavendish-Bentinck, House of Commons, 14 August 1917, *Hansard*, House of Commons, vol. 97, no. 116, c. 1008.

Howard's colleagues shared a romantic attachment to traditional agricultural methods and an appreciation of indigenous peasant knowledge. The publications by his colleagues at the IARI illustrate an active and abiding interest in the mycorrhizal process, and in the use of manures to restore soil fertility. More specifically, only two years after Howard arrived at the IARI his colleague E. Shearer published a detailed review in the IARI-published *Agricultural Journal of India* titled "Note on Agriculture in Japan." In this article Shearer reviewed in substantial detail those portions of a book by F. A. Nicholson that related to Japanese agriculture. Shearer, following Nicholson's lead, laid out a formula for composting that almost exactly corresponds to Howard's Indore compost method. There is no reasonable likelihood that Howard did not know of the interest, or the publication of his colleague, and it is very odd that Howard never referenced Nicholson's book or this article by Shearer. This does not detract from the remarkable accomplishment that Howard attained at Indore, because Howard clearly gave a scientific rationale and protocol for some of the methods practiced by traditional Japanese, Chinese, and European peasant agriculture. But the lack of candor about the debt that Howard owed to his colleagues at the IARI has obscured what is only now becoming clear: Curzon set up the IARI to apply western scientific knowledge to an eastern culture, and the IARI succeeded in this imperial synthesis with developments that Howard incorporated into organic farming, which has now proved such a central part of the modern environment movement and become embedded in global culture. In short, Howard's reticence to share credit has obscured the broader institutional origin of organic farming.[76]

While Howard's ideas at the IARI came together in collaboration with colleagues, there is very little hint of such indebtedness in his popular writing. In *An Agricultural Testament* the IARI at Pusa is blamed for hindering his work because it divided crop research "into no less than six separate sections." No progress could be made "without complete freedom" and the bureaucratic specialists at the IARI stood in the way of such freedom. He escaped these limitations, he wrote, by his move to the Indore research station where he could follow his own agenda. The biography of Howard, written after his death by his second wife, is partially responsible for the neglect of his colleagues' contribution, and for the exclusive focus on unique innovations pioneered by Howard. It also explains partially the heavy romantic focus on traditional methods by Louise and Albert Howard. On the other hand, Howard's imperial mission was not glossed over. It was taken for granted, Louise wrote, "that it was the function of the British Government in India to confer on the peoples of India all the advantages of Western scientific discovery."[77]

Unfortunately, an earthquake took down the monumental Pusa station in 1934, leaving the famous central dome, the Phipps Laboratory, in ruins. The viceroy

---

[76] E. Shearer, "Notes on Agriculture in Japan," *Agricultural Journal of India*, III (Calcutta, 1908): 52–64. In this article Shearer reviews Frederick Augustus Nicholson, *Notes on Fisheries in Japan* (Madras, 1907).
[77] Howard, *Sir Albert Howard in India*, 203.

Lord Lithgow then moved the IARI to Delhi in 1936, where it has remained ever since.[78] The earthquake can be seen as a tragic metaphor for the loss of prestige that would in the next few decades befall the narratives of wholeness and organic farming pioneered by the IARI and Albert Howard. While some scientists in and out of the Empire accepted the principles of organic farming well into the 1950s, the scientific community increasingly became suspicious of Howard's blend of science, romance, and orientalism, favoring instead the more practical mainstream model of specialization and the use of artificial chemicals that raised crop yields. The "Green Revolution" of the 1940s onward depended upon artificial pesticides and fertilizers as well as intensive plant breeding, and successfully raised yields in India, Mexico, and other parts of the world. Ironically, two streams emerged from the work accomplished at the IARI: the pioneering work on wheat varieties and farming techniques fed directly into the Green Revolution; and the innovative work on composting by Howard and his colleagues fed into the organic farming movement.

Publishing a summary of his work in 1924, Howard proudly reviewed the results obtained. This included improved varieties of wheat, methods for saving irrigation water (work mostly carried out in Northwest India), research on soil erosion and reducing surface drainage, as well as methods for sun drying vegetables that preserved vitamin content and thus fought Beriberi. These methods also had tangible benefits for military purposes because dried vegetables were "easily transported by mules and can be dropped from aero planes into beleaguered fortresses."[79] He also described how his work had improved varieties of gram, fibers, and soil seeds. This report he privately published and proudly included a letter from Mr. Bernard Coventry, his immediate supervisor as the Director of the Pusa Institute and Agricultural advisor to the Government of India. Coventry praised the wide effect of Howard's work. His letter mentions that Howard proposed plans for a new Institute of Plant Industry at Indore, which had been forwarded to the Secretary of State for approval and that "he had every expectation of full funding." At this juncture, Howard took his accrued leave, departing for England with the full expectation of returning to his new research station at Indore—a station completely under his control.[80]

INDORE

After many years working at Pusa, Albert Howard gained his own research station at Indore, as Director of the Institute of Indore Plant Industry, with funding from a number of key sources. The Indian Central Cotton Committee (ICCC) provided

[78] NA. *A Brief Survey of Three Decades of Research at the Institute* [Imperial Agricultural Research Institute] (New Delhi, 1937), 21–2.

[79] Albert Howard, *Work Done by the Botanical Section, Agricultural Research Institute, Pusa, from May 1905 to January 1923*, privately printed. (No location, 1924), 6.

[80] Ibid. The titles of the 93 papers published in this report are classified as *Memoirs of the Department of Agriculture in India (Botanical Series)* 1–18; *Bulletins of the Agricultural Research Institute, Pusa,* 19–37; *Bulletins of the Fruit Experiment Station, Quetta,* 38–48; *Articles in the Agricultural Journal of India,* 49–82; and *Other publications,* 83–93.

a grant to cover the construction of the buildings, roads, and other infrastructure.[81] This committee advocated research for improved cotton strains, usually with higher quality American cotton seeds that would replace Indian varieties that produced rougher and shorter cotton fibers.[82] An Indian prince of the Holkar line, Maharaja Tukojirao Holkar III, donated land.[83] The Central Indian States—a political office of the British Indian government and largely composed of the treaty states governed by hereditary princes under the Viceroy—provided operating funds. This gave Howard the resources he needed to conduct experiments as he saw fit. Here he worked from 1924 to 1931, where he experimented with the effect of composting on humus. The Indore Process or Indore Method is the term Howard used to describe the composting technique he devised at the Institute of Plant Industry, Indore.[84]

It has been widely assumed by organic farming activists, including Louise Howard, that Albert Howard invented the Indore method that lies at the heart of the organic farming protocol. Rather than inventing, however, it would be more accurate to say he perfected a process begun by his imperial associates in Pusa and his scientific colleagues at the Rothamsted research station in England—a research station that organic farming enthusiasts, including Albert and Louise Howard, greatly deplored. H. B. Hutchinson and E. H. Richards, both at Rothamsted, published an article in 1921 that revealed a critical finding of their research on composting. In "Artificial Farmyard Manure," published in the *Journal of the Ministry of Agriculture*, Hutchinson and Richards published a document, preceding the Indore method, laying out the basic scientific principles that lie at the heart of organic farming.[85] Despite its mundane title, the article was reviewed in *Nature* and its true significance was clearly understood: namely, that composting vegetable matter such as straw into a fertilizer as potent as animal manure in an age of a

[81] This committee ran under the leadership of B. C. Burt who served as secretary for the first seven years. Local provincial committees would advise this India-wide committee, hence the name, Central Cotton Committee.

[82] Originally only advisory, the ICCC published its first report in 1919 and operated under the authority of the Department of Revenue and Agriculture. Its role soon expanded with the passing of the *Indian Cotton Cess Act*. This act taxed two annas per bale on all cotton exported or purchased by mills in India. With a substantial budget, the ICCC expanded its remit to advance research into all aspects of the cotton industry, from agriculture, marketing, and technology. The success of this committee inspired a similar structure for the jute industry in India. See the *Annual Report of the Indian Central Cotton Committee, Bombay, for the year ending August 31st 1928* (Calcutta, 1929), 1–6; B. C. Burt, *Journal of the Chemical Society* (1943): 200.

[83] Based in Indore, Holkar ruled one of the princely states of the Central Indian States. The Maharaja was a strong anglophile and supporter of British rule, gaining a knighthood when he was awarded the Star of India. He traveled widely, and married several times, his last wife an American actress, Nancy Anne Miller, from Seattle Washington, who converted to Hinduism. He ended his controversial reign in 1926 by abdicating in favor of his son, still in regency, not long after Howard arrived at Indore.

[84] Albert Howard, *An Agricultural Testament* (Oxford, 1956), 40–1. Howard had lectured in the Imperial Department of Agriculture in Barbados. He continued to publish in West Indies scientific journals after his return from India. See "The Manufacture of Humus by the Indore Process," *The West India Committee Circular*, (April 23, 1936), 173–4, 180, 196.

[85] H. B. Hutchinson and E. H. Richards, "Artificial farmyard manure," *Journal of the Ministry of Agriculture* 28 (1921): 567–72.

decreasing supply of animal manure could change agriculture in a significant way. The anonymous reviewer wrote that the findings of this experiment offered by the Rothamsted Experimental Station, offered "the most notable advances in agricultural science." He recounted how farmyard manure had played a central role in the past for fertilizing crops—so important in fact that cattle dung has been judged by its grade of nitrogen enrichment. Cake-fed dung—that is the dung produced by cattle fed with seed cakes—had a high market value. Now a new method of composting could fertilize crops in the face of manure scarcity.[86]

This article by Hutchinson and Richards also demonstrated that the content of nitrogen in urine and dung does not automatically transfer to the crops when applied to the field. Instead it was necessary to compost dung with "carbonaceous matter" (litter or waste plant material such as straw). This enhanced the growth of fungi and bacteria that absorbed nitrogen from the urine and dung, and then when spread on the fields, transferred the nitrogen into the roots of the plant. Farmyard manure could thus be manufactured with only a small portion of manure—the bulk composed of plant material. By fermenting the straw, the process fixed nitrogen from the atmosphere. The key aerobic bacteria was *Spirochaeta cytophaga*. This agent required nitrogen in the form of ammonia, moisture, and air to rot the straw. More dung than was necessary simply went to waste—the excess nitrogen in the dung was lost as ammonia or other forms of gaseous nitrogen to the atmosphere. Further, if the nitrogen in the compost mix is in excess of this amount it also tends to pass into the atmosphere as ammonia. With an ample supply of air, dung, and the proper mix of carbonaceous matter, the compost mix produced fertilizer with 2 percent nitrogen—regardless of the initial content of excrement. A farmer, could therefore, with a little starter dung, "make an artificial product, closely resembling farmyard manure." The significance of this groundbreaking work was obvious to other scientists and to farmers. This innovation, when dung was scarce and expensive, could make valuable fertilizers from available vegetable matter through composting—without the use of any chemical fertilizers whatsoever.[87]

Howard and the followers of his Indore method did not deny the importance of the Rothamsted work. They did not, however, in later years credit Hutchinson and Richards for the central scientific breakthrough that it clearly was—perhaps because the perceived arch-enemy of the organic farming movement, the Rothamsted research station, produced it. In one passage, while Howard credits the work of Hutchinson and Richards, he emphasized his own original contribution. This contribution consisted of perfecting their composting method and then formulating—and popularizing—an easily replicated system. Howard himself had no key scientific breakthrough, certainly not on the level of Hutchinson and Richards. Rather he put the findings together into a unified and simplified process called the Indore Method—a practical and holistic approach that depended on key findings from Rothamsted. While Howard to his credit fully admits this is the case, he nonetheless remained relatively silent on the work of colleagues who laid the

---

[86] Anonymous, "Artificial Farmland Manure," *Nature*, 2704/107 (1921): 828–9.   [87] Ibid.

foundation for his own Indore method. He then popularized his work by pointing to the romantic notion that the origin of his own innovations were Indian and Chinese peasants.

Later, after retiring to Britain, Howard slowly began to link the problem of depleted soil to plant health and thus human health. As will be seen in a subsequent chapter, he followed enthusiastically the work of Robert McCarrison, a British physician in India, who, in the 1920s, observed widely divergent health features among Indian groups, from exquisitely healthy Hunzas in the north to the disease-prone Dravidians in the south. McCarrison arrived at this conclusion by simplifying the diets of six regions of India into six separate feeding regimes, and then applied these different feeding regimes to six discrete sets of rats. He observed that those rats with a diet high in whole grains and fresh vegetables had greater body weight with more resistance to disease and a significantly longer life than the other sets. The rats that ate only refined foods with few vegetables were unhealthy and short-lived. He concluded that this latter diet fitted the lifestyle of the English a hundred years into the Industrial Revolution and this fact, he concluded, explained the prevalence of disease among his countrymen back home.[88] Howard himself began to suspect, with his work at Indore, that more than plant health was involved in returning nutrients to the soil: that the Indore method, devised to solve the practical problem of providing inexpensive fertilizer to Indian peasants with little animal manure available, may also have implications for human health.

---

[88] Robert McCarrison, "Nutrition and National Health," *British Medical Journal*, I (1936): 427–30.

5

The Search for Pre-Modern Wisdom

Followers of Howard have attached a key romantic myth to Howard's organic protocols: that he arrived in India as a scientist who had to unlearn his formal training; that he humbly discovered the Indore Method from the inspirational peasant farmers of rural India. Indeed, Howard made passing reference to this idea in his later years and his second wife Louise picked up and expanded on these statements. The myth of the peasant origin of organic farming has given rise to the belief among his followers that Howard, along with Gabrielle and Louise, bequeathed to the West and a globalizing world—not a brilliant new conceptualization and methodology of compost—but the ancient wisdom of the East. As this chapter shows, however, the separation of the organic farming protocols and the myth of peasant tutelage throws the accomplishments of Albert Howard, Gabrielle Howard, and most especially Louise Howard, into clearer historical light—accomplishments that not only reveal the often-hidden role of women in science, but also illustrate the remarkable accomplishment of three people who changed land use, consumer habits, and ideas around the globe.

Organic farmers joined a wide array of individuals who claimed inspiration from eastern wisdom. Myth does not equate with ignorance, but rather is a narrative—an imaginative story—that combines history with romanticism, mysticism, and subjective values. Given the streams of romanticism, orientalism, and holism that inspired Howard's imagination, it makes sense that he made a number of passing references about peasant wisdom. It also makes sense that the organic farming movement seized on these statements, and that the only biography of Howard, written by his second wife Louise, drew attention to the peasant wisdom of the East illuminating and justifying Howard's accomplishments.

In addition to ecology and holism, the claim that eastern wisdom and peasants in particular provided the foundations of organic farming grew directly out of orientalism. Scholars employ the term orientalism to denote the literary and artistic depictions of the Middle East and Asia in a manner that sees a wide gulf between the scientific and rational West and a timeless, ancient, and static East; an East that cradles a treasure trove of lost knowledge and human experience preserved as if in amber from ancient times to the present. The praise that orientalists paid to the peasant and to the East also contained a back-handed compliment and reflect the sentiments of many imperialists, such as that of Lord Cromer, Consul-General of Egypt (and effective Governor) from 1883–1907, who stated that, the mind of the oriental … [that] like his picturesque streets, is eminently wanting in symmetry. His reasoning is of the most slipshod description … deficient in the logical faculty.[1]

To many orientalists Asians sported a close-to-nature ethic that more than balanced their non-western mental makeup. Asians moved with the rhythm of the seasons; possessed exotic faith traditions; preserved ancient agricultural customs; and harbored medical wisdom that had slowly amalgamated from generations of human experience, acting as a conduit from the ancient to the modern. All this wisdom, westerners discovered in the Orient, if they looked for it.

Scholars have debated whether orientalists genuinely admired the East. Literary historian Edward Said who declaims orientalism as a "certain will or intention to understand, in some cases to control, manipulate, even to incorporate, what is a manifestly different (or alternative and novel) world."[2] Others however understand orientalism as the inevitable result of globalization and that orientalists have often expressed a sincere appreciation of non-western cultures—to the point of transcribing and rescuing non-western culture from destruction in a modern world by salvaging traditions on the verge of extinction through translation, oral histories, archeology, and a wide array of conservation projects.[3]

Westerners have often ascribed to non-western faiths a plethora of ancient environmental values that stand as a model to emulate. For instance, some scholars of Hinduism have downplayed Hinduism as a faith system and emphasized instead the more universal aspects of Hinduism as a philosophy and way of life—an approach that appeals to western audiences. Further, because high Brahmanism developed a form of monotheism that served as an umbrella to local nature gods, and because the sum of practice and beliefs of Hindu people vary remarkably, scholars easily extract iconic ideas of nature from a wide pantheon of deities and practices.[4] The same can be said for Buddhism, which in the Theravada system practiced in South and South-East Asia, exhibits a syncretism that absorbs local spirits, gods, and myth. The more intellectualized Mahayana Buddhism practiced in East Asia also offers a multitude of schools and approaches to nature that mix with indigenous faith systems, such as Shintoism and Zen Buddhism. Orientalists have been tempted to read into these varied systems new ideas of recent origin— wrapped in an ancient and mystical halo. Unlike Christianity, Judaism, and Islam, Hinduism and Buddhism do not offer a single text or even an agreed upon canon, nor a central organization or an "orthodox" creed. Therefore, eastern faith systems

---

[1] Evelyn Baring Cromer, *Modern Egypt* (New York, 1908), 146.

[2] Edward Said, *Orientalism* (New York, 1979), 12.

[3] Gregory Barton, "The Appeal of Orientalism," *British Scholar*, 3/1 (2010): 1–4.

[4] For further discussion of the definition of Hinduism, see Joseph T. O'Connel, "Gaudiya Vaisnava Symbolism of Deliverance from Evil." *Journal of the American Oriental Society* 93 (1973): 340–3; Romila, Thapar, "Imagined Religious Communities? Ancient History and the Modern Search for a Hindu Identity," *Modern Asian Studies* 23 (1989): 224.

appeared plastic and amorphous and allowed westerners to stamp onto the East any number of useful ideas.[5]

The transcendentalist tradition in the United States had long drawn inspiration from Hinduism, creating its own version of the mystical East that, while misreading and misunderstanding Hinduism, created an American fantasy of eastern culture as a treasure house of mysticism that could unloose the human potential for universal brotherhood. Emerson and Thoreau spoke about nature and its immutable laws in a language that organic farming enthusiasts clearly mimicked. It also expressed a profound skepticism of science and all forms of logic chopping—advocating existential observation and practical experience over abstractions.

Contemporary to the rise of English romantic farm literature in the 1920s and 30s, many in the British Empire also wrote home about experiences abroad. Rudyard Kipling in the late nineteenth and early twentieth century depicted India as a storehouse of wonder and mysticism, prompting a renewed fascination with the Indian Empire, and Hinduism in particular. But Rabindranath Tagore in particular brought the East before western audiences. A western educated Bengali poet, Tagore presented a version of the East influenced heavily by western orientalism. His accolades in the press, the academy, and a Nobel Prize illustrated the rewards that awaited those who could translate the simple virtues of the East to western audiences. Tagore studied agriculture at the University of Illinois, Urbana, and—like Gandhi—deeply imbibed romantic farming literature that advocated peasant crafts and virtues. With the start of the First World War he lectured English and American audiences that the West would need the "sacred water" of India "to sweeten the history of man into purity."[6] That a number of early environmental activists, including those promoting organic farming, ascribed environmental ethics to Hinduism and above all to the peasants of India is not a surprise.[7]

The right-of-center cultural milieu of organic farming circles encouraged enthusiasts to romanticize the peasant. Conservatives in the 1920s and 30s often contended that a people (*volk*) carried wisdom and indigenous knowledge from generation to generation. On the continent this sprang from the ideas of the philosopher and historian Johann von Herder who during the Napoleonic occupation resisted enlightenment reforms and rationalization of laws and customs by arguing that societies thrive on the characteristics of a particular people, and that law should not be universal across cultures and societies, but rather that government and laws (and elites) should share the racial and cultural characteristics of the people they ruled. Napoleonic reforms, he believed, bred sterile cosmopolitan culture that

---

[5] Duara, Prasenjit, "The New Politics of Hinduism," *Wilson Quarterly* 15/3 (1991): 43.

[6] His presentation of the East to the West had little truck however in Japan, where audiences were not receptive to his persona as "wise man of the East." Stephen N. Hay, "Rabindranath Tagore in America," *American Quarterly* 14/3 (1962): 444–6.

[7] Ronald Inden, "Orientalist Constructions of India," *Modern Asian Studies* 20 (1986) 401–46; Peter Marshal, *The British Discovery of Hinduism in the Eighteenth Century* (Cambridge, 1970) 43–4; Peter van der Veer, "Introduction," *Orientalism and the Postcolonial Predicament*, eds. Carol A. Breckenridge and Peter van der Veer (Philadelphia, 1993): 1–23.

divorced people from the soil that nourished them. Universalism destroyed national culture.[8]

Marxists in particular found Herder's approach an anathema, not only because of the urban base for the vanguard of intellectuals who pushed for revolution, but also because Karl Marx had specifically, in his analysis of Napoleon III, identified the "reactionary peasant" as a backward force in society. The organic farming movement arose in a milieu of resistance to a number of modernizing forces: to unbridled capitalism, to urban consumer society, and to international socialism, all of which arose—at least partially—out of the ideals of the French enlightenment and a belief in the mass perfectibility of society. The myth of peasant wisdom has proved, and still proves, a powerful tool in attempts to resist globalization and dominant consumerist culture by organic activists and their allied health food and slow food movement adherents.[9]

F. H. King's hugely influential *Farmers of Forty Centuries* (1911) inspired many agricultural reformers, including Albert Howard. The imaginative influence of this book cannot be overstated. Howard often referred to it, as did romantic writers on the peasantry such as Robert McCarrison, G. T. Wrench, and many others. King taught and researched agricultural science at the University of Wisconsin, Madison, and then served as chief of the division of soil and management at the United States Department of Agriculture Bureau of Soils.[10] He launched a whirlwind tour of Japan and China and wrote his book in a white heat of unrestrained enthusiasm He argued that Asia had maintained soil fertility for thousands of years by returning nutrients to the soil—most particularly human waste—and that western nations ought to adopt this method to preserve soil fertility for the long haul. This book, more than any other single document, popularized the belief in romantic farm literature that peasant wisdom held the key to fight soil erosion and low agricultural productivity.[11]

King differs in many ways from organic farming in his prescriptions, however, and has many glaring holes in his argument that organic farming enthusiasts overlooked. He emphasized not the result of human health, but efficiency. Unlike the conservationists of his day, he saw the need to return nutrients to the soil as a way of using land even more intensively, and for accelerating economic and population growth. Where he imbibed his orientalist romanticism is not known, and a biography of his life would prove useful in this regard. While he took many photographs in Asia, he also utilized set stage photographs of romanticized and ideal peasants. He saw Chinese culture as both ancient and unified, stretching from the misty beginnings of human history, seemingly unaware of famines, upheavals,

---

[8] Gregory A. Barton, *Informal Empire and the Rise of One World Culture* (Basingstoke, 2014), 186–8.

[9] Lars Tragardh, "Varieties of Volkish Ideologies," *Language and the Construction of Class Identities,* ed. Bo Strath (Gothenburg, 1990) 31; Eugene Lunn, "Cultural Populism and Egalitarian Democracy: Herder and Michelet in the Nineteenth Century," *Theory and Society* 15 (1986): 496.

[10] C. B. Tanner, and R. W. Simonson, "Franklin Hiram King—Pioneer Scientist," *Soil Science Society of America Journal* 57/1 (1993): 286–92.

[11] F. H. King, *Farmers of Forty Centuries, or Permanent Agriculture in China, Korea and Japan* (Madison, 1911).

alien rule, importation of technology, and agricultural methods. He entirely overlooked the problems of massive deforestation and environmental damage. Rather he concluded that the agricultural practices he witnessed produced, among the Chinese, "a race which, with fortitude and rare wisdom, has kept alive the seeds of manhood and nourished them into such sturdy stock."[12]

King's argument that western nations should return night soil from the cities back to the farms appears to have been formed well before his trip to the Far East and to be derived from American, British, and European efforts to address soil fertility. Politicians and engineers have long recommended the use of night soil and the idea has a long and varied history that dates from the mid-nineteenth century, well before the publication of his book in 1911.[13] King also mentions, without deeper examination, that the international settlement in Shanghai—not Chinese peasants—arranged for the sale of urban wastes to fertilizer middlemen, who in turn delivered night soil from the cities to the farms. Further King drew heavily on European scientific literature to discuss the advantages of composting methods, through which he viewed Chinese efforts. Thus, King viewed China through a distinctly western lens. In fact, he entirely missed the fact that China was so rapidly industrializing that the importation of artificial fertilizers had already begun to change agricultural use, in the same way that it had in Europe and the United States. Merely touring and identifying composting in a peasant population in the Far East did no more to roll back these changes in China than European composting had in Europe. He also paid scant attention to the poverty that such labor-intensive methods produced. He lingered long in his book over foot pumps and labor-intensive hand tools, revealing a deep romanticism about medieval rural life that contributed little to subsequent organic farming. The main point—the return of night soil to the farms—though often touted by King as necessary, never formed the core protocols of organic farming.

Some of the influences on organic farming enthusiasts also influenced people with dissimilar ideas. Broad cultural influences, like orientalism or rural romanticism, did not flow in a unidirectional fashion. The Roosevelt administration, National Socialists, Communists, Japanese Fascists, Mongolian princes, Manchurian war lords, along with religious spiritualists such as Theosophists, agriculturalists such as the followers of Steiner, and utopian novelists all fantasized about the potential treasure house of eastern wisdom. But this shared fascination did not produce similar outcomes. Henry A. Wallace, Agriculture Secretary under Roosevelt (and future Vice President), also shared similar interests to F. H. King in a mystical Far East. After flirting with theosophy, he sponsored in 1945–46 an expedition to search for arid plant hybrids from the Gobi Desert, particularly strains of wheat that could be transplanted to the American Midwest—a particular concern given the dust bowl experience of the Midwest. Wallace and the Soviets he so admired pursued scientific farming, productivity, and hybrids. Even the East dreamed

---

[12] Ibid., 50, 67.
[13] Richard Wines, *Fertilizer in America: From Waste Recycling to Resource Exploitation,* (Philadelphia, 1985), 25–30.

about the East, as all regions and nations romanticize the past and put powerful images to utilitarian use.[14]

Organic farming draws upon scientific arguments that arose a cultural reaction against the perceived moral and physical degeneration brought about by industrialization and capitalism.[15] During the first half of the twentieth century many of the basic tenets of organic farming developed in response to an extended period of industrialization, imperialism, wars, decolonization, and globalization. To its first adherents, organic farming offered not merely a model for agriculture; it also proposed a new model for humans to relate to nature, one that sought harmony with natural processes. Many of the basic tenets of environmentalism developed in tandem with, and even out of, the early stages of organic farming, and constitute a middle stage of the environmental movement between global conservationism and modern environmentalism. Organic farming enthusiasts have persistently advocated peasants as a conduit for knowledge and ancient wisdom that moderns have forgotten or abandoned. The myth of the peasant origins of organic farming has therefore shaped the perception of generations of environmental activists and historians alike and concealed the remarkable accomplishment of the founders of organic farming, Albert Howard and his first and second wives, Gabrielle and Louise Howard.[16]

[14] Wallace had an interest in eastern mysticism, and played a role in persuading Roosevelt to assist in signing the Roerich Peace Pact of April 1935 to protect cultural monuments and artifacts. See James G. Boyd, "In Search of Shambhala? Nicolas Roerich's 1934–5 Inner Mongolian Expedition," *Inner Asia* 14/2 (2012): 260.

[15] The United States Department of Agriculture National Organic Standards Board defined organic farming in April 1995 as "an ecological production management system that promotes and enhances biodiversity, biological cycles and soil biological activity." See Mary V. Gold, "Organic Production/Organic Food: Information Access Tools" (June, 2007), National Agricultural Library. Available online at: https://www.nal.usda.gov/afsic/organic-productionorganic-food-information-access-tools [accessed September 22, 2016]. Gregory A. Barton, "Sir Albert Howard and the Forestry Roots of the Organic Farming Movement," *Agriculture History*, 75/2 (Spring, 2001): 168–87; Gregory A. Barton "Albert Howard and the Decolonization of Science: From the Raj to Organic Farming," *Science and Empire: Knowledge and Networks of Science in the British Empire 1850–1970*, eds. Brett Bennett and Joseph Morgan Hodge (Basingstoke, 2011): 163–86.

[16] Contemporary historians have absorbed and repeated the myth of the peasant as fountainhead of organic wisdom. Philip Conford in *The Origins of the Organic Movement* (Edinburgh, 2001) and *The Development of the Organic Network: Linking People and Themes, 1945–95* (Edinburgh, 2011) offers an uncritical account of this prevailing myth as does William Lockeretz in *Organic Farming—An International History* (Oxfordshire, 2007). William Beinart and Lotte Hughes published an important discussion on organic farming in *Environment and Empire* (Oxford, 2007). The authors however join Conford and Lockeretz in the understanding that Howard arrived at his organic protocols by observing peasant agriculture. See Philip Conford, *Origins of the Organic Movement* (Edinburgh, 2001); Philip Conford, *The Development of the Organic Network: Linking People and Themes, 1945–95* (Edinburgh, 2011); William Lockeretz ed., *Organic Farming—An International History* (Oxfordshire, 2007); William Beinart and Lotte Hughes, *Environment and Empire* (Oxford, 2007). See also James Beattie, "Book review: Environment and Empire," *New Zealand Journal of Asian Studies*, 11/2 (2009): 200. Roy H. Pearce makes a convincing case that the observation of native Americans reveals more about the observers than the subject. See *The Savages of America: A Study of the Indian and the Idea of Civilization* (Baltimore, 1953). See also Robert Berkhofer, *The White Man's Indian: Images of the American Indian From Columbus to the Present* (New York, 1978); Daniel Francis, *The Imaginary Indian: The Image of the Indian in Canadian Culture* (Vancouver BC, 1992). Attitudes from the nineteenth century are explored in: Sherry L. Smith, *The View from Officers' Row: Army Perceptions of Western Indians*, (Tucson, 1990); Alan Trachtenberg, *Shades of Hiawatha: Staging Indians, Making Americans, 1880–1930* (New York, 2004).

THE PRIME CASE STUDY: THE HUNZAS

The myth of the peasant in the organic farming movement also clearly overlapped with the idealization of the "noble savage." In many ways the idealization of the noble savage ran parallel to the idealization of eastern cultures, particularly among Europeans who put their imaginative stamp on hunter-gatherer societies, and on societies left relatively untouched by modernism. The noble savage myth both preceded and penetrated farther than the well-known classic novel by James Fennimore Cooper, *The Last of the Mohicans* (1826). The discovery of the Americas spawned publication of numerous accounts of American Indians, and spurred Thomas Hobbes theory of human brutality and savagery in *Leviathan* (1651), as well as Rousseau's image of utopian societies that boasted free love, peaceful coexistence with nature, and communal property.

Organic farming drew on its own version of the "noble savage" with the Hunzas. Enthusiasts held up the Hunzas as the prime example of wholesome peasants that over ions of time preserved a primitive agriculture unaffected by modern mechanism, fertilizers, or pesticides. The Hunzas still live in the Hunza valley in the Karakorum Mountains in northern Pakistan, in the western Himalayas. As Ismaili Muslims they practice a branch of the Shia faith and are related ethnically to gypsies; the Burusho people. They claim, romantically, to be descendants of the soldiers of Alexander when he invaded Northwest India in the fourth century BC. Albert Howard refers to the Hunzas as a people who enjoyed spectacular health because their food came from exceptionally fertile soil. However, he never worked with the Hunza, nor did he conduct experiments with them. But he did draw inspiration from them, primarily by reading the accounts of other authors.[17] Drawing on the popular romantic farm literature of G. T. Wrench (also a medical doctor) Howard wrote that

> The Hunzas living in a high mountain valley of the Gilgit Agency on the Indian frontier... [give a] demonstration of what a primitive system of agriculture can do if the basic laws of Nature are faithfully followed. The Hunzas are described as far surpassing in health and strength the inhabitants of most other countries; a Hunzas can walk across the mountains to Gilgit sixty miles away, transact his business, and return forthwith without feeling unduly fatigued... For thousands of years they have evolved a system of farming which is perfect.[18]

The Hunza example fulfilled the requirements of a movement that sought scientific validity for an ideal example of health that emanated from the application of organic protocols. Howard quoted favorably from the reports of a British medical officer in India, Robert McCarrison who claimed that,

> During the period of my association with these people I never saw a case of asthenic dyspepsia, of gastric or duodenal ulcer, of appendicitis, of mucous colitis, of cancer...[19]

---

[17] Albert Howard, *The Soil and Health: A Study of Organic Agriculture* (New York, 1947), 11.

[18] Ibid., 37.

[19] Ibid., 177. Howard took this quote from Robert McCarisson's Mellon lecture of 1921 "Faulty Food in Relation to Gastro-Intestinal Disorder," *Journal of the American Medical Association* 78 (January 7, 1922): 2–4.

Howard suggested that the Hunzas secret was a form of organic composting that mixed "vegetable, animal and human wastes…carefully returned to the soil."[20] Wrench, whom Howard read and cited profusely after his career in India, sums up the peasant mystique that many in the organic farming movement shared, stating that the Hunzas formed,

> An erratic block of an ancient world, still perhaps with its peculiar knowledge and traditions, and preserved in that profound cleft of theirs from the decay of time…Everything suggests that in its remoteness it may preserve from the distant past, things that the modern world has forgotten and does not any longer understand. And among those things are perfect physique and health.[21]

Wrench elsewhere argued that the Hindu doctrine of the migration of the soul gave a spiritual reflection of the organic farming Law of Return. Just as the soul returns again and again, so too do nutrients return to the soil. No wonder, he concluded, that Howard discovered the protocols of organic farming on Indian soil.[22]

In this regard the Hunza example ran parallel to the myth common throughout this period in central and eastern Asia that the "Shambhala" valley served as a reservoir of wisdom, long life, and perfect health. Various Hindu and Buddhist sources describe this myth. It first caught the attention of the early Portuguese explorers, as well as, later, British, Soviet, National Socialist, and American enthusiasts. Echoing the Hunza example, Shambhala inspired James Hilton's 1933 novel *Lost Horizon* about a land that time forgot, called Shangri-La. President Franklin Roosevelt, influenced by Hilton's novel, dubbed the later named "Camp David" as Shangri-La.[23] As the imaginative appeal of this legend illustrates, organic farming enthusiasts joined a wide array of individuals and groups that posited eastern wisdom overlooked by the West.[24]

Gabrielle's letters to her mother provide a window into the exciting years of research at Indore and throw light on the question of the peasant origins of organic farming. Soon after the construction and the establishment of demonstration plots, the Howards hosted conferences starting in 1928 that showcased their work to scientists, planters, and farmers, including Indian peasants.[25] As their work gained in popularity and recognition, Gabrielle's health unfortunately began to decline. But her enthusiasm, even in the last difficult years of her life, never abated. She tells in her letters how they hosted conferences and exhibitions, which went "very much better that I could have dreamed possible." She notes with great satisfaction

[20] Howard, *The Soil and Health*, 177. Howard further lays out his theory on the Hunza in "The people of the Hunza Valley," *Newsletter on Compost* supplement no. 9 (June, 1944), Howard Archive.
[21] Phillip Conford, *Origins of the Organic Movement* (Edinburgh, 2001), 50.
[22] G. T. Wrench, *The Restoration of the Peasantries: with Especial Reference to that of India* (London, 1939), 79–80. Many followers of Howard built on this myth, particularly the American disciple of Howard, J. I. Rodale, in his book *The Healthy Hunzas* (Emmaus, PA, 1955). Other popular works followed such as Renee Taylor, *Long Suppressed Hunza Health Secrets for Long Life and Happiness* (New York, 1964).
[23] David Eisenhower and Julie Nixon Eisenhower, *Going Home to Glory: A Memoir of Life with Dwight David Eisenhower, 1961–1969* (New York, 2010), 31.
[24] Boyd, "In Search of Shambhala?", 260.
[25] Louise Howard, *Sir Albert Howard in India*, 196.

that telegraphs streamed in "demanding more accommodation, with local hotels full, rest houses full, and with huts erected in gardens, people sleeping in the offices and six visitors in their own bungalow."[26] She wrote to her mother,

> The institute looks so nice—all the old building mess has been cleaned up—the buildings and wards finished. It is a treat to go round it. The watchmen have all been put into khaki uniforms with bright new turbans and salute in fine style. There are 4—one at each gate—all old sepoys. The scientific work has languished a bit but the agricultural aspect has gone not so badly. A lot of people are coming to see the place and the demands now outside for help are already almost too much. We have to start building again immediately. We have to put up six quarters for visiting plenipotentiaries and new labourers who are sent by the various states to learn our methods and 4 quarters for cationers who come for the same purpose. The states are sending men for a month or two months to learn from us and then go back and use the methods. It is a great compliment to the institute that this is already necessary—it is a nuisance to be in building again. We are also going to have a special week of demonstrations where cultivators will come and we shall make a camp for them just outside the area.[27]

Though Albert was the main attraction, Gabrielle played a vital role as speaker, which amazed the visitors "who I suppose had not heard a woman speak before."[28] A camp at the gate of the institute had the Indore Fire Brigade, and twelve boy scouts sent in to help. Demonstrations, lectures, lantern slides, and films illustrated the Indore Method.[29]

To this three-day conference and exhibition alone, the all-India Cotton Committee sent forty members. Over 400 peasant farmers were accommodated in large tents.[30] The servants, she notes "managed excellently" except for those "who got drunk." By this time, the Indore Method has become established as a protocol: "At any rate everyone at Indore seems to have heard of it and a very mixed account of it."[31]

After his retirement from India in 1935, Howard wrote a series of popular books that emphasized—in a way not found in his earlier scientific publications—the wisdom of the East and the lessons he learned from Indian peasants, whom he dubbed, "my professors." Alongside the Indore Method of composting, his followers have consistently asserted that the organic farming movement, through its central founding figure Albert Howard, repackaged indigenous peasant knowledge for a modern scientific world."[32]

While a careful comparison of his earlier and latter books contains clues to this rhetorical shift, a number of factors explain why scholars and enthusiasts have accepted at face value the peasant origin of organic farming. First, the papers of Sir Albert Howard had—until now—been missing. Instead of diaries, letters,

---

[26] Gabrielle Howard, Letters, 207.   [27] Ibid., 223, 224.   [28] Ibid., 208.
[29] Ibid., 209. No films produced at the Indore station have been discovered to date.
[30] Ibid., 208.   [31] Ibid., 207.
[32] As quoted in Howard *Sir Albert Howard in India*, 17. Albert Howard's popular books include, *An Agricultural Testament* (Oxford, 1940); *Farming and Gardening for Health or Disease* (London, 1945). The latter was reprinted in 1947 as *The Soil and Health: A Study of Organic Agriculture* (London, 1947).

and early reports from his professional work, scholars have been left with only his published books, including his later works that mix science, mysticism, and romanticism. Second, his wife Louise wrote the only biography of Howard but had not shared with Albert—as did Gabrielle—his early critical years in India when he developed the Indore process. Third, the peasant myth appealed to almost all the followers of organic farming, including scholars.

Gabrielle's many letters to her mother, who resided in England do not reveal, however, any particular regard for peasants. Working side by side during their time in India, the letters present a congruence of views between Gabrielle and Albert. They both shared a view of the peasantry that—though by no means negative—reveals no hint of learning from the bottom up, nor even a modicum of romanticism about peasant farming techniques. They both approached their work strictly based upon strict scientific observation and experimentation. Gabrielle's letters include many references to touring farmland, and general observations of life and culture in British India, and also of Indian incompetence.

Just a few examples give an idea of how Gabrielle and Albert Howard approached the peasantry. She found the Indian peasants in some districts to be living in "indescribably dirty huts" and she attributed their good health to constant bathing and the powerful Indian sun.[33] The Howards toured farmland extensively throughout India, and never mentioned peasant innovations or traditional practice that interested her. The following is a typical example:

> We went all over the farm which was very interesting as it was in a district with a type of agriculture we had not yet seen—the cultivators are said to be the laziest set in India but they seemed exceedingly friendly and good natured. They had very curious shoes...[34]

At one unidentified monastery in the foothills of the Himalayas, their guide introduced them to a prayer wheel with slips of paper attached that read "Om Man I Padme Hum" which the guide interpreted to the Howards as "Praise to the jewel in the Lotus." Each turn of the wheel counted as a repetition of the prayer. An old woman laboriously turned the six-foot high prayer wheel. Gabrielle tells facetiously how,

> Bert [Albert] was all for having a motor engine fixed up to whizz the wheel round continuously until he found out that it must go slowly to be efficacious.

She explains this to her mother, as "Buddhistic...nothing to do with the Koran which is Mohammedan."[35] Reading through the hundreds of letters one does not gain from the Howards a deep sense of either Christian or other religious sentiment, and no sense of a profound regard for eastern tradition. Rather one senses at best a mere passing cultural interest.

The Howards however did have a deep interest in agriculture and pursued this passion with their scientific experiments and their efforts to spread the results of

---

[33] Gabrielle Howard, Letters, 183.   [34] Ibid., 139.   [35] Ibid., 202.

their work to the peasantry, from the top down. Gabrielle and Albert Howard worked tirelessly to educate peasant farmers, along with other British imperial officials. At the many conferences they held at Indore, "Intelligent peasants were brought [who] really seemed to take an interest."[36] Her letters do not indicate anywhere that either she or Albert Howard learned from the peasants, however. Rather, they conducted scientific experiments, and passed the results on to the other agricultural experts, scientists, farmers, and then to Indian peasants.

After the death of Gabrielle, Albert Howard married her sister Louise when he retired from service in India and returned to Britain. Louise presented a picture of Albert Howard in India that read back into the past an "organic" Howard. She revealed a one-man show of brilliance, bravery, and audacity at almost every turn—her biography reading rather typically like a family memoir full of loving exaggeration that downplayed his IARS colleagues.[37] Having never visited India, Louise simply could not accurately describe the institutions where he served, nor the vast teamwork involved in imperial agriculture. She missed key publications, book reviewers, and other works by his colleagues that show concern for non-chemical fertilizer. She also overlooked the hard-headed and utilitarian economic policy that inspired most of Howard's work, and that of his colleagues.[38] Scholars and organic farming enthusiasts derive their widespread belief that Albert Howard learned his Indore Method from peasant wisdom from a selective sampling of only a very few sentences from Louise Howard:

> [It is] because he worked away from Western agriculture that Sir Albert gained that enormously wide understanding...[39]
>
> He considered that fortune had apportioned to him an exceptional favor in putting him to work among the peasants of the East.[40]
>
> His demonstration that the female hops of commerce could not be cultivated without the presence of the male plant alongside was an example of an instinctive awareness of the importance of natural principle.[41]
>
> More especially did he acknowledge the lessons to be got from the century-old experience of the Indian peasants, whom in later life he most happily named his "professors."[42]

These few statements form the core of the myth of peasant origins for Albert Howard's work, and scholarship on organic farming and popular culture has cited these passages widely.[43] A close co-worker of Howard from his first years in India, and a personal friend, H. Martin-Leake, makes clear the failure of Indian peasants as farmers who gave no wisdom to Howard. Published in a series of memorials

---

[36] Ibid., 208.   [37] Howard, *Sir Albert Howard in India.*
[38] G. A. Barton, "Albert Howard and the Decolonization of Science: From the Raj to Organic Farming," *Science and Empire: Knowledge and Networks of Science in the British Empire 1850–1970,* eds. Brett Bennett and Joseph Morgan Hodge (Basingstoke, 2011): 163–86.
[39] Howard, *Sir Albert Howard in India,* 17.   [40] Ibid.
[41] Ibid., 20.   [42] Ibid., 24.
[43] Conford for instance, characterized Howard as "attached to the traditional knowledge of peasant farmers." See Conford, *Origins,* 66.

after the death of Albert Howard, this appreciation of Howard's work gave no indication of the peasant myth.

> The studies of those early years gave to India the first Pusa wheats which spread throughout that granary of India, the mighty plains of the Indus and Ganges; wheats which might have supported the rapidly increasing population of the sub-continent of the present day if his less spectacular work on the plant-environment relationship had received greater recognition. Why it may be asked, did these wheats fail to develop their intrinsic merits when placed in the hands of the Indian cultivator; why is the yield now, after forty years, unrecognizably greater than that at the end of last century? . . . That is the position in India; a heavily indebted peasantry, with the family holding averaging five acres to give the maximum response . . . It is India's misfortune that other failed to see the lessons of his teaching with the result that now, with the crying demand for food for the increased population, the yields of wheat, as of most other crops, is stationary at the level of the end of last century.[44]

The question then remains: if Albert and Gabrielle Howard did not derive their organic protocols from Indian peasants, where did their ideas originate?

While Louise Howard indicated that Albert Howard consistently preferred the natural methods of nature, the published material produced by Albert Howard during his tenure in India reveal no aversion to artificial fertilizers or to pesticides. In 1924 he published a book that represented the culmination of his work with Gabrielle up to this time, *Crop Production in India*.[45] In this book Howard gives only a hint of his future work on compost. He does show a passing familiarity and respect for composting by peasants in China, gleaned from King's book *Farmers of Forty Centuries*. He also remarked, however, that Indian peasants lagged far behind the composting practices of the Far East.[46] He then made a pivotal remark that shows the limitation of these practices for India: "The use of human excreta in preparing composts, as practiced in China, is impossible in India." In India, due to the heat and poor transport, human waste spread disease easily. He could have also added that cultural and religious prejudice against the use of human manure, just as in England, made this a more difficult practice to implement.[47]

In *The Waste Products of Agriculture: Their Utilization as Humus* (1931), co-authored by Albert Howard and Yeshwant D. Wad, Howard discussed chemical fertilizers and pesticides without a trace of criticism. It must be kept in mind that this book laid out the complete Indore Method in its entirety—the key component of organic farming protocol—and marked the end point of his major scientific research to date. In this book he recommended the feasibility of using sulfate of ammonia, an important by-product of coal, taken from the Tata Iron and Steel

---

[44] H. Martin-Leake, "Sir Albert Howard—An Appreciation," *Organic Farming Magazine*, 13/8 (September, 1948).
[45] Albert Howard, *Crop Production in India* (Oxford, 1924).   [46] Ibid., 39.   [47] Ibid.

Company at Jamshedpur and from the coalmines in Bengal, Bihar, and Orissa. He pointed out that,

> The manner in which this source of supply is being developed is very satisfactory and it is still more satisfactory that a market for increasing quantities of the sulphate of ammonia produced in India is being found in the country.[48]

He lamented that the high price made this product too difficult for the majority of farmers to use. Nitrogenous fertilizers from "the establishment of synthetic process" have been "a matter of the first importance." Further, the cyanimide process "offered the best prospect of success in India" as a method of "obtaining synthetic sulphate of ammonia." But the high price again made this option difficult. He continued that,

> It is also to be hoped that, should the demand for artificial fertilizers in India make it worthwhile, private enterprise will come forward to erect synthetic nitrogen works in this country.[49]

He then takes a very balanced view of the prospect that artificial fertilizer companies may come into India to set up manufacturing. If financially feasible, he concluded, this would be a good thing.

> But we need hardly say that we would welcome the establishment by the two firms mentioned, or by any other fertilizer firms, of their own research stations in India working in the fullest co-operation with the agricultural departments, the Indian Tea Association, the Indian Central Cotton Committee and any other bodies interested in the fertilizer question.[50]

His main concern continued to revolve around not the safety or damage of industrial agricultural methods, but rather the affordability of artificial fertilizers and pesticides. Howard and Wad point to the fact that Howard developed the Indore Method out of economic necessity, as a way of raising soil fertility using techniques the Indian peasants could afford. Only cost forbade the widespread use of artificial fertilizers and pesticides. The authors raised only one concern that hints at Albert Howard's future objections towards industrial agriculture—the bias involved in taking money from corporate interests, such as the Rothamsted Experimental Station in England. Government agencies, they felt, offered the best hope for advancement of agricultural practice in India. He sounded this idea early in India; an idea picked up by his immediate followers of the Indore Method.

Howard and Wad never credit in this book the agency of the peasants themselves. Where Indian soils were fertile they made it clear that the fixation of nitrogen from the atmosphere kept the Indian soils fertile. They did not mention that Indian peasant methods of fertilization returned nutrients to the soil.

---

[48] Albert Howard, *The Waste Products of Agriculture: Their Utilization as Humus* (Oxford, 1931), 88. Yeshwant D. Wad joined the statff of the Insitute of Platn Idustry in 1928. See Yeshwant D. Wad, "The Work at Indore," in *Organic Gardening Magazine*, 13/8 (September, 1948).
[49] Howard, *The Waster Products of Agriculture*, 89.   [50] Ibid.

> It is sometimes forgotten that the combined nitrogen lost in the shipments of oil-seeds is automatically replaced by fixation of free nitrogen from the atmosphere. If this were not the case, the soil of India would have been exhausted long ago.[51]

They concluded that disease in plants could be fought with pesticides or better selection of breeds and soil aeration. They also suggested that copper sulfate made a useful pesticide, but one that the peasant could ill afford. This early work made clear that the poverty of the Indian farmers pushed Howard to the Indore Method, not his aversion to fertilizers and pesticides.

The widespread notion among historians of organic farming, and among organic farming enthusiasts, that Albert Howard founded the science of his Indore Method on the ancient peasant wisdom of India is clearly a myth. Many factors lay behind the adoption of this idea, not least a few statements made by Howard himself, and his second wife Louise in her biography. But the persistence of the peasant myth has obscured the startling originality of Albert Howard's work, and of the contributions of Gabrielle and Louise Howard to the founding of this global movement.

[51] Ibid., 148.

6

The Compost Wars

The work of Albert and Gabrielle Howard came to fruition only as Gabrielle neared the end of her life, stricken by an aggressive cancer. Rumors circulated about her bad health. She kept working and was delighted with the Indore conference because, speaking during one of these, "It has at any rate shown the committee that I am still alive and kicking."[1] But the cancerous growth required regular removal by her doctor. She then annoyed the doctor by scheduling a trip to Germany to seek other medical advice.[2] While she tried to keep an optimistic tone with Albert, she shared devastating news with her sisters. On December 17, 1929, still in India, she wrote to Marie and Louise that she had bad news. A growth had been removed by surgery and she had "had a hemorrhage." A "little tag" on the scar appeared to be the source.[3]

> There were no new papilloma anywhere. It may therefore be a small recurrence of the big growth which was so difficult to remove or it might be the scar breaking down and bleeding—which would be even less satisfactory than the former. Very small pieces come off now. One of which certainly looked like the piece of a papilloma. We are all naturally very worried…it all points however to my having to return very soon and probably for good.[4]

She subsequently went to Düsseldorf and wrote to Louise that Marie should make a booking for her at the clinic (unnamed) for March 15 or 16th in 1930, for a "single room and second class food." She did not care about the room's quality, "as long as I am alone." She noted that Albert would have to work alone in India, or retire earlier than he had planned. This had come at an unfortunate time—all his colleagues wished him to continue his work—and she knew "he really wants to stay."[5] Gabrielle penned her last letter to both Marie and Louise, just before her death, on January 1, 1930,

> I have just had another examination with a somewhat disastrous result. I had been having fairly heavy hemorrhages with the coming away of somewhat large pieces. The doctor found about five papillomata—small but one has no stalk. They have grown so quickly that he has advised me to go back this month. If the one without a stalk goes on growing at this rate it will soon be too big to cope with.[6]

Gabrielle died on August 18, 1930, in Geneva. Albert arrived only to bury her back in England, and retired, heartbroken. But in a few years he began his life

---

[1] Gabrielle Howard, Letters, 208.   [2] Ibid., 226.   [3] Ibid., 229.
[4] Ibid., 230–1.   [5] Ibid., 232–3.   [6] Ibid., 235–6.

anew, building on their life's work together in a crusade that slowly crystallized in his mind over the next decade—he determined to change the health of the world's soils, and the health of its people, in her memory.

Soon after his retirement from India in 1931 Albert Howard married Louise Ernestine Matthaei, thirteen months after the death of Gabrielle.[7] The depth of personal devotion that Albert and Gabrielle expressed for each other, in private and in their single-minded pursuit of work, suggests that Albert felt a deep need to be close to her, even after death. His marriage to Louise kept the likeness of Gabrielle in his life and Louise herself offered many attractions to Howard, in addition to physical resemblance. Louise, like Gabrielle, dedicated her life to work and to intellectual pursuits. She had also attended Cambridge University and Newnham College, as did Gabrielle. But rather than science, she excelled in the Classical Tripos and had been offered a research fellowship. She served as Director of Studies in classics at Newnham, from 1909 to 1916. Students remembered her as both a sympathetic and demanding instructor.

Early in her career in 1908 she published an article on arbitration and mediation in the ethics of the ancient world.[8] Ten years later she published a monograph, *Studies in Greek Tragedy*, which, though widely cited, had mixed reviews. Reviewers found it sincere with sparks of independent thinking and—what would become her hallmark—a thorough professionalism and master of detail. One reviewer, though, found the book simplistic and lacking in method. Because she examined four plays only, and extrapolated "the qualities which make the Tragic Spirit," he felt her conclusions too sweeping given the narrow range of evidence.[9] Despite her achievements as a classical scholar, her German heritage—and her German sympathies—haunted her many accomplishments in Britain. The university pressured her to resign due to an essay she published urging understanding and peace between Britain and Germany, titled *The Lover of Nations*—published in 1915 while still at Newnham College.[10]

Reflecting her childhood experiences in Europe, and her love of the German language and culture, the essay fought against the brutal war-time propaganda that dehumanized Germans. But given the suppression of free thought during this war period, she could only plead obliquely for peace. She wrote that ancient history bristled with examples where the voice of both sides of the combatants were not known. The loss of this voice is a loss to historical knowledge and deprived human history of further enrichment and understanding. Sparta served as one example. If it had produced a Thucydides the world would have heard both sides, and been richer for it.[11] She then applied this argument to the war fever that gripped Britain. We need to do more than produce propaganda, she argued, we need to explain ourselves better to Germany, and then in turn, "listen to her [Germany's] explanations." The rage

[7] They married on September 17, 1931.
[8] Louise E. Matthaei, "The Place of Arbitration and Mediation in Ancient Systems of International Ethics," *The Classical Quarterly* 2/1 (January, 1908).
[9] Review: "Miss Matthaei on Tragedy" by J. T. Sheppard, *The Classical Review*, 33/3–4 (May–June, 1919): 69–71.
[10] Louise E. Matthaei, *Lover of Nations* (London, 1915).   [11] Ibid., 1.

for war destroyed free speech, and "It is one of the most damning accusations against war that it places its ban on free communication."[12] She concluded that we need lovers of nations, not one-sided arguments, so that "a lover's insight" could spread peace throughout the world.[13]

The essay received very little public attention, but did gain the attention of her employer, Cambridge University. Soon forced to resign she found work where she could. She applied to work as an editorial assistant for Leonard Woolf, husband of the English writer and poet, Virginia Woolf, and a member of the Bloomsbury group.[14] Leonard needed help proofing galleys for his own and Virginia's writing while he labored to set up Hogarth Press, which soon began publishing a variety of works by influential writers, including the first edition of T. S. Eliot's *The Wasteland* (1922). Virginia recorded her impression of Louise in her diaries. Though she profoundly admired her courage for publishing her anti-war tract, she found much fault in her:

> Miss Matthaei arrived. I remember her at Newnham. She has left, we understand, "under a cloud." It is easy to see from her limp, apologetic attitude that the cloud has sapped her powers of resistance.

Leonard and Virginia attempted to talk about the war, but Louise demurred, eliciting from Virginia the observation that "it seemed altogether odious that anyone should be afraid to declare her opinions—as if a dog used to excessive beating, dreaded even the raising of a hand." But Louise offered a bold assessment of her own handicap as a dissenter that contradicts Virginia Woolf's assessment of her timidity. Before their interview ended she remarked that "I must tell you one thing…my father was a German. I find it makes a good deal of difference—it is a distinct hindrance commercially." The Woolf's agreed, as Virginia noted in her diary that despite this disadvantage, Louise had to make a living somehow and deserved a job. But true to Virginia Woolf's peculiar standard of aesthetics, she found the 35-year-old Louise to be "a lanky gawky unattractive woman…with a complexion that blotches red & shiny suddenly." Nor did she approve of how she dressed which, despite her best effort, "was inconceivably stiff & ugly."[15]

Still the Woolf's hired her. She had "a quick mind," enthusiasm and a love of writing. They budgeted between £200–250 a year for her salary. Instead of lecturing at Cambridge University Louise soon found herself proofing galleys in a cramped stall.[16] She took on more responsibility as the press expanded, including critiquing articles and proofing for the *International Review,* a new journal that blended political essays and journalism. As Leonard's assistant editor she ran the London office with efficiency. Virginia noted that Leonard felt the need to show up at least twice a week and "so appeasing the gaping maws of Green and Matthew [Louise

---

[12] Ibid., 5.   [13] Ibid., 7.

[14] The interaction between Virginia Wolf and her contemporaries in the Bloomsbury group are nicely laid out in *The letters of Virginia Woolf (Vol II 1912–22),* ed. N. Nicolson, (London, 1976).

[15] *The Diary of Virginia Woolf (Vol 1 1915–1919),* ed. Anne Olivier Bell (London, 1977), 136.

[16] Ibid., 136, 143, 190.

Matthaei]."[17] As Virginia saw more of Louise's highly competent work, both her esteem and her criticism mounted. One evening she found Louise working late and poured her a cup of tea. That night she wrote in her diary that she saw no reason why Louise carried around a sense of apology simply "because she is an unattractive woman." After all she "has more sense in her head that all the cropheads put together."[18] Given that Gabrielle, Louise's sister, was a celebrated beauty in her youth and that pictures of Louise in middle age show a handsome and respectable appearance, Virginia's estimation of her appearance must be taken with a grain of salt. Despite her mixed assessment of Louise, Virginia nonetheless counted her as an "intermittent" friend, along with such notables as the economist John Hobson, and the Fabian activists Sydney and Beatrice Webb.[19]

Sometime after working for the Woolfs, Louise gained a job as a researcher in Geneva.[20] In London she had taken a highly competitive examination to work for the newly formed International Labour Organization (ILO) established in 1919. The signatory governments of the Treaty of Versailles established the ILO to gather facts and statistics on international labor conditions and to facilitate guidelines for working conditions. The ILO operated as a de-facto agency of the League of Nations, from whom it also had financial support. Eager to avert a Bolshevik uprising outside of Russia, the signatories of the treaty charged the ILO with improving working conditions for workers and with facilitating peaceful resolutions to disputes. From 1926 to 1974 the ILO secretariat was housed in Geneva in what came to be called the "Old ILO Building."[21]

After losing her job with Cambridge and then suffering the drudgery of proofing galleys in a cramped stall, her new employment provided a refreshing contrast. She began her new research duties in 1921 under Dr. Walter A. Riddell, Chief of the Agricultural Service of the ILO. Within a few years, in 1924, she took over as Chief of the Agricultural Service when Riddell became the Canadian delegate to the League of Nations.[22] Anti-war idealism and a social conscience were hardwired into the mission of the ILO, and the League of Nations. The location helped her heal from her emotional wounds. The ILO building sat on the very edge of Lake Geneva. She could walk from her office along the pristine blue waters and view the Alps rising in the distant to the majestic snowcapped peaks of Mont-Blanc. The campus itself boasted gigantic cedars and oaks and provided an ideal location for walking, thinking, and planning her future. The building was splendid. With a classical Florentine design, fronted by feminine statues of peace and justice framing the entrance, it boasted a sweeping staircase crowned (in 1931) by a massive mural illustrating Christ in his carpentry workshop in Nazareth talking to contemporary

---

[17] Ibid., 254.   [18] Ibid., 225.   [19] Ibid., 234.

[20] Annuaire de la Société des Nations, "International Labor Organization/Bureau International Du Travail Members." Available online at: http://www.indiana.edu/~league/ilomembers.htm [accessed August 21, 2017].

[21] Today the building is the headquarters of the World Trade Organization. Construction began in 1923 and it was the first in Geneva to contain an international organization. Since 1995 it has housed the headquarters of the World Trade Organization.

[22] The ILO personnel file for Louise Matthaei has been lost. I owe this information to Dr. Amalia Ribi Forclaz who has worked extensively on the ILO archives in Geneva.

workers, both men and women. Blue tiled panels from Portugal, inlaid stone murals, an ornamental library with paneled walls, seashells carved into the colonnades between bookcases, stained glass, patterned marble floors, ornamental brass light fittings, and wrought iron railings were all donations from member nations. The atmosphere exuded peace between nations and the dignity of labor. Here in this healing space of concord and rest, she found her life's work as a researcher and administrator.[23]

While Louise' superiors highly respected her competent work, no employee at the ILO had the ability to completely fulfill the mission at the ILO. The broad base of the stakeholders and the limited budget and administrative authority hindered what could realistically be accomplished. Part of the difficulty lay in the fact that the ILO served as an information gathering center that advised the League of Nation, but one which—it had been optimistically assumed—would eventually gain legislative authority in the family of nations and thus implement the ideas and suggestions that it advanced. Therefore, the limitation and indeed failures of the League of Nations impacted the reach and authority of the ILO. Louise saw first-hand the failures of an agency that balanced input from labor unions, peasants, government workers, and industry. She also saw how little real change the statistical data that her agency gathered and distributed actually produced. A former official of the ILO, G. A. Johnson, remarked that,

> no survey of the pre-war activities of the ILO in the agricultural field could lead to any other conclusion than that agriculture had been both misunderstood and neglected by it.[24]

Johnson referred to the contradictions between the interests of the stakeholder and the success of the League of Nations, not to competency of the staff

One of the factors that lay behind Louise's admiration of Albert Howard's work was the practical nature of his Indore Method that directly addressed the mission of the ILO. She comprehended how the Indore Method could raise productivity for the kaleidoscope of labor relations; if implemented, it could work for plantations, large farms, small farmers, gardeners, and every aspect of the complex world of global farming—whether agricultural laborers on wages, small farmers living off of yearly harvests and profits, or whole families including women and children. Nor did organic farming completely rely on the approval of government agencies, though both Howard and Louise later lobbied hard to gain institutional backing. Another attraction of Albert's work was his disdain of bureaucratic obfuscation and forms—a refreshing antidote to her daily work. Albert's protocol, and the appeal to farmers of all stripes to adopt it, cut through the red tape and gave her a

---

[23] NA., "The World Trade Organization Building: The Symbolic Artwork of the Centre William Rappard," *Headquarters of the World Trade Organization* (Geneva, World Trade Association, 2008).
[24] Amalia Ribi Forclaz, "A New Target for International Social Reform: The International Labour Organization and Working and Living Conditions in Agriculture in the Inter-War Years," *Contemporary European History*, 20 (2011): 311. See also A. Johnston, *The International Labour Organization: Its Work for Social and Economic Justice* (London, 1970), 254.

powerful sense of having made a difference in the livelihood and the health of farm workers. Albert Howard acted as a kind of Occam's Razor: cutting to the quick and solving problems of soil fertility, productivity and health, with one clear and simple answer; a scientifically sound Indore Method of composting.[25]

Albert and Louise together cared for Gabrielle at the end of her life in Geneva. When Gabrielle died August 18, 1930 they comforted each other in their mutual loss. Howard then returned to his Indore research station to wrap up his lifetime work. They exchanged letters though none have as yet come to light. Rather quickly, Howard and Louise began consulting each other on personal and professional questions. Outside of their growing romantic interest, Louise brought from her professional life a broad knowledge of international law, economics, and the labor challenges facing rural workers around the world.[26] She also brought with her— from her time at Hogarth press—a critical eye for prose narrative. She tutored Albert on how to turn bureaucratic and scientific writing into popular books that turned the uninspiring topic of composting into flaming and passionate texts of romantic farm literature which amateur enthusiasts and professionals of all stripes, from medicine to botany to agriculture, would enjoy reading. There can also be little doubt that Louise enabled Albert to expand his vision of how the Indore Methods impacted the world, in more ways than merely increasing productivity while doing away with the use of chemical fertilizers.

Louise discovered that Albert had exhausted himself in India. There, he would rise at 3:00 a.m. to do his writing before the day's work began—exhausting himself, until he "staggered on to the homeward-bound vessel" alarming his companions, by coughing up blood. That did not stop him from working, however. Having embarked from Bombay, he set sail around Africa on his return trip fully intending to rest and enjoy retirement. But as news of his trip preceded him, invitations from plantation owners in Kenya brought him ashore, delaying the return visit home. He could not resist inspecting for himself to see how coffee growers applied his ideas, originally developed for Indian cultivators. Then came Rhodesia and South Africa. The explosive enthusiasm for his methods in Africa fired his imagination. He began to dream of a worldwide application of the Indore Method. The idea of wrapping up his life's work began to fade; the seed was planted for a new expanded mission. And then there was Louise.

They had agreed by letter that she would arrange her own holiday so as to meet him in May 1931 at the vacation resort of Rimini on the east cost of Italy. The city had long been known for its bathing therapy and Howard felt the need for healing. He slept long hours once there. Rimini boasted Roman ruins and renaissance buildings that sat peacefully along long stretches of sandy beach and enjoyed an average

---

[25] Forclaz "A New Target for International Social Reform," 307–29 details a history of the Agricultural Section of the ILO in the 1920s and 30s, its structure and how it operated within the framework of growing internationalism.

[26] See Sybil Oldfield, "Howard, Louise Enrestine, Lady Howard (1880–1969)" *Oxford Dictionary of National Biography*. Available online at: http://www.oxforddnb.com/index/101037576/Louise-Howard [accessed August 21, 2017].

daytime temperature in May of 31 Degrees Celsius. Their romantic relationship began in earnest at this time and they married shortly after, on September 17, 1931. Louise, usually reticent in personal matters, paints a romantic view of this holiday and dates the founding of the organic farming movement from this moment—conflating their personal milestones in life as the milestone of the movement.[27] Years later, after Albert's death, she wrote that,

> The organic farming movement was born on the lovely shores of the Adriatic at the seaside resort of Rimini. In May, 1931 before the tourist season had opened, with the sunbathed stretches of sea and sand on either side, not a soul in sight, Mr. Howard as he then was, sat and corrected the proofs of his book *The Waste Products of Agriculture: Their Utilization as Humus*. We had agreed to meet for a holiday, having fortunately been able to arrange our official vacations to coincide.

Presumably she dates the start of the organic farming movement at this place and time because *The Waste Products of Agriculture* has been acknowledged widely as the founding document of the movement. Putting the final touches on this manuscript at Rimini marked the end point of Albert's work on the book—with her active involvement—right before publication. It also marked the beginning of their courtship, probably indeed of their engagement, and Louise can be forgiven for equating her engagement to Albert and the completion of the book as the official launch date of the organic farming movement. There can be little doubt, that Louise' time at Hogarth Press as an editorial assistant only sharpened her already developed abilities as a writer, and proved highly useful to her role as critic and supporter of her future husband's writing. Louise lovingly portrays his remarkable humility already apparent at Rimini, in his fully accepting her critique on how he needed to rewrite. She offered in fact, "considerable corrections of form." This almost tender description of a critique of his manuscript and his grateful acceptance, brings from her the declaration that his humility was a sign that he sought truth overall, though this humility was not apparent "to the outside observer"; it was "a part of his character" that few saw. Few indeed have complimented Albert Howard for his humility, so we may safely surmise that Albert openly displayed this trait only to those he loved.[28] Resting from his labors with Louise back in England, Albert fully recovered from his exhaustion, no doubt helped by the planning of their future wedding and homemaking.

As Albert Howard began work in England on the second and last phase of his career, Louise wrapped up her own work in Geneva. She had left the ILO in 1932 to live with her new husband back in England. But she took with her the notes she had meticulously gathered while at the ILO in Geneva. In 1935 she published with Oxford University Press a book that summed up her understanding of labor relations and agriculture: *Labour in Agriculture: An International Survey*.[29] It received favorable reviews, more so than her earlier effort with

---

[27] Lady Louise E. Howard, "The Birth of the Organic Farming Movement," *Organic Gardening Magazine*, 13/8 (September, 1948).
[28] Ibid.   [29] Louise Howard, *Labour in Agriculture: An International Survey* (Oxford, 1935).

Studies in Greek Tragedy.[30] A former colleague of Albert's, Daniel Hall, of Wye College, who then directed Rothamsted, read the manuscript, advised her on its revisions, and gave his endorsement. Her former supervisor at the ILO, Walter Riddell, also offered advice. The Chief of the Agricultural section who followed her at the ILO, F. W. von Bülow, offered further advice and access to recent statistics and material. She also acknowledged the help of her husband Albert for his knowledge of tropical agriculture. Appropriately the Royal Institute of International Affairs (known also as Chatham House), which had its origins in the same Paris Peace Conference that produced the Versailles treaty and the ILO, arranged publication.

Her book gives hints of her leaning toward the Indore protocol and she often used the word "Nature" with a capital "N." It included a philosophy close to that of the organic movement broadly laid out though not specified:

> In general, man can start, stimulate, and encourage; he can eradicate, check, and prune; he can mate, feed, rear, or separate. In the long run, he is never able, nor is he in fact trying, positively to contradict or to evade natural processes...We invariably return to the truth that ultimate conformity with Nature is the agriculturalist's salvation, as well he knows, [he is a] member of an industry where nothing can be made or manufactured, where everything has to grow and to become.[31]

The position she takes in this book might however surprise organic enthusiasts. She did not foresee peasant farmers or small landowners maintaining their way of life, nor that they should do so. Agriculture, she argued, should rather be run like a business with economy of labor. The goal of farmers "should then be exactly the same as the aim of industrialists, namely, to produce the greatest abundance in the most economical way and with the least expenditure of human effort."[32] These large farming businesses should then have guaranteed representation in "parliaments and on international councils, her Ministries and Departments" as well. There needed to also be a closing of the gap "between town and country in which all of the poetic values are with the country, and all the hard facts which count are with the town."[33]

This position echoes the political platform of many fascist parties in the 1930s that sought to dilute the power that urban polities held over the entire country by guaranteeing rural representation. While she constantly expressed sympathy to farmers, and to the need to work within the rules of nature, she harbored in this book no romance for the peasant. She saw a clear gain from big agricultural businesses and international competition. As for the industrial farming aided by Justus Liebig's innovations and so hated by advocates of traditional farming and organic farmers, she has only praise:

> The nineteenth century...shook agriculture out of its national complacency. The results of self-sufficient and subsistence agriculture were far too poor to have justified

---

[30] "Review by: Josiah C. Folsom," *Journal of Farm Economics* 18/2 (May, 1936): 439–41. Folsom regretted that limited available material meant Louise Howard could not give more information about the social experiment underway in communist countries, or in Latin America. But Folsom praised the thoroughness of the scholarship and remarked that the book was the most complete global work on labor and agriculture ever published.
[31] Louise Howard, *Labour in Agriculture*, 4.　　[32] Ibid., 267, 268 to 269.　　[33] Ibid., 269.

their continuation without some further advance. International competition has proved, as it always does, an unrivalled stimulating force.[34]

Nevertheless, the amount of labor expended by poorer cultivators on simple cultivations is extravagant. This extravagant expenditure is a waste. Better information and training, the imitation of a more advanced technique learnt from elsewhere, should tend to abolish as unnecessary, we might say as unseemly, methods which make agriculture so incredibly laborious to thousands of human beings.[35]

And as for learning from peasants,

In effect his [the peasant] is to state the fundamental problem of the European States to-day, and what we may expect and indeed may hope will soon become also the fundamental problem of such continents as Africa and Asia: how are all these regions of the world to transform their peasant farming into industrialized or at least modernized farming, with the same output from a quarter of their present labour force?[36]

By the time she wrote this book, and had helped Albert Howard rewrite *The Waste Products of Agriculture*, she surely believed that the Indore Method raised productivity per acre and did so affordably to peasants, particularly in Africa and Asia. Was she here thinking that organic farming methods may play a key role in eliminating peasant labor and cultures around the world? Other than her suggestion that the industrialization of farms would and should cut the majority of peasants out of a livelihood, it is not possible to know exactly her thoughts at this stage regarding the possible role of organic farming. It does not mean that she lacked sympathy or did not care. As she writes,

As always, such adjustment spells disaster to a number of existences, and the pressing problem therefore is to seek means at present for furthering and encouraging these developments without incurring too many tragedies.[37]

She lambasts the tariffs put up to protect agricultural markets, such as in France and Switzerland: "by these means, have been able—so far—to leave their peasant systems untouched." In North America this was done [during the American depression] "at the expense of an almost complete hold-up in the rural social development of the United States and Canada."[38] She suggested that,

The survival of a peasant system, untransformed, without radical modification, is not, in view of the types of social existence now everywhere available to highly cultivated peoples, a sufficient aim to justify defence at all costs.[39]

In addition to her support for industrial agriculture she also advocated economic liberalism and free trade.

It has been a cardinal mistake that in the turnover from the old unimpeded commerce to the universalized tariff system more effort was not made to rescue the moral content—shadowy enough perhaps—of the nineteenth-century free-trade ideal and carry it over,

[34] Ibid., 285.   [35] Ibid., 286.   [36] Ibid.
[37] Ibid., 287.   [38] Ibid., 288.   [39] Ibid., 288.

in a different but substantial way, into what is apparently going to be the trading method of the twentieth century.[40]

She then links all subsidies of agriculture, which she dislikes, to the conditions of free trade and the need for farmers to willingly submit to foreign competition and modern standards—presumably by adopting the necessary mechanization, fertilizers, and pesticides, along with the consolidation of small landholdings into larger units. She makes clear that subsidies to farmers should be paid—and only paid—to accomplish the industrialization of agriculture. All agricultural research must insist on this necessary change to abolish peasant agriculture, which is "backward" and a global problem.[41]

> In the first place, it should have been the clear design of the tariff-imposing authority to insist on a reasonable but thorough raising of the standard of efficiency of their national agriculture; it would be possible to argue that all further state experimental work in agriculture should be stopped until the majority of farmers in each country had adopted the bulk of the existing improvements made available for them by the good work of these services, paid for, it must be remembered, not only by farming interests but by the community at large, and not least by past generations, who, with their endowments, have made possible that pursuit of scientific truth at the universities which is the foundation of all help to the technique of agriculture. Only if higher standards of efficiency were demonstrably being sought could the question of direct money subsidies of agriculture, whether for experiments, for education, or for the simple maintenance of some branch of production, be entertained.[42]

Louise Howard's book, published four years after her marriage to Albert Howard, raises interesting questions. It is difficult to imagine the two of them in disagreement— no instance of disagreement between them has been recorded. These passages show that the major currents of modernization and development, prominent in British and British Empire scientific networks, were shared by Louise and Albert Howard. These passages also reveal an earlier and later phase of the development of their ideas. They suggest that Louise and Albert learned to attach the Indore Method to the ideals found in romantic farm literature, and that they shifted in the 1930s toward a neo-traditionalist approach to agriculture and health—beginning sometime after the publication of Louise's book.

Only with the publication in 1940 of Albert Howard's *Agricultural Testament* do we see coming into prominence the link between the Indore Method and the romantic ideals of the wider organic farming movement. One can clearly see in his earlier writing very little difference, if any, to the approach taken by the United Nation's Food and Agricultural Organization (that absorbed and built on the work of the ILO) or by the World Bank that advocated an "integrated rural development strategy" for the third world that unfolded in the 1960s and 1970s—a position that by 1940 and afterwards both the Howards and the organic movement vehemently

---

[40] Ibid.   [41] Ibid., 291.   [42] Ibid., 289.

opposed.[43] To interpret this earlier phase as hypocrisy, however, would be a misreading. Rather it is natural to see that Albert and Louise Howard moved through stages of intellectual development and change, and only came to absorb many of their neo-traditionalist agricultural positions in the late 1930s. It becomes clear that the organic farming movement emerged as the marriage of the Indore Method developed by Albert Howard in India with romantic, ecological and neo-traditional approaches to agriculture.

As Louise finished writing *Labour in Agriculture*, Albert's work began again in earnest. He wrote and answered letters from farmers throughout the British Empire, gave papers to agricultural and scientific societies, including the Royal Society, and published opinions in the *London Times* and a myriad of regional and local newspapers. He also began inspecting compost operations and consulting to plantations and large farmers. As Howard faded from the scientific attention he had enjoyed in India, he gained a new popular following. Removed from the laboratory he relied on his own experiments and older studies from forestry on the mycorrhizal process to answer critics. While the days of his own scientific discoveries were behind him a steady trickle of new work—such as the importance of the mineralization of organic matter in the soil through composting—continued to appear that backed up his claims. In the 1930s his prophetic preaching began in earnest.

The initial growth of Howard's organic method occurred precisely where Louise had predicted major advances in agricultural efficiency: with corporations and large farms. Large-scale applications of compost were implemented on tea gardens in Assam and Ceylon, coffee plantations in Kenya, and fruit plantations in South Africa—using the Indore Method to produce thousands of tons of compost every year in order to reduce plant disease and raise productivity per acre. This was no accident: labor costs were lower in tropical and sub-tropical regions of South Asia and Africa and his primary concern was not to save labor, which these regions had in abundance, but to raise productivity on the available agricultural land. Albert also engaged in a frenzy of correspondence, lectures, publications, and paid tours of inspection. His practical experience in India proved vital as he ran into many of the same problems that he had faced in British India; the difficulties of finding enough vegetable matter to produce the compost; the need to break down vegetable matter that was resistant to bacteria; and problems of communal arrangements, village commons, and—less common in colonial Africa—small individual plots not large enough to implement a strict protocol of organic management. Overall his method cut against peasant agriculture by favoring the more successful farms that were well managed and could carefully reproduce the conditions necessary for compost bacteria to thrive.

Howard's work was translated and published in a number of German venues in the 1930s. His influence on the continent came from the widespread application

---

[43] Joseph M. Hodge, "Science, Development, and Empire: The Colonial Advisory Council on Agriculture and Animal Health, 1929–43," *The Journal of Imperial and Commonwealth History*, 30/1 (January, 2002): 20, 21.

of his Indore Method in the German colonies, and thus back home, as well as direct translation of his work and ideas in articles and newspapers. In 1935, *The Tropical Planter*, a magazine that promoted the economic development of land in the German tropics published a substantial article by Howard of forty-eight pages that laid out his Indore process. As usual with most of his publications, this article elaborated both the theory of organic farming and the practical methods required to implement the Indore Method, replete with photographs and hand-drawn illustrations. Howard concluded with a strong pitch for the adoption of the Indore Method throughout the German empire.[44]

In 1937 Howard toured tea plantations in India as a paid consultant, and to advocate his methods. He banked not only on his reputation as the former director of the Indore research station, but also on his book—the Madras manager of Oxford Press told Howard that his book *Waste Products of Agriculture* had sold 1,500 copies so far in India alone.[45] Rather than a scientific fact-gathering exercise, the tour had all the hallmarks of a victory lap to re-confirm the validity of the Indore Method.[46] He gave little time to contradictory evidence. His major objective was to convince the Finlay Group—a large tea corporation and one of the largest producers of tea in the world—to adopt his methods.[47] He hoped that the successful examples he encountered on this tour would provide the incentive Finlay needed to make the Indore Method a requirement of all the planters and managers operating under the company, which he believed "is the only really effective answer to the critics of the Indore Process."[48]

On September 24, 1937, Howard met with Mr. W. B. Bruce, Estates Inspector for James Finlay and Co., Ltd. at 1 Clive Street, Calcutta. Considered the Wall Street of the East, the imposing Finlay building marked the beginning of Clive Street. This building stood three stories high with Corinthian pillars supporting an imposing pediment. It looked more like a bank or a government ministry than a company headquarters that traded in tea and jute. This initial meeting gave Howard hope that he could persuade Finlay to adopt the Indore Method for all the tea estates in the company. Bruce warmly welcomed Howard. He immediately let him know that he thought "nothing of Tocklai." This comment, heart-warming to Howard referred to a newly re-structured research station for tea that did not advocate Howard's methods but instead reflected the values of the Rothamsted Experimental Station and advocated fertilizers and pesticides over the Indore Method. Bruce told Howard that the Deanston estate that he managed in Balisera Valley in Sylhet (today in Bangladesh) would not use "an ounce of artificials" after April 1938.

[44] See Von Sir Albert Howard, "Die Erzeugung von Humus nach der Indore-Mehode," *Der Tropenpflanzer: Zeitschrift für das Gesamtgebiet der Land und Forstwirtschaft warmer Länder*, 39/2 (February, 1935): 46–88.

[45] Albert Howard, *Diary: November 13, 1937 to February 2, 1938, Notes on a Tour to Tea Estates in Sylhet and Cachar*, 22, File: 1938, *Matthaei Family Archive*, Birmingham, UK. On this tour Howard visited company offices, estates, English clubs, and met individuals of interest.

[46] Ibid.

[47] A good history of the company is found with NA., *James Finlay & Company Limited: Manufacturers and East India Merchants 1750–1950* (Glasgow, 1951).

[48] Albert Howard, *Diary: Sylhet and Cachar*, 5, 6.

This, to Howards mind, offered an ideal trial run of his methods that the company could not ignore. He gleefully recorded in his travel diary that Bruce assured him that "Compost is the sole topic of conversation" at this estate. Howard pulled root samples from his briefcase to show the difference between tea roots grown on artificial fertilizer versus tea roots on the Indore Method. The office staff all expressed amazement.[49] Bruce, Howard wrote that evening, proved to be an ardent "compost-wallah" and promised to transplant these methods to Sylhet, Assam, and the Dooars. Howard then had another encouraging meeting with James Jones, a Calcutta director and "another keen organic matter man." It was "a very successful visit" he concluded.[50]

Howard managed to gain access to high ranking government officials as well company directors. His diary records lunch at the Government House in Calcutta that included a personal talk with Lord Brabourne, Governor of Bengal, (1937–39). He followed up with a visit to Bradbourne's Private Secretary L. G. Pinnell and his advisor, Sir Harold Stevens, Chief Secretary with the Government of Bengal, meeting at the Bengal Secretariat (Writers Building). He left them with some briefs on compost and what needed to be accomplished in Indian agriculture.[51] While explaining his Indore Methods to Lord Brabourne he also offered his ideas on solving the problems created by water hyacinth (*Eichhornia crassipes*). This perennial aquatic plant from Brazil had invaded waterways after its introduction in the nineteenth century. It clogged the waterways, blocked light in the water, and absorbed oxygen, in turn pushing out native plants and killing fish life. It also slowed the movement of water and led to silting, making navigation of canals and waterways a massive administrative problem. He suggested they turn an out-of-control invasive species into useful compost and thus turn an ecological disaster into an advantage. He followed this advice with concrete examples from farms and plantations in Bengal. This creative suggestion opens a window into Howard's parenthetic thinking. Slowly he was beginning to link his Indore Method with broader environmental solutions—a deliberate strategy carried to great success by Louise Howard after his death.[52]

Despite his access to the highest channels in India, opposition abounded. The newly expanded Tocklai research station dogged his steps and defied his mission. The Tocklai Experimental Station, named after its location near the Tocklai river in Assam, was founded in 1911. The Jorehaut Tea Company Limited, along with the

---

[49] This tour gave him the opportunity to take more samples of roots, judging the mycorrhizal differences between tea grown with compost and those without, and he sent the results to Dr. Rayner by air mail.

[50] Albert Howard, *Diary: Sylhet and Cachar*, 10.   [51] Ibid., 21.

[52] The problem had been growing globally for a number of decades. Water Hyacinth affected steamboat traffic in the 1880s in Florida. It had spread east to Egypt by 1879, and to Asia by 1888, Australia by 1890. See USDA Natural Resources Conservation Service, Plants Profile (2002). Available online: http://plants.usda.gov/cgi_bin/plant_profile.cgi?symbol=EICR [accessed August 21, 2017]; Herbert J. Webber, *The water hyacinth, and its relation to navigation in Florida* (Washington, 1897); Howard anticipated contemporary research on methods to use water hyacinth for energy and other practical purposes. For a summary of some contemporary research see James A. Duke, *Handbook of Energy Crops* (unpublished, 1983). Available online at: https://hort.purdue.edu/newcrop/duke_energy/Hymenaea_courbaril.html [accessed August 21, 2017].

states of Assam and Bengal, donated the land, and the tea industry in India contributed funds for its operation. From 1930–33 the Empire Marketing Board paid for its ongoing expenses until funding cuts during the depression terminated the Board and threw the research station into financial crisis. The British government initiated a Commission of Enquiry in 1936 to review its function, chaired by a Cambridge scientist, Frank Engledow. Without visiting India, Engledow recommended that a London Advisory Committee oversee the station and that Tocklai no longer sponsor ad hoc research but instead specialize its work on the chemical composition of tea. He also recommended an annual conference of planters and scientists to share information and expected them to conform to the new mission of the station and to correlate research with empire-wide efforts by focusing on theoretical and statistical problems.[53]

Engledow, an agricultural botanist, stood squarely against Howard's philosophy and proved a formidable opponent. Like Howard, he had graduated from St. John's College in Cambridge. Younger than Howard he nonetheless had published extensively on the genetics of wheat, and had also investigated the quality of wool production. After a stint in the Middle East during the First World War, he returned to Cambridge as a researcher at the School of Agriculture. In 1930 Cambridge engaged him as Draper's Professor of Agriculture and Head of the School of Agriculture. He traveled extensively on royal commissions.[54] Engledow engaged in a number of intrusive bureaucratic activities that offended many traditional farmers: he sat as a member of the Agricultural Research Council, served as Director of Plant Breeding and Genetics of the Executive Council of the Imperial Agricultural Bureaux, and also sat on the Committee on Higher Agricultural Education, the Agricultural Improvement Council for England and Wales, and the Design of Farms Building Committee.[55] He tirelessly crusaded for the development and modernization of agriculture in the British Empire and promoted a theoretical and systematic approach to scientific research that downplayed practical problem solving *in situ*. He feared that natives in the colonies caused severe ecological damage, and the time would soon come,

> when those responsible for Colonial Administration would be called to account for having allowed the native populations to misuse the natural assets of their countries by continuing to practice agricultural methods which were wasteful and wrong under present conditions.[56]

Howard despised this kind of top down interference. Bureaucratic commissions meddled from afar and interfered with practical research, demanding conformity to theoretical questions unrelated to the real needs of farmers. Ironically Howard

[53] The first conference was held in 1937. The Second World War interrupted these plans, with the army actually taking over buildings. The independence of India ended oversight by London. Available online at: http://www.tocklai.net/ [accessed June 10, 2016].

[54] See L. F. Easterbrook ed., *Farming and Mechanized Agriculture 1944–45* (London, 1946), 396. This book showed an excessive regard for high tech farming, including adverts that idealized the science fiction vision of farming from a control tower.

[55] Ibid., 227, 229, 317, 318, 331, 400.

[56] As quoted in Joseph M. Hodge, "Science, Development, and Empire," 1.

himself had benefited from precisely the same impulse toward colonial development initiated by Joseph Chamberlain in the 1890s and when Lord Curzon launched a centralized and top-down structure with the founding of the IARI that hired Howard in 1905. Colonial development initiatives continued to advance in the 1920s and 30s, but with a twist—at what were often loose networks of research stations, such as Pusa that employed Howard and allowed him to set up his own Indore research station, the emphasis shifted away from application of research and toward questions of fundamental knowledge and statistics. The Colonial Office in the 1930s launched a plethora of "specialized, advisory committees, whose members included many of the most prominent scientific figures in their respective fields."[57] Howard loathed the new direction.

Skepticism of Tocklai was not limited to Finlays. Howard found a similar attitude at the Duncan Brothers & Company tea trader, also in Calcutta. Regarding a recent Engledow report issued by the Tocklai research station in India, Howard recorded that "all [were] convinced that the Tocklai and the Engledow Report are washouts."[58] In a particularly telling comment after the inspection of the greenhouses owned by Messrs. Lowe and Shawyer, Ltd, he remarked that,

> [Mr. Mosley, a member of the firm] agrees with me that the mycological and entomological work now being done is useless, and that the advice given to practical men is generally of no value. Mycology and entomology will have to be looked at from a new point of view—prevention rather than cure. For this to be effective, the research officers will have to learn practice, and practical growers will have to employ suitable research officers on their staffs. The experiment station work will have to be designed to help men like Mr. Mosley to solve their problems, not to publish papers on life histories [of plants].[59]

Many in the tea industry shared Howard's suspicions about Tocklai. Nor was Albert Howard the first in the tea industry to steer away from artificial fertilizers and recommend composting from plant material produced on the estate itself. Harold H. Mann, Scientific Officer to the Indian Tea Association, recommended as far back as 1901 that not only should companies prioritize fertilizing tea estates but that "the nucleus of whatever manuring is done must be found on the spot." This included the mix of plant and animal wastes as Howard proposed, as well as composting from a wide array of farm waste—cattle dung, ashes, clippings from the tea bush itself, and even "road sweepings." [Howard also approved the use of rich topsoil and other material from the nearby jungles as an option—in one case, at Oodlabari Tea Estate, using fresh humus dug up from the surrounding forest floor, "with good effect."[60]] This, as Mann had suggested, should be done *in preference* to artificial chemicals which "should be reduced to the lowest quantity" not

---

[57] Ibid., 2.　　　　[58] Howard, *Diary: Sylhet and Cachar,* 10.

[59] Albert Howard, *Diary: Visit to Messr. Lowe & Shawyer, LTD... Uxbridge, Middlesex,* 2–3, File: 1937, *Matthaei Family Archive,* Birmingham, UK.

[60] Albert Howard, *Diary: Tea Estates,* 12.

only because of their cost, but because the artificial fertilizers tended to degrade the soil in the long run and produce only short-term gains.[61]

Not all compost produced equally effective results. A common mistake, Howard found, was the application of too much water. The compost pile needed adequate drainage and plenty of air to properly encourage the growth of fungi and bacteria. This meant monitoring the pile and turning it over to aerate it. Throughout most of his tour he critiqued the methods of composting he saw, which failed to maximize the benefit of the Indore Method. He did not want to see composting fail by improper practice. He needed highly successful demonstrations of the Indore Method on a large scale in order to squash "talk based on the NPK mentality [i.e. the approach that relied on industrial nitrogen-phosphorus-potassium fertilizers]."[62] If all went well, the Tocklai research station would be made redundant. He could accomplish this quickly, he believed. With only twelve months of proper compost-ing "all this replication, randomization, and statistical analysis" could be ignored.[63] He could then win the debate by example. At the end of one lecture he intoned that mother earth herself would "give the verdict on the suit of Compost v. Ammonium Sulphate. Not the lawyers on each side!"[64]

His inspection reconfirmed his conclusions. Each of the "NPK nurseries" and tea estates not composting fared poorly.[65] He happily reported that the managers of the Shamshernagar Tea Estate were "firmly convinced the Indore Process had come to stay."[66] In one entry he waxed eloquent, describing the "tea estate of my dreams" that gave a foretaste of coming glory and a living example "of what the earth will be like when it has been made ready to receive her children!"[67] Even worldly gain would back up his methods because they worked. Not only Mother Earth but "The final verdict on such matters is given by Main Street and the housewife" who wanted not theory, but results.[68]

He encountered some opposition however. Lecturing at the Nagrakata Club in West Bengal, near Darjeeling and the foothills of Bhutan, he was challenged by "one [anti] compost Lawyer present who had to be squelched. The only time I had to deal with a compost lawyer in N. E. India."[69] On another occasion, a director of a small tea company, Mr. Richards, challenged him to make a scientific test of the Indore process on tea against a control group using artificial fertilizer. Howard debated with the director till 1:00 a.m. in the morning, but did not take up the challenge. Howard countered that he did not want small-scale trials "to test [only] some of my ideas." It would be too easy for the artificial manure interests to bribe the subordinate staff of the estate and to also bribe the staff at the Tocklai research station "to obtain any result they wanted." His reticence showed the depth of pas-sion on both sides that made him fear a total lack of objectivity.[70] Howard pressed the director as to why he wanted to do these tests. Richards replied that "humus might interfere with quality," though he gave Howard no clear scientific reason for

[61] Harold Mann, *The Tea Soils of Assam and Tea Manuring* (Calcutta, 1901), 61, 62.
[62] Albert Howard, *Diary: Tea Estates*, 13.   [63] Ibid.   [64] Ibid., 14.
[65] Ibid.   [66] Ibid., 2–3.   [67] Ibid., 5.   [68] Ibid., 15.
[69] Ibid., 16.   [70] Ibid., 45.

this suspicion. Howard concluded in his diary, "I suspect he is interested in the sale of artificials" and told him so. Howard repeated to Richards that the verdict "would be given by Mother Earth" and not by experiments nor discussion late into the night. He concluded privately that those opponents who cross-examined him had a "pedestrian mind."[71]

A hint of his formidable character comes through as he relates that at a Finlay tea estate near Madupatty in the Western Ghats a manager by the name of J. Whiteley Tolson was a "tyke pure and simple" who made composts in heaps too wet, without aeration, allowing the fungus only on the outside of the pile.[72] Howard demanded to know why he hauled yet more water to his composts when 150 inches of rain fell a year. "The Tyke had no reply and soon began to eat out of my hand. It is always well to stand up to a Tyke."[73] In another instance meeting with company officials of the Tea Research Institute in Ceylon he discussed compost with officials Roland V. Norris and Thomas Eden. Both of these, but particularly Eden, had experimented with fertilizers and pesticides, and neglected composting. Eden had corresponded extensively with Ronald Aylmer Fisher who worked at Rothamsted from 1919 to 1933, and afterwards as Professor of Eugenics at University College London. Fisher was a biologist and statistician and considered the founder of the New Synthesis, which is today accepted as the dominant paradigm of evolutionary biology. Fisher's prestige was immense, but he represented precisely the type of theoretical science that Howard despised. No doubt the problems faced by tea growers in Ceylon—particularly with blight—brought Eden into correspondence with Fisher. However, much of the correspondence dealt with the failure of artificial fertilizers on the tea plantations.[74] Eden eventually became disillusioned with Fisher's advice, which calculated tea production responses to Nitrate and Potash applications from mathematical formulas. Howard noticed this discouragement and advanced his own ideas on composting as an alternative:

> They [Norris and Eden] agreed to push the Indore Process and that no matters of disagreement remained. They appeared to be thoroughly frightened and to have realized what fools they had made of themselves.[75]

They had reason to be afraid. They had just heard the news that two estate directors who had not implemented the Indore process as per company instructions had lost

[71] Ibid., 49.
[72] Merriam Webster dictionary defines "tyke" as "(a) chiefly British: a clumsy, churlish, or eccentric person; (b) a small child." Available online at: http://www.merriam-webster.com/dictionary/tyke [accessed June 12, 2016]. See the entry "J. Whiteley Tolson" *James Finlay & Co—Managers and Assistants Letter Books Index, Volume 1–15.* Available online at: http://www.gla.ac.uk/media/media_169147_en.pdf [accessed June 12, 2016].
[73] Ibid., 26.
[74] See Correspondence with Thomas Eden (Tea Research Institute of Ceylon) and Ronald Aylmer Fisher, particularly March 1930–May 1934, University of Adelaide. Available online at: hpttp://hdl.handle.net/2440/67664 [accessed June 16, 2016].
[75] Albert Howard, *Diary: Tea Estates,* 39. For a description of the Tea Research Institute in Ceylon see Roland V. Norris, "The Work of the Tea Research Insitute," *Tea Research Institute* (Thalawakele, 1949): 4–10. Available online at: http://tri.nsf.ac.lk/bitstream/handle/1/778/TQ-20_4.pdf?sequence=2&isAllowed=y [accessed June 16, 2016].

their jobs. As with managers at another estate, they "had not heard that Shaw and Jones of the U. P. A. S. I. Experimental Station had just been sacked, largely on account of obstructing the Indore Process." This comment reveals the animosity over the agitation between advocates of the Indore Method and artificial fertilizer: failure in a highly competitive market could mean dismissal and managers needed desperately to choose the winning side.[76]

Nor did Howard brook variations on the compost theme, even when it involved the Indore Method. He had a serious contender for composting methods in Commander A. D. G. Bagot, who published in 1936, a year before Howard's tour, a small book, *Composting Tea Estate Wastes*.[77] His book created a stir in Ceylon and directly challenged Howard. Bagot argued like Howard that leaves from the tea bush, branches, weeds, wood ash, and jungle vegetable matter could all be composted. But because Ceylon received so much rainfall, little water needed to be added. Further, he argued that unlike the Indore Method, animal waste was largely unnecessary because the plant material itself contained all the nitrogen needed to successfully compost.[78]

Howard visited Bagot at his Park Tea Estate and directly confronted him. He demanded to know "where he got the idea" of altering his formula by not including animal manure. Bagot replied that because cattle were rare in areas of Ceylon he had "modified the original Indore Process accordingly." Howard replied that this would delete the very substances needed to compost the vegetable matter. He reminded Bagot that in world history no system of agriculture had ever been sustained without at least some animal dung, and that Bagot simply evaded "its correct solution." Howard insisted that Bagot convince him that "all I had learnt on this subject was incorrect." According to Howard, Bagot capitulated at once and said "he could not do this." Bagot "took it all very well" and wrote a conciliatory letter to Howard after the discussion. The recent dismissal of employees who refused to use the Indore Method may have led to Bagot's conciliatory attitude but Howard generously credited Bagot for admitting that despite the claims in his recent book, his compost simply did not break down properly.[79] There is no indication that Bagot's book made any further inroads against the Indore Method.

Howard's trip was not all work, however:

We got to Malabar Hotel on Willingdon Island about 6 p. m. Hotel new with cool rooms overlooking a most heavenly old world oriental harbor surrounded by coconut groves. There were no gondolas, alas![80]

After resting there he overcame his fatigue and "got all my papers in order and diary written up to date."[81] Traveling from there to Calicut he enthused "Scenery magnificent, the finest forest and mountain views I had so far seen in India."[82]

---

[76] Howard did express regret when his friends and allies were dismissed. He and a friend were "depressed as poor Mackenzie had just got the sack and they were preparing to leave their lovely house. Very sad." Albert Howard, *Diary: Tea Estates*, 24.

[77] A. G. D. Bagot, *Composting Tea Estate Wastes* (Fort Columbo, 1936).

[78] Albert Howard, *Diary: Tea Estates*, 39, 41.   [79] Ibid., 42.   [80] Ibid., 33.

[81] Ibid., 34.   [82] Ibid., 35.

In Ceylon the managing director of the Galaha Tea Estates Company arranged a Pontiac convertible with driver, which took him 966 miles around the island.[83] Howard was in his element, back in India, and gaining an ever-wider audience, thoroughly enjoying himself—though he did confess on his sixty-fourth birthday, that though enjoyable, the visit had been "rather a strenuous one."[84]

The trip however did not attain his main objective. While many tea estate managers adopted his method, Finlays did not adopt a company-wide policy on the Indore Method. Indeed, many estates were "forbidding the making of compost."[85] Concerns for profit kept Finlays from mandating the Indore Method. Howard's conservation bias abetted this failure: he counted soil fertility as being of as much importance as making money. At the Finalys head-office in Madras he told one of the directors that "they laid too much emphasis on cost and should now aim at getting the best product and then consider cost [of] production."[86] Though he gained a great deal of private support for taking such a long-term view, ultimately, the directors at Finlay could not justify mandating the Indore Method if it lowered profits and displeased stock holders. Ultimately fertilizers and chemical pesticides still held out the best hope for raising production and fighting plant disease with vastly lower labor costs than the Indore Method.

In 1937, Howard was not a purist on the use of artificial fertilizers and pesticides. He lets slip in his diary that he supported the use of artificial chemicals on tea plantations at least until the compost heaps were in place and ready to improve soil fertility. He may have worried about the uncertainty of success of the Indore Method in all circumstances, and worried that if "artificials had been given up too quickly" the transition to composting could fail. This is a rare admission.[87] When he visited a tea estate that used both artificial fertilizers and the Indore process he could not help enthusing that

> The tea on this estate was in excellent condition; soil very open; artificials had been cut down. One of the best estates I had so far seen…Very good healthy plants and in excellent root development.[88]

He proclaimed this success without analyzing the implication that mixed use of chemical fertilizers and natural compost served as a departure to his own theories. This is a position that he admitted in a diary but never published, nor publicly advocated. After his death Louise never raised the serious possibility of mixed-use either.

SHIFT FROM FARMERS TO GARDENERS

In 1939 the ideas of Albert Howard for the first time gained a substantial public audience. A group of medical professionals in Cheshire, northwest England, dramatically linked Howard's Indore Methods to the restoration of human health.

[83] Ibid., 36.   [84] Ibid., 20.   [85] Ibid., 50.
[86] Ibid., 26, 27.   [87] Ibid., 39.   [88] Ibid., 41.

These medical men did not consist of scientists but practicing country doctors, along with some farmers and health officials. On March 22, 1939, five hundred people crowded into the neo-Baroque Town Hall in the small city of Crewe where Dr. John Kerr chaired the Cheshire Panel Committee, a county branch of the Association of Scientific and Clinical Medicine. Robert McCarrison and Albert Howard, both with knighthoods gained for their research in India, spoke in favor of the document—the "Medical Testament"—that came out of the meeting. *The British Journal of Medicine*, published by the British Medical Association, published their statement—not as an article, or even under correspondence—but rather only as a supplement that recorded the proceedings. The "Medical Testament" attracted public attention as newspapers and a host of writers sympathetic to neo-traditional farming picked up the story and the central argument. Scientific professionals kept largely silent. The "Medical Testament" was folksy, anecdotal, practical, and even bombastic, a perfect recipe for attracting public attention. Except for Albert Howard and Robert McCarrison, mainstream scientists did not lend their name to the project. It marked however, the coalescing of ideas and like-minded people around the core of the Indore Method.

The "Medical Testament" implicitly criticized the National Health Insurance Act. This act, always suspect to conservatives and farmers because it appeared to undermine a hardy yeoman independence, had been in operation since 1911. Passed by Lloyd George's Liberal government, it provided medical insurance to workers at a nominal fee. The Cheshire Panel Committee represented 600 general practitioners, most of them rural family doctors. The committee focused its critique on the phrase—taken from the Act—to engage in the "Prevention and Cure of Sickness." The "Medical Testament" conceded that while lifespan had increased since 1911, it had only resulted in the proliferation of illness. Therefor the Act had signally failed in prevention, and "it is not possible to say that the promise of the Bill has been fulfilled." By the time the patient came to the doctor for help it was usually too late. Illness "results from a lifetime of wrong nutrition!"[89] In England malnutrition began at conception with unfit mothers bearing unfit babies, producing babies with "big heads, tumid abdomens, flaccid skins, bulged joints and pinched chests" and anemic children deformed by rickets and spinal curvatures: a C3 nation (that is unfit for military service), and suffering from "gall-stones, appendicitis, gastric ulcer, duodenal ulcer, colitis, and diverticulitis." Almost the whole population was constipated. Even dog breeders raised healthier animals.[90] The cause? Poor food, poorly cultivated, poorly chosen, and poorly prepared.

Lionel Picton clearly influenced this report. Himself a medical doctor and an advocate of traditional farming methods, he acted as a conduit for ideas that had percolated for two decades through romantic farming literature. The document referenced the contrast between the health of societies that used traditional farming

---

[89] "Medical Testament: Nutrition, Soil Fertility and the National Health: County Palatine of Chester: Local Medical and Panel Committee, 22 March, 1939," *British Medical Journal,* (April 15, 1939, London): 157.

[90] Ibid., 157, 158.

methods (or were hunter-gatherers) and those in advanced civilizations. It pointed to the observation of explorers like Captain Cook who came across perfectly healthy islanders observed to be eating copious amounts of fresh fruit, vegetables, and fish. It also referenced the robust European islanders on Tristan da Cunha who lived primarily off locally raised vegetables, meat, seafood, and the eggs of seabirds.

For scientific backing the "Medical Testament" relied on McCarrison and Howard. McCarrison served in the Indian Medical Service as an army medical officer, stationed in the north-west of India. There he soon became fascinated with the health of mountain tribes and clans, discovering that water supplies in certain areas worsened iodine deficiency. He quickly gained honors for his findings, and the government of India appointed him to the Pasteur Institute of India in 1912 and he went on to win the gold Kaisar-i-Hind award [as had Gabrielle Howard] for public service and election to the Royal College of Physicians. He made his public mark however through his work on deficiency diseases, and brought fame to the inhabitants of the Hunza valley who demonstrated, he claimed, longevity and stamina. McCarrrison based much of his work on the newly minted theory of "vitamins" by Frederick Gowland Hopkins who published his research in 1912.[91] McCarrison's work in India overlapped with Howard's work in important ways; both argued that agricultural practices and health were intimately linked. His conclusions inspired Lord Linlithgow, Viceroy of India, to fund McCarrison's own independent laboratory. After his return to England, following his retirement in 1935, he lectured together with Albert Howard at the Crewe meeting.[92]

The *Medical Testament* quoted McCarrison at length and gave a precis of his accomplishments. In particular it focused on his experiments in India that compared the various diets of the "Indian races" to the health of rats fed on these diets. The result: "Some are of splendid physique, some are of poor physique, and some are of middling physique." The healthiest diet proved to be that of Northern India, among the Hunza, Sikh, and Pathan populations, whose diet was,

> composed of freshly ground whole-wheat flour made into cakes of unleavened bread, milk, and the products of milk (butter, curds, buttermilk), pulses, peas, beans lentils, fresh green leaf vegetables, root vegetables (potatoes, carrots), and fruit, with meat occasionally.[93]

Fresh vegetables, fresh raw milk, and butter, he argued, composed the essence of the healthiest diets. However, rats fed on a diet common to England of "bread and margarine [made with hydrogenated oils] tinned meat, vegetables boiled with soda, cheap tinned jam, tea, sugar and a little meat" all fought amongst themselves and resulted in diseases of the "lungs, stomach, intestines, and nerves... diseases from which one in every three sick persons among the insured classes in England

---

[91] F. G. Hopkins, "Feeding experiments illustrating the importance of accessory factors in normal dietaries," *The Journal of Physiology*, 44/5 (1912): 425–60.

[92] He was knighted in 1933. See H. M. Sinclair, "McCarrison, Sir Robert (1878–1960)," Andrew A. G. Morrice, *Oxford Dictionary of National Biography*, (Oxford University Press, 2004). Available online at: http://www.oxforddnb.com/view/article/34678 [accessed August 21, 2017].

[93] "Medical Testament," 158.

and Wales suffers."[94] While the authors of the "Medical Testament" did not specify the exact diet of the Hunza, Sikhs, Eskimos, and the inhabitants of Tristan Island, they argued that they held in common food that was,

> fresh from its source, little altered by preparation and complete, direct from animal and vegetable waste [compost] to soil, to plants, to food and then to animals and humans.[95]

The report then delved directly into Howard's work. It lauded his pioneering role in the discovery of plant nutrition and his experiments at Indore that had been "carried from India to many parts of the world" and had proved central to the cycle of nutrients from soil to humans.[96] The "Medical Testament" then quoted Howard at length, giving a summation of the Indore Method:

> It is not difficult to understand that the use of artificials in feeding the crop direct side-tracks a portion of Nature's essential round: artificial stimulus applied year after year at the same times but inevitably breed evils, the full extent of which are as yet but dimly seen.[97]

They pointed to how some municipal governments had begun to recycle wastes using the protocols of the Indore Method.

> Mr. E. F. Watson, superintendent of the Governor's Estates in Bengal...Bodiam in Sussex, at the large hop garden of Messrs. Arthur Guinness, Son and Co., Ltd.... [and] Captain R. G. M. Wilson's Iceni Estate in Lincolnshire.[98]

After the meeting at Crewe and the publication of "Medical Testament," Albert Howard emphasized with a newfound clarity and force the link between the Indore Method and human health, cementing this key concept of the organic farming movement. Further, the meeting also brought together Lionel Picton, McCarrison, and Howard, whose influence and collaboration were vital in the founding of the Soil Association, which in turn became a key organic farming advocacy group in Britain.

Though his views were now reaching a broader audience, Howard still had great hopes for the mainstream acceptance of his program, both from the bottom up by farmers and from the top down by government officials. He presented the evidence collated in the "Medical Testament"—along with his own work—before the Conservative Agricultural Committee of the House of Commons, at its meeting on March 23, 1939. His address to the committee emphasized the shape of the public health system of the future, based on the principles of the Indore Method and the health benefits that would accrue.[99] He emphasized the dangers of the Ministry of Agriculture, and the chemical industries that opposed natural composting.

---

[94] Ibid.   [95] Ibid.   [96] Ibid.   [97] Ibid.   [98] Ibid.
[99] Albert Howard, "Speech, Report of the Garden Competition," File: 1940, *Matthaei Family Archive*, Birmingham, UK. 1. See also, Albert Howard, "Report on Garden Competition and other Nutritional Interests" File: 1941, *Matthaei Family Archive*, Birmingham, UK. 1941. Howard had first read the rough draft of the "Medical Testament" while vacationing at the Riviera in 1939.

I left the House of Commons convinced that no opposition from Parliament need be feared when the time comes for adopting an agreed policy for agriculture and a reformed public health system.[100]

His optimism did not last. In 1940 Howard wrote a think-piece for the Chester Local Medical and Panel Committees that he republished in a pamphlet titled, *The Next Step*. In this Howard praised the committee that had published the "Medical Testament" but confessed to a sense of failure: he had not succeeded in convincing significant numbers of farmers, scientists, or politicians to follow his vision.[101] Farmers too easily sought safety first, with "matters like the relation between nutrition and health... not their immediate concern."[102] Further while they did care about the fertility of the soil they did not care enough to take action. Howard opined that some new "Coke of Norfolk" would be required to really illustrate the prosperity that can flow from an organic farm. While the niece of a former Prime Minister, Eve Balfour, had established a demonstration farm based on his principles, he pointedly did not mention the fact—probably because Balfour offered more amateur enthusiasm than scientific knowledge in her approach, and had imbibed a smattering of mysticism from Steiner's biodynamic movement seeping in from the Continent. Howard was clearly disappointed after attending a Young Farmer's Coalition meeting in February 1940. His speech, "The Reform of the Manure Heap" garnered little enthusiasm and he could not see,

> even a glimmer of hope that the average young farmer possess either the vision or the audacity to do for his farm what the peasants and workmen of Cheshire are willingly doing for their small patches of garden.[103]

He then confessed darkly,

> There is obviously little or nothing to be hoped now from the farming community taken as a whole.[104]

He had a back-up plan, however, though it no doubt devastated Howard that big agriculture and governmental bodies would not endorse his methods. He put forward "the second alternative" to support "the broadening of the garden competition."[105] Here he saw that schools could have garden projects, and that the distance from the garden to the school would be short, allowing children to "enjoy the real bread of their grandfathers."[106] This was a far cry from his vision of remaking agriculture from the top down. But it gave a vent for his energy, and some hope, however slim, for the future.

We can also see in this shift from large-scale farming to gardening a further shift from emphasizing scientific findings to personal testimony. This shift illustrated a strategic design to preserve a movement in clear decline. Having gone from acceptance in the highest circles of research in the British Empire after the war to rejection in official circles, he felt the need to preserve the dream of organic

---

[100] Howard, Report of the Garden Competition, 2.
[101] Albert Howard, *The Next Step* (1940), File: 1940, *Matthaei Family Archive*, Birmingham, UK.
[102] Ibid., 2.   [103] Ibid.   [104] Ibid., 3.   [105] Ibid.   [106] Ibid., 6.

farming among the willing—the meek and humble workmen and housewives with a bit of garden in the back. Depressing as such a comedown must have been, the new strategy kept Howard's dream alive. It also led Howard to give one final push for his ideas in a new book published in 1940, aimed at the common man and populist in tone, written with Louise's advice and guidance: the *Agricultural Testament*. In this we see a final stage of Albert Howard's development as a scientist that absorbed many of the characteristics of the movement he helped to found, fusing the cultural romanticism around romantic farm literature with the Indore Method, and buttressing the holism and rhetoric of his followers with his own scientific expertise. In the *Agricultural Testament* we can see the mature Albert Howard that we now know as the founder and leader of the early organic farming movement.

7

To the Empire and Beyond

In 1940 Albert Howard published his magnum opus and the culmination of his life work, the *Agricultural Testament*. In this volume he reached out to the general public with a treatise on the importance of the Indore Method, and he allied his own work seamlessly with the question of national health, and the work of Robert McCarrison. *Agricultural Testament* clearly built on the influence and approach of the *Medical Testament* by tying the Indore Method to questions of individual and national health. Almost everything in this book he had published before; but now he consciously applied his work to the question of national health and forged for the first time all the key elements we now associate with the organic farming movement.[1]

He reviewed again the key points made over the lifetime of his career: that plant and animal disease on the farm is a verdict by Nature on agricultural practice; that nutrients must be returned to the soil; and that the natural action of bacteria and the myccchorizal process must be properly harnessed through the compost pile. But a new note was added, by asking "how does the produce of an impoverished soil affect men and women who have to consume it?"[2] He admitted the evidence for this connection still lay in the future, when the effect of organic crops would be observed on humans.[3]

His magnum opus did not produce instant change. Further disappointment lay in global developments. After the Second World War the allies and axis powers shifted from a war economy to a peacetime economy, and faced severe shortages of food. Allied bombing devastated the economy on the continent. Further, a global food shortage included much of Asia as well and highlighted the need for chemical fertilizers to raise productivity, making the case for organic agriculture put forward by Albert Howard and the growing coteries of organic food enthusiasts vastly more difficult to promote. Organic farm advocates were not defeated by science or argument at this stage, however. Rather they were ignored—a far deadlier and more effective treatment for sending a nascent movement into abeyance. They were ignored primarily because newly founded international organizations like the Food and Agriculture Organization (FAO), governments, and industrial cartels perceived

---

[1] See the review by R. O. Whyte, "Soil Fertility and National Health," *Nature* (May 17, 1941): 590–1.

[2] Sir Albert Howard, *An Agricultural Testament* (1943), Project Gutenberg Australia. Available online at: http://gutenberg.net.au/ebooks02/0200301.txt [accessed August 23, 2017].

[3] Ibid.

threats to the world food supply and also saw opportunities to expand production and economic development through the use of chemical fertilizers.

The world wanted more food. Franklin Roosevelt launched the FAO at a conference in Quebec, Canada in 1945, with its newly minted motto, "let there be bread." The FAO absorbed the International Institute of Agriculture (IIA) which had been founded by the King of Italy, Victor Immanuel, in 1905. It collected literature and statistics on agriculture and built a sizable library repository in Rome. The FAO campaigned under the authority of its parent organization the United Nations to increase agricultural production; and chemical fertilizers played a central role in its mission.

Factories could fix nitrogen as nitrate almost anywhere because nitrogen was extracted from the atmosphere which is 78 percent nitrogen by volume. One caveat however was the availability of coal, electricity, and natural gas near nitrate factories to fuel the industrial process. The lack of expertise and training was also a limiting factor. Further, the other components of chemical fertilizers, phosphates and potash, were not equally distributed around the globe. These limiting factors also meant that the goal of forcing traditional agriculture to transition to chemical fertilizers required international trade and modern transportation to deliver supplies—at least to core densely populated regions. Therefore, raising crop yields with chemical fertilizers required the pre-conditions of broad economic development and free trade.

Europe produced and consumed half the world's fertilizers in 1946, followed closely by the United States. Outside of northwestern Europe and the United States, Japan alone manufactured and consumed large quantities of nitrogen— hampered only by the need to import phosphate rock and potash. FAO officials believed that in addition to "high pressure selling" by chemical industries, significant education measures could persuade farmers around the world that the increased yield from fertilizers would more than pay for the initial investment.[4]

Scientists had not settled on the precise mix of fertilizers to recommend to farmers. The required ratio of nitrogen, phosphate, and potash varied, due to the types of crops grown, the deficiencies in the soil, and often the character of the salesman that promoted a particular mix found in the product for sale. Before 1914, Germany primarily utilized potash as the lead ingredient in fertilizer, then nitrogen in the 1920s, and phosphates in the 1930s. Geography also played a role. Most of Europe by the 1940s, including the USSR, consumed more nitrogen fertilizers than the rest of the world combined.[5] The United States produced and consumed the most phosphate, followed by the USSR and North Africa. By contrast India and China, though quickly adopting, still used very little chemical fertilizers at the end of the Second World War.[6] Large tracts of the USSR, Latin America and Africa still had virgin soils with sparse populations who used no fertilizers, and in the Middle East the lack of water made arable cropping less amenable to chemical fertilizers.

---

[4] FAO, *Use of Commercial Fertilizers Past, Present, and Future* (February 25, 1946): 13, 15.
[5] Ibid., 20.   [6] Ibid., 16.

Some areas, like Canada and South Africa, although already heavy consumers of fertilizers, faced soil exhaustion that would soon require even more.[7]

In the 1930s–40s international cartels controlled the lion's share of the world's fertilizer supply. Focusing on nitrogen, phosphate, and potash production and distribution, the alliances between companies shifted many times in these volatile decades.[8] For instance, in 1929, three main corporations—the German Nitrogen Syndicate, Imperial Chemical Industries (British), and a few Chilean nitrate producers—controlled 80 percent of global nitrogen supplies.[9] The control of supply by cartels and the constantly shifting alliances among leading producers to control markets only added to the suspicion by traditional farming advocates and early organic farmers that cartels did not have the best interest of the soil or the health of plants and people in mind.

Cartels were not alone in the push for chemical fertilizers. The FAO, with its voluminous literature on fertilizers, enthusiastically urged fertilizing on government agencies and fed the mass media a steady diet of reports that highlighted the need for chemical fertilizers. The Second World War, the need for development, and the expanding human population provided a backdrop for the FAO to spread its pro-fertilizer reports, often penned by current or former executives of the chemical cartels:

> Wars, although causing untold human suffering, often do bring about certain developments and stimulate certain interests which, if carried through into peacetime conditions, benefit the human race. This last war is no exception in this respect... more food had to be grown per acre and this stimulated a greater interest in fertilizers.[10]

This report provides a glimpse into how entangled industry and war had become in agriculture. In Britain, the war led to a 350 percent increase in the amount of nitrogen applied to fields between 1935 and 1938 compared to pre-war conditions.[11] Other areas such as Australia and New Zealand, already heavy users of phosphates, suffered a loss of phosphates due to the Japanese occupation of Oceana with its abundance of raw material, but with the cessation of hostilities these countries made up and then surpassed this loss.[12] The United States, like Britain, also massively increased chemical fertilizer use during the war.[13]

By 1946 two visions emerged from FAO documents on fertilizers. One—in the eyes of the FAO—was a dark vision of a static world anti-globalist in nature, with nations largely self-sufficient and raising most of their own food. This dystopian world used very little chemical fertilizer and would rely for the most part on traditional agricultural methods. In this scenario the nations of the world faced "considerable unemployment... and a shrunken volume of international trade." A second and brighter vision projected massive increases in chemical fertilizer plants in "an expanding world economy with high levels of employment" and the "rapid development" of the non-industrial areas of the world.[14] This second vision

---

[7] Ibid., 17.   [8] Ibid., 27.
[9] Ibid., 28. See also United States Tariff Commission, *Digest: Chemical Nitrogen*, 114/SS (1947).
[10] FAO, *Use of Commercial Fertilizers*, 33.   [11] Ibid., 36.
[12] Ibid., 37, 38.   [13] Ibid., 40.   [14] Ibid., 51.

could, with proper government policy and generous development aid, hasten urbanization and global modernization to produce a world free of "little England" style protectionism, or worse, fascist visions of self-sufficiency and cultural identity. It would herald a world open to international corporations, cartels, and capitalism. In this better tomorrow farmers on every continent could "increase their production for export" and allow each part of the world to specialize in crops bound for a global market.[15]

The global climate for organic farming was not entirely hostile. Not all regions of the world had access to elemental sulfur or oil supplies needed for fertilizer plants—particularly in areas of Latin America and parts of Asia. These challenges led the FAO to advocate, alongside chemical fertilizers, the "efficient conservation and production of fertilizers from natural organic sources." This included plant material, animal manure, and municipal waste and would have provided a unique opening for organic farming advocates like Howard to press for a mixed-use approach.[16] But by the end of the war, the Indore Method had already been overlooked except by small groups of enthusiasts that did not include leading scientific and governmental bodies. The call for natural use of organic materials in farming, though often mentioned in FAO documents, rarely materialized. Indeed, as one report enthused, "commercial fertilizers came of age" from 1939–1951, and this new age proved to be a juggernaut that organic farming advocates could not stop.[17]

In 1946 the FAO and chemical fertilizer manufacturers projected success. Europe was expected to reach triple its nitrogen consumption by 1960; the Soviet Union increasing nitrogen consumption twelve times; North America four times; Asia, over twenty times. Officials at the FAO predicted world consumption of nitrogen fertilizer would rise from 2,243 million metric tons to almost 7,000 million metric tons. The vast markets of Asia and India particularly stood out as shimmering open markets in which development would allow their teeming populations to westernize. Fertilizers in these regions, the FAO predicted, would "rise to a height which would dwarf the requirements of all other areas of the world."[18] In this scenario, Albert Howard's Indore Method (very rarely mentioned in FAO reports) was no more than a quaint throwback to traditional agriculture methods impeding the world's progress.

The glowing predictions were not far off the mark. The demand for fertilizers spiked after the war in Europe, Asia, and Latin America. Production and consumption peaked in 1939, dropped during the war, reached a new high in 1949, and then began to climb year on year. Improvements followed quickly: pelleting and granulation, higher concentrations of chemicals that made transportation cheaper, and better storage, allowed the cartels to penetrate deeply into Africa, Asia, and Central America.

In China, as in numerous countries, temporary "soil fertility collaborators" were identified in relevant research facilities—usually in government agencies or universities—who prepared studies for the FAO and in turn acted as conduits of

[15] Ibid., 52.
[16] G. J. Callister, *Developments in World Fertilizer Production* (FAO: Rome, July 24, 1951): 11.
[17] Ibid., 12.   [18] FAO, *Use of Commercial Fertilizers*, 53.

FAO reports and expertise to further the importation and also the manufacture of chemical fertilizers. In China chemical fertilizers had been imported since 1904. The University of Nanking also launched a series of plot experiments to demonstrate the efficacy of NPK. The British-owned Imperial Chemical Industries (ICI), the largest manufacturer of fertilizers in Britain and the British Empire, sponsored demonstration trials to farmers in Kwangtung, Fukien, Chekiang, Kiangsu, Shantung, and Hopei. It worked hand in hand with the Republican government through the National Agricultural Research Bureau, even throughout an intense period of civil war, until 1949.[19]

The FAO only recommended traditional farming methods as a stop-gap measure until rural communities had access to chemical fertilizers. The weight of experimental data fell solidly behind chemical fertilizers for the most important crops in Asia—rice, wheat, and millet, along with cabbage, cotton, mulberry trees, and tea. While night soil, barnyard manure, oil cakes, and green manuring in some cases yielded similar results they were found in most instances to underperform against ICI fertilizers.[20]

Due to low transportation costs, fertilizer cartels in the 1930s–40s penetrated the coastal areas of China with ease. They also had the support of the Republican government which strongly recommended the use of imported fertilizers to raise agricultural productivity. Farmers gravitated to the new methods and were largely willing to pay the costs of fertilizers to attain a higher yield. Only a small group of conservative farmers resisted the suggestion, worried that the use of chemicals exhausted the soil, but the education efforts of the FAO, government officials, and the British-owned company Imperial Chemical Industries (ICI), the largest headway against the belief.[21]

Traditional methods eroded steadily under the chemical onslaught. In the northwest of China, farmers fallowed the soil to recover productivity; in the wheat regions of the north they rotated crops with manuring; and in the rice regions of the south they plowed in crops for "green" manure. Chemical fertilizers however challenged these methods.[22] The Farmers' Bank, which handled the distribution of fertilizers and channeled agricultural loans, wielded immense influence and often made the availability of credit and funds conditional upon the implementation of modern farming methods. In Taiwan, by 1947, over 150,000 tons of fertilizers were imported, with the United Nations both giving away fertilizers as well as selling at reduced prices to help the remainder of farmers still using traditional agriculture to make the switch.[23] On the mainland, development aid from the United States funded the establishment of ammonium sulfate plants, which, along with expanding railways, pushed the distribution of fertilizers further inland.[24]

The victory of the Communist Party in China only deepened the commitment to chemical fertilizers. After an initial period of instability, the first five-year

[19] K. K. Yao, *Fertilizers in China* (FAO: Washington, 1948): 1.   [20] Ibid., 1, 2.
[21] Ibid., 11.   [22] Ibid., 15.   [23] Ibid., 18.
[24] Ibid., 18. See also Government of the Republic of China to the Conference of the Food and Agricultural Organization of the United Nations, "Annual Progress and Program report on Food and Agriculture for China-1947" (August, 1947).

plan from 1953–57 announced substantial targets for agricultural and industrial progress, including heavy investment in the chemical industries that produced fertilizers. While these targets were highly unrealistic and were not met, fertilizer use nonetheless still rose quickly for a few years. However, the Cultural Revolution enforced a commune system and massive agricultural mobilization that devastated agricultural and industrial productivity, bringing famine in its wake. Yet farmers still used even more chemical fertilizers for a number of reasons. Fertilizers raised yields quickly and more cheaply than mechanization and the results curried favor with the Communist bureaucracy.

Even as industrial production fell in China from 1960–62, funding, expertise, and equipment from Russia jump-started new fertilizer plants.[25] Two fertilizer plants had already been built in China: one in Port Arthur built by the Japanese in 1935 and another in Nanking built in 1949 with help from the United States. The government then launched five more large industrial plants with Russian help. By 1957, nitrogen and phosphate production had increased by 500 percent in just five years. While the government also encouraged the use of piggery waste and green manuring, these natural methods of composting proved to be a stopgap measure until chemical fertilizers were widely available. By 1963 farmers employed ten times the amount of nitrogenous and phosphate fertilizer than they had in 1953, with China leading the world in the growth rate of chemical fertilizers.[26]

With new global demand came new factories. Between 1938–51 governments and private companies launched chemical fertilizer plants around the world. One example was a new nitrogenous plant in Egypt, at Suez, operating in 1951 with a capacity to produce 40,000 metric tons of synthetic nitrates a year. The new plant raised hopes at the FAO that every region of the world could produce their own nitrogenous compounds, phosphoric acid, and potash so that new production facilities could be sited near at hand to the farmers who needed it.[27] The population expansion added to the erosion of traditional agricultural methods. The world's population stood at 2.3 billion people in 1951 and was growing by 23 million a year. In the twelve-year period between 1938 and 1951 eighty-five countries produced or imported chemical fertilizers—representing the vast majority of the land surface of the world. Add the cold war efforts by the United States to aid development and fend of Communist expansion and it is clear to see why the FAO felt that the momentum toward industrial agricultural methods would prove unstoppable.[28]

[25] Jung-Chao Liu, "Fertilizer Supply and Grain Production in Communist China," *American Journal of Agricultural Economics*, 47/4 (1965): 916.

[26] Ibid., 918. Liu cautions that figures put out by the government also served propaganda value and could not be relied upon for exactitude, but concluded that the figures published still indicated exponential growth.

[27] Callister, *Developments in World Fertilizer Production*: 3.

[28] Ibid., 6. See also, FAO, *Commodity Report: Fertilizers: A World Report on Production and Consumption* (Rome, August, 1951); NA, *The Latin American Fertilizer Supply and Resources for Improving the Supply* (Washington, March 26, 1951, United Nations). In 1945, the Meeting of the Fertilizer Working Committee of the Emergency Economic Committee for Europe held a series of meetings that highlighted a post-war strategy that included stripping Germany of fertilizer machinery and supplies of fertilizers to compensate other European countries. See NA, *Minutes of Meeting of the Fertilizer Working Committee: First Meeting of the Fertiliser Working Committee of the Emergency Economic committee for Europe*, (July 30, 1945): 2.

Howard's response to the spread of chemical fertilizer use in China is illustrative of the limitations of his activism. He signed a note in 1942 along with a former colonial medical officer in Singapore, J. W. Sharff, and Lionel J. Picton, objecting to the importation of artificial fertilizer by the Government of China. He published the note in response to a statement by Dr. Wellington Koo, Chinese Ambassador to Britain, who spoke glowingly of "Western ideas of agriculture" imported into central China. Howard and his co-signers declared that the application of western science to agriculture had, in many respects, been a failure and that for China to keep its peasant agriculture intact it required the application of the Indore process, that is, "of what the peasants of China are already doing." That his letter was published in the *Report on Garden Competition*, a booklet printed by the Chester Local Medical and Panel Committee, only illustrates how far his work had become detached from the corridors of power. It also illustrated that Howard had profoundly misjudged "the East." Elites in China were not interested in preserving a romantic, and primitive agriculture. China was rapidly industrializing and no longer resembled the practices traced by F. H. King's *Forty Centuries of Farming*.[29] Ironically, the pro-industrial view that Louise Howard advocated in her 1935 book *Labour in Agriculture*, which neither Louise nor Albert still endorsed, had won the field.

THE GROWTH OF ORGANIC FARMING ACTIVISM

The efforts by Albert Howard to fight the drift toward industrial agriculture failed on all fronts except one: a small but growing number of environmental activists around the world who (though including many professional farmers) tended to be gardeners and very savvy consumers of organic products. Albert Howard's secretary, Ellinor Kirkham, gave an outline of the first frontiers of expansion for organic farming. She recounted how in the early war years she read an advertisement for a private secretary to work for Albert Howard in Heversham, England, where he lived during the war years. She reached for her copy of *Who's Who*, and read that he was the author of *The Waste Products of Agriculture* which, understandably, "did not sound of absorbing interest." But when she met her genial and enthusiastic employer in September, 1941, he inspired her with the importance of the mission to restore life to the soil. When she took her place at her desk, she found that Howard operated at the hub of a global wheel of enthusiasts, and that prodigious amounts of letters arrived from around the world. She helped see to it that he answered them all. She scheduled the lectures, organized the letters and ledger books, and kept track of the paperwork in the office. She was in a unique position to sum up the progress of the movement from this time forward and in

---

[29] The County Palatine of Chester Local Medical and Panel Committee, *Report on the Garden Competition and other Nutritional Interests* (1942), 19. An account of J. W. Scharff's experience with compost and the health of Singaporean workers before the fall of Singapore to the Japanese can be found in Ibid., 12–13.

a memorial after his death in 1947, outlined the early stages of the growth of Howard's movement.[30]

In this memorial Kirkham reveals that the organic movement spread first and foremost in parts of the British Empire: in South Africa, where its "adherents were foremost in the field"; then "close on their heels" the New Zealand Humic Compost Club; after this Costa Rica, "through the whole-hearted support of senor Don Mariano Montealegre, editor of the *Revista del Institutode Defensa del Café de Costa Rica*" who used his journal to propagate the ideal of organic farming and the Indore Method.[31] After that, there were a cluster of followers in India, where "a number of confirmed disciples among Sir Albert's friends" carried on his work. She then confesses—something that is never heard from Louise, or Howard himself—that in North America and Australia in the early war years "no great attention was at that time given" to anything like the Indore Process. She confirmed a clear pattern that, except for Costa Rica, the organic farming movement had not spread to any substantial degree outside of continental Europe, Britain, and parts of the British Empire. Only well after 1945 did organic farming spread to any appreciable extent to other areas of the world. By 1947 a few more examples emerged in the Middle East (through the British Middle East Office, the world's first development agency), European countries, the West Indies, and a few places in the Pacific.[32]

By 1948, however, Howard's ideas took root in Australia and the United States, and spouted enthusiasm, publications, and a flourishing of new societies. Ellinor Kirkham predicted, with prescience, that the post-war growth in the United States "bids fair to take a world lead in propagating Sir Albert's creed."[33] Howard himself, right before his death, confirmed her view and his optimism about growth in the United States, primarily through the efforts of J. I. Rodale. He related how in 1942 Rodale launched *Organic Gardening*, a new journal dedicated to the Indore Process, with Howard joining as Associate editor. Howard writes,

> The history of Organic Gardening makes interesting reading. At the beginning there were no sales, but Mr. Rodale persisted and was soon rewarded by a growing roll of subscribers and by a steady rise in the revenue from advertisements. Today the paper has over 60,000 subscribers and is well on its feet.
>
> Several other schemes have been launched. A series of booklets known as the Gardeners Book Club has been issued. In 1945 an important work entitled *Pay Dirt* (in which Mr. Rodale condensed his agricultural experience and his wide reading) was published by Devin-Adair Company of New York. Four editions have appeared and

[30] See Ellinor Kirkham, "Sir Albert Howard: Prophet and Champion of the Soil," *Organic Farming Magazine*, 13/8 (September, 1948).
[31] South Africa had an advanced conservation movement and a special concern for soil conservation. A good source for understanding the conservation ideals promoted by officials in South Africa, and how officials used Albert Howard's work for educational purposes, is found in C. J. J. van Rensburg and E. M. Palmer, *New World to Win* (Bloemfontein, 1946), 131–42.
[32] See Gregory A. Barton, "Environmentalism, Development and British Policy in the Middle East 1945–1965," *Journal of Imperial and Commonwealth History*, 38/4 (December, 2010): 653–74.
[33] Ellinor Kirkham, "Sir Albert Howard."

18,000 copies have been sold. He has now taken up the publication of cloth bound books and has acquired the American rights of *The Earth's Green Carpet*, which is now on the market.[34]

The movement was stirring on the continent of Europe as well. After the Second World War a number of voices began to call for a return to natural methods of agriculture. These cultural movements, like the biodynamic movement discussed earlier, blazed a philosophical path that emphasized the virtues of traditional agriculture and thus opened up new opportunities for the adoption of Howard's Indore Method. The Life Reform movement produced a writer of note and influence in the person of Ewald Könemann. His three-part work, *Biologische Bodenkultur and Düngewirtschaft* (*Biological Soil Cultivation and the Fertilizer Economy*) published between 1931–1937 raised the problem of municipal waste, and the draining of fertility from the soil to the sea.[35] Könemann also edited a journal, *Bebauet die Erde* (*Cultivate the Earth*), which kept his ideas alive from the 1920s to 1950s. He argued that in the past most Germans lived on the land and thus human waste and manure cycled back into the local ecosystem and maintained an equilibrium of fertility. However, the growth of large urban areas meant that national populations literally consumed the nutrition found in the soil by flushing the waste out to sea. Building on the work of two earlier biologists, Felix Lohnis and Raoul Francé, Könemann did much to popularize the understanding of the soil as a living entity, as did a number of other writers of the 1930s.[36] Könemann adopted Francé's "Edaphone" (life of the soil) concept and recommended developing the humus with the use of shallow ploughing and the return of manure, human waste, and mulch back to the fields. He did not, however, oppose the use of synthetic fertilizers or other chemical treatments, which distinctly separated him from organic advocates in Britain.

In Switzerland Hans Müller led the Schweizerrische Bauern-Heimatbewegung (Swiss Farmer's Movement for a Native Rural Culture) that sought the restoration of a faith-based Christian lifestyle deeply rooted in peasant culture. He called it "organic-biological agriculture."[37] Müller promulgated traditional farming methods that preserved the Christian ruralism of a Europe that prevailed before the age of industrial agriculture.[38] Müller also edited a journal, *Kultur und Politik* (*Culture and Politics*) in which he regularly aired his view that the farmer must not be judged on a materialistic basis only, or judged by statistics on economic outputs. The age of the machine killed the human spirit, he argued, and will always win on

[34] Albert Howard, "The Progress of Organic Agriculture in the U. S. A.," *Organic Farming Magazine*, 13/8 (September, 1948).
[35] Ewal Könemann, *Biologische Bodenkultur and Döngewirtschaft* (Tutzing, 1939).
[36] Felix Lohnis investigated the seasonal variation of bacterial activities in the soil, at the University of Leipzig. He also contributed to the science of nitrogen fixation and the role that decomposition played. The British Association for the Advancement of Science invited him to speak in 1912. See NA, *Nature*, 127/99–100 (17 January, 1931).
[37] Gunter Vogt, "The Origins of Organic Farming," *Organic Farming: An International History*, ed. William Lockeretz (Wallingford, Oxfordshire, 2007): 18.
[38] H. Müller, *Technik und Glaube: eine permanente Herausforderung* (Göttingen, 1971).

an economic score. But the machine age had introduced idolatry and the worship of mammon—a world dedicated to the false gods of materialistic production. Lost were the songs that farmers sang in the fields; lost the family life that cheered and sustained the peasants working in the Swiss valleys; lost to the aesthetics of simplicity, such as the chestnut brown horses pulling wooden carts along a muddy track. In such a life meditation was the native air that the peasant breathed; in such a life the poetry of song and story sweetened and soothed the hardships of labor and was the cardinal value of human work without the aid of advanced machines. Sowing seeds in the traditional way weaved a tapestry of tradition, habits, and culture that put humans close to their own families, and to the family of God—that is, the Christian community, working in harmony under God, the Father. Traditional farming was therefore more than the output of economic units: it was a lifestyle that had to be preserved in order to preserve human culture and meaning itself.[39] Müller worked closely with his wife to build his own version of a Swiss Shangri-la and like the followers of Steiner added his own cultural and mystic ingredients to the Indore Method. As a number of scholars have pointed out,

> Based on extensive scientific reading and their own experiences, the Müllers created the "organic-biologic agriculture and gardening method." This method drew upon Sir Albert Howard's ideas as well as those from Rudolf Steiner and his biodynamic attention to humus, soil organisms, composting and the cycling of systems. The Müller's approach to compost, in contrast to Howard's use of the Indore Method, focused on promoting a system of surface composting and mulching.[40]

Könemann helped popularize the idea of sustaining biological activity of the soil that had been explored by German, French, British, and American scientists, but this alone did not amount to what we would today call organic farming. However, the protocols that are today considered vital to the organic farming movement found greater acceptance in Europe after the Second World War because of the cultural background that these leaders offered. Many of the principles of the Life Reform movement were abandoned in the 1930s and later, dropping vegetarianism, the ideal of farming without animals, and dropping also the peasant romanticism that promoted the health-giving virtues of living on the land and the necessity of recycling municipal wastes.[41] Most in the movement never found the mysticism of Steiner's biological farming palatable or intellectually valid. This shift in values opened continental Europe up even more to the ideas and simple protocols of Albert Howard, which implicitly appealed to those inclined toward mysticism and native culture, but spoke the language of science and practical application.

---

[39] H. Müller, "Glaube und Technik," *Kulture und Politics* (1949/50): 1–5.
[40] See Bernhard Freyer, Jim Bingen, and Milena Klimek, "Ethics in the organic movement," *Re-thinking organic food and farming in a changing world*, ed. Bernhard Freyer (Dordrecht, 2015): 27.
[41] Vogt, "The Origins of Organic Farming," 17.

ALBERT HOWARD'S LAST YEARS

From the publication of *Agricultural Testament* in 1940 to his death in 1947, Howard addressed an astoundingly wide range of audiences in writing and lectures. Sensing that he no longer had the ear of scientists, he wrote for an eclectic array of societies, journals, and newsletters. For his growing number of disciples in the organic farming movement, he kept a constant output of lectures, articles, and short essays. Howard wrote for Lionel Picton, the founding member of the Cheshire Panel Committee that issued the *Medical Testament*, and founded and edited *News-Letter on Compost*. He also wrote for J. I. Rodale's magazine *Organic Gardening and Farming* in the United States. His output cascaded into newspapers, journals, and newsletters of every sort, including, for instance, a piece for the Roman Catholic *Magazine for the Lay Apostle* in which he contextualized compost in its proper placement "in the scheme of creation."[42] He read papers to any society who wished to hear his message: medical societies, farmers clubs, and an array of organizations seemly unrelated to the Indore Method, such as the Annual Meeting of the British Dental Association, where in June 1947 he opened the session with an invited paper titled "nutrition and dental health." He always carefully tied the interests of his audience to organic farming, and near the end of his life gained poetic power and fervency, using language far removed from the clinical science of the Indore research station, as seen below,

> Ever since the year 1879, when a combination of the worst season on record and the importation of cheap wheat from the New World put an end to the system of mixed farming, which Coke of Norfolk did so much to establish, insufficient attention has been paid to the earth's green carpet and to the work of the green leaf. We have tried to make our proteins on the cheap, as it were. A famine of quality has gradually set in which has been accelerated by the vast supplies of bastard nitrogen in the shape of sulphate of ammonia placed on the market by the makers of the explosives needed in the world war of 1914–18.[43]

Howard was not a vegetarian but he took his message to the London Vegetarian Society meeting in 1947 at Conway Hall, in Bloomsbury, that held an audience of 500. The published version of his address, printed in *Vegetarian News*, includes one of the few photographs we have of him after his retirement from India. The article does not make clear whether the statements derive directly from Howard himself or whether they are, in fact, substantially rephrased by the anonymous author—clearly an enthusiastic disciple of Howard. Either way, however, the lecture illustrated a clear transition from the early Howard carefully conducting scientific experiments

---

[42] Arguing from natural theology, he applied the law of return to our observation of the forests that, if obeyed, allowed humans to fulfill God's will. Soil, he preached, "is God's good gift to the human race" that required in turn good stewardship. See Albert Howard, "Compost and Creation," *The Magazine for the Lay Apostle* (1947): 60–3.

[43] See the *British Dental Journal*, LXXXIII/29 (July 18, 1947): 1–3. Also, Public Relations Officer, British Dental Association to Albert Howard, Certificate of Thanks, [Letter 2, May, 1947] File: 1947, *Matthaei Family Archive*, Birmingham, UK.

in India to the Howard that emerged after the 1940 publication of *Agricultural Testament*—from scientist to scientific skeptic; from bureaucrat to prophet.

The simplification and enthusiasm which turned off scientists and policy experts had the opposite effect on a growing popular base, and proved a necessary means of selling and building the movement. In the 1940s he built his base by turning away from the professional elites who were needed to keep the organic farming ensconced in the mainstream. While the statements made in the report of his lecture to the London Vegetarian Society may indeed simplify and exaggerate elements of his lecture, nonetheless the article gives insight into how his lectures were received, and how his charismatic presentations kindled the visions and even the myths that fueled the organic movement from this time forward.

The author enthused that Howard "let the land teach him" and led him out of orthodox science rather than "experiment in laboratories." He "made the peasants his professors" and thus picked up the secrets of a "six-thousand year old tradition" and followed the voice of Nature. He discovered that "disease would disappear" if the crops and then the animals were fed on organic produce, including the tripling of agricultural output. Because of the application of his ideas, India "became self-supporting in sugar." The reader is further informed that after retiring from India he returned to England to launch his ideas on the world. He had no interest in dealing with governments, universities, or vested interests but rather sought out "the creative minority" who are practical and try out things for themselves. To this creative minority he taught that "disease . . . is unnatural and unnecessary." With a new health service in Britain, planning to spend £150 million a year, the time had come for national change. The article praised the Rhodesian Natural Resources Act that mandated composting through legislation, and would light the way for a revolution where governments, from the top down, would change the world with composting.[44]

The Autumn 1947 issue of *The Farmer* published another account of this lecture and, while slightly more careful in the language employed, reconfirmed that Howard as he neared the end of his life waxed eloquent in his message, with a prophetic fervor. The report showed him pushing the limits of his thesis, which the early Howard would have rejected. Disease, he stated, appeared because Nature needed to remove an organism that had been improperly fed. Sickness was the "intermediate state between life and death. The majority of the population are in this state—half dead." He capped this observation by saying that "Disease does not attack the fit." And, if fit, "you need never worry about disease." Humans, he claimed, will remain sick as long as we use chemical fertilizers, which have so entranced the Ministry of Agriculture, whom he dubbed "Celestial Chemistries Ltd." for the miraculous claims they made for deadly chemicals.

Howard laid out his hopes for the future, and the way forward to completely transform society. First, the path to success ran through the creative minority, who would write their success on the land and on their bodies with their superior

[44] Anonymous, "Sir Albert Howard: Soil Food and Health," *Vegetarian News*, XXVI/257 (Autumn, 1947): 65–6.

health. The movement would grow in stages: first, with whole-wheat bread, then in small garden plots, then finally in farms. Sanitariums and other spas would then pick up on the new health-inducing trend until Britain, just as Rhodesia had done, wrote organic farming into the law. That, and the composting of municipal sewage, would complete the revolution in health. It would solve economic distress as well, not only through increased yield, but "if people were properly fed they would want to work and there would be no strikes." Hence industrial conflict in the modern economy would end.[45]

Howard built on his earlier themes and honed his message by poetic simplification that may have guaranteed enthusiasm among the growing cadres of dedicated followers, while at the same time exiling the movement he launched into a lonely abeyance for a number of decades. As a strategy for long-term survival it may indeed have been the one thing that he could do in the face of scientific and government rejection of his principles in the 1940s–50s. In the short run, however, his prophetic and poetic fervor buried all hopes of mainstream scientific and professional acceptance.

It seems likely that some of his followers oversimplified and exaggerated Howard's statements. But it is characteristic of his enthusiastic presentations that followers came away with such impressions. Given his active lobbying of city councilmen and members of parliament, it is doubtful Howard said he abhorred laboratories and point-blank refused to influence government policy—particularly also given his activism on the issue of urban composting. Howard certainly praised the Rhodesian Natural Resources Act. Indeed, this act discussed shortly, gave Howard hope that his dream of a global revolution that would return waste to the soil and forever change agriculture could succeed.

Howard had great hopes for Rhodesia. In 1946 he had written to the *Farmer's Weekly*, a South African weekly, complementing African farmers for being progressive and "compost minded." He had considerable correspondence with farmers, newspapers, and journals in the region, and praised farmers, commenting that "evidently the spirit of Cecil Rhodes is still active in the land."[46] Rhodesia pioneered the world's first government-sanctioned policy that implemented Howard's Indore Method and thus was the first governmental body to not only regulate, but mandate organic farming. The South African botanist, Illtyd Buller Pole-Evans, Director of the Botanical Survey of South Africa, played a key role in a report that underlay the establishment of the Rhodesian 1942 Natural Resources Act. He may have also been responsible for the overt reference to composting by Howard's methods. Pole-Evans studied mycology and plant pathology under Howard's mentor, Harry

---

[45] Anonymous, "We Must WRITE RESULTS on the LAND," *The Farmer* (Autumn, 1947) 37.

[46] The following citations are found in File: 1947, *Matthaei Family Archive*, Birmingham, UK. Full bibliographic information not always available: Albert Howard, "Improving Permanent Pasture," *The Rhodesian Farmer* (1947); Albert Howard, "Letter," *Farmer's Weekly*, (December 31, 1946); Albert Howard, "Good Farming Only Cure for Erosion," *The Rhodesian Farmer* (June 21, 1947): 15; Albert Howard, "Improving Permanent Pasture: Sir A. Howard's Suggestion to Colony's Farmers," *The Rhodesian Farmer* (August 27, 1947); Albert Howard "Leys and Green Crops," *The Rhodesian Farmer* (September 10, 1947): 17; Albert Howard, "Manure," *The Rhodesian Farmer* (October 22, 1947).

Marshall Ward, graduating in 1905, only a few years after Howard, and had great sympathy with his Cambridge colleague.

The report that preceded the act, published by the Natural Resources Commission, highlighted in 1939 that soil erosion had ruined the best land in Rhodesia "beyond repair."[47] The commission recommended that the colony give authority to a Natural Resources Board with broad powers over all the natural resources in Rhodesia. The board could raise prices for agricultural products and demand higher standards for farmers—something that appealed to Albert Howard. It described "formerly valuable tracts of country" now ruined that "could be brought back to big scale production."[48] The sheer scale of authority for the new Board understandably raised concerns among farmers. An historian of this act, Simeon Maravanyika, writes, "The Board was empowered to give orders to any land owner in the colony to take measures to conserve natural resources in the colony."[49] While farmers were suspicious of the government "mucking about with people's land" the severity of a drought overcame the initial reluctance to the Act that followed.

The report that led to the Act could not have been more pro-organic farming. It mentioned the problems associated with monoculture, and the "overuse of artificial fertilizers." One farmer, Duncan Black, testifying before the commission stated that when people,

> continually use artificial fertilizer to a certain piece of ground…well, even the ground gets sick of fertilizer. I find that you must rotate it in some way and not perpetually grow maize with artificial fertilizer.[50]

The Chairman of the Beatrice Food Production Committee told the Natural Resources Board,

> The basic requirement of good farming is finance. Good farming cannot be practiced unless adequate prices are paid to the farmer for his produce. The prices of farm produce should be fixed at an economic level, and should not be left to the buyer to fix. The wishes of the consumer should have no bearing on this subject.[51]

The report specifically recommended composting, and Howard's Indore Method. It highlighted the value of farmyard manure and the shortage of manure for composting that therefore needed to be specifically solved by composting plant material:

> These are fully described by Sir Albert Howard, exponent of modern compost methods in his book "*The Waste Products of Agriculture*." An excellent bulletin by the local Department of Agriculture describes how the process can he adapted to Rhodesian

---

[47] Southern Rhodesia Commission on the Natural Resources of the Colony, *Report of the Commission to Enquire into the Preservation of the Natural Resources of the Colony*, C.S. R. 40 (Salisbury, 1939). See Simeon Maravanyika, *Soil Conservation and the White Agrarian Environment in Colonial Zimbabwe c. 1908–1980*, PhD Thesis: Department of History and Heritage Studies at the University of Pretoria (September, 2013): 186.
[48] Ibid., 187.   [49] Ibid., 191.   [50] Ibid., 193.   [51] Ibid., 195.

conditions. The important point is that all waste vegetable matter such as grass, leaves, weeds, etc., may be used in its composition.[52]

Rhodesia, the report concluded, could double its agricultural output by using Howard's methods "without breaking up any more land." Further, environmental degradation could be halted by stopping shifting cultivation "among the natives" if they could use the Indore Method. Even at the time of the report in 1939, government sponsored community demonstrations had produced 871 "model rural villages." Further the government advised on the planting of tree plantations and the "digging of 3,176 compost pits."[53] So widespread was the effect of the Act that a member of the British parliament grilled the Undersecretary of State for Dominion Affairs "whether steps are being taken to secure the good-will and consent of the Africans concerned."[54]

As the ideas as well as the writings of Albert Howard circulated in his final years, they were often debated by authors in the press and in the letter columns of newspapers. One case caught the national attention at the highest level. A Dr. Franklin Bicknell, consulting physician at the French Hospital in London, wrote an article titled "Dying England" in *The Medical Press* supporting Howard's idea that modern Englishmen faced slow starvation—not from lack of food but lack of nutrition. This ignited Evelyn Strachey, Minister of Food for the Labour Government, to counter attack that the British consumed more than enough calories for health. Strachey was a prominent Marxist politician and writer who felt abhorrence at an organic farming movement that smacked of many of the fascist ideals of the defeated Nazis. Lord Addison, leader of the House of Lords, appointed by the Labour Prime Minister Clement Attlee, took the attack on the quality of British food as a personal insult to the Labour government and joined in the attack on Bicknell.[55] He particularly took umbrage at the quotation of Bicknell by Lord Woolton, the former Minister of Food during the war years and Conservative Party Chairman. Woolton quoted Bicknell that "England is dying of starvation." Addison remonstrated,

It is not true, and it ought not to have been quoted. This Dr. Bicknell goes on to say that the unemployed before the war were better fed than most of the nation to-day.[56]

Addison then quotes Sir John Boyd Orr, Director-General of the FAO, who stated that 17 percent of the population before the war did not have adequate food, and that this was not the case in the present time. He then fumes,

Heaven knows, we should like a better diet, but it is wrong—and I say the noble Lord has no right—to disseminate statements of that character, which are manifestly untrue. It does great harm to the country.[57]

[52] Southern Rhodesia Commission, *Report of Commission*, Section 354.
[53] Ibid., Section 355.
[54] House of Commons (HC) Deb 05 (August, 1941), vol. 373, cc.1764–65, 1765: 4. Mr. David Adams.
[55] House of Lords (HL) Deb 08 (May, 1947), vol. 147, cc. 462–561.
[56] Ibid.   [57] Ibid.

Addison then suggested such "gruesome" remarks, when quoted in parliament, were heard on the radio around the world, and gave the impression that Britain was "down and out" and would deleteriously affect Britain's foreign policy, because the statements affected their perception of strength and prestige, claiming that "if you want the rest of the world to do what you would like, you do not let them think that you are feeble and helpless."[58] To counter the assertion, Addison asked Lord Rothschild to visit the Ministry of Food, who then came back with the figure that the average citizen consumed 2,900 calories daily. This debate drove more readers to the letters that followed in *The Medical Press*, where Howard's ideas were thoroughly aired, and through Bicknell, to Howard. Howard himself wrote in to justify Bicknell's reliance on his own work, stating that, while the British were not starving to death from lack of calories, "England is now suffering from a famine of quality."[59]

Welcome as such a national debate appeared to Howard, it nonetheless alienated organic farming advocates from official circles, and placed them on the fringe of the dominant scientific narrative—simultaneously strengthening the growing organic farming movement among its core adherents, but isolating the movement from mainstream institutions.

Albert Howard died, unexpectedly, October 20, 1947. Though his cause of death is not recorded in the papers Louise collected, it is likely that Howard died of a heart attack. Gabrielle, writing to her mother from India, recommended to her "Huxley's Syrup of acid glycerophosphates" because Albert took them for his health, and "it has done him a tremendous amount of good." Glycerophosphates were prescribed for tachycardia—an accelerated heart beat—and also for any type of heart arrhythmia, or what today would be called degenerative heart disease. He also took the product Sanatogen, invented by Bauer in 1898, which had been advised by two physicians in India and was used for heart conditions, anemic conditions, or weakness and exhaustion from overworking.[60]

THE DEATH OF IMPERIAL SCIENCE

It did not take long for small circles around the British Empire, as well as in England and the United States, to pick up on Howard's scientific narrative. The way that amateurs interpreted Howard's work partially explained its popularity and sheds light on a crucial point in environmental history after the Second World

---

[58] Ibid.

[59] For the exchange of letters see *The Medical Press*, CCXVII/Weds (May 14, 1947), 20, 402, 421, 465, 466.

[60] Gabrielle Howard, Letters, 92. Frederick Hugh Clark, "Epileptoid attacks In Tachycardia," *British Medical Journal* (August 10, 1907): 308. Albert Howard also took a product that contained concentrated milk proteins and glycerophosphates. Gabrielle wrote that "Sanatogen has also been recommended to us very strongly by 2 doctors and he is going to try it after he has finished the bottle of the other." See Gabrielle Howard, Letters, 193. See also "Sanatogen," National Museum of American History. Available online at: http://americanhistory.si.edu/collections/search/object/nmah_714696 [accessed August 23, 2017].

War when the environmental movement began a slow and steady shift from the right of the political spectrum to the left. In the late 1940s and early 1950s, organic farming literature arose as part of a larger quest for pre-industrial wholeness, and a return to traditional agricultural methods. This literature often promoted a sharp distinction between a noble "imperial science" that seemed to capture the virtues of public service and objectivity, even aristocratic ethics of duty, over and against an industrial age of "capitalistic science" that served a new elite of large industrial combines and cosmopolitan financiers.

Although the early followers of Albert Howard tended to express far right inclinations, they could nonetheless be found all over the political spectrum; from former fascists and ultra-Tories, to Labourites in Britain, or Labourites and Liberals in Australia. All however had a profound political appreciation for the importance of race and soil. These overt fascist sympathies, however, evaporated slowly during and after the Second World War, as did overt support for the British Empire as decolonization set in during the 1950s. We see this clearly in the first journal to use the word "organic" in its title, the *Organic Farming Digest*. Howard's followers, nostalgic for an old order, often credited his work to the British Raj, while those who disagreed with Howard, they firmly believed produced, a suspect scientific narrative influenced by ill-intentioned chemical manufacturers. However, in the years following the independence of India, and against the steady drumbeat of decolonization, references to an imperial science faded, leaving behind a deep residue of hostility to large-scale industrial capitalism and a penchant for scientific outsiders that remained an indelible characteristic of the modern environmental movement.[61]

Examples of this abound. A cattle grazer, H. F. White, and a farmer, V. H. Kelly, started the *Organic Farming Digest*, published in Sydney, New South Wales, Australia.[62] William John McKell, the Premier of New South Wales and the future Governor-General of Australia, introduced the *Organic Farming Digest* in its first article, linking the preservation of trees with the preservation of farmland.[63] Albert Howard served as the honorary patron of the society. The journal adapted Howard's ideas to the local Australian scene, along with fellow travelers of the organic farming and nutrition movement, such as G. T. Wrench, Robert McCarrison, and others. It lasted only a few years, from 1946 to 1952 and disbanded due to lack of funds. But this early organic farming journal, like a handful of others around the British Empire, inspired a populist affinity to scientific narratives that originated in the British Raj.[64]

---

[61] Rachel Carson is an example of a scientist who, like Howard, also worked for government agencies but took her concerns to a popular market. See Rachel Carson, *Silent Spring*, (New York, 1962).

[62] The observation that the *Organic Farming Digest* is the first to use the word "organic" in its title has been noted by John Paull in "The Lost History of Organic Farming in Australia," *Journal of Organic Systems*, 3 (2008): 2.

[63] W. J. McKell, *Organic Farming Digest*, 1/1 (April, 1946): 1–2.

[64] When Albert Howard retired from service in India, he visited farmers and researchers throughout the British Empire who experimented with his methods, and quickly found supporters around the world, including in Britain. These supporters included activists for traditional agriculture such as; the

Australian farmers suffered from very particular challenges unique to the great southland. The continent, with the exception of a narrow strip of land along its indented coast, most of it on the eastern side, had had nutrients leached from the soil for millions of years. The soils of this ancient land in particular lacked phosphorus, and after a few years of good crops soon produced lower yields. Therefore, the introduction of artificial fertilizers with phosphorus, and the remarkable success of the Correll family who introduced to south Australia the use of seed drills simultaneously with phosphorus use, led to the wholesale abandonment of traditional methods of farming. This occurred despite a cultural bias against "experts." Scientists and company salesmen who had recommended nitrogenous fertilizers for Australia based on results in Europe or the United States had cost obliging farmers dearly— the soil, as Alfred Pearson, chemist of the Victorian Department of Agriculture had warned, was actually high in nitrogen and potassium. But the application of phosphorus proved so successful that by the 1920s its use, along with improved methods for dealing with drought and weeds, turned Australia into a powerhouse exporter of agricultural products, particularly wheat.[65]

Problems with chemical fertilizers soon followed however. As both Michael Williams and Lionel Frost have pointed out, modern farming methods accentuated problems with drifting sand and American-style erosion similar to the dust-bowl desertification that drove thousands of small farmers off the land. Soil exhaustion led to soil problems which after the First World War affected large swathes of agricultural land that stood well outside Goyder's line in south Australia—the geographical delineation of the zone suited to agriculture.[66] Thus in the aftermath of the Second World War many farmers were receptive to solutions to soil fertility, yield, and plant health that did not rely on the same chemical fertilizers that had contributed to soil degradation. This explains, in part, why the *Organic Farming Digest* was so well received in Australia.[67]

What is of particular interest in these early articles however is how the editors and readers of this pioneering organic journal translated the scientific narrative from India into "imperial science" and "capitalist science," though these were not always the terms specifically used by the authors. The flashpoint of conversation

Earl of Portsmouth, Lady Eve Balfour, Sir George Stapledon, as well as the nutritionalist Sir Robert McCarrison and the visionary writer G. T. Wrench.

[65] The traditional methods of agriculture that Australian settlers practiced were derived from Ireland and Britain. See Ted Henzell, *Australian Agriculture: The History and Challenges* (Victoria, 2007), ix; Lionel Frost, "The Correll Family and Technological Change in Australian Agriculture," *Agricultural History*, 75/2 (Spring, 2001): 238–41; Department of Agriculture, *Annual Report 1900–1* (Melbourne, 1901), 5–24. The young Commonwealth government of Australia sought advice from officials in Britain and the British Empire to raise agricultural productivity. Especially readable is the Scottish Agricultural Commission to Australia, *Australia: Its land, Conditions and Prospects: The Observations and experiences of the Scottish Agricultural Commission of 1910–11: A Report with Numerous Illustrations* (Edinburgh, 1911).

[66] George Goyder, Surveyor-General of South Australia, suggested in 1865 that the Mallee scrub south of the suggested line was most suitable for agriculture.

[67] Lionel Frost, "The Correll Family," 240–1. For a good overview of the challenges faced by settlers in Australia see Michael Williams, *The Making of the South Australian Landscape: A Study in the Historical Geography of Australia* (London, 1974).

that led to the emergence of these two scientific genealogies, often (but not always) revolved around the doctrines of the Liebig era and the Rothamsted Experimental Station in England, both of which were seen by his followers to contradict the work of Albert Howard. The Liebig era was associated with doctrines that explained plant nutrition through simple chemical analysis, and arose in the latter part of the nineteenth century when chemical fertilizers became the norm for most farmers in Europe and the United States.[68] But it was the challenge of the Rothamsted Experimental Station that aroused the greatest fury in the organic farming movement. John Lawes, the founder of Rothamsted in 1843, also manufactured and sold artificial fertilizers. As the oldest agricultural research institution in the world, this station in the 1930s investigated genetics and developed statistical methods of experimental design and analysis. After 1943, under the directorship of William Ogg, Rothamsted added yet more specialized departments in biochemistry. It stood in the minds of organic farming supporters as the symbol of the triumph of industrial chemistry over botany, biology, and ecology. It was, in their minds, the Liebig movement run amuck.[69]

The *Organic Farming Digest* manifested a theme of hostility toward the Rothamsted Experimental Station from the start. One writer, A. S. Neeham, highlighted an argument repeated throughout the journal:

Howard had the unique opportunity in India of carrying out a lifetime of research with public funds and no interference from vested interests. His conclusion was that chemical manures are anathema. Sir Albert has shown that animals fed on food grown with chemical manures are disease-ridden, while comparable animals on the same diet grown on soil treated with organic manure are healthy. Such vital research gets no publicity, and the food we eat is mostly grown with artificials.[70]

Needham also pointed out that in the Rothamsted annual report "you will find that considerable sums are received from the Fertilizer Manufacturer's Association, the United Potash Co., Imperial Chemical Industries, the Association of British Chemical Manufacturers, British Basic Slag Companies, etc." He argued pointedly that "Agricultural research in Britain is largely supported by, and its direction controlled by, the Chemical Combine." While good work had been done at Rothamsted, he observed, "it has always been largely concerned with methods of using chemical manures." This science of the vested business interests has been behind modern agricultural practice, and "vast tracts of the earth's surface was being turned into desert by mechanized chemical farming." Behind it all was the

[68] Justus von Liebig (1803–73), a German chemist, has been credited with launching the modern fertilizer industry. He demonstrated the role of nitrogen in plant growth and identified key elements of plant nutrition. The role of humus in soil fertility interested him little. See Justus Liebig, *Organic Chemistry in Its applications to Agriculture and Physiology* (Cambridge, 1841). The use of chemical fertilizers did not become the norm in the English speaking world until the 1880s. See Richard A. Wines, *Fertilizer in America: From Waste Recycling to Resource Exploitation*, (Philadelphia, 1985), 160–1.

[69] Albert Howard, *The Soil and the Health: A Study of Organic Agriculture*, (New York, 1947), 77–81. E. B. Balfour, *The Living Soil and the Haughley Experiment* (London, 1943), 134–6.

[70] S. Needham, "Rothamsted Experimental Station," *Organic Farming Digest*, 1/ 2 (July, 1946): 10–11.

fact that "Agricultural research in this country is concerned mainly with devising methods of using chemical manures so that their long-term destructive effects are not immediately apparent."[71]

Articles in the journal argued repeatedly that vested interest ruined scientific enquiry, and that usury had ruined the soil. Excerpts from the *Alternative to Death*, by the Earl of Portsmouth (previously Viscount Lymington) lambasted a financial system that led to the indebtedness of farmers. This debt forced farmers to mine the soil instead of farming it properly for long-term sustainability.[72] Examples from the Empire abounded, Portsmouth argued, of ruined soil caused by capitalist monocrop cultivation. Albert Howard, in a review of an article by D. J. Salisbury, from the *Journal of the Royal Horticultural Society,* lamented that Barbados in the West Indies had been ravaged by "forty years [during which] artificials have steadily replaced pen manure" and this was followed inevitably by "virus disease ... [and] the loss of productive power in the cane." This compelled the imperial government to seek a grant of £171,810 under the authority of the Colonial Development and Welfare Act to develop "mixed farming based on animal husbandry."[73] In North Bengal he had witnessed tea plantations in 1937 rejuvenated by "nature's law of return" when the "Indore Process" was implemented without "artificials." The tea was then, "to all intents and purposes free from disease."[74]

Vested interest, it was argued, ruined science. In a reprinted article titled "Milk and Soil Fertility," F. Sykes opined that "enormous vested interests" were behind chemical fertilizers, which produced "conniving and extremely clever propaganda" that had all but abolished natural manures, devastating the soil of the farms. The effect of big business on human nutrition was equally deleterious. Those "interests employed in the making of artificial concentrates for humans, sold in packets and tins" deprived the "whole germ and life-giving qualities [of grain]." Then the same business interests turn around to sell these "extracts of wheat (the germ) and sell these foods at ridiculous prices as real vitalizing foods." The result is the devastation of human health and the enrichment of the "pill and drug trades, whose immense wealth is built upon" unhealthy soil. He concluded that "these manifold forces of immense power stand right in the way of food reform."[75] However Sykes suggested an alternative: "Government enforcement of ... composting processes using animal residues for their activation" that would restore health to the soil and to the humans depending upon the soil.[76]

---

[71] Ibid. The criticism by organic enthusiasts was highly tendentious. Rothamsted maintained for more than a century some of the most famous agricultural experiments in the world, not involving fertilizers, including pasture treatment and ploughing regimes. I owe this suggestion to Dr. Frederick Kruger.

[72] Ibid., 13.

[73] E. J. Salisbury, "Organic and Mineral Fertilizers," Review by Albert Howard, *Organic Farming Digest*, 1/2 (July, 1946): 18.

[74] Ibid., 20.

[75] F. Sykes, "Milk and Soil Fertility," *Organic Farming Digest*, 1/4, (January, 1947): 20.

[76] "Poison Sprays Destroy Bees," *Organic Farming Digest*, 1/4, (January, 1947): 25.

This vested interest created a capitalistic science that placed a premium on chemistry, because chemistry could raise crop yields but at the expense of nutritional quality. One article titled "Cheapness is Expensive" argued that "the really important point [was] that statesmen, scientists, farmers, consumers, wholesalers, and retailers alike, would get cheapness out of their minds—cheapness necessarily concentrates attention on gross yield per acre—and consider first and foremost ultimate nutritive value."[77] Another entry reprinted from a speech delivered at the Hawkesbury Agricultural College in New South Wales in 1946, saw disconcerting connections between chemistry and capital. The science of chemistry, so easily dominated by vested interests, neglected the biological activity in the soil, including the mycorrhizal process, and thus missed the value of the process that lies behind organic farming. Biology is not about cheapness and capital. There were "disconcerting biological facts which utterly destroy chemical theories." Chemistry misses the "interrelation of living things—plant, animal, insect, etc.—[which] is termed ecology."[78] Can anyone doubt, he concluded, that human health "depends more upon food than upon any other single factor in our environment?"—and thus upon biology, and not upon chemistry.[79]

One entry reprinted an introduction to a New Zealand seed catalogue from Arthur Yates and Company, which sold a wide variety of fertilizers. The introduction by this small company concluded with "Yours sincerely, for our country against 'rackets.'" The article, penned no doubt by Arthur Yates, the business owner, made a clear distinction between small enterprises like his own and the "vested interests" with their "hundreds of millions of pounds capital," that they use to "buy or kill serious opposition." Yates claimed that these capitalists had even bought off the government departments in New Zealand through financial influence. Superphosphate companies, he said, received £1,500,000 of subsidies each year, yet none came to the manure based fertilizer companies, such as his own.[80]

The editors of the *Organic Farming Digest* offered readers a brilliant contrast with scientists from India. These imperial scientists were praised as lavishly as the Rothamsted Research Station and the Liebig system were condemned. On the publication of G. T. Wrench, *Reconstruction by Way of the Soil*, a book reviewer gushed that "it is refreshing to encounter this latest work...an inspiring account of what might well be the norm for a healthy humanity, the now oft-quoted Hunza race [in India] so lauded by Sir R. McCarrison...and other investigators."[81] These investigators of wholeness in British India, the review suggested, approach the

[77] "Cheapness is Expensive," *Organic Farming Digest*, 1/5, (April–June 1947): 15.

[78] Sir Stanton Hicks, "Food Production is Everybody's Business," *Organic Farming Digest*, 1/6 (July–September, 1947): 11. This article is a transcript of a lecture delivered by Stanton Hicks at Hawkesbury Agricultural College, New South Wales, in 1946.

[79] Ibid., 12.

[80] Arthur Yates, "A New Zealand Message," *Organic Farming Digest*, 1/6 (July–September, 1947): 19–20. The author may be referring to mining concessions which would appear as either free or nearly so, compared to manure based fertilizer companies that had to purchase raw material at considerable expense. Yates owned Arthur Yates and Co., Ltd, in Auckland, New Zealand.

[81] D. M. Lewis, "Review of *Reconstruction by Way of the Soil* by G. T. Wrench," *Organic Farming Digest*, 1/6 (July–September, 1947): 31.

world like Howard—ecologically and as a unified whole. The review concludes by lauding travel as a key to understanding these differences:

> The traveler comes to the opinion that the modern scientific farm, and especially the experimental farm, is a mixture of forcing house and hospital. It fragments the lifecycle. It is the offspring of a defect of thought, the splitting or departmentalizing of the mind, which disables it from seeing wholeness and that men, animals, plants and soil are inseparably united.[82]

The journal praised Lord Louis Mountbatten who like Curzon had admonished broader visions of scientific investigation to solve the ills of society. The journal quoted Mountbatten in an address to radio engineers in which he suggested that "the scientist has been too much inclined to sit in his ivory tower, washing his hands of the results of his discoveries and inventions. The world is moving fast, and it is up to the scientist to see that it does not move downhill."[83] Weston Price stood as a perfect example beside Albert Howard of a scientist not bought off by capitalist industry; who investigated nutrition among hunter-gather societies in and outside the British Empire. He had "found all over the face of the earth, groups of so called primitive peoples who had learned to live in harmony with their surrounding."[84]

In a book review of *Thoughts on Feeding* by Lionel Picton, another reviewer pointed out the distinction between true agricultural interests, and "our Ministry of Agriculture." Government agencies in Britain almost always represented vested interests versus the honor roll of true scientists, most of whom worked in the British Empire, and the Indian government in particular. Into the hallowed ranks of such true scientists as Rayner, Howard, and McCarrison, the author placed Picton.[85] In a defiant note, the author of the review concluded that,

> If a Government cannot be persuaded to express this new knowledge of human nutrition in a practical form, even if it means a complete regulation of our national agriculture, even if it means war with Big Business and the financial interests, then that Government must go.[86]

When Albert Howard died October 20, 1947, the *Organic Farming Digest* reprinted an obituary from an English magazine, *The Guild Gardener,* that contrasted the "two schools of agricultural science."[87] One school, as Howard had put it, learned more and more about less and less, while the other learned more and more about nature, and took, as Howard had, "the Indian peasant, the cattle, and the whole army

---

[82] Ibid., 32.
[83] Harold White, "Whiter Civilization," *Organic Farming Digest*, 1/7 (October–December, 1947): 22.
[84] Ibid.
[85] A. G. Badenoch, "Review of *Thoughts on Feeding*, by Lionel James Picton, *Organic Farming Digest*, 1/7 (October–December, 1947): 26–7.
[86] Ibid., 29.
[87] "A Tribute to the Late Sir Albert Howard," *Organic Farming Digest*, 1/9 (April–June, 1948): 5. See also Louise Howard, File: 1947 Biography Sheet, *Matthaei Family Archive*, Birmingham, UK. Another compilation of the basic ideas and finding of Howards career, by Louise Howard, is "The Green Leaf: A Selection of Extracts from the Writings of the late Sir Albert Howard," *The Albert Howard Foundation of Organic Husbandry* 4 (Undated, 1948?).

of underground workers—earthworms, bacteria, and soil fungi" for its teachers. "England preferred the first type of agricultural school, the specialist. But the great outer world has accepted him [Howard] wholeheartedly... Reports pour in from every part of the British Empire giving vivid accounts of plantations which were wearing out and crops becoming disease-ridden, now cured through practising the full cycle of soil fertilization." The "democratic government" in Britain however was run by "rackets" and "the very force of this movement has, of course, brought reactions from what are known as vested interests."[88]

As the term "Commonwealth" began to replace references to the British Empire, a similar unique role for agricultural science along organic lines was articulated. The editor of the January–March 1949 issue of the *Organic Farming Digest* cited with approval the comments made by John Boyd Orr, who served as the first Director-General of the United Nations' Food and Agricultural Organization. The British Commonwealth had "more manpower," Orr argued, more land, and more nations, than any other entity, and she could lead the world in "good husbandry which can bring salvation." America looked down on Britain, and treated her as of "little account in world affairs." But America had run out of land, and Americans were ruining the land they had. "We are the people who can give the lead. We in Britain must stop looking to America."[89] Interestingly the separation between an imperial and capitalist science expressed by the *Organic Farming Digest* was a reflection of a worldview that was anti-finance, anti-bureaucratic, and pro-empire.

We see in the *Organic Farming Digest* and a select list of organic journals throughout the British Empire an archival bridge that has been largely missing in the historical literature. They reveal how the organic farming movement on the political right adopted a critique of capitalism that would soon segue into a broader environmental movement situated largely on the political left. How did this come about? After the Second World War, the loss of the Empire in the next few decades led to the loss of a positive imperial science that had served to oppose the narratives of vested capitalist interests. Soon not imperial science, but scientific outsiders provided this opposition, many, but not all, on the left of the political spectrum: they spoke appealingly to popular audiences and replaced the role of pro-imperial spokesmen who had offered such devastating critiques of vested capitalist interests. Outsiders like Rachel Carson—also mentioned in the *Organic Farming Digest*— and thousands involved in the counter-culture movement of the 1960s joined in the critique. Of the imperial and aristocratic elements little remains, with the exception of a few very high-profile figures like Prince Charles, whose support for organic farming continues to tap into an environmental tradition of scientific narrative on the sidelines of mainstream professional and scientific institutions. Having moved from right to left, organic farming and the rising environmental movement began to move to the center of the political mainstream.

[88] Ibid., 6.
[89] "The World Food Situation," *Organic Farming Digest*, 1/12 (January–March, 1949): 1–4.

DESICCATION THEORY AND SOUTH AFRICA

Debates in Australia and South Africa raged over land degradation, most particularly, soil erosion, the loss of soil fertility, and desiccation. Links between encroaching desertification and farming practice had already been made by a Drought Commission in 1923 and a Native Economic Commission of 1932.[90] These commissions raised the fear that the dunes of the Kalahari that crossed the border with Botswana and Namibia threatened to march southward, and the southern semi-arid Karoo—where South African famers practiced pastoral agriculture—threatened to expand outwards and destroy prime agricultural land. Officials advanced the conservation movement in South African with a special concern for soil conversation, finding the principles of organic farming a useful allied cause. Many feared that dustbowls—as happened in the United States during the 1930s—would soon devastate South African farmland and threaten the civilization that white settlers had built.[91]

Organic farming in South Africa overlapped with conventional farming practices, and drew from the global network of organic experts and enthusiasts in the British world. Policy developed and practiced in South Africa in turn affected policy in other parts of Africa and the British Empire, influencing the environmental movement at large.[92] Articles in the *Veld Trust News*, which reached a large body of readers involved with farming, and the bulletin of the *Organic Soil Association of South Africa* highlighted the dangers of desiccation. The threat divided into four main concerns: (1) deforestation lessoned rainfall; (2) pastoral overgrazing led to the destruction of grasses, shrubs, and trees, with effects similar to deforestation—loss of water retention, erosion, and bare hills and valleys incapable of supporting farming of any sort; (3) industrial farming methods created erosion because chemical fertilizers did not return nutrients to the soil and thus destroyed the humus, the top layer of farmland; and (4) stock or crop farming on the edges of dunes and deserts stripped away the protective barriers that held the deserts within natural limits.

Organic farmers argued that abusive practices threatened agricultural production, the nutritional health of the plants, and thus also the animals and people by increased desertification and decreased rainfall. The immanent collapse of civilization, or at least of national health and security, was at stake. With these arguments in hand, organic farmers picked up on the main threads of the conservation movement and extended the thrust of the conservation movement into the 1950s and 60s, linking it with the growing environmental concerns of these decades. Organic farmers sought "all around reform" to put the pieces of environmental issues together: forestry and soil conservation, organic farming protocols, and the burgeoning health food movement, which provided a market for their produce. The Indore Method

---

[90] William Beinart and Lotte Hughes, *Environment and Empire* (Oxford, 2007), 304.
[91] A valuable study of these concerns is laid out in William Beinart, *The Rise of Conservation in South Africa: Settles, Livestock, and the Environment 1770–1950* (Oxford, 2008).
[92] Ibid., xvi, xix.

of Howard, along with reforestation, soil conversation methods, and a concern for the whole cycle of health from soil fertility to plants, animals and humans, checked "the advance of deserts" while "an increase in consumer co-operation" for organic foods would allow civilization to survive.[93] As one writer (Rolf Gardiner) claimed in *Organic Soil Association of South Africa*, a conversation with "Field Marshal Smuts in Cape Town" elicited the statement,

> Unless we take care, the white population of South Africa will be driven back to the coastal belt, and the interior will become a howling wilderness.[94]

In 1945 the *Veld Trust News*, a farming journal for both Afrikaans and British farmers, described the dreadful "march of the dunes" across South Africa. The "hungry sands of the Kalahari...spreading and increasing in the dry hot winds; the patches of drifting sand of the Free State where vegetation is gone" and the threat to the Cape meant farmers had to change their practices immediately. Such sand, blown by wind, "will eat through iron and steel." In Persia, it warned, a telephone pole lasts only eleven years; in Australia, "steel rails have been eaten away." This destructive force "has been let loose over large areas in South Africa today."[95]

Another writer warned that "death stalks" the land, with "'floods, drought, [and] destruction' as South Africa's constant companions." Hippos and crocodiles once abounded, it continued, where now all is dry, and earlier memoirs revealed the drastic changes that had taken place. The article described how the early explorer Francois le Vaillant penetrated a veld "more beautiful, the earth richer and more fertile" than he had seen before, with "nature more majestic" than seen today. Much of this, the author concluded had been swept away by poor grazing practices and bad farming.[96]

The pages of the *Veld Trust News* often repeated the exploits of empire foresters. It highlighted the suggestions of among others, E. P. Stebbing, an empire forester, who suggested planting a shelterbelt around the south Sahara to protect against the southern drift of the desert. This hugely ambitious and bold plan had not been implemented due to the Second World War and now "Death and the Desert were on the march. Drought was both a household word and a national problem." The same article quoted a 1916 South African Association for the advancement of Science report that stated,

> It is an established fact that for the last two hundred years or more there has been a steady and persistent decrease in the rainfall and an equally steady change in the character of it. The result we see today is the conversion of many parts of South Africa into what may almost be designated as desert. With these desert conditions extending, the whole productivity of the country is threatened.

[93] NA, *Organic Soil Association of South Africa* (Winter, 1957), 7.
[94] Rolf Gardiner, "Letter," *Organic Soil Association of South Africa* (Winter, 1957): 18.
[95] D. W. G. Shuttleworth, "Past, Present and Future," *Veld Trust News* (July, 1945): 3.
[96] Ibid.

While scientists debated how much of the climate change was an act of nature and not of man, the author concluded,

> Let us fully realise that alone they (windbreaks and dams) will not restore the rich and beautiful country the pioneers found. Since the earliest days, we have been destroying the vegetation of our country and so weakening our resistance to drought and erosion. Until we make a determined effort to restore to the country a thick blanket of veld and forest, any other attempts to hinder the drying up, washing away and impoverishment of our soil will prove to have been temporary measures.[97]

Geologists, taking a long-term view of climatic changes, often challenged these statements, telling instead a tale of climate change that spanned thousands of years and involved natural cycles in the expansion and contraction of deserts. Geologists explained the phenomenon, especially in the report of the Drought Investigation Commission in 1923, as a series of long-term cycles unaffected by the activities of man. This Commission contradicted farmers who remembered in their lifetime how climate had changed, rainfall lessened, and land dried out. Geologists "like Wayland, Leaky, and Nilsson" postulated "interpluvial" epochs where periods of dryness occur through global climate change. But farmers, including organic farmers, disagreed vehemently, and based their claims of massive environmental damage on their own experience on the land. In an article titled "All of Africa is Drying up" T. C. Robertson traced the history of how desiccation theory arose, relying on observations of the last 100 years. He noted that the missionary David Livingston, in his private journal, had observed that the shallow waters of Lake Ngami were a result of the drying out of the continent that had been happening "throughout the whole country." He wrote that, in the experience of farmers,

> The change could hardly be so rapid that a famer, basing his conclusions on the personal experience of one lifetime, would be able to trace its course.[98]

Other geologists and conservationists agreed however with the experience of farmers. Professor Schwartz, another geologist, showed that the water levels of Lake Ngami had risen and fallen many times in more recent human history. D. R. V. L. Bosazza wrote in "Are Deserts on the March?" that the geologists missed the definition of what a desert is. In the journal *Nature*, he argued that a desert is more than just the outcome of less rainfall. He posited that "The definition of a desert as being a landscape where the rate of soil erosion is greater than the rate of soil formation." He cited also J. MacDonald Holmes in "Soil Erosion in Australia and New Zealand" to argue that deserts come and go, and that this was caused greatly by the activity of humans.[99]

One of the key groups that advocated for organic methods in South Africa was the Organic Soil Association of Southern Africa (OSASA). It formed on July 13, 1948, in a public library in Johannesburg. A Mr. R. L. McKibbin gave a talk titled, "Life is in the Soil" and the people who gathered around him formed a committee

---

[97] Ibid., 9, 12.
[98] T. C. Robertson, "All of Africa is Drying up," *Velt Trust News* (November, 1949): 19, 20.
[99] D. R. V. L. Bosazza, "Are the deserts on the March?" *Velt Trust News* (December, 1949): 21, 23.

that then launched the OSASA bulletin, by the same name, one month later.[100] OSASA hammered away at the theme of desertification and soil loss, along with broader issues of nutrition, and the cycle of health from soil to plants, animals, and people. Like the movement in Britain, the other Dominions, and the United States, it presented a strong dose of amateur enthusiasm for a romantic attachment to rural values, and a mixed approach to science—supportive when evidence lent towards organic farming, and critical when it did not.

The response to William Ogg, Director of Rothamstead and President of the Society of Chemical Industries, is instructive. He had stated that there is "no scientific evidence to support views that fertilizers were injurious to soil, or to the health of plants, animals or human beings."[101] This provoked a question from the editor at OSASA, that was not calculated to endear scientists to the organic movement.

> What constitutes "scientific" evidence in the eyes of Sir William? . . . One is tempted to reply to such dogmatism that [quoting Shakespeare] "There are more things in Heaven and Earth than are dreamt of in thy philosophy!"[102]

Many scientists however did advocate views that appeared to support organic protocols. The OSASA bulletin highlighted the visit of Dr. Hugh Bennett, former head of the United States' Soil Conservation Service, when he surveyed soils in South Africa to remedy the erosion he found. He predicted that South Africa would lose 50 percent of its fertility in the coming twenty years if the government did not take drastic action.[103] Another source of official support proved to be the Extension Officers of the South African Department of Agriculture. The country was divided into Conservation Districts that were then subdivided into Extension Areas each under the direct supervision of a separate officer. A District Committee supervised each district with the committee composed of farmers, government members, and scientists.[104] The organic farming community had a far more positive view of this bureaucratic structure in South Africa than in the United Kingdom, because rather than pushing for more fertilizers, Conservation Districts tended to support organic protocols. Besides advocating for improved farming and soil conservation movements, they also recommended composting with Howard's Indore Method as the prime protocol. They functioned as "vigilantes, assuring adherence to rules and regulations." Organic farming enthusiasts viewed the Extension Officers as they had viewed officials of the British Empire, "withdrawn from the web of vested interests and political intrigue."[105]

---

[100] NA "10th Year Anniversary Number," *The Organic Soil Association of Southern Africa* (Winter, 1958): 2–3.

[101] As quoted in NA, *Organic Soil Association of Southern Africa* (Winter, 1955): 1.

[102] Ibid.

[103] Ibid., 3. B. Dodson, "A Soil Conservation Safari: Hugh Bennett's 1944 Visit to South Africa," *Environment and History* 11 (2005): 35–53.

[104] The South African 1948 Soil Conservation Act, reflecting similar legislation in the United States, made provision for Districts and their Committees.

[105] Ibid., 4–6.

The OSASA bulletin presented a clear bridge between the conservation movement and the burgeoning environmental ideas that began to form in the 1950s. Reading through the journal from 1955 to 1962 reveals the insights that would within a decade become standard ideas of the modern environmental movement. OSASA advocated that: (1) the conservation movement had been too utilitarian; (2) nature existed for its own sake and for its own rights and enjoyment; (3) that food processing and chemicals were a danger to human health and to the whole environment, particularly wildlife;[106] (4) that food should be eaten raw as much as possible;[107] (5) that the radiation of the atomic age presented a unique and new danger to human survival and health;[108] (6) that television threatened our health; (7) that consumerism left us spiritually dead and empty; (8) and that ecology taught us that humans are too successful in our struggle for survival against nature—to such an extent that humans and all life on earth were in imminent danger.[109]

The OSASA bulletin sounded an apocalyptic alarm linking Howard's Indore protocols to the survival of the human race.

> The Association is, in many ways, a crusade in support of a conviction. This conviction is that unless we do something positive fairly soon to maintain or restore the fertility to our soils, there won't be many really healthy human beings living, except in isolated places.[110]

Eve Balfour also credited OSASA as "one of the very first national or regional associations to become affiliated with the world [Soil Association] organization."[111] Louise Howard acknowledged their work and fervency, predicting that the devoted pioneers in South Africa would eventually bring success with a "snowball effect" for the ideas of Albert Howard.[112] She could not but have been impressed with a group that argued that the Indore Method gave such "pure delight" from composting making that it "should be declared a sport."[113]

LOUISE HOWARD AND THE ENVIRONMENTAL MOVEMENT

A series of organic farming related newsletters and magazines came and went in the 1940s–50s but one in particular, run personally by Louise Howard hugely impacted the growth of organic farming and, in particular, served as a bridge between the conservation movement, the first stage of the environmental movement, and the broadening consciousness of modern environmentalism. As mentioned previously, Lionel Picton edited *News-Letter on Compost*. When Picton dedicated himself to

---

[106] NA, *Organic Soil Association of Southern Africa* (Winter, 1957): 8–16.   [107] Ibid.
[108] NA, *Organic Soil Association of Southern Africa* (Winter 1956): 17–18.
[109] NA, *Organic Soil Association of Southern Africa* (Winter, 1955): 62.
[110] NA, *Organic Soil Association of Southern Africa* (Christmas, 1959): 1.
[111] Eve Balfour, *Organic Soil Association of Southern Africa* (Winter, 1958): 17.
[112] Ibid., 17–18.   [113] Ibid., 11.

other writing projects, Albert Howard took over the editing of the journal and renamed it *Soil and Health*. The first issue appeared in February 1946 and he edited it until his death.[114]

Louise built on a phrase Howard had used in public speeches, "writing our answer on the land" and turned it into a publication series. Albert suggested that experiments and official sponsorship for the Indore Method were no longer necessary because they could write the answer on the land with demonstrated results. Taking this phrase, Louise launched a new series of publications that would show how mother nature would make the case for organic farming by successful examples that could not be ignored. The Albert Howard Foundation of Organic Husbandry, founded by Louise, published the series of *Our Answer to the Land*, from 1950–53. The first issue gave a summary of Howard's work, and was followed with testimonies from gardeners. It detailed the global impact of the Indore Method, tracing out a list of countries where farmers and gardeners had success-fully practiced the Indore Method, including Britain, North America, Australia, New Zealand, and then numerous British imperial holdings in Africa, Asia, and a few European countries such as Italy, France, the Netherlands, Germany, Denmark, and Sweden.[115]

The sources of these testimonies point to the lack of scientific and professional bodies sponsoring organic enterprises, as the movement went into abeyance during decolonization from 1947 onward. The series did point to some limited successes at the governmental level. Some urban councils in England had sponsored the composting of sewage waste, a key component of Albert and Louise Howard's strategy to revolutionize agriculture. W. S. Baldwin, Agricultural Executive Officer of Manchester City Council, made a contribution on a demonstration compost pile that gathered interest in a city exhibition. Manchester in fact had used com-posting as a form of waste disposal—less to return nutrients to the soil and more as a way of "controlled tipping," that is, using bacteria to properly break down waste to reduce noxious odors and disease threat.[116]

The Union of South Africa sponsored an education effort aimed at encouraging composting, highlighted in *Our Answer to the Land* which reprinted in 1950 a 1942 article from the South African *Farmer's Weekly*. A Captain J. M. Mowbray in Southern Rhodesia discussed how many Africans had been taught composting, and more examples like this abounded including letters from composting and gar-dening societies. An obscure publisher in the United States, J. I. Rodale, converted to organic farming after reading these examples, and would soon become a major player in the organic movement in the United States. What this series illustrated was how a movement operating only a few years after Albert Howard had turned its hopes for a breakthrough from commercial farming, to gardening. Rodale had asked Albert Howard to be associated with his new venture, *Organic Farming and*

[114] Philip Conford, *The Development of the Organic Network: Linking People and Themes, 1945–95* (Edinburgh, 2011), 95.

[115] Louise Howard, *Our Answer to the land* (1950), 1.

[116] The city of Manchester published a monograph on the subject. See Bertram B. Jones and Frederick Owen, *Some Notes on the Scientific Aspects of Controlled Tipping* (Manchester, 1934).

Gardening, and this soon changed to *Organic Gardening,* strategically dropping "farming" from the title and focused on a wider audience of homeowners who wished to raise fruits and vegetables in their back yards.[117]

After Albert's death, Louise founded the Albert Howard Foundation of Organic Husbandry, and changed the name of the newsletter from *Soil and Health* to *Health and the Soil,* which then closed down in 1951. Louise then launched *The Albert Howard News Sheet (AHNS)* in May 1953 which ran to December 1965. The *AHNS* is especially interesting because it details a murky era after Albert Howard's death, and reveals the central role played by Louise Howard in promoting the organic farming movement in its this new middle stage. The optimism of the early movement under Howard still existed: indeed, allied organizations such as the Soil Association in Britain and its growing number of international affiliates gained in membership and influence during this period with a small but growing number of small farmers, gardeners, and enthusiasts. But Albert Howard did not join the Soil Association, much as it owed its very existence to his ideas. He objected to its disregard of exact science. Louise also kept her distance from the Soil Association for a number of years and worked on her own. Her role in promoting organic farming and a host of broader environmental issues has never been investigated, and the recovery of the full *AHNS* archive, along with her other papers, highlights for the first time her central contribution to the early environmental movement in the 1950s.

The *AHNS* stood in a web of broad conservation and environmental contacts. It had international reach, and became an indispensable clearing house of information that collected letters and observations from many contributors. It also republished a plethora of articles and news of allied concern—it highlighted any breakthroughs on environmental issues. The *AHNS* kept Albert and Louise Howard's approach to organic farming at the center of the small but growing environmental movement, influencing other activists and organizations, and carefully keeping the focus on the call for massive societal change. Through detailed news clippings, reports, and testimonials Louise kept a readable and folksy tone to the news sheet, but one that eschewed mysticism and naïve statements that could discredit the movement, such as notions from Steiner's bio-dynamic movement or sloppy assertions of sentiment or simplistic health cures that could not be substantiated.

Louise had a grand strategy, as did Albert Howard. They focused on municipal composting as the keystone of their grand plan for societal change that, if adopted, would change the entire way humans conducted agriculture and disposed of waste. Howard's Indore Method had been shown to work not merely for composting vegetable matter for the fields, but also as a system that could take urban human waste and, mixed with a wide variety of plant wastes, transform it into a quality fertilizer for the soil.[118] In 1946 Howard gave a paper to the

[117] See Louise Howard, *Our Answer to the Land* (1950–53). See also Eric C. Gilles, "Composting" reprinted from *Farm and Forest* 2 (1946): 92–102. See also Letter, E. C. Gilles to Louise Howard (March 24, 1950), File: 1950, *Matthaei Family Archive,* Birmingham, UK.

[118] For how the Indore Method was modified to process Bangalore sewage into compose see C. N. Acharya, *Preparation of Compost Manure from Town Wastes* (Delhi, 1946). This was followed up

Annual General Meeting of the Institute of Sewage Purification. In this paper
he argued that sewage should not merely be purified, but fully utilized so that it
produced fertilizer for raising "high-quality food" that would form, in the future,
"the public health system of tomorrow." He could hardly speak to a more friendly
audience, effectively telling the engineers of municipal sewage systems that their
work could form the basis of future agriculture and improve human health. Howard
predicted that municipal composting would soon be "the rule in this country."[119]
An encouraging discussion followed. But the practical challenges were massive:
the plan required hiring more engineers, spending more money, convincing city
governments to take action, and overcoming the reluctance of the British population
to eat food grown with human waste.[120]

In 1947, right before his death, Albert Howard published a last article praising
the effects of treated sewage sludge on his garden in Blackheath. He recommended
water hyacinth and other weeds as perfect plant material to mix with the composted sewage sludge produced. If an "alert" country such as the United States with
a growing progressive community could lead the way, he was sure Britain and then
the British Empire would soon follow. A world revolution in agriculture and
human health could then be within reach.[121] Interestingly, not municipal composting, but the wider focus in the newsletter had the greatest impact. Albert and
Louise had a habit of commenting on all things environmental and this in turn
linked up their readers to broader environmental concerns, and concurrently hitched
organic farming to a growing web of readers and activists who shared a broader
environmental focus. The grand project that envisioned widespread municipal
composting, however, never materialized outside of a few isolated successes.[122] But
the broader concerns gained ground.

by a conference in India on compost, held at New Delhi, in December 1947. The *Hindustan Times*
(December 20, 1947) covered the opening of this meeting. The conference discussed composting both
cow dung and human excreta to improve crop production and was chaired by the Minister of food and
agriculture. See *Proceedings of the First All India Conference on Compost Held at New Delhi, December
16–17*, (New Delhi, 1947). See also C. N. Acharya, *Preparation of Compost Manure from Farm, Village
and Town Wastes* (ND). File: 1947, *Matthaei Family Archive*, Birmingham, UK.

[119] Albert Howard, "Activated and Digested Sewage Sludge in Agriculture & Horticulture," *Soil
and Health* 2/1 (1947): 19.

[120] Ibid., 13. Howard cited an earlier source for the discovery of "activated sludge"—that is, sewage
sludge fully aerated and reduced by bacteria and other micro-organisms to form a clear liquid, separate
from the solids, and not given to putrification. Arden and Lockett, "Experiments on the Oxidation of
Sewage without the Aid of Filters," *Journal of the Society of Chemical Industry*, 30/10 (May 30, 1914):
523–39. Howard also cited a medical colleague Lionel J. Picton. For a discussion that followed this
paper see Albert Howard, "Activated and Digested Sewage Sludge in Agriculture & Horticulture," *Soil
and Health* 2/2 (1947): 65–78.

[121] Albert Howard, "Dried Activated and Digested Sewage Sludge for the Compost Heap," *Organic
Gardening*, (February, 1947): 13–14. Albert Howard published one more article before his death in
1948 in the *Organic Gardening* magazine—"The Animal as our Farming Partner," *Organic Gardening*,
(September, 1947): 17–19. This method was used on a small scale for 1,600 municipal areas in India
by 1952. A broad discussion of this process in India can be found in *Compost and Sewage Bulletin*, 5/2
(Delhi, 1952). See also *Compost and Sewage Bulletin*, 5/1 (Delhi, 1952).

[122] A good history of the experiments and technology of municipal composting in the twentieth
century is found in L. F. Diaz, M. de Bertoldi, W. Bidlingmaier and E. Stentiford eds., *Compost Science
and Technology (Volume 8 of Waste Management)* (London, 2011).

As a widow, Louise personally followed up on Albert's work. She, like Albert, focused on municipal composting because of its potential to globally change the foundation of agriculture. Louise understood that organic composting in gardens would continue to advance, as would local markets for organically grown food. But she did not feel that massive structural change could be expected from the bottom up with only a few demonstration farms or farming enthusiasts hawking their fruits and vegetables in market stalls. Critics eagerly pointed out that in the age of the machine farms did not produce enough manure—or even vegetable wastes—to produce the composting required for organic farming on a large scale. Louise understood that the widespread transformation of industrial farming to organic farming could only happen if the wastes of major urban cities could be recovered and returned to the soil. She focused therefore on urging a small coterie of lobbyists to persuade city councils to adopt composting of sewage sludge on a widespread basis. This alone could provide the compost for large enterprises, and truly fulfill Howard's dream of changing the face of farming from an exploitive enterprise of mining minerals from the soil to a sustainable relationship between human consumption and the soil. Strategically, municipal composting was the biggest gamble the Howards took—one that, if it succeeded, would fulfill their dreams, and fulfill them quickly.

In addition to steering lobbying efforts toward city councilors, Louise tried to personally win over James Griffiths, Secretary of State for the Colonies, as a convert to municipal composting. In his position Griffiths oversaw vast territories in the British Empire, and could push for policy changes in the processing of urban wastes. She approached him as a representative of the Albert Howard Foundation for Organic Husbandry (AHFOH) and recommended two readings on municipal composting, one from Hugh Martin-Leake, a scientist and former colleague of Albert Howard in India, and another from an engineer, L. P. Brunt, who had published a pamphlet titled *Municipal Composting* with the AHFOH.[123] She also pointed Griffiths to Howard and Wad's *The Waste Products of Agriculture*. She wrote that the "moment is suitable for a wide extension of the practice of town and village composting" as evidence came back from successful trials in Nigeria and Kenya that had productive ramifications for agricultural production. Merely his encouragement alone, she urged, without the expenditure of extra funds from the Colonial Office, could spur local officials to instigate municipal composting. There is no evidence, however, that she received a response to her letter.[124]

---

[123] L. P. Brunt, *Municipal Composting Albert Howard Foundation of Organic Husbandry* (London, 1949).

[124] See Letter: Louise Howard to James Griffiths (May 20, 1950), File 1950: *Matthaei Family Archive*, Birmingham, UK; Draft Letter: Louise Howard to James Griffiths amended by Mr. Haynes (1950), *Matthaei Family Archive*, Birmingham, UK; Letter: Lousie Howard to Viscount Bledisloe (May 8, 1950), *Matthaei Family Archive*, Birmingham, UK; Letter: Louise Howard Letter to Lord Douglas (May 8, 1950), *Matthaei Family Archive*, Birmingham, UK; Letter: Louise Howard Letter to Earl of Portsmouth (May 8, 1950), *Matthaei Family Archive*, Birmingham, UK; Letter: Louise Howard Letter to John Patterson (May 8, 1950), *Matthaei Family Archive*, Birmingham, UK; Letter: J. H Patterson, to Louise Howard (May 17, 1950), *Matthaei Family Archive*, Birmingham, UK; Letter: Lord Douglas to Louise Howard (May 13, 1950), *Matthaei Family Archive*, Birmingham, UK. An account of

Albert Howard's Indore Method appeared to solve a major problem when applied to municipal composting—how did one return liquid sewage sludge to the fields? The *AHNS* published a contribution from a consulting engineer, J. C. Wylie, who played an important role in advocating municipal composing in Great Britain. Wylie notes that when Howard returned from India in 1935 he was shocked at how, in the quest for public hygiene, the sanitation services destroyed organic matter that could have returned fertility to the soil. Howard's ideas advanced very little, however, until he presented a paper at a conference sponsored by the Institute of Public Cleansing in June 1939 at Scarborough. Howard purported to have solved the problem of turning wet sludge into usable fertilizer while simultaneously killing off the dangerous bacteria. The conference generally agreed that inciner-ation of sewage sludge, the current practice, burnt too much fuel and destroyed the good bacterial and with it any hope of a useful fertilizer. Composting according to the Indore Method (mixing the sludge with vegetable matter), solved the problem. One disciple, J. L. Davies, applied his method to the small municipality of Leatherhead, in Surrey. Rather than merely laying out sludge in drying beds, he mixed the sludge with plant material and then pulverized the mix into a mush. He then fermented the sludge not in drying pans but in compost piles using the Indore Method. This dried out the sludge while killing the dangerous microorgan-isms. The compost had the added benefit that it could be stockpiled in large amounts and was ready for application to the fields.[125]

During the Second World War research at Reading University had confirmed Howard's claims that the Indore Method produced compost ready for application as a fertilizer. But the lead researcher, Professor Stoughton, concluded that the compost thus produced contributed little of nutritional value to the soil. Research at the University of Bristol by a Dr. Bould confirmed this finding and argued that the value of the compost was negligible because it contained low levels of nitrogen, potash, and phosphates. Howard and his followers however rejected these findings, particularly the last observation. The Indore Method, they argued, was never designed to compete with chemical fertilizers in terms of the level of nitrogen, pot-ash, and phosphates. Rather the Indore Method was predicated on the idea that organic composting promoted bacteria that through the mycorrhizal process allowed plants to absorb nutrients at a higher rate.[126]

J. W. Scharff's experience with compost and the health of Singaporean workers before the fall of Singapore to the Japanese can be found in The County Palatine of Chester Local Medical and Panel Committee, *Report on the Garden Competition and other Nutritional Interests* (1942), 12–13. Louise's communication to Griffiths came with letters of support from Sir John Patterson, K. B. E., and Viscountt Bledisloe.

[125] Wylie summarizes the history of Howard's impact on municipal composting in an issue of the *AHNS*. The *AHNS* bulletins are numbered but not dated, though the approximate date can be inferred from references in the text. Many of the items also have no title. See J. C. Wylie, *AHNS* 64: 1.

[126] A colleague of Albert Howard's, formerly Director of Agriculture, United Provinces, India, and Principle of the Imperial College of Tropical Agriculture, Trinidad, wrote a treatise on behalf of the Trustees of the Albert Howard Foundation of Organic Husbandry in 1949 summarizing the experiments and trials on municipal composting around the world. See H. Martin-Leake, "How can we use our Sewage and our refuse?", *Albert Howard Foundation of Organic Husbandry*, 2 (1949).

There were some limited successes. Various municipal localities took on composting to solve their particular problems. The Rural Water Supply and Sewage Act of 1944, passed by Britain's coalition government, attempted to address a shortage of water by discouraging the dumping of sewage into streams and rivers. To comply with this, the historic County of Dumfries in Scotland launched seventy-nine small sewage plants that produced sludge. The county councilors, consisting largely of farmers, supported the proposal to mix the sludge with straw and compost it by the Indore Method in order to dispose of the waste. Needing to add no microorganisms but only those indigenous to the waste saved time and money and handling. A few more successes followed. A composting plant was constructed at the small town of Kirkconnel in southwest Scotland on Indore lines, and a similar installation followed in Jersey. The introduction of new composting plants that adopted the "Dano" system proved both compact and labor saving. This system rotated cylinders that blew air into the sewage and speeded the composting process. In 1955 the Edinburgh Corporation proceeded at Seafeliedl with a "Dano" plant as did a few other municipalities.[127]

Further advances met strong headwinds. The Natural Resources Technical Committee in 1954 supported the Bristol and Reading research and concluded that the resulting compost, though harmless, was not helpful to plant nutrition. Louise Howard complained that local municipalities that carried out composting schemes faced hostility. "It has to be recorded," she wrote many years after the Scarborough Conference, that one project in Radcliffe, as in so many others,

> had to be carried through by the local authorities...in the teeth of opposition from the Ministry of Housing and Local government, who refused loan sanction in 1957. Only after two years of "long and determined negation" was sanction obtained in 1959.[128]

However, these small successes proved temporary. In 1963 after decades of effort, she admitted that in Britain and the USA there was almost no widespread municipal composting. After twenty-five years Louise could look back and remark that while there was still hope, little advance had been made.[129]

While the push for municipal composting largely failed, Louise Howard oversaw a small but robust movement that fed into a broadening environmental consciousness in the late 1940s and into the 1960s. Louise ran the *AHNS* long enough to witness the organic farming movement impact society far beyond the small organizations it spawned around the globe. The *AHNS* contained in embryo form, almost all of the later characteristics that we define in the modern environmental movement from the 1960s to the present. It illustrated that organic farming literature in this period not only kept alive the ideals of the conservation movement, but also formed the core of the later environmental movement, revealing not two separate stages of environmentalism, but rather one single growth. The *AHNS* while focusing

[127] Others at Craigmillar and Poswerhall, and then Dumbarton, followed, in 1960, as did the Borough of Radcliffe and Midlothian County Council. See Wylie, *AHNS* 64: 4.
[128] Louise Howard, *AHNS* 68: 1.   [129] Louise Howard, *AHNS* 90: 1.

most of its stories on the United States, UK, Australia, and South Africa, also included copious reports from almost every other part of the world. The reports included reprinted news found elsewhere. Usually the reports involved in the *AHNS* featured organic farming activists synthesizing new information from journals, newsletters, and scientific papers from around to the globe. The *AHNS* assessed and analyzed disparate data and synthesized discrete information into a single environmental world view that revealed a comprehensive and balanced environmental consciousness well before the 1970s.

The *AHNS* reported optimistically, even naively, on composting and reforestation in Communist China. This contrasts with the realism shown by the FAO reports that fully understood that the use of manure and the introduction of pigs for fertilizer in China during the 1950s were stopgap measures until chemical fertilizers replaced composting. One writer in the *AHNS* however, found encouragement in the temporary agricultural policies. Cleve E. Sandy reported the results of two visits to China in 1952 and then in 1960. The advance in eight years, he enthused, was amazing. "Deforested hills were covered with trees," and "literally millions of trees almost all of them under six years old" showed the government had carried out "the grandiose official re-afforestation program" to cover one third of China in trees. Additionally, reservoirs and dams checked the flooding of the Yellow River. Terracing protected the soil and irrigation had increased.[130] "These measures go hand in hand with plans to step up supplies of animal manure and above all of compost." The government aimed to place a pig on every farm. With green manure and other compostable material Mao had launched a new "shock movement." This report however admitted that "chemical fertilizers are also to be increasingly manufactured to boost the fertility of worn-out areas, but their role is always secondary to that of compost." Sandy romantically and erroneously concluded that "Chinese agriculture is on the road to true organic farming and the Chinese peasant at his best remains, as he has been through forty centuries, the organic farmer par excellence."[131]

The AHNW was equally optimistic on the Soviet Union. Louise reported on an article in *The Times*, March 6, 1964, of an interview with Nikita Khrushchev. He claimed that in order to avoid dust-bowl conditions, such as those that affected North America in the 1930s, 100 million acres would be alternated between growing grain and the husbandry of animals, such as sheep and horses. The *AHNS* titled this "Russia sees the red light," by which Louise indicated that Russia had to stop industrial farming and begin some form of natural composting. This, however, did not happen. Only small private plots (that produced 30 percent of Soviet agricultural output) resorted occasionally to composting.[132]

Broader issues abounded in the *AHNS*. It often focused on the effect on birdlife of spraying insecticides on crops around the world. In one example, it traced the

---

[130] Louise Howard, *AHNS* 65 1.   [131] Ibid., 2.

[132] For an account of how the agricultural rhetoric and actual reforms differed, see Auri C. Berg "Reform in the Time of Stalin: Nikita Krushchev and the Fate of the Russian Peasantry" Dissertation, Doctor of Philosophy, University of Toronto, 2012. Louise, Howard, *AHNS* 93: 1, Louise Howard, *AHNS* 78: 1.

Audubon Society survey from field inspections that found wildlife devastated by aerial spraying, in this case, in the south-eastern states of Alabama, Georgia, Louisiana, Mississippi, Florida, Teas, Arkansas, North and South Carolina. It noted that,

> Almost all wild life was affected. Even two months after spraying animals newly dead were picked up. Insects were the first to die in alarming numbers, including predator species useful for the control of other species. The effect on bird life was terrible. Quail were decimated or wiped out in the treated areas of Alabama and Texas. In the first-named States in a sixty acre clover field out of 41 birds' nests with eggs 38 were abandoned or destroyed. Losses in bird population up to 85 and even 93 per cent were registered in some places.[133]

The *AHNS* reprinted or summarized studies that traced the growing alarm about DDT (along with other chemicals) and its devastating effect on wildlife—birds in particular—and human health. These reports were widespread before Rachel Carson published *Silent Spring*. In addition, the *AHNS* carefully recorded the debate on toxic sprays in agriculture in the House of Commons.[134]

The *AHNS* also focused on the dangers of pesticides in food and the danger of hormones in meat. Hexoestrol, an estrogen steroid, sprayed onto animal feed, increased the body mass of cattle and sheep. While the authorities at the United States Department of Agriculture (USDA) felt that residual amounts of hormones like hexoestrol would have a negligible effect on human health, the *AHNS* pointed out that hormones in milk and meat built up over time and could have unforeseen effects in humans.[135] Three decades later studies revealed the adverse human effect of this chemical and led the European Union in 1985 to ban the use of these products in meat.[136] The *AHNS* was also strewn with references to factory meats and reported widely on protests against factory farming, particularly protests from the National Farmers Union of England and Wales.[137] Louise and her organic farming associates raised the alarm on how vaccines not only threatened the quality of the meat from cattle and sheep, but—in the effort to wipe out diseases that spread in factory meat conditions—led to the "ruthless slaughter" of millions of animals to stop disease such as foot and mouth disease.[138]

The *AHNS* also served as a clearing house for legislation affecting chemical additives to food and water. Activists wrote in with progress reports keeping tabs on the global movement for whole foods free from chemicals. In one example, from West Germany, the *AHNS* reported on a Foods Act proposed by Member of Parliament Kate Stroel. Parliament passed the Act which established the principle that "all food additives are forbidden unless previously authorized by statutory regulation." This placed the burden on producers to get approval for additives

---

[133] Louise Howard, *AHNS* 51: 1–3.　　[134] Louise Howard, *AHNS* 57: 1.
[135] Louise Howard, *AHNS* 49: 1–20.
[136] N. T. Crosby, *Determination of Veterinary Residues in Food* (Cambridge, 1997), 162–4. See also "The European Union's Ban on Hormone-Treated Meat," CRS Report for Congress. Available online at: http://congressionalresearch.com/RS20142/document.php?study=THE+EUROPEAN+UNIONS+BAN+ON+HORMONE-TREATED+MEAT [accessed August 23, 2017].
[137] Louise Howard, *AHNS* 96: 3.　　[138] Louise Howard, *AHNS* 74: 4.

rather than merely waiting for evidence of damage.[139] Water purity also greatly concerned the *AHNS*. Louise argued caution in the use of fluoride in water, predating the widespread opposition of this mineral to water supplies. When an Edinburgh physician, A. G. Badenoch, in 1949 summarized the progress of the organic farming movement under the leadership of Albert and then Louise Howard, he presented his findings to the Royal Society of Arts, London and argued that fluoride—which circulated broadly in nature—rarely concentrated naturally and was often totally absent in water supplies. He noted,

> Fluorine is obviously not an element to be played with, either literarily or metaphorically, and the introduction of fluorides, even in small doses, as a method of hardening the enamel of children's teeth is probably not without risk.[140]

Other environmental concerns, such as the use of alternative energy, abounded. Louise Howard co-authored with Hugh Martin-Leake, a former colleague of her husband, a pamphlet promoting the use of methane gas composted from farmyard manure. Louise and Leake pointed out the noble history of the idea, when Pasteur recommended creating methane from manure to the French Academy of Sciences in 1884. The method had multiple advantages they argued. Decentralization of energy supplies gave more independence to small farmers and put less strain on the national resources—particularly the use of oil. The Second World War had brought to the fore the need for farming to be independent of outside supplies. The Inter-African Information Bureau for Soil Conservation and Land Utilization, a French Colonial organization, forwarded a comprehensive historic bibliography of alternative methane production. The *AHNS* reprinted the bibliography. These few examples highlight the fact that a wide array of global organizations with environmental concerns actively used and depended on the *AHNS* as a clearing house of cutting-edge ideas for environmental reform.[141]

Louise published accounts of global water pollution, and reported on pollution control efforts in the United States, Britain, Canada, Europe, and elsewhere. The newsletter also preached for landscape beautification after mining, suggested solutions to growing landfill problems, and even raised the alarm about the build-up of garbage on the South Pole.[142] The *AHNS* was also strewn with references to the dangers of exotic species and the threat of non-indigenous animals and plants to local ecosystems.[143] The *AHNS* kept tabs on almost every issue that many erroneously assume originated in a later environmental movement.

---

[139] Louise Howard, *AHNS* 53: 2.

[140] A. G. Badenoch, "The Minerals in Plant and Animal Nutrition," *The Albert Howard Foundation of Organic Husbandry* (June, 1949).

[141] H. Martin-Leake and Louise E. Howard, "Methane Gas from Farmyard Manure," *The Albert Howard Foundation of Organic Husbandry*, 9 (1952): 1–10.

[142] Louise Howard, *AHNS* 73: 1; Louise Howard, *AHNS* 78:4; Louise Howard, *AHNS* 48: 2.

[143] Louise Howard, *AHNS* 76: 4. An exception seemed to be Eucalypt plantations, which Louise supported because the reduced the strains on native forests. See Louise Howard, *AHNS* 94: 3. This follows Albert Howard's suggestion of using Red Gum (exotic eucalypt) to break up a hardened soil pan in parts of India. See Albert Howard, *Diary: November 13, 1937 to February 2, 1938, Notes on a Tour to Tea Estates in Sylhet and Cachar*: 30, File: 1938, *Matthaei Family Archive*, Birmingham, UK.

CONCLUSION

Howard's initial optimism that he could persuade the governments and farmers around the world to adopt the Indore process en masse faded in his latter years. The activism of the coterie of reformers he built around him did not however give up, even as hopes faded for official recognition. Rather the compost wars transitioned, with Howard at the lead, into more subversive and guerilla tactics that would prove to hold the movement steady for decades until broader acceptance finally came.

While the organic farming movement appeared to be in abeyance in the late 1940s and into the early 1960s, under the surface connections and issues formed that laid the foundation for not only the long-term success of the organic farming movement, but also for a growing environmental movement that grew directly out of the conservation movement, and then out of organic farming. The organic farming movement, particularly under Louise Howard's stewardship after 1947, was the middle stage of the *longue durée* of environmental consciousness, which had its roots in the early and mid-nineteenth century and continued to the present time. No comparable movement in the late 1940s and 1950s put all the issues of environmentalism together in this manner until the 1970s. Louise understood that the organic farming movement had launched something completely new and different, though when she wrote the following words in 1947, the phrase "environmental movement" had still not been in wide use.

> The history of the first ten years of the organic farming movement are above all interesting for the number and importance of the apparently extraneous topics which have gradually been collected and fitted into a great theory of natural law: these additions have eventually proved to be part of the whole.[144]

She could hardly have seen her own influence, and that the collective she helped build would support the most influential cultural change since the Industrial Revolution.

Louise had optimism for the future of this new movement. She noted that in Paris, a July 1964 conference of biologists emphasized,

> learning more about natural processes with a view to making more intelligent use of them and to working with rather than against, nature as far as possible.[145]

She also saw in this same issue, a change of attitude in the United States of America in 1960. The USDA had asked for an appropriation of $29 million to aid the non-chemical control of insects that are agricultural pests. These funds would be spent on research and sponsor studies on the effect of pesticides on food.[146] Even the mass media had picked up on the themes so prevalent in organic farming, with *The Times* lamenting the "slow poisoning of the land" in 1960—showing growing awareness of the very issues fervently pushed by the organic farming movement.[147]

---

[144] Louise E. Howard, "The birth of the organic farming movement," *Organic Farming Magazine*, 13/8 (September, 1948).
[145] Louise Howard, *AHNS* 97: 2.   [146] Ibid.
[147] As quoted in Louise Howard, *AHNS* 61: 2.

8

The Globalization of Organic Farming

From 1950–80 the environmental movement continued to evolve towards a more emphatic emphasis—but by no means a new one—on air pollution, water pollution, and the further protection of wildlife. One enduring theme between the earlier and later environmental movement—in which organic farming played a lead role—was the focus on ecology and human health. The environmental historian Samuel Hays argued that the middle period of the environmental movement in the 1950s and 60s, while "prompting some legislation victories...generated only limited institutional capability or political staying power."[1] Until the 1980s, despite some remarkable legislative advances, the movement in this middle period grew on the strength of "the citizen environmental movement."[2] Although gaining little access to scientific funding, having very little media support (other than letters to the editor or occasional media stories on interesting figures), and having almost no official support from government agencies, specialized groups on a plethora of environmental issues still continued to grow. Organic farming, more than any other allied environmental movement, preserved intact the older issues of the conservation movement—the perils of deforestation, the belief in ecological interdependence, and the fear of the toxic pollutants that undermined human health and wildlife. Organic farming activists communicated these concerns to other allied environmental movements and absorbed in return, other new trends. The period from the Second World War to the 1980s, however, marked a major shift in terms of acceptance of the organic narrative in many key parts of the world. Britain, the United States, South Africa, and Japan represented those parts of the world where the organic movement made the most startling progress in terms of membership, influence, and growth of consumer markets.

ORGANIC FARMING IN BRITAIN

A small group of organic farming enthusiasts, inspired by Eve Balfour's book *The Living Soil* (1943), founded the Soil Association on May 3, 1946, with Charles Kerr, a former member of parliament for the National Liberal Party, as President.[3]

---

[1] Samuel P. Hays, *Explorations in Environmental History* (Pittsburgh, 1998), 382–3.
[2] Ibid.
[3] The National government raised Kerr to the peerage in 1940 and he is often referred to as Lord Teviot. From 1951 to 1970 Lord Bradshaw served as President.

Out of 109 founding members, almost all of them supported Howard's Indore Method for organic farming, with any number of variations, linking the health of "soil, plant, animal and man."[4] While infighting limited its influence in the first few decades of its existence, the Soil Association substantially aided the efforts of Louise Howard to expand the influence of the Indore Method. The society sought,

> To bring together all those working for a fuller understanding of the vital relationships between soil, plant, animal and man. To initiate, co-ordinate and assist research in this field. To collect and distribute the knowledge gained so as to create a body of informed public opinion.[5]

Albert Howard attended this initial meeting, but then stopped actively supporting the group when he realized that a number of the founders combined his organic protocols with the decidedly unscientific and often mystical beliefs of Steiner. Louise also kept her distance too, though after Albert Howard's death she did agree to serve as Vice-President of the society for a few years. Balfour hinted at the difficulty she had working with Albert Howard in her memoir of him, "The Late Sir Albert Howard."[6] She suggested that he remained aloof from any organizations he did not found (though this is not actually true as he had worked closely on projects initiated by J. I. Rodale and many others). On Albert Howard's character, she pinpoints the difficulty of trying "to give an account of the man" who she felt was impatient and argued even when others "differed only in points of detail." This no doubt referred to their own disagreements—the mixing of mystical and non-scientific ideas with the science behind the Indore Method. But she remarked that, by the same token, he never took things personally and, while uncompromising, was "always courteous and charming." She confessed that "it is doubtful whether the Association would have come into being save as a result of the seed he had planted."[7]

The English fascist Jorian Jenks edited the new journal of the Soil Association, *Mother Earth*, until 1963.[8] Much like the *Albert Howard News Sheet* (*AHNS*), *Mother Earth* published and republished on almost every aspect of environmental thought, with a strong ecological concern that included the effect of chemicals on wildlife and the effects of pollution. The editor from 1964 to 1972, Robert Waller, also tackled environmental issues, but with a bent toward mysticism that both attracted and repelled.[9]

The Soil Association also made the occasional educational film. In 1950 it produced *The Cycle of Life* that dramatically played on the fear of desertification to support the Indore Method. The narration is apocalyptic, drawing on the conservationists' fear of global desertification. It stated that, "the deserts of today were the green pastures of yesterday" and portrayed Sahara-like scenes of sand dunes and arid lands with top soil blowing off, and houses swept out to sea by swollen

---

[4] Philip Conford, *The Origins of the Organic Movement* (Edinburgh, 2001), 101.
[5] As quoted in Phillip Conford and Patrick Holden, "The Soil Association," *Organic Farming: An International History*, ed. William Lockeretz (Oxfordshire, 2007): 187.
[6] Lady Eve Balfour, "The Late Sir Albert Howard," *Organic Gardening Magazine*, 13/8 (September, 1948).
[7] Ibid.   [8] Conford and Holden, "The Soil Association," 190.   [9] Ibid., 192.

floods. It rehearsed a well-known genealogy of conservationist ideas about desertification: Rome, Egypt, and Babylon all falling through the misuse of the soil. Britain, it concluded, was well on its way to becoming a desert. Interviewing Robert McCarrison on the connections between organic food and health, the film highlighted a segment on Albert Howard and his composting protocols, assuring the viewers that, when adopted by farmers, organic farming would save the earth from the fate of desertification. It concluded dramatically that the peoples of the earth had no idea of the grim future of famine and death that threatened them if industrial farming methods continued.

Lord Bradford served as President from 1951 to 1971, and under his leadership the Soil Association saw slow and steady growth, but with few breakthroughs that caught the national attention. However, this changed in 1971 when E. F. Schumacher—author of the ecological best seller, *Small is Beautiful: A Study of Economics as if People Mattered*—became President. Schumacher, one of the most important voices of the environmental movement in the 1970s, learned much of his environmental awareness from the organic farming movement. He joined the Soil Association in 1951, seeking advice on gardening. His biographer, Barbara Wood explains that his membership in this organic farming group "opened his eyes to a whole new way of thinking."[10]

Schumacher's father was a professor of economics at the University of Berlin and the family had the money, despite the devastation caused by the First World War, to send Ernst Schumacher to London for a visit. During his visit he immediately felt the anti-German attitudes of the English who, he complained in a letter to his mother, were "frightened of German recovery" and hell-bent on power and gold. Schumacher won a Rhodes scholarship to England to attend Oxford. Once in England he took his role as a representative of Germany very seriously and answered questions from fellow Oxford students who demanded an explanation for German support of Hitler. He vigorously defended his country. He explained that the Treaty of Versailles all but guaranteed support for someone like Hitler. Debating in the Union Club, he supported the motion "This House believes that England needs a Hitler" and explained that Hitler merely wanted to redress the slavery imposed by the allies on Germany and to free Germany from the lie of German war guilt.[11] Germany had a serious Jewish problem, he argued, and "Hitler's party will become less extreme the more it [the economy] grows." In the meantime, given the problems created by the allies and the Jews, "there is no doubt that in this respect something has to be done."[12]

His politics in youth were rightwing in a number of other respects. Staying at the International House at Oxford, he was irked by the "rather too many coloured people" and complained that "for God's sake, I am not allowed to say that here" and he added sarcastically, "that brotherhood may prevail."[13] He disapproved of Roosevelts "New Deal" and saw in Germany the example of the rampant inflation

[10] Philip Conford, *The Origins of the Organic Movement* (Edinburgh, 2001), 101.
[11] Barbara Wood, *E. F. Schumacher: His Life and Thought* (New York, 1984), 32–3.
[12] Ibid., 33.   [13] Ibid., 45.

that occurred with government spending, noting wryly that Roosevelt was the "greatest president since Hoover…"[14] His political views may have perhaps prepared him for an appreciation of organic farming decades later. He wrote in 1933 to the Warden of New College, G. K. Allen, that patriotism meant gratitude and a debt to the Fatherland for "we must never forget the soil upon which we have grown, and the organism of which we are part"—a sentiment, very much in line with not only fascism, but also the romantic farm literature prevalent in the 1930s.[15] He gladly accepted in England an invitation to speak at the pro-Nazi society, Friends of the New Germany, to justify the economic policies of the National Socialists.[16] While visiting the United States, he addressed an American crowd in New Jersey—unidentified by his biographer—explaining Hitler's policies in a favorable light, though he seemed politically aware of the need in the United States to reject overt anti-Semitism. When a number of Jewish members of the audience objected to his support of National Socialism, he replied sarcastically that "so far I have not been anti-Semitic" to silence them. After hecklers threatened violence, the police escorted Schumacher from the hall.[17]

But his politics took another turn, as he increasingly made England his home. He began developing his own economic view, one he dubbed in 1934 as the "Fritz's World Improvement Plan." He proposed that to lower unemployment, the government should pay for a basic minimum wage directly into the coffers of manufacturing firms, who in turn would pay that wage to the employee and then "top up" the salary to a higher level to attract recruits. Whenever employees left the firm, the employer would pay a tax to the government. Those firms that hired more people and, by implication, used less machinery, saved the most money, and also lowered unemployment. He shared his new plan with his uncle and father, but his uncle dismissed the idea. He expressed surprise that his nephew would spend his time on such a trivial project. His father did not bother to read it, deeply upsetting Schumacher.[18] He went back to work in Germany but decided to again return to England, perhaps, among other reasons, because he felt the English gave a hearing to his views. His politics also began a slow shift to the left. He advocated the intermarriage of Europeans and Jews into a single people to secure peace between Germany and Anglo-Saxon countries—a position advocated by his favorite philosopher Frederick Nietzsche. After a few years he felt no desire to return to Germany as war approached and wanted to desperately to stay and work in England.

While he turned increasingly against National Socialism this did not save him from being interned as an enemy alien. In May 1940 he was arrested and interned on Prees Heath, near Shropshire, along with 1,400 other prisoners.[19] While in prison he met Communists who argued persuasively for the ideas of Karl Marx, which he soon adopted wholeheartedly and then added his own conservative ideas to the mix—particularly a strong conviction for the need of eugenics. Because the prisoners engaged in farming, he then conceived his own agricultural policy for

[14] Ibid., 43. [15] Ibid., 50. [16] Ibid., 52.
[17] Ibid., 54. [18] Ibid., 60. [19] Ibid., 89.

Britain. The problems of modern agriculture were not due to low soil fertility, he concluded, or the high cost of farm labor, but, rather, to the problem of "negative selection" where the most intelligent and hard-working people left the farm for the city whilst "the dullest stayed behind." If intelligent young people could be channeled into farm work this would improve the human stock and agriculture along with it.[20] After his release from the camp, he began writing for newspapers while still forced to perform manual labor during the course of the war. By this time, he had become firmly convinced of the need for state capitalism, with its uniform standardization of mass industry.[21] He dreamed of returning to Germany after the war to lead a new Communist revolution of workers against the capitalistic elites.[22] He also came down firmly against Christianity, and saw its doctrines as "the most terrible and savage superstitions of a barbarous age."[23] He broadcast his new ideas through freelance publications with the *Observer* and *The Times*.

He kept, however, his penchant for outraging his audiences. He attended a Fabian conference on reparations that debated the price that Germany should pay for the war, suggesting that,

> if it goes according to the socialist principle of "each according to his need and from each according to his capacity" then, as Germany is ruined, and America is so rich, the Americans should pay reparations to the Germans.[24]

He maintained an active correspondence with two of Britain's premier economists—Maynard Keynes and William Beveridge—and he kept his name circulating as an "ideas man" in conferences and newspapers, eventually catching the attention of the socialist leaning Attlee government. He held no grudge against Britain for his imprisonment. After the war he sought and then gained citizenship and signed up to join the British Control Commission in Germany to aid the allied occupation. On the continent he discovered that no central plan for reconstruction had emerged among the allies. Rather their efforts involved a mix of both rebuilding and dismantling Germany, with attempts to strip equipment and industrial plants from Germany and ship them piecemeal to allied or former axis-dominated countries. Many in the British Control Commission also sponsored plans to return Germany to a simple agricultural economy—a peasant economic base for Germans that emphasized simplicity and pastoralism—so that it would become a defanged tiger that would never rise to economic power again. To what extent this vision for a defeated and de-industrialized Germany planted the seed in Schumacher for his later book, *Small is Beautiful*, is unclear, but the similarity is striking.

Back in England he moved in 1950 to Caterham, in Surrey, to a large rambling house with four acres of prime garden land. There he raised his own vegetables, chickens, rabbits, and made bread for his own family. He then began making compost and joined the Soil Association, eagerly consuming organic farming literature.[25] He read Albert Howard, Lionel Picton, Robert McCarrison, and Eve Balfour, among others. His receptive mind absorbed the new ideas of organic

---

[20] Ibid., 97.   [21] Ibid., 112.   [22] Ibid., 113.
[23] Ibid., 117.   [24] Ibid., 128.   [25] Ibid., 172.

farming as he had earlier absorbed Marxism. He became obsessed with wholeness and health, and the proper handling of soil. In the words of his daughter and biographer, who summarized his new views, if "you have healthy and nourishing plants, vegetables, fruits salads, and grains...you will also have healthier animals and people."[26]

He had limits however. He wrote to his sister Edith in November 1951 that while pursuing this new vision of wholeness in organic farming, "we must try not to let ourselves be pulled into all the useless hocus pocus."[27] He rejected the mystical and unscientific ideas that swirled around some of his fellow travelers in the Soil Association, particularly that of biodynamic farming. However organic farming literature did lead him into the conservation and early environmental movement, and soon after joining the Soil Association he began expressing concerns about global deforestation, desertification, and soil erosion.

As with Howard, Schumacher also romanticized peasant culture in the East. But unlike Howard he added in a number of personal foibles such as a sincere belief in the efficacy of astrology, a fascination with flying saucers, and a belief in the teachings of George Gurdjieff, a Greek and Armenian guru who expounded a mystical system of belief based on discovering a higher hidden spiritual reality through the channeling of secret trans-historical brotherhoods leading to higher consciousness. A trip to Burma further inspired him. Within weeks he was convinced that poor peasants were happy and stress-free because of the simplicity of their life. Schumacher recycled the myth of peasant wisdom found widely in organic circles and advocated a new economic system based on these ideas, which he dubbed "Buddhist economics."

In *Small is Beautiful: A Study of Economics as if People Mattered*, Schumacher laid out a vision remarkably reminiscent of the ideas circulated by organic farming enthusiasts.[28] The book consisted of a series of rambling essays that extended the core ideas of the conservation and organic farming movement through the lens of economics. In the first half of the book—arguably the most influential part—he persistently used the word "conservation." While most of his readers assumed his ideas were new, many of his basic themes were the stock in trade of the earlier environmental movement as it had formed in the mid- and late nineteenth century. While still calling himself a socialist, Schumacher's positions on agriculture and nature drew largely on the right-wing cultural milieu of organic farming. His ideas also drew from the innate conservatism he inherited in Germany—updated with Keynesian analyses. He also called for the nationalization of large industries and balanced his leanings toward big industrial schemes with suggestions for local control through community councils.

Schumacher still held traditional and conservative views on society. While he himself enjoyed world travel, he harbored a nostalgia for a pre-modern order, where people traveled only for a "special reason" such as "Irish saints or the scholars

[26] Ibid., 173–4.　　[27] Ibid.
[28] E. F. Schumacher, *Small is Beautiful: A Study of Economics as if People Mattered* (London, 1973).

of the University of Paris."[29] Pre-modern society allowed people to intimately interact with families, friends, and real people instead of "states and other anonymous abstractions."[30] He rejected the mystical pantheism that often colored the environmental movement, and emphasized instead a Descartian eternal soul "apart from the body" in a relationship with a transcendent God—very much in the Christian tradition.[31] He opposed women working: "Women, on the whole, do not need an 'outside' job, and the large-scale employment of women in offices or factories would be a sign of serious economic failure." Letting "children run wild" without discipline and a traditional education, he believed would be a grave mistake.[32]

It is no accident that he wrote this book during his tenure as President of the Soil Association. The similarities with organic farming—and Howard's ideas in particular—are striking. Like Howard, he rejected overspecialization as an end in itself and believed that scientists needed to balance specialized knowledge with human wisdom and practical experience, emphasizing not merely expertise but "the organic, the gentle, the non-violent, the elegant and beautiful."[33] His admonition that workers act as their own bosses, with independence and pride, reflected the ethic of agrarian land reform and the ideal of the sturdy yeoman farmer that he then applied to the entire economy.[34]

> It is moreover obvious that men organized in small units will take better care of *their* bit of land or other natural resources than anonymous companies or megalo-maniac governments.[35]

His distrust of large urban environments and industry, and the mass media that reinforced urbanism as "bread and circuses," also reflected common tropes among conservative organic farmers.[36]

Schumacher's view of the soil, on which all economics depended, is taken direct from Howard's work,

> A cubic centimeter of fertile soil contains milliards of living organisms, the full exploration of which is far beyond the capacities of man. The fundamental 'principle' of modern industry, on the other hand, is that it deals with man-devised processes which work reliably only when applied to man-devised, non-living materials. The ideal of industry is the elimination of living substances.[37]

In the second chapter, "The Proper Use of Land," Schumacher argues that when man "circumvent the laws of nature, he usually destroys the natural environment that sustains him." He echoes strongly the common trope among organic farming enthusiasts that as man's environment deteriorates so "his civilization declines."[38]

Schumacher, like Howard's followers, romanticized and fundamentally misunderstood eastern cultures. While he coined the phrase "Buddhist economics" to describe his approach to economics and nature, his ideals expressed in *Small is Beautiful* reflected more the ideals of the conservation movement that arose in the

29 Ibid., 63.   30 Ibid., 68.   31 Ibid., 34–5.   32 Ibid., 51–2.
33 Ibid., 29.   34 Ibid., 30.   35 Ibid., 31–2.   36 Ibid., 33.
37 Ibid., 101.   38 Ibid., 93.

British Empire and that in turn fed into the organic farming movement. He echoed the particularly colonial tone of the Men of the Trees movement of Richard St. Barb-Baker when he suggested that followers of Buddhist economics "ought to plant a tree every few years and look after it until it is safely established," which would then result in "a high rate of genuine economic development independent of any foreign aid."[39] Modernization, he wrote, resulted in a list of ills (which could just as easily have been formulated by organic farming advocates):

> A collapse of the rural economy...a rising tide of unemployment in town and country...the growth of a city proletariat without nourishment for either body or soul...Millions of people...moving about, deserting the rural areas...to follow the city lights...causing a pathological growth.[40]

In early 1955 Schumacher left England for an "Oriental adventure" to the Union of Burma as an economic advisor, funded by the United Nations, to issue a report. The National Coal Board, his employer, gave him a few months unpaid leave. He arrived with high expectations that he could "bridge...the East and the West" and help the Burmese with economic development without harming their indigenous culture.[41] Based on the cheerful temperament of Burmese, who had very little money but still seemed remarkably happy, he concluded that the Burmese needed self-sufficiency along the lines Gandhi had proposed for India. The Burmese should emphasize renewable industries, such as forestry and peasant agriculture, and avoid basing new industries on "oil, coal, metal, etc." (even though Burma had the largest oil reserves and production in Asia).[42] He emphasized that the Burmese should not industrialize like the West, but should instead keep their local indigenous culture intact by small enterprises. In his report he argued that Burmese should "reverse all its development policies" and exclusively emphasize rural development. His orientalist view of a romantic and unchanging peasant culture based on a brief visit did not gain traction. The Economic and Social Council of Burma to whom he reported, "was not impressed."[43] The Burmese government dismissed the report—they were not interested in lagging far behind the global trends of modernization.

Schumacher derived many of his ideas from organic farming. *Small is Beautiful* brought the 1930s anti-cosmopolitan politics of ruralism, indigeneity, and attachment to the soil to a new generation during the 1970s. A generation after the end of the Second World War and the defeat of fascism, and well after dissolution of the large overseas European empires, his ideas seemed fresh, and distinctly unlike the laissez faire conservative parties in Britain, Europe, and the United States. His opposition to capitalism and his distrust of vested interests and overspecialized science echoed the fundamental world view of organic farming enthusiasts prior to and immediately after the Second World War. In *Small is Beautiful*, Schumacher struggled to express clear points, and this opaqueness, coupled with his public support for the British Labour party and his opposition to free market conservatism, eased his acceptance by individuals in the 1960s and 70s counter-cultural movements. Thus, the reader

[39] Ibid., 54.   [40] Ibid., 54, 61.   [41] Woods, *E. F. Schumacher*, 191.
[42] Ibid., 193.   [43] Ibid.

could infer that Schumacher advocated a new revolutionary order because his environmentalism assailed corporatism, capitalism, and consumerism. In fact, Schumacher echoed most of the fundamental positions of the 1930s–40s far right, repackaged for a new generation.

Schumacher became President of the Soil Association the same year that he converted to Catholicism, in 1971. His conversion illustrated a deep attachment to his middle-class conservative roots in Germany that, in spite of his many ideological shifts, never abated. Paradoxically, despite his appeal to the left of the political spectrum, Schumacher turned the Soil Association in the UK toward a more commercial orientation. Along with Eve Balfour, he successfully pushed the society to launch a new marketing strategy to place organic farming on a viable business footing.[44] When Schumacher died in 1977, Balfour returned as President and served until 1982. The new commercial emphasis launched by Schumacher paid off over time. By 1986 five million pounds of organic produce sold in grocery stores throughout Britain. The UK Register of Organic Food Standards established in 1987, issued organic food standards in 1989—modelled on the recommendations of the Soil Association.[45] While the older *Mother Earth* journal published by the Soil Association took no advertising money, a reincarnation of the magazine as *Living Earth* in 1993 (after it underwent tumultuous changes and new names) actively sought advertising money and corporate patronage. These changes and the public acceptance of organic farming in the United States added new momentum. Conford and Holden, in a brief summation of the history of the Soil Association, wrote that,

> By 1996 there were 44 [active groups of the Soil Association]...of which nearly one-third had been founded in the 1990s. Some contained only a handful of members, others anything up to two hundred; the overwhelming majority of them had links with environmental groups.[46]

The links between organic farming and a new phase of the environmental movement, in Britain as in most of the industrialized world, were strengthened by the 1980s. Organic farming, as a central feature of the middle stage of the environmental movement, successfully bridged the first phase of the movement (the conservation movement) with the new modern environmental movement from the 1970s to the present.

ORGANIC FARMING IN THE UNITED STATES

The period from 1940 to 1978 has been called by one scholar, "the era of polarization" when the organic farming camp had little support from academic and mainstream agriculturalists.[47] *Reader's Digest* captured a commonplace sentiment when, in 1952, it published an article by R. I. Throckmorton, Dean of Kansas State College,

---

[44] Conford, *The Origins of the Organic Movement*, 107.
[45] Ibid., 112.   [46] Ibid., 113.
[47] J. Heckman, "A History of Organic Farming: Transitions from Sir Albert Howard's *War in the Soil* to USDA National Organic Program," *Renewable Agriculture and Food Systems* 21/3 (2005): 146.

titled, "Organic Farming—Bunk!" Throckmorton argued that since all chemicals, including pesticides derive ultimately from nature, there is no such thing as "unnatural" fertilizers or pesticides.[48] Ten years later in July 1962, Harland Manchester, a popular writer on science and nutrition, published another article in *Reader's Digest* titled "The Great Organic Gardening Myth" that argued a similar position, suggesting that vitamins are vitamins, and cannot be distinguished between those with a natural or unnatural origin. Further, the growing world population needed food and chemicals boosted agricultural output.[49] Academics and chemical companies reinforced this critique. The Woolfolk Chemical Works Ltd. issued a pamphlet declaring that the "condemnation of chemical fertilizers and pesticides is unjustified." Monsanto Company in a brochure, "Plain Talk, Pesticides and the Environment," highlighted how an acre growing corn on chemical fertilizers far out-stripped that of a similar "Nature's acre" which would produce a mere 25–30 bushes against 130 bushels per acre using chemicals.[50] Academics also downplayed the significance of organic farming. Arthur W. Galston, a professor at Yale University, titled a piece in *Natural History*, "The Organic Gardener and Anti-Intellectualism," in which he argued that the counter-cultural trends among youth led many to accept the emotional appeal of a close-to-nature ethic—young people revolt against "the establishment" and feel the urge to unreasonably reject "the synthetic, plastic world" that authority figures created.[51]

A steady trickle of letters to the press, however, supported organic farming and posed questions to academics at agricultural colleges. Small farmers and gardeners wanted more information about organic farming and methods, and this made the movement difficult to ignore. Firman E. Bear, a soil scientist at Rutgers University responded to these inquiries in a 1947 article titled "Facts...and Fancies about Fertilizer," in which he classed Howard, Balfour, J. I. Rodale, and the American farmer and writer E. H. Faulkner as "gloomy prophets." Many officials and scientists hit back hard against the annoying inquiries on organic farming, as in 1963, when a scientist from the University of Wisconsin, Emil Truog, called the organic farming movement a "Cult."[52]

A film produced in 1950 by the American Medical Association (AMA), *The Medicine Men*, gives an idea of the hostile caricature of organic farmers and health food that enthusiasts faced.[53] It began with a swipe against breads mixed

---

Heckman, the son of a prominent organic farmer in Ohio, is a professor in the Plant Biology and Pathology Department at Rutgers University.

[48] R. I. Throckmorton, "Organic Farming—Bunk," *Reader's Digest* (October, 1952): 46.

[49] Harland Manchester, "The Great Organic Gardening Myth," *Reader's Digest* (July, 1962): 102–5.

[50] As quoted in Carlton Jackson, *J. I. Rodale: Apostle of Non-conformity* (New York, 1974), 114.

[51] Arthur W. Galston, "The Organic Gardener and Anti-Intellectualism," *Natural History* (May, 1972): 28. As quoted in Jackson, *J. I. Rodale*, 112.

[52] As quoted by J. Heckman, "A History of Organic Farming," 146. See also F. E. Bear, "Facts...and Fancies about Fertilizer," *Plant Food Journal* (April, 1947): 1–6; E. Truog, "The Organic Gardening Myth," *Soil Survey Horizons* 4 (1963): 12–19; E. Truog, "Organics only?—Bunkum!" *The Land* 5 (1946): 317–21.

[53] "The Medicine Men" [Film], circa 1950, American Medical Association. Available online at: https://www.youtube.com/watch?v=3Aw9ucp2dMs [accessed December 26, 2016].

with vegetables or nuts in an apparent attempt to mock whole wheat bread. An investigative journalist, the hero of the piece, interviews a scientist in a white jacket. The scientist explains to the journalist that there is "a food faddism sweeping the country, it is sort of a big lie technique" used by their promoters. When asked why people would double their food bill on such items, the scientist explains that people are gullible and vulnerable to superstition and magic. The film cuts to a Hollywood film clip where an African medicine man places the heart of a lion and the brain of a wolf in a boiling pot, to produce both courage and cunning. In an office of the Food and Drug Administration an inspector tells the journalist that society indulges quacks peddling "fear superstition and ignorance" because,

> on the surface their crimes don't seem so violent as kidnapping or murder. But when one of these birds gets ahold of a patient who could be cured with proper medical care, and as a result of that, the patient dies, then to me that is manslaughter or even murder.

The film presents the sellers of vitamin supplements as criminals, "preying on sick kids" and, when caught making unscientific medical claims, yet unfortunately only getting "light sentences." Meantime the AMA, the FDA, and the Better Business Bureau do all they can to put quacks out of business. The film then portrays a fictional vitamin seller, "spotted in a restaurant behaving like the rest of us mortals," hypocritically enjoying white bread, meat, and potatoes, and guzzling down beer. Cornering the supplement maker, the investigative journalist hurls at him, "how many people have died of your treatments? How many victims have you left in broken health? How much money have you made from this racket? What about the rights of the people you swindle?" The besieged vitamin seller retorts that the journalist was hired by the AMA and big investors. No irony was intended in this line even though the AMA did indeed produce the film.

One explanation for this hostility is that the period 1940–78 was one of "scientific optimism" that looked to science for answers to societal ills.[54] In 1961 *Time* magazine dubbed the contemporary era as the "age of science." Everything from atomic power to the Green Revolution seemed to offer more solutions than problems. At the same time resistance to this scientific optimism continued to grow in small circles—and not only from organic farmers, but also from a broader swathe of professionals and amateurs who were disillusioned with chemicals, the most famous example being that of Rachel Carson's *Silent Spring* (1962).[55] That the counter-current of doubt and pessimism regarding chemical agriculture gained ground in this period is clear, as the work and influence of J. I. Rodale, discussed shortly, illustrates. Rodale's magazine *Organic Gardening* increased from 260,000 readers in 1960 to 1,300,000 by 1980.[56] He was not alone in his efforts to avoid the ills of industrial agriculture.

---

[54] Heckman, "A History of Organic Farming," 147.   [55] Ibid.
[56] Ibid. See also W. C. Kelly, "Rodale Press and Organic Gardening," *HortTechnology* 2 (1992): 270–1.

A number of key figures helped herald a slow acceptance of natural farming methods in the United States. Henry Wallace, Secretary of Agriculture from 1933–40 and Roosevelt's Vice President from 1941–45, brought attention to the problem of soil fertility during the Dust Bowl. His own father had served as Secretary of Agriculture under the Harding and Coolidge administration. He led efforts to fight soil erosion through proper land use planning and improved farming techniques. He emphasized early in his tenure as Secretary of Agriculture the coordination of local farming with newly established soil conservation societies to protect and establish woodlands and integrate forest areas into agricultural land-use. This integration of forestry and farming in demonstration farms, long advocated by Howard, served as an educational tool for ecological principles and had the practical effect of preserving topsoil, protecting farms from adverse weather, and returning nutrients to the soil.[57]

William Albrecht, a professor of soil science at the University of Missouri, promoted research that emphasized soil fertility and the return of organic matter and minerals to the soils. While not an organic farmer he saw, like Howard, a connection between healthy soil, grass, animals, and people. He understood soil to be more than an inert substrate for fertilizers. Rather soil was either a vulnerable fabric that fed nutrition into healthy organisms or it was a lifeless skin that lacked even the minimal elements necessary to sustain a healthy chain of life up the steps of the food chain. In 1957 he wrote,

> Unfortunately, the human species has not yet condescended, generally, to see itself (when hungry) as just another animal in the biotic pyramid. Instead of appreciating the precariousness of our high nutritional position in the evolutionary scale, we have assumed that high perch to be one of authority and control over the lower life forms. It has encouraged our exploitation of everything below, even to the increasing destruction of the soil that provides nutrition and health and serves as the foundation of the entire pyramid.[58]

While he did not advocate a full system of organic farming, Albrecht was very open to the concept. J. I. Rodale, after establishing the Soil and Health Foundation to research organic farming, testified before a congressional commission in December 1950 that almost all the universities in the country had turned down his proffered funds for research—except the University of Missouri where Albrecht worked, which had accepted $1,400 to experiment on the utility of rock fertilizers. "At least this institution," he wrote, "has accepted a grant from us, whereas the others treat us, more or less, as crackpots, and refuse to do any experimental work."[59]

Another prominent American, whose work anticipated the organic farming movement, was the 1927 Pulitzer Prize winning novelist, Louis Bromfield. In his

---

[57] See John F. Preston, "Lessons from the Farm Forestry Projects," *Journal of Forestry* 44 (January, 1946): 9–10; Harold T. Pinkett, "The Soil Conservation Service and Farm Woodland Management, 1938–1945" *Agricultural History* (April 1, 1985): 280–9.

[58] William Albrecht, "Soil Fertility and Biotic Geography," *Geographical Review*, 47/1 (January, 1957): 102.

[59] As quoted in Jackson, *R. I. Rodale*, 116.

novel, *The Farm*, he captured the ideals of the Country Life Movement that advocated the cultural and spiritual advantages of rural living. He recounted in fiction the biography of a piece of land owned by generations of the MacDougal family in Ohio, from the settling of the Western Reserve before Ohio became a state in 1803 up to the 1930s. Bromfield advocated a Jeffersonian ideal of small independent land owners and traced the decay of the Anglo-Saxon industrial and cultural elites in the United States—not unlike the Indiana novelist Booth Tarkington. Both in *The Farm* and his previous novel, *Early Autumn*, he chronicled the chaos of elites who had grown far removed from the land that originally gave prominence to their families, and the gangrene that beset the culture and politics of a nation with new immigrants that did not share their identity or values.

After years living as an expatriate in Paris and hobnobbing with Hollywood celebrities like Humphrey Bogart and Ernest Hemmingway, Bromfield had returned to his roots in Ohio, where as a boy he had worked on his grandfather's farm, and which inspired much of his writing. On 900 acres he established "Malabar Farm" to employ conservation methods, particularly deep plowing with the Graham plow to break up the hardened soil pan. Shallow plowing with the Moldboard plow and the use of chemical fertilizers had over generations produced a hard layer of degraded soil. While speaking well of organic farming methods in his 1945 novel *Pleasant Valley*, Bromfield began to turn away from organic methods as he gained more experience in farming. Stung by this, Rodale charged—without evidence—that this was due to his ambition to be Secretary of Agriculture if Dewey had won the 1948 presidential election. Undoubtedly Bromfield did change his mind regarding organic methods, which he had once praised as an antidote to factory farms. In the introduction he wrote to another book, *Roots in the Earth: the Small Farmer looks Ahead* by P. Alston Waring and Walter Teller, he referred to organic farming enthusiasts as "cultists."[60]

Aldo Leopold, another key figure whose ideas presaged organic farming, linked the first phase of the environmental movement—the conservation movement—with post-Second World War environmentalism. He began his career in the US Forest Service and, as a forest ranger in Arizona and New Mexico, practiced the "wise use" doctrine of nature management pioneered by Gifford Pinchot. However, a visit to Germany added a new ecological concern to his work. On a forest management tour in National Socialist Germany in 1935 he made a special study of the "Naturschutz" program that protected endangered species and attempted to reintroduce animals into their natural habitats. Leopold encountered in Germany the antithesis to "scientific forestry" in the idea of Der Wald, the organic forest. One scholar claimed his German trip inspired Leopold to conceive—at least in part—of the Wilderness Society and also contributed to his conception of a "land ethic" that linked a community of humans and wildlife to the soil.[61] Leopold became Professor of Game Management at the University of Wisconsin. In the

[60] Ibid., 76.
[61] See Boria Sax, *Animals in the Third Reich: Pets, Scapegoats, and the Holocaust* (New York, 2000), 79. I owe the suggestion of the organic forest concept to Dr. Fred Kruger.

Sand Country Almanac—a book which widely impacted the conservation movement as it evolved into the modern environmental movement—he described his efforts to reclaim nine acres of degraded land in Wisconsin. His thoughts on organic farming have been overlooked. They show how the new ecological thinking advocated by A. G. Tansley at Oxford University, and Frederic Clements at the University of Kansas, spilled into the analyses not only of forest management, but of agriculture as well.[62] Leopold writes,

> . . . the farmer, by the very nature of his techniques, must modify the biota more radically than the forester or the wildlife manager. Nevertheless, there are many discontents in agriculture which seem to add up to a new vision of "biotic farming."
>
> Perhaps the most important of these is the new evidence that poundage or tonnage is no measure of the food-value of farm crops; the products of fertile soil may be qualitatively as well as quantitatively superior. We can bolster poundage from depleted soils by pouring on imported fertility, but we are not necessarily bolstering food-value. The possible ultimate ramifications of this idea are so immense that I must leave their exposition to abler pens.
>
> The discontent that labels itself "organic farming," while bearing some of the earmarks of a cult, is nevertheless biotic in its direction, particularly in its insistence on the importance of soil flora and fauna.[63]

It is possible that the reference to organic farming as a cult sprang from the methods and language of the man most responsible for bringing the ideas of Albert Howard to the American public: Jerome Irving Rodale. Though Howard had many admirers in the United States, Rodale played the central role in raising public consciousness of organic farming in North America; he merged enthusiasm with entrepreneurial energy reaching millions of Americans with the message about the Indore Method, and the health benefits of eating organic fruits and vegetables. His colorful and controversial character attracted amateur gardeners, farmers, and consumers—while in many cases also offending scientists and professionals by his intemperate language. Rodale credited Howard as the founder of the organic farming movement and considered himself his disciple. Rodale, however, in his own right, as a publicist, became a central figure in the history of the organic farming movement in the United States.

Rodale studied accounting, attending but not finishing a degree at New York and Columbia University. He then worked as an accountant for the Internal Revenue Service in Washington DC. He felt at the same time however a powerful pull toward the land, expressing to a friend a desire in 1918 at twenty years of age "to get out [of the city] as quick as we can to God's land." In addition to his dream of farming he dreamt of starting businesses and making money. He admired such American heroes as the industrialist Andrew Carnegie and the novelist Horatio Alger.[64] After leaving his job with the Internal Revenue Service he founded with

---

[62] Gregory A. Barton, "Introduction," *American Environmentalism*, ed. Gregory A. Barton (San Diego, 2002): 17.

[63] Aldo Leopold, *A Sand County Almanac: and Sketches Here and There* (New York, 1949), 187.

[64] Jackson, *J. I. Rodale*, 21. Quote from Ibid., 22.

his brother in 1923 an electrical manufacturing company in New York—a business he then moved to a small town in 1930 close to a rural area he loved: Emmaus Pennsylvania. In nearby Allentown, where he lived, he began gardening, and then publishing.[65]

His published torrent of titles, from books on humor to verb and synonym finders and cross word puzzles. Almost all of his sales came from mail order.[66] He ventured into health publications in August 1935 with *Health Digest* which— unlike the earlier titles—turned a profit. *Health Digest* primarily reprinted studies on a wide number of health-related issues. He also ventured into policy questions and politics. *Health Digest* reprinted excerpts from the fiery speeches of Huey Long in the United States Senate. Huey Long had opposed the American entry into the First World War and spoke stridently against the Federal Reserve. He supported a "net asset" tax to redistribute wealth from large corporations and wealthy individuals whom he claimed raped the economy and stripped money from hard working Americans and farmers. Staunchly anti-communist, Long allied with Father Coughlin—who expressed openly his opposition to Jews as an abusive oligarchy.

By republishing Long's speeches, Rodale continued the tradition started by organic farming enthusiasts in Britain and Europe of mixing populist and often far-right politics with farming and health. Rodale's affinity to Huey Long fitted easily within the cultural milieu of romantic farm literature, but did not accord with his actual background. Born of Jewish parents, and the son of a rabbi, few of his extended family members would likely have agreed with Rodale in his support for Long. As in most of the causes Rodale adopted, he cared little about offending his audience, earning the reputation among admirers of a free-thinking maverick willing to take on Goliath. To his many critics in the media and sciences, however, he was a crank.

Rodale's biographer, Carlton Jackson explained the moment that Rodale converted to organic farming,

> One day in the late 1930s, while reading an English publication, *Health For All* he came across an article written by Sir Albert Howard, the famous British agriculturalist. So excited was J. I. [Jerome Irving Rodale] about what Howard said that he wrote to him. From this correspondence there developed a friendship between the two that led J. I. closer to his long-time dream of working directly with the land.[67]

After this point, Rodale concentrated almost all his publishing efforts on advancing the organic farming movement in the United States. He reprinted many of Howard's articles and summarized the arguments of the Indore Method in countless articles he himself authored. He launched a new magazine, *Organic Farmer*, that later changed its title to *Organic Farming and Gardening*, in May 1942. He persuaded Sir Albert Howard to join as associate editor, a position Howard held till his death. The magazine then split into two formats, *Organic Farming* and *Organic Gardening*, which by 1954 merged into *Organic Gardening*

[65] Ibid., 26.   [66] Ibid., 27.   [67] Ibid., 63.

and Farming. By the end of the 1960s it had almost one million subscribers—a massive number compared to the relatively smaller numbers in Britain and other parts of the world.[68] Rodale also launched *Prevention* magazine in June 1950, which traced a broader outline of health food concerns that still kept organic farming as a core solution to the ills of modern society. *Prevention* grew to over one million subscribers by 1970.

Even with the explosive growth of his publications and outreach, Rodale maintained the centrality of Howard's ideas to the organic farming movement, never deviating from his 1948 tribute published in his *Organic Gardening Magazine* where he stated that the movements success in England and the United States "will, in large measure, be due to the basic discoveries and labors of Sir Albert Howard." He continued,

> It is due to Sir Albert Howard that there is taking place in the United States at the present moment an extensive and up surging movement, a zealous rebellion against accepted "orthodox" scientific agricultural practice...Is it not a vast and irrefutable debt that our nation owes to this celebrated Englishman, a high-minded gentleman and a penetrating scholar with his eyes ever set on a high horizon?[69]

In his book *Pay Dirt*, Rodale laid out Howard's full philosophy of organic farming as well as a number of ideas unique to himself. The health of plants, animals, and humans were threatened by chemical fertilizers, he wrote, and he declared, "what we are getting is more and more *chemical* in food." We are eating less living food that the body needs, he continued, but it is killing more than our health—it is killing birds and wildlife.

> Many birds like to scratch in the earth and snare insect larvae. One peck in sour soil that has been dressed with ammonium sulphate should be sufficient to tell them they are in the wrong place and to fly to greener pastures. The farmer then loses valuable allies in this war against destructive insects.[70]

He called factory food the cycle of death, from soil all the way to humans. He detested DDT and fought hard against its use, as did many other organic farmers. Rodale methodically listed thirty-six reasons why Howard's organic methods should be used in agriculture, prompting Howard, at Rodale's request, to write a generous appraisal of *Pay Dirt* in the book's introduction.

These ideas emanating from the organic farming movement decisively influenced Rachel Carson. Organic farming activists had broadly aired their opposition to pesticides, including DDT, well over a decade before *Silent Spring*. Rodale's biographer suggested that Carson regularly read Rodale's *Health Bulletin* and that she communicated with him on the malign effects of pesticides. One year after the publication of *Silent Spring* she wrote to Rodale on April 3, 1963,

[68] Ibid., 64.
[69] From J. I. Rodale, "Sir Albert Howard: A Tribute," *Organic Gardening Magazine*, 13/8 (September, 1948).
[70] Jackson, *J. I. Rodale*, 32. J. I. Rodale, *Pay Dirt: Farming & Gardening with Composts* (New York, 1946), 24.

I am of course most interested in your items on pesticides, and general atmospheric pollution. These have given me several useful tips on situations I have then followed up with interest.[71]

While Carson did not come out publicly in favor of organic farming or associate officially with Rodale, her work mimics the positions of organic farming advocates on the effect of pesticides on wildlife, most particularly birds. She shared also a distrust of scientism and the unnatural arrogance that humans can control nature with certainty. She wrote,

The chemical weed killers are a bright new toy. They work in a spectacular way; they give a giddy sense of power over nature to those who wield them, and as for the long-range and less obvious effects—these are easily brushed aside as baseless imaginings of pessimists.[72]

She also displayed a defensive posture about pessimism, fanaticism, and cultism. This suggested that she identified with the organic farming movement that felt the sting of these accusations. In the words of a biographer she,

... quite self-consciously decided to write a book calling into question the paradigm of scientific progress that defined post-war American culture.[73]

Strong opposition from chemical companies followed, a point that Carson seems to have expected perhaps from reading the *Health Bulletin*. She wrote in *Silent Spring* that:

There is a strong tendency to brand as fanatics or cultists all who are so perverse as to demand that their food be free of insect poisons.[74]

She also echoed Rodale's *Prevention* magazine, founded twelve years before the publication of *Silent Spring*, as well as the Audubon society and a host of other conservation groups. Like organic farming advocates, she questioned the persuasive role that money from chemical companies played in the testimony of scientists. Rodale's many warnings about pesticides and their effect on human health could easily have been written by Carson's pen:

As we pour our millions into research and invest all our hopes in vast programs to find cures for the established cause of cancer, we are neglecting the golden opportunity to prevent, even while we seek to cure.[75]

Both Carson and Rodale testified before congressional committees. In 1950 Rodale served as a witness for the *House Select Committee to Investigate the Use of Chemicals in Foods and Cosmetics*. The chair of this committee, Congressman James Delany, succeeded in amending the Food and Drug Act, including the Pesticides Amendment (1950), the Food Additives Amendment (1958), and the Color

---

[71] As quoted in Jackson, *J. I. Rodale*, 33.
[72] Rachel Carson, *Silent Spring* (New York, 1962), 68–9.
[73] Mark Hamilton Lytle, *The Gentle Subversive: Rachel Carson, Silent Spring, and the Rise of the Environmental Movement* (New York, 2007), 166–7.
[74] Rachel Carson, *Silent Spring*, 178.   [75] Ibid., 242.

Additives Amendment (1960).[76] Additionally both Carson and Rodale had a select group of prominent scientists who supported their positions. A plant ecologist, Frank Egler, an independent scholar and maverick scientist, spoke in support of Carson and, obliquely, of organic farming enthusiasts. An article in the *American Scientist* (March, 1964) gives a clue as to his sympathies. He followed the seminal work of ecologists Arthur Tansley and Frederick Clements, but he also appreciated the "holism" of J. C. Smuts and the downstream affect this had on not only scientific, but cultural movements.[77]

Almost fourteen years earlier, in 1950, before a congressional committee investigating the impact of chemicals on human health, Egler publicly agreed with Rodale that the organic farming movement was a unique and modern innovation, not merely a throw-back to pre-modern farming methods.[78] In his 1964 article, Egler sympathetically portrayed organic farmers as having made "little impression on government, little impression on other social groups except for gardening and horticulture, but considerable impression on the general public."[79] He then praised Carson for having broken through with *Silent Spring* the established governmental and scientific barriers that silenced opposition to the overuse of chemicals in agriculture and in the manufacture of food. Carson's position as a best-selling author and marine biologist gave her a credibility that Rodale lacked and this, in addition to her literary style, and the support of a select group of academics and scientists, no doubt contributed to the impact of *Silent Spring*.

New research has uncovered letters that indicate organic farming enthusiasts tutored Carson on many key issues, particularly the dangers of DDT, and supplied significant material for her book *Silent Spring*. Environmental historian John Paull examined Carson's correspondence in the Beinecke Rare Book and Manuscript Library at Yale. He traced the letters between Carson and two women on Long Island, Marjorie Spock and Mary T. Richards—both organic farmers (they were possibly a couple, though this is not known for certain). They vehemently objected to the United States Government aerial spraying DDT mixed with fuel oil over their small farm in an effort to battle a gypsy moth infestation devastating three million hectares of forest in the Northeast.

The President of the national Audubon Society, Richard Murphy, "together [with] organic gardeners and a chiropractor" unsuccessfully sought an injunction to force the federal Government to cease spraying DDT. The trial ran twenty-two days and the *New York Times* printed front page news accounts.[80] Because of this publicity, Rachel Carson initiated correspondence with Spock and Richards and a lively exchange followed that led all the way up to the publication of *Silent Spring*. Carson dubbed them as her "chief clipping service." Crucially, she also received transcripts of the trial. Paull writes that the overlap of sources in her book and the material supplied to her, the discussion of arguments and

[76] Jackson, *J. I. Rodale*, 107.
[77] Frank Egler, "Pesticides in our Ecosystem," *American Scientist* 52/1 (March, 1964): 111.
[78] Jackson, *J. I. Rodale*, 95.   [79] Egler, "Pesticides," 127.
[80] John Paull, "The Rachel Carson Letters and the Making of *Silent Spring*," *Sage Open* (July–September, 2013): 2.

ideas that appeared shortly afterwards in her book, and her fear of being attacked and dismissed lead to the conclusion that she not only gained many of her sources and ideas from organic farmers (some of whom were also biodynamic farmers), but that she also feared having her work dismissed if she ever revealed the source.

She had reason to fear revealing her organic farming sources. The trial Judge Bruchhausen had discounted testimony from one expert because "He conducts an organic farm."[81] Though Paull does not accuse Carson of plagiarism, he writes,

> *Silent Spring* was a joint effort and their common cause, and Carson wrote their evidence into, but their names out of, the script entirely. Their "common cause" was the construction of *Silent Spring* and this was the consuming passion of Carson in the final years of her life. There is no evidence revealed in the correspondence to indicate that Carson shared or explored the interest of Spocak and Richards in either anthroposophy or the writings of Rudolf Steiner.[82]

The success of Carson's book helped both Rodale and Schumacher advance the commercial application of organic farming, which in turn broadened its consumer base to include those who never gardened or farmed, but were passionately committed to eating fruits and vegetables grown with the Indore Method and free of chemical pesticides. Rodale also advocated, as Schumacher did in Britain, the commercialization of organic farming, and praised the trend in supermarkets to set aside an organic section for fruits and vegetables. The growing reach of his media empire also helped inspire the proliferation of health food stores across the country. Health food stores only added weight to another phenomenon—the establishment of approximately 2,000 communes across the United States that largely modeled their farming methods on Howard's protocols. The *Saturday Review of Literature* (April, 1971) announced that:

> ...many of these communes cultivate crops [such] as organically grown grain, vegetables, and other produce, which are then sold to health-food store, health-food wholesalers, or supermarkets.[83]

Rodale's success caught the attention of major news and entertainment venues. In 1971 *Penthouse* trumpeted Rodale as the "Pollution Prophet," while in March 22, 1971, *Time* magazine, in an article titled "Catching up to Rodale Press," described him as the leader of an "esoteric group" who built his empire on selling rose-hips, kelp, and clay based toothpaste products, along with his condemnation of DDT and polluting soaps that contained phosphate detergents. This same article quoted him as boasting that "the health magazines are growing fast and the cash register is ringing."[84]

---

[81] As quoted in Ibid., 8.   [82] Ibid.

[83] Herbert A. Otto, "Review: Robert Houriet, *Getting Back Together*," *Saturday Review of Literature* (April, 1971): 17. As quoted in Jackson, *J. I. Rodale*, 112.

[84] As quoted in Jackson, *J. I. Rodale*, 80. See also G. Bryant, "J. I. Rodale: Pollution Prophet," *Penthouse* 2 (1971): 28–32; "Catching up to Rodale Press," *Time* (March, 1971): 22.

Rodale's publications like Schumacher's work in Britain broadened the tide of support for the organic farming movement and built clear bridges to a broader environmental movement in the 1960s–70s that grew—in part—directly out of the organic farming movement and the many causes it espoused, from pollution control, to desertification, soil fertility, and wildlife preservation. Slowly more scientists in the late 1960s warmed toward organic farming. This warming began the process of thawing out the wall of exclusion that separated organic farming protocols from scientific communities. A Professor of Biology at the University of Texas, John J. Biesele, Professor of Plant Physiology at Washington University, Barry Commoner, and the Professor of Population at Stanford University, Paul Erlich among many others, made supporting comments toward Rodale and organic farming.[85]

Near the end of his life Rodale saw Howard's ideas spreading into a large movement, one that he predicted would eventually impact the global culture of the world in a significant way. In *Organic Merry-Go-Round* he observed that:

> Critics will come and go, but the organic method will progress steadily because it has a truly scientific basis—more so than our so-called present day scientific agricultural methods. Each year we see more farmers taking up our method and I have yet to see the first farmer who, having begun to practice it, has abandoned it.[86]

J. I. Rodale did not live to see the movement gain official sanction from the government, or grow into a mainstream industrial and consumer market. While stating that he fully expected to live to the age of 102 he instead died the same age as Albert Howard, 73, from a heart attack. He went out with a bang. He died dramatically while giving an interview on the Dick Cavett Show. Most parts of the country did not see his death, though a few stations aired the show before the tapes could be recalled. Cavett introduced Rodale dramatically,

> My next guest used to be known as a food freak. Now that he's rich and famous—a *New York Times* article called him—"Guru of the Food Cult"—a lot more people are listening to him. J. I. Rodale is his name. He's an unusual man with a lot of opinions which the U. S. Department of Agriculture, to mention one, doesn't agree with.

Rodale gave a basic sales pitch for organic farming, discussing the ideas of Sir Albert Howard and crediting Howard as the originator of the movement. After an intermission, Rodale boasted to Cavett that, "I am so healthy that I expect to live on and on. I have no aches or pains. I'm full of energy..." He then laid out the evils of sugar and the corruption of the chemical companies. Then, after discussing a pet theory on how electricity worked in the human body, he slumped in his chair, his chin on his chest. The audience laughed, thinking he was feigning sleep, and playing a joke. Cavett asked "Mr. Rodale, are you all right?" When Cavett realized something had gone terribly wrong, he called for a physician. Rodale died a few minutes later at Roosevelt Hospital.[87]

[85] Ibid., 110–11.
[86] J. I. Rodale, *Organic Merry-Go-Round* (Emmaus, 1954), 37. As quoted in Ibid., 104.
[87] Ibid., 225–36.

JAPAN

In addition to the United States, Britain, and its settlement dominions, Japan also became a key player on the global organic scene after the Second World War. A number of historical precedents served to arouse interest. The abolition of feudalism in 1868 launched a period of agricultural and industrial development under the Emperor Meiji. Rather than farming land as serfs under the aristocratic class (the *Daimyo*), more peasants owned land privately or worked as paid laborers on large estates. By the 1930s chemical fertilizers and pesticides, along with mechanization, cooperatives, and research stations, changed the farming landscape of Japan to resemble that of other westernized countries. The move away from animal power with horses and oxen eliminated most animal dung for fertilizer and led to an uncritical adoption of chemical fertilizers and pesticides. Farmers used the traditional methods of returning nutrients to the soil—such as the composting of human waste—only when they could not afford the new methods.

On September 27, 1940, Japan, Germany, and Italy signed the Tripartite Pact. The new alliance heightened the interest of Japanese officials in the agricultural policy of Germany. The National Socialists experimented with a number of natural farming methods in the 1930s to steer a middle ground between the tractor-centric collectivization in the Soviet Union and the streamlined agricultural production from farm to factory as seen in the United States. Neither Germany nor Japan had vast tracts of land and needed to make smaller farm plots more efficient. In addition, Japan and Germany both envisioned settling land in their new colonies—the Germans in Eastern Europe and the Japanese in Manchuria. Manchuria beckoned as a relief valve for depressed rural conditions in Japan, and as a way for settlers to solidify the Japanese empire. The new settlements also reinforced agrarian ideals of a self-sufficient citizenry that would—it was hoped—promote pan-Asian racial harmony with Japan and thus cement the imperial mission.[88]

One advocate of natural farming methods emerged in the northern island of Hokkaido, Japan's second largest island. Colonists farmed land in Hokkaido seized from the Ainu peoples under the authority of the Meiji government. The soil, however, had lower fertility than Japan's main island and, as a result, farmers often used cattle manure to raise productivity. The successful dairy farmer Torizō Kurosawa espoused ideas that addressed problems of soil fertility. As a director of the Hokkaido Cooperative Creamery Association and its successor company Snow Brand Milk Products Co. Ltd., he emphasized the primacy of agriculture and rural life as the bedrock of the state.[89] Kurosawa rejected chemicals in agriculture and advocated "cyclic farming"—that is, returning cattle manure back into the soil (also known

[88] The Kōki Hirota cabinet proposed the "Plan for Manchuria Agricultural Emigration of One million Households" which started in earnest in 1934. See Tatsushi Fujiwara, *Nachisu Doitsu no yuki nogyo: "Shizen tono kyosei" ga unda "minzoku no zetsumetsu"* [Nazi Germany's Organic Farming: "The Extinction of Ethnicity" born of "Coexistence with Nature"] (Tokyo, 2012), 25. See also Sandra Wilson, "The 'New Paradise': Japanese Emigration to Manchuria in the 1930s and 1940s," *The International History Review* 17/2 (1995): 249–86.

[89] Hokkaido Seiraku Kumiai and Yukijirushi Nyūgyō Kabushiki-Gaisha respectively.

as "Hakkaido farming"). As an early environmentalist he also lobbied the government (along with Japan's foremost and earliest conservationist, Shōzō Tanaka) to help pollution victims of the Ashio Copper Mine Pollution Incident.[90]

Kurosawa pushed hard for the adoption of the "Hakkaido Farming" method for new Japanese settlers in Manchuria. He wrote a pamphlet titled *National Policy on Strong Soil and Livestock Machine Agriculture* in May 1943 and sharply criticized standard agricultural practice.[91] He argued that the government's plan to colonize Manchuria with "one million households" would entail millions of Japanese settlers in Manchuria. While an admirable goal, he predicted that using current industrial methods the project would fail abysmally. Farmers today, he argued, are too detached from the natural methods and too insensitive to issues of soil fertility. While the land and the soil in the past had "nurtured today's Japanese race," if the farmers in Japan and Manchuria "partake of food produced in unhealthy soil, inevitably, their physique will be smaller." Chemical fertilizers only temporarily helped crop production and ultimately failed the farmer and the consumer. "Natural cycle" use of manure—not tractors—was needed in Manchuria. The "Jewish civilization" of industrial western agriculture only poisoned the Japanese.[92]

In the 1950s ideas about organic farming began to seep into Japan, through Albert Howard's own work and through the representation of Howard's ideas in Rodale's book, *Pay Dirt*, titled in the Japanese version, *The Golden Soil* [Ogon no tsuchi].[93] Though *Pay Dirt*, first published in 1950, attracted only a small readership, the translator enthused that the book "should have been written by somebody Japanese, and because there was no such book, I think that we have to substitute it with this translated book."[94]

The director of the school that published *Pay Dirt* did so upon the enthusiastic recommendation of Frank S. Booth (1880–1957). Booth wrote the foreword titled "Dedicated to Japan's Farmers." He was Director of the Ferris School in Yokohama, a Presbyterian founded educational institution designed to teach English and western cultural values to the Japanese. An American raised and educated in Japan, he had attended Rutgers University and returned to Japan to work for the Sale Frazer Company and then the Nichiro fishery company. Interned by the Japanese government during the war, he held no grudges and negotiated with the Allied General Headquarters to gain favorable terms for Japan and, after his death, was

[90] F. G. Notehelfer, "Japan's First Pollution Incident," *Journal of Japanese Studies*, 1/2 (1975): 361; Tanaka Shozo, *Tanaka Shozo senshu* (7 vol.), ed. Anzai Kunio, Kano Masanao, Komatsu Hiroshi, Sakaya Junji and Yui Masaomi (Tokyo, 1989): 4: 159; Robert Stolz, "Nature over Nation: Tanaka Shōzō's fundamental river law" *Japan Forum* 18/3 (2007): 417–37.

[91] Torizō Kurosawa, *Kendo kokusaku to yuchiku kikai nogyo.*

[92] Fujiwara, *Nachisu Doitsu no yuki nogyo,* 248, 249.

[93] This book was published by Rakuno Gakuen Correspondence Education Publishing Department. [This school was headed by Torizo Kurowawa, first as director from 1942–46, and then as President of the school from 1950–82, then as the director again in 1957–1966]. See Michio Uozumi, "Introduction," in Albert Howard, *Nogyo Seiten* [An Agricultural Testament], trans. Shigeru Yasuda (Tokyo, 2003), 313.

[94] Teruo Ichiaku, "Afterword," in J. I. Rodale, *Yuki noho: shizen junkan to yomigaeru seimei* [Organic Farming: Natural Circulation and Life that Revives], trans. Teruo Ichiaku (Tokyo, 1974), 379.

awarded the Third Class in the Order of the Sacred Treasure. His enthusiasm for Albert Howard, and then Rodale's publications, led him to advocate organic farming and places him as a key figure in the history of organic farming in Japan.[95] The craze for modernization, however, meant that sales remained small. But more publications soon followed. In 1959 the Council for the Productivity Improvement of Agriculture, Forestry and Fisheries published Howard's book, *The Waste Products of Agriculture*.[96] This brought Howard's ideas to a wider readership in Japan.

During the American occupation of Japan (1945–51) General Macarthur instituted a policy that brought widespread and radical land reforms. Large landowners surrendered most of their land to their tenants. Almost overnight the number of independent farmers doubled, and they managed the lion's share of arable land available in Japan.[97] They also provided a potential base of farmers open to new niche markets like organic farming who were concerned about soil fertility and human health. To stay in business, however, most farmers increasingly adopted chemicals and mechanization to raise yield. Set agricultural prices kept profits low and labor costs continued to rise in the 1950s and 60s due to migration into the large urban areas—largely Tokyo, Osaka, and Nagoya.[98] By 1961, one scholar estimated that agriculture had thoroughly modernized and was "mono-cultural, mechanized, well-equipped, specialized, and dependent on chemical and fossil fuels energy."[99]

Low profits led to consolidation of farmland and distribution networks to gain efficiencies. This in turn led to the growth of a small number of corporate monopolies that distributed food to stores, and led also to the consolidation of retail chains that monopolized meat, milk, rice, fruit, and vegetables. Many small farmers went bankrupt or sold out to corporate farms.[100] Those small farmers that survived increasingly turned to farmers' markets, selling directly to consumers which enabled them to claim 80–90 percent of the retail price. It also put farmers in direct contact with consumers who communicated their concerns for food safety to the farmer (or to the farmer's family staffing the stall). This new communication, sidelining the monopolies, fed into existing consumer led cooperatives in Japan and gave rise

[95] See "Booth, Frank S.," *20th Century Japanese Dictionary of People*. Available online at: https://kotobank.jp/word/%E3%83%96%E3%83%BC%E3%82%B9-124755#E3.83.87.E3.82.B8.E3.82.BF.E3.83.AB.E7.89.88.20.E6.97.A5.E6.9C.AC.E4.BA.BA.E5.90.8D.E5.A4.A7.E8.BE.9E.E5.85.B8.2BPlus [accessed August 26, 2017].

[96] Albert Howard, *The Waste Products of Agriculture*, trans. Ken Yamaji (Tokyo, 1959). This book was published by Zaidan Houjin Nourinsuisangyo Seisansei Koujou Kaigi [The Council for the Productivity Improvement of Agriculture, Forestry and Fisheries]. It was republished again in 1985 by Nihon Keizai Hyouronsha with a translation and foreword provided by the Japan Organic Agriculture Association (JOAA).

[97] Shyuzou Teruoka, *Nihon no nougyou 150 nen: 1850–2000 nen* [150 Years of Japanese Agriculture: 1850–2000] (Tokyo, 2003), 87. Pan Jie, "The Ethics and Business of Organic Food Production, Circulation and Consumption in Japan," PhD Dissertation (Submitted August, 2014), The University of Hong Kong, 31–2.

[98] Chie Nakane, *Social aspects of Japan's Industrialization* (Hong Kong, 1981); Jie, *Organic Food Productioni*, 35.

[99] Ibid., 37.

[100] Farmer population reduced from 5,430,000 in 1985 to 2,600,000 in 2010. See Ibid., 41.

to the "teikei" movement, discussed shortly, that underpinned the growth of organic farming in Japan.[101]

Large distributors and retailers had few concerns for food safety or the protection of the environment.[102] Along with the increased production and the streamlining of food production, the modernization of Japanese farming also led to soil infertility, which in turn led to instances of crop failure, increased disease, and insect damage. Further expansion of industrialized livestock led to increased use of antibiotics.[103] With mass industrialization also came pollution of water and air, exemplified by the outbreak of Minamata disease—a mercury driven neurological disorder caused by high mercury levels in fish that broke out in the region housing the Chisso chemical and Showra Denko chemical companies.[104]

Increasingly, small groups of consumers worried about the health of their food. Consumers and farmers united in a grass roots "teikei" (partnership) movement to buy vegetables, rice, milk, and eggs directly from the field.[105] Teikei partnerships began in 1972 when a group of Tokyo consumers visited farmland just outside the city to contract for fresh supplies sold directly from farm to table. The group persuaded seventeen initial farmers to raise organic crops and sell their produce only to the group. Farmers benefited because the teikei clubs promised to buy all the produce at an agreed price. They also benefited because it gave them a variety of crops to grow and helped small farms stay afloat on higher prices. The personal health of the farmers and the soil fertility of their farms were also concerns.[106]

Concurrent with these efforts, in 1971 Teruo Ichiraku founded the Japan Organic Agriculture Association (JOAA). Ichiraku organized the steering committee and ran seminars and workshops, as well as the annual meeting. The JOAA established ten goals or points, which included: mutual assistance; crop planning; the agreement to buy all a farmer produced; fair prices; self-delivery; democratic governance; education; transparent management; and working toward the ethics of teikei.[107] The JOAA on its founding issued the following statement,

> A close inspection of current farming techniques which reveals them to be on the one hand efficacious and rational, but on the other hand questionable in terms of product quality, safety and taste, or threatening to farm workers' health...if the management of crops and animal waste in some way hinders the cultivation of soil fertility or environmental preservation, these techniques must be ruled out...we must develop alternative technologies.[108]

---

[101] Ibid., 44–5.   [102] Ibid., 41.   [103] Uozumi, "Introduction," 313.

[104] See Jeffrey Broadbent, "Japan: A Forword," *Forging Environmentalism: Justice, Livlihoods and Contested Environments*, ed. Joane R. Bauer (London, 2006): 177.

[105] Notes from Cayce Hill and Hiroko Kubota, "Thirty-five Years of Japanese Teikei," *Sharing the Harvest: A Citizen's Guide to Community Supported Agriculture*, eds. Elizabeth Henderson and Robyn Van En (Vermont, 2007): 267.

[106] Kazumi Konrod, "The Alternative Food Movement in Japan: Challenges, Limits, and Resilience of the Teikei System," *Agriculture and Human Values* 32 (2015): 145–6.

[107] Ibid., 146.

[108] Tatshushi Fujiwara notes that organic farming only came into prominence due to the founding in 1971 of the JOAA. See "Foreword," *Nachisu Doitsu no yuki nogyo*, 22–3.

The 1970s and 80s witnessed a rapid growth in teikei groups as a result of the JOAA, growing to around 1,000 groups by 1990. The new teikei groups created a ready audience for organic farming books. Finding no equivalent in Japanese literature, Ichiraku translated Rodale's *Pay Dirt* into Japanese in 1974. In order to make it more attractive to Japanese readers, he changed the title to *Organic Farming: Natural Circulation and Life that Revives*. In the afterword, Ichiraku gave an estimate of its influence. He notes that one of the main impetuses behind organic farming in Japan was Howard's book *Agricultural Testament*. In addition, he noted, the 5,000 or so health food stores in the United States that Japanese visitors had encountered on their trips had raised demands for similar stores selling organic produce in Japan.[109]

The publication of a book of essays by Sawako Ariyoshi, *The Complex Contamination [Fukugō Osen]*, brought organic farming to a wider public audience in Japan. Ariyoshi was a Catholic who spent the early years of her childhood in Dutch Indonesia. She traveled widely in her lifetime, enjoying long stints in the United States where she may have been exposed to organic principles, first at Sarah Lawrence College in New York and then at the University of Hawaii. A morning newspaper, *Asashi Shimbun*, serialized *The Complex Contamination* in 1974–75. It contained interviews with experts, food manufacturers, and organic farmers, and surprisingly for a best-selling book, contained "no handsome men or beautiful women…no love…no story nor main character."[110] Instead, Ariyoshi's book raised critical concern for the amount of pollutants in Japan, similar to Rachel Carson's work *Silent Spring*. Her book was a folksy yet pioneering study of the impact—present and future—of chemical fertilizers, detergents, carcinogenic dyes, exhaust fumes from cars and other polluting agents. She traced through common items in the kitchen and home how poisons accumulated in the body—through detergents for dishes and clothes, automobile emissions, and polluted water from factories, pesticides that poured through the facets, and through chemical fertilizers and pesticides that degraded food in the refrigerator. These toxins had, she argued, been accumulating since the 1950s and all this became "complex contamination"—that is, contamination from many sources.[111]

Ariyoshi's book brought attention to another advocate of organic farming, Giryo Yanase. Yanase, born in 1920, studied medicine at Kyoto University. Upon graduation he served as an army medical doctor during the Second World War in the Philippines. On his return to Japan in 1946 after the war he worked at the Amagasaki Hospital in Hyogo Prefecture, and then, in 1952, set up his own practice in his hometown of Gojo. He developed a private passion for organic farming and sought to preserve the purity of his boyhood environment threatened by industrialization. The Kongo Mountains fronted Gojo—a region lionized by the classic Manyo poets from the eighth century and a land described as "the open field

[109] Teruo Ichiaku, "Afterword," J. I. Rodale, *Yuki noho: shizen junkan to yomigaeru seimei* [Organic Farming: Natural Circulation and Life that Revives] trans. Teruo Ichiaku (Tokyo, 1974): 377.
[110] Fujiwara, "Foreword," 23.   [111] Ibid.

where serenity sublimates the soul."[112] Running his own medical clinic he came to the conclusion that pollution affected the health of his patients. He reminisced that "in the autumn of 1952 I began to notice that agricultural science was heading in the wrong direction." On his own he researched organic principles and decided to begin farming. He promoted the direct sale of organic produce in stores and to consumers and became convinced that industrial farming led to an increase in "cancer, leukemia, stomach ulcers liver disorders, kidney and endocrine problems, rheumatism, and other metabolic disorders."[113] In 1975, he wrote *Revolution for Organic Farming: Sow on Unpolluted Soil [Yuki nogyo kakumei: yogore naki tsuchni ni make]*, noting that modern civilization and modern farming both kill humans and deprive society of natural resources. He wanted, he wrote "to advocate a civilization that is presupposing not to deprive or kill, but to give and make alive."[114]

Organic farming had many fellow travelers in Japan. In the 1940s Masanobu Fukuoka began "natural farming." He is appreciated around the world by a small and dedicated group of readers for his book *The One-Straw Revolution*, published in 1975. In this book, he presents a deeply Buddhist religiosity merged with a faith that nature is self-regulating and proposes that, when crops are allowed to grow with minimum interference, it heals both the land on which the food is grown and the farmer. He came to agriculture obliquely, resigning from his work as a micro-biologist in Yokohama and returning to his family's farm in 1938. Believing (in accordance with classical Buddhist doctrine) that the material world was an illusion and all our experiences in this world amount to nothing, he used his farm to illustrate "do-nothing farming," to show that diminished intervention with nature produced bountiful harvests. He showed how radically reducing time and labor spent on making composts, spreading fertilizers and pesticides, or even tilling the soil to plant seeds could save effort and money. He preached that seeds encased in soil could be scattered almost effortlessly and could still produce a bountiful harvest. Weeds helped, and did not harm the crop. At most, chicken manure could be spread on the soil, if needed. His methods were simple. He writes,

> To plant, I simply broadcast rye and barley seed on separate field in the fall, while the rice is still standing. A few weeks later I harvest the rice and spread the rice straw back over the fields.[115]

By rejecting traditional science, and what humans think they know about nature, he claimed high agricultural productivity for his farm. While this contradicts basic human knowledge—both professional and even amateur—Fukuoka reminds the reader that humanity "knows nothing at all."[116] Like Rudolf Steiner, Fukuoka had more of a cultural influence on consumers than any measurable practical success. There are very few documented instances of his followers applying his methods and successfully running farms to bring produce to market. His method of attaining high yields with no tilling, no planting, no chemicals, no fertilizers, no weeding,

---

[112] As quoted in Jiko-Kai, "What is the Jiko-kai?". Available online at: http://www.jiko-kai.org/en/about.html [accessed December 10, 2016].
[113] Ibid.   [114] As quoted in Fugiwara, "Foreword," 23.
[115] Masanobu Fukuoka, *The One-Straw Revolution* (Goa, 2014).   [116] Ibid., 4.

and no pruning are difficult to replicate outside of his own farm in Japan. Yet his profoundly romantic and intuitive approach to nature played a role in inspiring urban consumers to seek out organic products. Like Steiner's biodynamic methods, most farmers around the world who incorporate aspects of Fukuoka's ideas are organic farmers adding a few cultural or philosophical touches from Fukuoka to their work. Where he has had his greatest impact may have been in inspiring some followers of permaculture.

Interestingly, consumers—not gardeners, farmers or government officials—launched organic farming in Japan. This differentiates the organic farming movement in Japan from Britain and the United States, where, though consumer interest always existed, organic farming was largely driven by the desire of farmers and gardeners themselves to raise healthy food. Three causes set Japan apart from this pattern. The first is that the organic farming movement in Japan never spread widely in the 1950s and 60s and, thus, the organic farming movement gained popularity in Japan only in the 1970s and 80s when retail health food store networks were already prominent in some western countries. Therefore, the visibility of organic farming in other parts of the world, particularly the United States, caught the attention of those who traveled as tourists or did business overseas—and few of these were farmers by profession. Secondly, in large urban areas, land was scarce, and the average middle-class Japanese house did not include a large lot or back yard, as did houses in the growing suburbs of the United States. Thirdly, a large network of consumer cooperative organizations already existed in Japan and quickly picked up organic food as a niche market. The Rochdale-Pioneers-Cooperative model, founded in Britain in 1844 had already laid the base for cooperative societies around the world and especially in Japan.[117] Japan opened its first Rochdale cooperative in 1879. Buying clubs also spontaneously organized to feed hungry populations after the Second World War and this further built up a network of cooperative societies.[118] These food cooperatives provided a broad network of consumers experienced in the concept and practice of cooperation between small farms and buyers. When in 1971, Tokyo consumers approached farmers to join a small organic cooperative movement, called, teikei, both farmers and consumers understood how cooperative organizations worked and were ready apply organic principles to a known and trusted method of networking.

CONCLUSION

The examples above from Britain, the United States, and Japan do not capture the whole global story of organic farming in this period: societies throughout the non-communist world also boasted individual farmers, plantations, and certainly gardeners who practiced organic protocols. Most of them were scattered individuals who remained in the former British Empire, or who had stumbled

[117] Johnston Birchall, *The International Co-operative Movement* (Manchester, 1997), 1–6.
[118] Konrod, "The Alternative Food Movement in Japan," 147.

across the writing of Albert Howard or his many fellow travelers. As in Europe, the passion to practice natural or traditional methods of farming could not be contained in a single coherent movement. But from the 1980s and afterwards, as we will see in the final chapter, there began the integration of organic farming—already an international movement—into government policy and certification standards that, with world trade, created a new global encomium that standardized the Indore Method in government policy and international trade agreements—a dream that Albert and Louise Howard never lived to see fulfilled.

9

The 1980s to the Present

While a few positive stories on organic farming appeared in the 1970s most mainstream press coverage mocked or dismissed organic farmers and consumers. However, the growing army of consumer shoppers at health food stores in the United States made the movement impossible to ignore. The *Washington Post*, for instance, ran the occasional piece by Sidney Margolius on organic farming in the 1970s and early 1980s. The North American Newspaper Alliance syndicated his work in over 100 newspapers and dubbed him the "Dean of consumer affairs."[1] He gained the spotlight by seeking out and revealing hacks and frauds, including those who peddled natural solutions to allay fears of chemical fertilizers and pesticides. A few decades earlier he had championed DDT as "great stuff" and in *Collier* magazine lovingly gave directions for applying DDT inside the home, on mattresses and furniture—including directly applying DDT dust on clothing and on pets.[2] He had not changed much by the 1970s when he reviewed a book heavily influenced by organic farming titled *Unfit for Human Consumption* by Ruth Harmer. He summarized how the public perception on chemicals had evolved. We are caught, he wrote, between two fears: (1) of foods poisoned by chemicals; and (2) the fear that food costs will rise without chemicals. He caricatured the organic farm enthusiast as an "all-out organic foodist who envisions mental health through a daily gram of niacin, and sexual vitality through halvah."[3]

Margolius conceded that not every single organic food purist could be written off as paranoid or as a cultist munching on sesame seeds. Too many scientists had joined the movement to do that. But Harmer, he opined, had gone too far. While she correctly told the dramatic story of the 1969 courtroom drama of the United Farm Workers Organizing Committee—that demanded unsuccessfully to see the agricultural records for the chemicals used on crops—she missed the credit due to the Food and Drug Administration (FDA) for banning many harmful chemicals. In 1959 the FDA banned aminotriazole on cranberries, taking considerable heat from congress, farmers, and the *Journal of the American Medical Association*. Margolius concluded by calling for an independent commission to examine the organic food charges raised by Ruth Harmer.[4]

[1] Marian Burros, "A Tribute to Sidney Margolius," *Washington Post* (February 7, 1980).
[2] Sidney Margolius, "DDT is no Cure All," *Collier's Weekly* (November 17, 1945): 27–35.
[3] Sidney Margolius, "Review: Unfit for Human Consumption," *Washington Post, Times Herald* (December 9, 1971).
[4] Eisenhower appointed Arthur Flemming Secretary of Health, Education and Welfare in 1958. Flemming supported the ban, announcing that tests on rats showed it caused thyroid cancer.

The *Washington Post* in early 1972 took a more bemused approach towards consumers of organic products. In another article the paper related how consumers hunted wormy apples, puny potatoes, and dirt encrusted carrots. They were "longhaired self-styled 'freaks,'" but also "close-cropped conservatives." These "suspicious shoppers," who avoid the "chemical feast" of conventional food, believed that organic food contained more nutrition and tasted better. The article measured the listings under "health food" and found stupendous growth, with 10 inches of space in the 1969 Yellow Pages grown to 42 inches in 1971. The article then quoted the Director of the Bureau of the FDA, Dr. Virgil O. Wodicks, who said that "nobody has actually proved there's any real difference between organic and non-organic foods." Though deprecatory of organic farming, the article emphasized the real issue of concern over certification and pointed out that the health food industry depended largely on trust, with many within the movement calling for an objective standard enforced by the federal government.[5]

Many scientists took a very public stance against organic farming. Thomas H. Jukes, a molecular biologist at the University of California, Berkeley, and a regular columnist in *Nature* between 1975 and 1980 declared organic farming to be "scientific nonsense." He declared in a meeting of the American Association of the Advancement of Science in 1974 that the alarming growth of the organic farming movement had made "significant inroads into the attitudes of the general populations." This new myth undermined the maximum production of foods. A colleague on the same panel, Daniel I. Arnon, Professor of Cell Physiology at Berkeley, agreed and suggested that organic and conventional produce delivered no identifiable nutritional difference "because all plant food enters roots in an inorganic form."[6]

Earl Butz, Secretary of Agriculture under Richard Nixon and Gerald Ford, took a final stand against the growing tide of the organic farming movement. Oddly, he often advocated the very agrarian values that appealed to organic farmers—the belief in sturdy, independent, and virtuous farmers as the bedrock of a stable republic. An article in the *Washington Post* on June 13, 1976, drew attention to the fact that the majority of farmers saw Butz as "the greatest Secretary of Agriculture in the history of the Republic." He was so popular in Iowa that the 1972 election campaign of Richard Nixon advertised the slogan, "Vote for Nixon or lose your Butz." Nixon himself ate wheat germ and did not disdain the health food movement. He signed into law the Environmental Protection Agency, the Endangered Species Act, and the National Environmental Protection Act—thus establishing the EPA as one of the most powerful tools for the protection of the environment. Nixon

[5] Hank Burchard, "The Great Hunt for the Puny Potato: Despite High Prices, Ranks of Organic Food Buyers Swell," *Washington Post, Times Herald* (February 28, 1971). See also Sidney Margolius, "Eating for Health: HEALTH FOODS—FACTS AND FAKES," *Washington Post* (April 25, 1974); Jean Mayer, "The Nondefinition of 'Organic Foods,'" *Washington Post* (April 28, 1974).

[6] For a short biography of Thomas H. Jukes see Watson M. Laetsch, Kevin Padian, and Roderic B. Park. "Biography of Thomas H. Jukes." Available online at: http://content.cdlib.org/view?docId=hb1r29n709&doc.view=content&chunk.id=div00029&toc.depth=1&brand=calisphere&anchor.id=0 [accessed December 27, 2016]. "Organic Farming 'Scientific Nonsense,'" *Washington Post* (February 28, 1974).

also supported a broad range of bills that fought pollution of water and air, reduced pesticides, and protected marine environments.[7] Without a doubt Nixon adopted more green legislation than any President since Teddy Roosevelt, who championed the conservation movement and the mass protection of forests. But his Secretary of Agriculture Earl Butz nonetheless took the side of large corporate farms and pushed for higher efficiency and modernization in farming, warning farmers to "get big or get out." He did not oppose small farms, but wanted the small farms to consolidate when necessary and to become efficient enough to get off government subsidies. To help farmers he also arranged large grain purchases by the Soviet Union, and a number of other states, including North Korea, South Korea, and South Vietnam, inviting charges that he was soft on Communism as well as right wing dictators. Butz hoped through these deals to bring stability to the price of grain for American farmers while also acting as a force for peace in world affairs. Butz idealized farmers and the role they played in the world. He reminded them in true agrarian fashion that "you are the peacemakers, you are the most productive part of America."[8]

He could not, however, slow down the closure of small farms that had been underway since the 1950s any more than Republican or Democratic Secretaries of Agriculture could do before or after his term in office. While the burgeoning organic farming market may have been an option for many small farmers, he did not see the potential of the organic farm movement and missed the opportunity to support it. He opposed the reduction of nitrates in bacon and the banning of diethylstilbestrol—an estrogen hormone that fattened animals—to cattle. Organic farming "would condemn hundreds of millions of people to a lingering death by malnutrition and starvation," he claimed (which of course was technically true if conventional farming were to end abruptly).[9] Earl Butz reflected the fact that the agrarian ideal attracted both Republicans and Democrats and that the ideal was also under extreme pressure in a globalized world. The massive changes arising from the migration to cities and the globalization of farm markets meant that many small farmers either depended upon subsidies for price supports and payments to keep land out of production or, without the supports, went bankrupt, giving way to larger corporate farms.

THE USDA AND ORGANIC CERTIFICATION IN THE UNITED STATES

A breakthrough in mainstream acceptance of organic farming came in 1980, from the USDA. The Secretary of Agriculture who followed Butz and Robert Bergland, sponsored a report that brought together an interdisciplinary team of scientists to

[7] Gregory A. Barton, "Introduction," *American Environmentalism*, ed. Gregory A. Barton (San Diego, 2002): 18.
[8] James Risser and George Anthan, "Why they love Earl Butz: Prosperous farmers see him as the greatest," *New York Times* (June 13, 1976).
[9] Ibid.

study sixty-nine organic farm case studies. In a surprise to most of the scientists involved, they came away with a high regard for the success and professional management of these organic farms.[10] Bergland's background prepared him to lead this remarkable team. He ran a 600-acre farm producing wheat and lawn seed. He also served as an advisor to the FAO annual conference in 1973, which, through its continued interest in forestry and conservation ideals, could not have failed to impress him. In 1961 Bergland chaired the Minnesota Conservation Service, which, given its emphasis on soil conservation, further instilled his sympathies toward a more ecological basis of farming. He then served as the Midwest Director of the United States Conservation Service. His father, Selma Bergland, influenced him. He had lost his farm during the depression and told his son that politics is power, and he needed to "get in it." Winning a seat in Congress in 1971 he served on numerous committees—for conservation, small business, and agricultural debt. Then in 1977 President Carter appointed Bergland as the new Secretary of Agriculture.[11] As it turned out, he used his political position to advance organic farming.

Under his leadership, the USDA Study Team on Organic Farming issued the *Report and Recommendations on Organic Farming* in 1980.[12] It served as the first important step in bringing organic farming out of the wilderness of institutional and professional isolation and into the mainstream. Dr. Anson R. Bertrand, Director of Science and Education at the USDA, led the study team. After approaching the Rodale publishing house for advice, they decided on a list of sixty-nine organic farms in twenty-three states as case studies. The study team then reviewed organic farming literature and practice in the United States, England, Germany, Switzerland, and Japan. Interviewing the farmers and inspecting on-site, they grappled with the reasons farmers chose to switch from conventional to organic methods. The team also investigated instances of success and failure to understand the economics of the organic farming movement, and how costs, prices, and profits affected both the farmer and the consumer. The study team uncovered a number of concerns that lay behind organic farming: the energy cost of inputs from chemical fertilizers; the decline in soil fertility; the devastating environmental pollution caused by industrial agriculture; the deadly effects of pesticides on humans and animals; and the continued demise of small farms.[13] Most importantly, the report called for more study and more dialog, and then suggested increased research funding to help organic farmers and consumers. In a foreword, Bergland wrote that,

> We in USDA are receiving increasing numbers of requests for information and advice
> on organic farming practices. Energy shortages, food safety, and environmental concerns

---

[10] William Lockeretz "Introduction," *Organic Farming: An International History*, ed. William Lockeretz (Oxfordshire, 2007): 2.

[11] Robert Bergland, "Toward a National Food Policy," (September 9, 1977), The 38th Alfred M. Landon Lecture Series. Available online at: https://www.youtube.com/watch?v=qI0xGNqaLSo [accessed February 11, 2017].

[12] The USDA Study Team on Organic Farming issued a *Report and Recommendations on Organic Farming* (Washington, 1980).

[13] Ibid., x.

have all contributed to the demand for more comprehensive information on organic farming technology.[14]

He mentioned that small farmers and gardeners, as well as large enterprises, had developed "alternative farming systems" that needed a better understanding of their practices and impact. He ended hopefully that "we look forward to increasing communication between organic farmers and the U. S. Department of Agriculture." The report was a far cry from the earlier accusations from the FDA that organic farmers and health food enthusiasts are swindlers—even murderers—undermining the health of gullible consumers. This breakthrough with the USDA for the first time brought the organic farming movement out of the cold, and though continued progress proved fitful, the organic farming movement grew exponentially in the United States and, increasingly, around the world.

The states of Oregon, Maine, and California had adopted legal definitions of "organic." The Bergland report analyzed particularly the California Organic Food Act of 1979 (COFA). COFA defined organic farming broadly in terms of food grown naturally—or ecologically—and mandated that the label "organic" only be applied to food produced "without application of synthetically compounded fertilizers, pesticides, or growth regulators."[15] Other stipulations of COFA applied. For twelve months the fields yielding products to be labeled organic had to be free of synthetics, and COFA specified the compounds that could be used and those prohibited. Meat, poultry, or fish had to be free of chemicals and drugs for ninety days before slaughter or thirty days before milk production. The definitions of "organic" used in California, as well as in Oregon and Maine, divided organic enthusiasts. Some felt legislators had adopted overly strict guidelines, and others feared that the law so watered down organic principles that "agribusiness interests will be able to pass off their chemical grown produce as organic."[16] With these issues in mind, and so as to guide future research and legislation, the Bergland report suggested its own carefully worded definition of organic,

> Organic farming is a production system which avoids or largely excludes the use of synthetically compounded fertilizers, pesticides, growth regulators, and livestock feed additives. To the maximum extent feasible, organic farming systems rely upon crop rotations, crop residues, animal manures, legumes, green manures, off-farm organic wastes, mechanical cultivation, mineral-bearing rocks, and aspects of biological pest control to maintain soil productivity and tilth to supply plant nutrients and to control insects, weeds, and other pests.[17]

The study team did little in the way of an historical review of organic farming. The report mentioned that many in the organic farming movement assumed that organic methods were a throwback to the agriculture of the 1930s. Garth Youngberg makes a similar statement in an oral interview with the National Agricultural Library, claiming that farmers in the 1940s largely practiced alternative and sustainable agriculture. Youngberg stated that farmers "began to adopt them [chemicals] in the late 50s and 60s." Even a cursory look at the books

---

[14] Ibid.   [15] Ibid., 6.   [16] Ibid.   [17] Ibid., xii.

produced by Albert Howard, Eve Balfour, or Rodale's mass circulated *Prevention* magazine would instantly dispel such notions that sustainable agriculture only retreated in the mid-twentieth century. Where the Bergland report and Youngberg were correct is in their assertions that some pockets of farming—particularly among small farmers—had not entirely adopted the use of synthetic fertilizers and pesticides and that in the 1960s and 70s the saturation of industrial agricultural methods eliminated almost all remaining mixed farming.

Youngberg played an important role in the Bergland report. He had earned a PhD in Political Science, focusing on agricultural public policy, in 1970. The publication of his article titled "The alternative agriculture movement" in the *Policies Study Journal* caught the eye of officials in the USDA who in 1979 then invited him to join the study team that produced the 1980 Bergland report. Youngberg emphasized that the decision to interview organic farmers proved key to the insights gained by the study team—a report based on library and laboratory research would have produced a much different and less momentous report. The scientists came to the team open minded, he believed, though still presuming that organic practitioners avoided sound scientific and professional management. Visiting farmers on their own turf and conducting "on-farm" case studies changed their thinking. The scientists "frankly, were very impressed by what we found." As they concluded interviews over the course of the summer and fall of 1979 their enthusiasm began to build. Youngberg relates,

> These were high level top, top level scientists who were finding some things in the soil structure, soil quality, life of the soil, in the soil microbiology, in these organic farms that had obviously been using green manures, rotation, applying animal manures and reincorporating crop residues properly...that were just very, very impressive. The feeling on the team at least, by the time we were ready to write the report was that this is something worth looking at...there was a clear feeling that this was a productive, viable option, or alternative for farmers that deserved some support. And so we recommended ten pages of research that we thought could usefully be done by USDA.[18]

The report was translated into eight languages, and was met with requests for copies from around the world, including many developing countries. Negative responses flooded in as well, as Youngberg pointed out, from vested interests. The election of 1981 also brought in a new Secretary of Agriculture, John Block, under President Reagan, who "had less enthusiasm for organic farming that secretary Bergland had." Budget cutting at the USDA sent a "chill through the department" and led scientists and policy makers in the USDA to shy away from the controversial Bergland report. But, even so, he pointed out that the report created momentum for organic farming. The 1980s accordingly saw major growth in acceptance of the movement, largely because the USDA gave the movement its stamp of approval. It was, he related, "a revolutionary step" that opened up a dialog long overdue.

---

[18] Garth Youngberg, Alternative Farming Information Center, National Agricultural Library (June 27, 2012). Available online at: https://www.youtube.com/watch?v=imBzVGzbEJY [accessed February 11, 2017].

Youngberg also relates how scientists in many land-grant universities read the report, and that this encouraged the blossoming of new research projects. In 1983 Youngberg left the USDA and founded the Institute for Alternative Agriculture (IAA) to develop farm-policy options and suggest ways the federal government could advance the organic movement. His group became a new lobby group for organic farming, and the only organic lobby group at the time with a presence in Washington DC.[19] Youngberg makes the point, as did Albert and Louise Howard decades earlier, that organic farming is a scientific practice.

> If people have the perception that this is a non-productive, non-scientific regressive kind of primitive agriculture then obviously they are not going to support it. Scientists are not going to try to find research funds, and policy makers are not going to vote for legislation.[20]

Youngberg also shared a concern about the broader acceptance of terms such as organic, alternative, or sustainable agriculture, arguing that a legalistic approach risked manipulation of the definition and production techniques that could go far afield from the original ecological ethic of organic farming.

Partisan politics added weight behind the Bergland report. Because a Democratic administration had sponsored the report and a Republican administration chose not to pursue its recommendations, the Democrat-leaning *Washington Post* lamented that too few had adopted organic principles. Secretary of Agriculture John Block had even dismissed organic research as a "dead end." In "Seeds of Organic Farming Falling on Barren Ground These Days" (June 13, 1982) the *Washington Post* forgot its very recent caricature of organic farmers as "food faddists" and lamented the change at the helm of the USDA. It also lamented the plight of Garth Youngberg who had formerly worked full-time on organic research. Block had reduced by half the workload Youngberg devoted to organic farming.[21] The *Washington Post* followed up on April 3, 1983, with a more optimistic article titled "More Farmers Taking the Organic Route: Organic Farmers Must Plow Through Information Desert."[22] The newspaper was not alone. Within only a few years of the Bergland report positive reports on organic farming reverberated through newspapers and other media forms.

---

[19] Mrs. Gene and Doug Wallace of the Wallace foundation supported the IAA, with a number of other foundations joining in to support. They started the *American Journal of Alternative Agriculture*.

[20] Garth Youngberg, Alternative Farming Information Center, National Agricultural Library (June 27, 2012). Available online at: https://www.youtube.com/watch?v=imBzVGzbEJY [accessed February 11, 2017].

[21] The *Washington Post*, so critical of Block on organic farming, neglected to mention a number of issues. It did not mention the Conservation Reserve Program that Block instituted to buy out soil eroded farmland, nor how this program conserved land for ecological purposes. Nor did the *Washington Post* give him credit for lifting Carter's 1979 grain embargo, or restricting farmers' debt to save family farms. The *Washington Post* however correctly depicted Block as no ally of organic farming. See Ward Sinclair, "Seeds of Organic Farming Falling on Barren Ground These Days," *The Washington Post* (June 13, 1982).

[22] Ward Sinclair, "More Farmers Taking the Organic Route: Organic Farmers Must Plow Through Information Desert," *Washington Post* (April 3, 1983). See also Tom Kapsidelis, "Organic Farming is Accepted As Part of the Agricultural Mainstream," *Washington Post* (June 27, 1983).

Certification concerns had dogged organic farmers and consumers from the beginning of the movement. Some form of certification had been a key policy element advocated by Albert Howard in the 1940s. While private third-party organizations attempted to fill the void of absent government oversight, this often led to confusion because each group defined different methods and protocols. This changed however, with the Organic Foods Production Act (OFPA) of 1990.[23] This bill, signed by President George Bush, established the National Organic Standards Program (NOSP). Housed in the USDA, the NOSP regulated organic farming guidelines and required the USDA to implement uniform national standards for organic goods—the National Organic Standards (NOS)—that would govern organic and livestock labeling. Implementation went slowly, with organic standards only introduced in 1997 and then—after a concerted public protest by organic groups that the rules were not stringent enough—the USDA tightened the protocols and implemented the law in October 21, 2002. After this period the USDA provided for the registration of other state and private organic certifiers (none could by law operate outside of the official USDA rules).[24]

The protest that occurred after OFPA and the final changes that led to the 2002 implementation of the act, revealed the competing model to the organic farming ideal: the concept of "sustainable" or "alternative" farming. One specialist in agricultural policy suggested that only a matter of degree separated sustainable and organic farming. Sustainable agriculture focused on the long-term effects of chemical use, but was open to flexibility and compromise, while organic procedures prohibited chemical usage altogether.[25] The conflict between these two approaches came to a head in 1997 when a coalition of organic groups lobbied the USDA to tighten the standards of the OFPA. A number of groups joined in the crusade including Rodale publishing house, Whole Foods Market, and the Organic Trade Association—the latter representing the organic business community in North America, including retailers, such as the giant corporate retail chain, Whole Foods, which established its first store in Austin Texas in 1980.[26]

The passage of OFPA brought the organic farming movement into the mainstream, codified it, and also protected it, almost sixty years after Howard published his Indore Method in the *Waste Products of Agriculture* in 1931. But it proved a dangerous moment. If the legal definition of "organic" was too loose and undefined it risked turning loyal consumers off the organic label. Further the authenticity of the organic ideal could have threatened the many followers of organic farmers and activists. Who, for instance owned the word, or defined it: the USDA or the contemporary network of organic enthusiasts who still followed the protocols of Albert Howard? The compromise reached by OFPA between farmers, activists,

[23] Title XXI of 1990 Farm Bill: "Food Agricultural Conservation and Trade Act of 1990," pub. L. No. 101-624, 104 Stat. 3359 (November 28, 1990).
[24] Robyn O'Sullivan, *American Organic: A Cultural History of Farming, Gardening, Shopping and Eating* (Kansas City, 2015), 134–5.
[25] Frye, *The Transnational Origin, Diffusion, and Transformation of "organic" Agriculture: A Study in Social Movement Framing and Outcomes* (Lafayette, OH, 2007), 135.
[26] Ibid., 96.

and business groups satisfied most stakeholders. With legal definitions in place corporations then expanded into the burgeoning market, as did Whole Foods grocery chain growing from its base in Austen Texas into upscale markets in cities across the United States. But with corporate growth came another disadvantage. Farmers who marketed their products as organic then had lengthy, detailed and expensive protocols to follow, including the requirement to show receipts for the purchase of approved inputs on the farm, and of course, the inspections that went along with it. The informal and free adoption of the name "organic" for food changed abruptly, denying many enthusiastic amateurs a market for their uncertified goods. The professionalization of small-farm operations often denied small producers the means of bringing their goods to market as organic.[27]

CERTIFICATION IN THE EUROPEAN UNION

These same concerns about certification roiled organic farming organizations in Europe. One advocate for certification regimes and for institutional acceptance of organic farming has been the International Federation of Organic Agriculture Movements (IFOAM), a global organization but one that was most active in Europe in the 1980s–90s. IFOAM was founded in 1972 in Versailles, France. The President of *Nature et Progres,* Roland Chevriot, drew together a few likeminded organizations to launch the new Federation—including the Soil Associations of both the UK and South Africa, Rodale Press, and the Swedish Biodynamic Association. The new organization regarded "biodynamic" to be a subset of organic farming. The sponsoring organization, *Nature et Progres,* was itself founded in 1964 to promote organic methods. Chevriot conceived of the idea of starting IFOAM while talking with Robert Rodale in May, 1972, on a trip to the United States. He later sent out a letter to over 50 organic groups. He wrote,

> At the time when industrial expansion is questioned and notions of "Quality" and "Survival" are raised, it seems necessary to me that organic agriculture movements make themselves known and coordinate their actions.[28]

To bring solutions to food quality and the ecological crises he proposed that "scientific and experimental data" cross borders and become a federation for the benefit of "all of us and humanity."[29]

Only 10 percent of recipients responded to his call for an inaugural meeting. But, by 1975, IFOAM had grown to fifty members representing seventeen countries and, by 1984, over 100 members representing fifty countries, including countries from Asia, Africa, and Latin America.[30] Just as in the United States with the Bergland

---

[27] O'Sullivan, *American Organic,* 134.

[28] Roland Chevriot, "Creation of an International Federation" (ND). Available online at: http://infohub.ifoam.bio/sites/default/files/page/files/founding_letter.pdf [accessed August 25, 2017].

[29] Ibid.

[30] John Paull, "From France to the World: The International Federation of Organic Agriculture Movements (IFOAM)," *Journal of Social Research & Policy,* 2 (December, 2010): 95.

report, the year of 1980 was also a breakthrough one for organic farming in Europe. IFOAM worked in partnership with the European Community to establish organic farming certification. IFOAM built on the pre-existing influence of organic farming groups and articulated the need for carefully conceived organic certification standards. Four countries in the European Union—Finland, Denmark, France, and Spain (joined by non-EU Switzerland)—instituted their own certification procedures.[31] In France organic farming went under the name of *Agriculture Biologique*, with procedures for the labeling of organic farming livestock in place by 1992. Austria followed with the *Austrian Codex Alimentarius* in 1983; the Danish in 1987 mandated public certification for the organic label. Spain and Finland instituted strict legal standards for the organic label in 1990. Almost all member countries in the European Union had private certification for organic farming (Greece an exception) by the time the European Union superseded privately defined organic protocols. This regulation, *EC Reg. 2092/91*, was published by the European Commission in 1991 and enforced as law in 1993.[32]

IFOAM's "Basic Standards" for certification played a leading role in guiding the EU to adopt the EU-wide certification program in 1991.[33] Under this program, member states are permitted to put stricter standards in place for certification, but they cannot be weaker. The imprint of the organic label, backed by law throughout the EU, gave consumers greater confidence in organic produce, and helped increase sales. Further, the private labeling by organic groups continued, with a logo marked on products side by side with EU approval. Consumers in Europe buy organic goods as a statement of ecological wholeness, in addition to meeting their desire for food with higher nutrition and free of chemicals. Slowly, organic farming products at the supermarket came to be seen as an aspect of a wider environmental consciousness.

THE GLOBAL ORGANIC WORLD

In most of the English-speaking world, particularly Canada, Australia, New Zealand, and South Africa, organic farming ran parallel to organic farming developments in Britain and the United States. Journals, newsletters, and magazines proliferated in the mid-1970s.[34] Organic societies saw past gardens and farms, and lobbied for the protection of the entire ecosystem, which included national and also

---

[31] S. Padel and N. Mampkin, "The Development of Governmental Support for Organic Farming in Europe," *Organic Farming: An International History*, ed. W. Lockeretz, (Cambridge, MA, 2007): 96.

[32] O. Schmid, "Development of Standards for Organic Farming," *Organic Farming: An International History*, ed. W. Lockeretz, (Cambridge, MA, 2007): 156.

[33] Sandra Schwindenhammer, "Global organic agriculture governance through standards: When inter-institutional policy-making oscillates between global harmonization and regional integration," paper presented at the International Conference on Public Policy, Milan (July 1–4, 2015): 9–11. Available online at: http://docplayer.net/27895891-Sandra-schwindenhammer.html [accessed August 25, 2017].

[34] Rebecca Jones, *Green Harvest: A History of Organic Farming and Gardening in Australia* (Collingwood, 2010), xii.

global challenges. Deforestation, wildlife conservation, and the greenhouse effect of industrial gases that led to global warming were all highlighted. In Australia the Organic Farming and Gardening Society (formerly the Victorian Compost Society) advocated for the preservation of the Great Barrier Reef in Queensland, as well as for cleaning up the Mordialloc Creek in Melbourne. A new and growing addition to the list of environmental demands by organic groups began in this period, including the protection of native plants and animals against invasive species. One submission to the Commonwealth Government House of Representatives Select Committee on Wildlife Conservation in 1971 by an organic spokesman is typical, stating that "the public aim should be to make the country viable for the natives [flora and fauna] that remain; and to make the whole an ecological entity."[35]

As in the United States, a back to the land movement in Australia ran parallel to the growth of organic farming, often with the eager participants little aware of the romantic farm literature tradition and the distrust of the big industrial vested interests that had preceded them decades earlier. The magazine *Grass Roots*, published in Victoria, Australia, also emphasized an idyllic rural existence and household self-sufficiency that merged seamlessly with the counter-cultural movement. The first edition of *Grass Roots* recast the language of rebellion against modernism that had begun before the Second World War for a new generation of the 1970s and 80s. By the 1990s the Australian Quarantine Inspection Service organized—through discussions with organic organizations and stakeholders—minimum certification standards that placed Australian organic exports in line with the European Union standards, resulting in a Ministerial Export Order from January 1, 1992.[36]

Certification standards rapidly moved from the United States and Europe to Japan and the rest of the world. In 1999 the Japanese Diet replaced "The Agricultural Basic Law" of 1961 with "The Basic Law on Food, Agriculture and Rural Areas."[37] This included, helpfully a "sustainable Agricultural Development" segment that encouraged sustainable agriculture for the twenty-first century, including the use of manure and straw to make compost fertilizers.[38] Michio Uozumi lamented, however, that even with this new law, "the research on organic farming is hardly conducted at national agricultural research centers or prefectural test centers."[39] The bulk of the budget was "pumped into genetic modification techniques and clone techniques with increasing tendency each year."[40] Consumer

[35] As quoted in Jones, *Green Harvest*, 60.
[36] E. Wynen and S. Fritz, "NASAA and Organic Agriculture in Australia," *Organic Farming: An International History*, ed. W. Lockeretz, (Cambridge, MA, 2007): 234–40.
[37] See Aurelia George Mulgan, "Agricultural Policy and Agricultural Policymaking: Perpetuating the Status Quo," *Japanese Governance: Beyond Japan Inc.*, eds. Jennifer Amyx and Peter Drysdale (London and New York, 2002): 171–95.
[38] Michio Uozumi, "Introduction," in Albert Howard, *Nogyo Seiten* [An Agricultural Testament], trans. Shigeru Yasuda (Tokyo, 2003), 315.
[39] Japan has forty-seven prefectures, including Tokyo as the capital state. A prefecture is equivalent to a state in the United States or Australia.
[40] Uozumi, "Introduction," 315.

demand, not government support, continued to drive organic farming in Japan as it had decades earlier.

The harmonization of organic certification through initiatives in the multilateral agencies of the UN helped spread the process of certification to most of the world in a relatively short period of time. As standards proliferated in the 1990s, these same standards became obstacles to international trade, with different countries requiring different protocols for attaching the organic label to food products. Further, because organic farming offered the prospect for developing nations to export goods at a premium price to the industrial centers of Europe, North America and Japan, the UN stepped in to resolve the regulatory fragmentation. The Food and Agriculture Organization (FAO), the United Nations Conference on Trade and Development (UNCTAD), and IFOAM established the International Task Force on Harmonization and Equivalence in Organic Agriculture (ITF) in 2002 to design and harmonize organic standards. In 2009 these same organizations launched the Global Organic Market Access Project (GOMA),

> to increase awareness of the need and opportunity for harmonization and equivalence for organic trade, to facilitate regional initiatives for cooperation, to promote IFT tools and offer technical assistance for using them, and to follow up on other recommendations and results of the ITF.[41]

In addition to global forums sponsored by the UN to hammer out differences in standards for organic farming, the UN established regional agreements as well. These numerous projects included the East African Organic Products Standard (EOPS), maintained by IFOAM and UNCTAD, the Pacific Organic Standard (POS), sponsored by IFOAM, the Asia Regional Organic Standards (AROS) and the ASEAN Standard for Organic Agriculture (OSOA), and the Harmonized Organic Regulations for Central America, Panama, and the Dominican Republic.[42] Beginning with the Bergland report the organic farming movement had, by the year 2000, experienced a sea of change. Institutional and government acceptance had become a reality.

By 2014 organic produce totaled over $80 billion in sales globally. Late comers to widespread global production in the first decade of the twenty-first century aggressively entered the market. China, Korea, Africa (outside South Africa), and Latin America became large producers of agricultural products, largely due to the globalization of certification standards and export centered economies.[43] NGOs played a particularly important role promoting organic farming in Latin America, primarily as a development tool that allowed small farmers to maximize profit on small plots with minimal economic cost—in line with Howard's attempt to provide Indian farmers with low-cost efforts to raise output. This has in recent years included government attempts to pay for conversion costs to organic agriculture

---

[41] As quoted in Schwindenhammer, "Global organic agriculture governance," 14.
[42] Ibid.
[43] "Worldwide sales of organic food from 1999 to 2015 (in billion U.S. dollars)," Statistica. Available online at: https://www.statista.com/statistics/273090/worldwide-sales-of-organic-foods-since-1999/ [accessed August 25, 2017].

and to encourage, through export agencies, the sale of coffee, bananas, and other goods to the European and North American markets.[44]

Marginal landscapes have in some regions provided the greatest swaths of territory devoted to organic farming, particularly through grazing. The higher price available for organic beef and lamb, combined with the necessity of grazing over large territories where the cost of fertilizers and pesticides would be prohibitive, allowed easier application of the organic label. This is the case in Australia, with its low nutrient soils, where almost 30 percent of the landmass is given to organic grazing.[45] Other regions, such as Europe, with high fertility and smaller farms have in the last decade increased organic farming to almost 30 percent of their farmland—a profound transformation.

[44] Salvador V. Garibay and Roberto Ugas, "Organic Farming in Latin America and the Caribbean," *The World of Organic Agriculture—Statistics and Merging Trends*, eds. Helga Willer, and Lukas Kilcher (Bonn, 2010). Available online at: http://orgprints.org/17931/1/garibay-ugas-2009-world-organic-agriculture.pdf [accessed February 11, 2017].

[45] Paul Kristiansen, Acram Taji, and John Reganold, *Organic Agriculture: A Global Perspective* (Canberra, 2006), 2.

10

Organic Farming and the Challenge of Globalization

In 2014 Marcelo Laurino, a Brazilian, walked into the information centre at Bishop's Castle, the small town where Albert Howard grew up. Laurino was an agronomist from Brazil working for the Ministry of Agriculture, Livestock and Food Supply in the province of Sao Paulo. He asked a very simple question. Where is the statue for Albert Howard or the plaque on the wall of the farmhouse that marked his childhood home? The employees at the information center, working in the corner of England where Howard spent his boyhood days and whose farming and landscape had so inspired him, had not heard of the founder of organic farming. Nor had they any idea that organic farming and Shropshire were connected. They referred Marcelo to the Bishop's Castle Heritage Resource Centre where one of the trustees later contacted him by email. Laurino later wrote back and described his surprise that the population of Shropshire had not heard of Albert Howard, particularly given Prince Charles' enthusiasm for organic farming at Highgrove House, in Gloucestershire. Laurino added,

> After all, we are talking about Britain's global role in bringing an alternative dialogue between food production and environmental conservation, which is more than urgent to preserve human life on this planet.[1]

This interaction between a Brazilian scientist and locals in Shropshire leads to a larger point: namely, that the global organic farming movement has not had a proper history, which traces the origins of this movement around the globe, written about it. This book has attempted to do just that. But this book also has implications for how we understand the history of a number of other globalizing phenomena, such as: the history of the British Empire; the rise of environmentalism; and, finally, the future challenges that lie ahead for organic farming.

ORGANIC FARMING AND EMPIRE

What might seem surprising to many general readers—that organic farming arose in an imperial setting—is actually part of a long history of environmental reforms initiated within the British Empire. Organic farming shared many similarities

[1] Private correspondence, "Marcelo Laurino to Trevel Chalkely" (2014).

with, and even grew from, the empire forestry movement, which constituted the world's first major attempt to set land aside for conservation. Organic farming also played an important role in the growth of environmental consciousness around the world during the key transition between conservation and environmentalism. It transmitted a deep suspicion of corporations and big science into the broader environmental movement—especially a distrust of those whose expertise was "bought off" in the name of profit.

Organic farming had a significant reach throughout many regions of the British Empire, especially in Australasia and Africa. It offers an important example of how experts gained popular influence in formal colonies such as India, the Northern and Southern Protectorates of Nigeria and also in settler colonies like Canada, Australia, New Zealand, and South Africa. As a general rule, histories of empire have tended to create strict historiographical divisions between formal and settler colonies because of the stark political and demographic differences. This goes all the way back to Sir John Seeley's *The Expansion of England* (1883), in which it was argued that Britain should jettison the formal imperial holdings for the more valuable settler empire. Most histories of agriculture and farming have tended to focus primarily on either formal or settler colonies.[2] A number of contemporary imperial historians, and especially the historian Tony Hopkins, have sought to break down these barriers, because they recognize rightly that the British Empire was not so strictly divided. The British Empire facilitated transnational flows linking together every part of the empire as a whole. From the mid 1850s onwards, Britons naturally thought about the empire as one common emporium for trade and cultural influence.

As a trusted imperial expert, Albert Howard, along with his second wife Louise, used his position as a colonial expert to create trust and respect for his methods among the general public. Howard was in many respects unique in that he was able to communicate to the public in a clear way on a subject—growing plants—that was of considerable interest given the prominence of gardens through the twentieth century.[3] Working for the British Empire gave him credibility in a way that working for the Rothamsted research station would likely not have done. This is because many Britons and their descendants in the settler dominions shared traditionally conservative viewpoints, including a skepticism of big-business and overly theoretical science. Howard's science tapped into many peoples' anxieties about lost rural values, industrial change, and the rise of corporations. He was a scientist, but he applied his ideas in a practical way that everyone could understand. He got his hands dirty and carefully laid out in his lectures and in his books the practical methods of composting according to the methods he developed in India. His second

---

[2] See James Bellich, *Replenishing the Earth. The Settler Revolution and the Rise of the Anglo-World, 1783–1939* (Oxford, 2009); Anthony Hopkins, *British Imperialism: Innovation and Expansion, 1688–1914* (Harlow, 1993).

[3] Andrea Gaynor, *Harvest of the Suburbs: An Environmental History of Growing Food in Australian Cities* (Perth, 2006).

wife Louise then kept his ideas prominent and in the public eye after his death, spending decades retelling his homely truths in a way that appealed to the public.

Howard received respect because he was one of thousands of experts who gained employment throughout the British Empire in the first half of the twentieth century in any number of technical positions (such as forester, veterinary doctor, or agronomist). Joseph Hodge describes this expansion as the "triumph of the expert" because towards the end of empire experts received a considerable amount of power to make decisions about land use.[4] What is unique about Howard is that he was able to reach a wider audience beyond the narrow circle of colonial scientists. While other agricultural researchers elsewhere in the British Empire learned from and built on indigenous farming systems, they had no real public audience. Their legacies are found in archived annual reports and obscure technical bulletins and await future historians to tell their stories.

Organic farming also gained initial support in part because it fit within a wider imperial discourse on health and wholeness. After the Second World War many people associated these viewpoints with conservative and even extreme right politics. Decolonization fueled the emergence of strong civil rights and environmental movements, which many adherents imagined to be anti-colonial. Organic farming suffered because of its imperial and far-right associations. Scientists in these countries looked to industry and new technology for new insights into agriculture and health and looked down on how organic farming advocates appealed to culture, biology, and place—categories that where synonymous with racism or empire. The loss of pro-organic imperial scientific research pushed organic farming activists into the academic wilderness. After decolonization, organic advocates lacked institutional sponsorship—such as Howard had at Indore—and lacked also all the prestige and influence that went with it.

In short, therefore, the same reason why organic farming succeeded in its initial phases—the prominence of imperial science—explains why decolonization sent the movement into abeyance for decades. In time, however, organic farming regained popularity, but only by changing its narrative and social base. To understand why and how it changed, we must understand how profoundly decolonization reshaped the politics and culture of former colonies in the matter of two decades. New nation-states were established out of the formal British Empire. In the settler colonies, the transition from empire to independence was more gradual, but equally profound. Many historians now claim that "effective decolonization" occurred in the 1960s and 1970s because these decades saw the emergence of ideas of citizenship and national identity, the inclusion of indigenous peoples into politics and cultural life (except in South Africa), and the decline of British preferential trade, common defense, and migration. As Brett Bennett has argued, a shift occurred from appreciating exotic empire-wide plants to celebrating indigenous plants as populations

---

[4] Joseph Hodge traces this shift of authority from the district administrator in the British Empire to technocratic scientists and experts in *Triumph of the Expert: Agrarian Doctrines of Development and the Legacies of British Colonialism* (Athens, OH, 2007).

in the settler colonies felt the need to emphasize their independence from Britain. Organic farming fit neatly into this new emphasis on gardening.[5]

THE ENVIRONMENTAL MOVEMENT

This book has hopefully dispelled the myth that the organic farming movement was a continuation of traditional agriculture into the modern age or that it arose from peasant wisdom. Organic farming was a new movement with its own unique roots and protocols and, like the environmental movement itself, much more than a mere backlash against industrial society: it was a movement to reinstate lost cultural and spiritual values. Organic activists found their initial home in conservative and far right circles. Their successors adjusted to the defeat of fascism and decolonization and repurposed these cultural values within new movements, especially a new phase of modern environmentalism. They did so by importing ideas and values that resisted patterns of mass industrial production and the standardization of consumption habits. They also imported ideas that resisted those aspects of modernism that denied the individual's connection to nature and natural processes.

While the dream of Albert and Louise Howard to change the world through municipal composting largely failed to materialize (due to cost and public revulsion at the idea of recycling sewage onto farmland), the steady growth of the Indore Method of composting nonetheless had a major impact. Little could Louise know at the time of her death that the incremental efforts of gardeners, small farmers, and small markets would, over the next few decades, reach a tipping point and swiftly convert not just millions of people, but also numerous governments and international organizations to the ideas of her late husband. After such discouragement in the 1950s and 60s, it would surprise her to have learned, that authorities would from 1980 onwards transform the reach of organic farming so radically, bringing the movement she once led in exile into a global system of agricultural management. Nor could she have foreseen that the accumulation of market forces would finally, through large corporate enterprises (and, yes, hated vested interests), produce organic farming on an industrial scale.

It has been thought until recently that the environmental movement can be roughly divided into two parts—the earlier global conservation movement and the modern environmental movement. The earlier phase focused on the preservation of resources, soil preservation, and a growing realization of ecological interconnectedness. The modern environmental movement emphasized pollution and a wide range of issues from the protection of wildlife, to air and water purity. Tracing ideas is notoriously difficult, and it is important not to overstate links. For convenience we speak of a single environmental movement, when in fact it is possible to trace a diverse range of civic groups, policy makers, and individuals advancing

[5] Brett Bennett, "Decolonization, Environmentalism and Nationalism in Australia and South Africa," *Itinerario* 41/1 (2017): 27–50.

ideas of health, wholeness, and responsibility toward nature in this period. What this book has shown, however, is that the middle period between the conservation movement and the environmental progress of the late 1960s, often missed by historians and the public, is at least partially bridged by the organic farming movement.

The organic farming movement carried on most of the basic tenets of the conservation movement by trumpeting the dangers of deforestation and global desertification. It added a vocal advocacy for the link between soil, farming practice, and human health. With organic farming taken into consideration it becomes possible to view environmentalism as a whole—perhaps not unified or codified, or even as a coherent social movement, but certainly as a rising tide of environmental consciousness. Organic farming, as advocated by Albert Howard and many diverse allies (particularly Louise Howard), clearly played a leading role in this middle period after the Second World War, including providing many of the core ideas for Rachel Carson's *Silent Spring*. With the discovery of the Howard archives, on which this book is based, it is also clear that this rise in environmental consciousness after the Second World War owed much to Louise Howard as an organizer, intellectual, and activist. Historical narrative tends to overstate a few key figures by simplifying the past and overlooking other actors. Louise Howard stands out in the web of environmental influence in the 1950s and 60s as a leading figure that connected past ideas of wholeness to scientific narratives. This combination of wholeness and science influenced a broad range of groups and individuals that figure prominently in the modern environmental movement. In the opinion of this author, Louise Howard must be seen as not only one of the leading figures of the environmental movement in this middle stage, but—though hitherto unacknowledged—as the single most influential women in the global environmental movement.

Challenges to organic farming lie on the horizon. Genetically modified crops offer the prospect of still higher yields, while using less pesticides; synthetic biological agents offer pest fighting potential that may be far less harmful to human health. On the other hand, certified organic pesticides themselves often contain such heavy metals as copper sulfate that may be harmful to human health.[6] Mixing organic and conventional methods of agriculture—anathema to many in the organic farming movement—may yet provide a path for furthering the reach of the methods pioneered by Howard. Ironically, the "early Howard" approach promoted precisely such a blend of organic and conventional methods in India before he converted wholly to the views of his more radical followers.

THE FUTURE OF ORGANIC FARMING

What does the future hold? It is not the historians' task to answer this question, but a few observations are tempting. First, the environmental need for organic farming is likely to drive its expansion in the future. Industrial agriculture takes a toll on

---

[6] Christie Wilcox, "Are lower pesticide residues a good reason to buy organic? Probably not," *Scientific American* (September 24, 2012). Available online at: https://blogs.scientificamerican.com/science-sushi/pesticides-food-fears/ [accessed June 1, 2017].

water catchment areas. Wildlife and human health can suffer from the use of chemical fertilizers and pesticides. Industrial agriculture also does not sequester carbon in soils as well as organic farming, and this in term implicates the problem of global warming. Soil erosion affected almost a third of arable land between 1950 and 1990 and this will continue to be a major concern in the future.[7] As consumers are increasingly submerged into an urban, consumer, and digital lifestyle, the desire to achieve balance will increase, and the desire for a healthier lifestyle that mimics the conditions of our evolutionary past will keep the desire for romantic association with nature alive.

There may however be practical limits to the dream of wholeness that is embedded in organic farming. Corporate farming will push out yet more small freeholds around the world and organic farming will evolve further into ever larger business interests. These interests will play a dominant role in the future in terms of defining protocols and methods of organic farming, meaning that the cultural ethics that gave birth to the movement may continue to fade or, worse, increasingly be manufactured into slogans and images that have reality only in marketing. Ultimately, the fight against vested interests may be lost as organic farming grows into a larger business lobby, leaving less room for the small producers and for trusted scientific outsiders. There may indeed be practical and structural limitations to the dream of wholeness that drove organic farming as a movement and, more disturbing, there may be in our future even less room for innovations from new figures like Albert Howard (or for organizers and popularizers like Louise Howard). In a globalized world, governed by a distant managerial elite, it is likely that outsiders will have less and less of a voice.

The challenges facing the organic vision that Howard laid out were summarized well by Garth Youngberg in 1991. Youngberg predicted that the big question for organic farming was—how far can the movement go? How far can these organic systems displace conventional agriculture?[8] We can add to the question and ask, what is the right balance between organic and conventional agriculture, for consumers, for nature, and for farmers? What is needed to secure its future so that social scientists—as well as scientists—can together map out a macro-approach to organic farming around the world?[9] There is much more work needed to integrate ideas about wholeness and the law of return broadly into human society.

The challenge to organic farming in the future is also a challenge to science itself, as the debate over global warming exemplifies. Scientific findings often proceed through winding pathways, with little credit given to the initial discovery and often with little impact on the public. Howard and many of his followers turned Rothamsted into a symbol of vested and corrupt scientific interests, bought off by

[7] H. Steinfeld, P. Gerber, T. Wasenaar, V. Castel, M. Rosales, and C. de Haan, *Livestock's Long Shadow* (Rome, 2006). Available online at: http://www.fao.org/docrep/010/a0701e/a0701e00.HTM [accessed April 29, 2014].

[8] "Garth Youngberg Interview Part 1" [video] (June 17, 1991), Alternative Farming Information Center, National Agricultural Library, June 27, 2012. Available online at: https://www.youtube.com/watch?v=imBzVGzbEJY [accessed February 11, 2017].

[9] Ibid.

industry and government funding to the detriment of human health and the environment. Since there today exist hundreds of millions of organic consumers around the globe, this image has stuck in the public imagination. Conversely, Howard's work at the Indore research station has been presented by organic enthusiasts as a symbol of honest and trustworthy science, not bought off by vested interest, but done for the benefit of the Indian people and the world. In the case of organic farming, however, it actually, and ironically, owed much to the research done at Rothamsted, and, in particular, to the study by Hutchingson and Richards that discovered how to turn plant-based compost into valuable fertilizer that used very little manure. However, this discovery in 1921 had limited impact because it lacked the propaganda, or cultural appeal, of a popular movement until Albert Howard picked it up and connected the findings with widely held fears of chemical fertilizers and pesticides.

New findings and new knowledge often require a positive public perception that the scientists and the sponsoring institutions share the cultural values of the public it serves. The lesson for scientists and policy makers in the future is that, in order to have impact, science must connect with deeply held values. Today, the public is deeply divided on the issue of global warming. The debate often centers around who we can trust: Which scientists? Which institutions are reliable? Which institutions have an ulterior motive? Which scientists have been corrupted? Which ones are objective and trustworthy? The ideas held by the public—whether rooted in informed opinion, traditional spirituality, or even prejudice—must be taken into account. Science must speak to the heart, and not just to pure rationality, in order for its findings to be taken seriously and to impact and transform society. In an age of global mega-cities, we have all become urban environmentalists, whether we like it or not, and we owe the values that we share to those who pulled together the vanishing strands of the past—in this case organic farming—and tied them into an integral part of our modern life by merging science with human needs.

Economic growth and industrial production will remain central to scientific funding and research. But if we disconnect science from the needs of human culture—including spiritual values—science loses impact on the public. Albert and Louise Howard both clearly understood this. Theory and laboratory findings must produce results in the field, and in the hearts and minds of consumers. The organic farming movement made precisely such a connection and that is one of the ways to explain its remarkable success. It connected theory to practice, the past to the present, and science to the heart. Its ability to do so in the future will determine its success or failure.

Bibliography

ARCHIVES CONSULTED

India Office Private Papers, British Library, London, UK.
Matthaei Family Archive, Birmingham, UK.
Willis Collection, Shropshire Archives, UK.

CONTEMPORARY NEWSPAPERS AND
PERIODICALS CONSULTED

Albert Howard News Sheet
American Farmer
British Dental Journal
Collier's Weekly
Compost and Sewage Bulletin
Country Life
Farm and Forest
Highland Agricultural Society Transactions
Journal of the Chemical Society
Journal of the Society of Chemical Industry
Kentish Express
Kentish Gazette and Canterbury News
Kentish Observer
London Gazette
Nature
New York Times
Newsletter on Compost
Organic Farming Digest
Organic Gardening Magazine
Organic Soil Association of Southern Africa
Penthouse
Plant Food Journal
Plough, Loom and Anvil: An American Farmer's Magazine
Reader's Digest
Soil and Health
The Agricultural Journal of India
The Albert Howard Foundation of Organic Husbandry
The Farmer
The Farmer's Magazine
The Guardian
The Indian Medical Gazeteer
The Land
The Magazine for the Lay Apostle
The Medical Press
The Organic Soil Association

The Rhodesian Farmer
The Times Trade and Engineering Supplement
The West India Committee Circular
Time
Vegetarian News
Velt Trust News
Washington Post

OFFICIAL AND GOVERNMENT REPORTS

Callister, G. J. *Developments in World Fertilizer Production*. FAO, Rome, July 24, 1951.
Department of Agriculture. *Annual Report 1900–01*. Melbourne, 1901.
FAO. *Commodity Report: Fertilizers: A World Report on Production and Consumption.* August, 1951.
FAO. *Use of Commercial Fertilizers Past, Present, and Future*. February 25, 1946.
Fletcher, T. Bainbrigge. "Note on Plant Imports into India." *Proceedings of the Third Entomological Meeting 1052—held at Pusa 3–15th February 1919*. Calcutta, 1921.
Imperial Agricultural Research Institute. *A Brief Survey of Three Decades of Research at the Institute*. New Delhi, 1937.
Imperial Agricultural Research Institute. *Scientific Reports*. London, 1906.
NA., *Annual Report of the Indian Central Cotton Committee, Bombay, for the year ending August 31st 1928*. Calcutta, 1929.
NA., *Food, Agriculture, Conservation, and Trade (FACT) Act of 1990*. November 28, 1990.
NA., *Minutes of Meeting of the Fertilizer Working Committee: First Meeting of the Fertiliser Working Committee of the Emergency Economic committee for Europe*. July 30, 1945.
NA., *Proceedings of the First All India Conference on Compost Held at New Delhi, December 16–17*. New Delhi, 1947.
NA., *Prospectus of the Agricultural Research Institute and College, Pusa*. Calcutta, 1906.
NA., *Report and Recommendations on Organic Farming*. Washington DC, 1980.
NA., *Report of the Agricultural Research Institute and College, Pusa (including report of the imperial cotton specialist) 1910–11*. Calcutta, 1912.
NA., *Report of the Agricultural Research Institute, and College, Pusa 1907–09*. Calcutta, 1911.
NA., *Report of the Agricultural Research Institute, and College, Pusa (including report of the imperial cotton specialist) 1909–10*. Calcutta, 1911.
Organization of the United Nations. *Annual Progress and Program report on Food and Agriculture for China-1947*. August, 1947.
Scottish Agricultural Commission to Australia. *Australia: Its land, Conditions and Prospects: The Observations and experiences of the Scottish Agricultural Commission of 1910–11: A Report with Numerous Illustrations*. Edinburgh, 1911.
Southern Rhodesia Commission on the Natural Resources of the Colony. *Report of the Commission to Enquire into the Preservation of the Natural Resources of the Colony*. Salisbury, 1939.
The County Palatine of Chester Local Medical and Panel Committee. *Report on the Garden Competition and other Nutritional Interests*. 1942.
United Nations. *The Latin American Fertilizer Supply and Resources for Improving the Supply*. Washington, March 26, 1951.
United States Department of Agriculture (USDA) and Tennessee Valley Authority (TVA). *Superphosphate: Its History, Chemistry, and Manufacture*. Washington DC, 1964.

United States Tariff Commission. *Digest: Chemical Nitrogen* 114/SS. 1947.

World Trade Association. *World Trade Organization Building: The Symbolic Artwork of the Centre William Rappard, Headquarters of the World Trade Organization.* Geneva, 2008.

BOOKS, ARTICLES, AND OTHER SECONDARY LITERATURE

Abrams M. H. *The Mirror and the Lamp: Romantic Theory and the Critical Tradition.* Oxford, 1953.

Acharya, C. N. *Preparation of Compost Manure from Town Wastes.* Delhi, 1946.

Akiyama, Y. *Feeding the Nation: Nutrition and Health in Britain before World War One.* London, 2008.

Albrecht, William. "Soil Fertility and Biotic Geography." *Geographical Review* 47/1, January, 1957.

Allen, Robert C. "Agriculture and the Origins of the State in Ancient Egypt." *Explorations in Economic History* 34/2, 1997.

Anderson, Clifford B. "The Metamorphosis of American Agrarian Idealism in the 1920's and 1930's." *Agricultural History* 35/4, October, 1961.

Ayres, Peter G. *Harry Marshal Ward and the Fungal Thread of Death.* St. Paul, MN, 2005.

Badenoch, A. G. "Review of *Thoughts on Feeding* by Lionel James Picton." *Organic Farming Digest* 1/7, October–December, 1947.

Badenoch, A. G. "The Minerals in Plant and Animal Nutrition." *The Albert Howard Foundation of Organic Husbandry*, June, 1949.

Bagot, A. G. D. *Composting Tea Estate Wastes.* Fort Columbo, 1936.

Balfour, E. B. *The Living Soil and the Haughley Experiment.* London, 1943.

Balfour, Lady Eve. "The Late Sir Albert Howard." *Organic Gardening Magazine* 13/8, September, 1948.

Barge, Laura. "Pastoral in Southern Poetry." *The Southern Literary Journal* 26/1, Fall, 1993.

Barnard, F. M. *Herder's Social and Political Thought.* Oxford, 1965.

Bartlett, Charles L. *Guano: A Treatise on the History, Economy as a Manure and Modes of Applying Peruvian Guano.* Boston, 1860.

Barton, Gregory Allen. "Sir Albert Howard and the Forestry Roots of the Organic Farming Movement." *Agriculture History* 75/2, Spring, 2001.

Barton, Gregory Allen. *Empire Forestry and the Origins of the Environmental Movement.* Cambridge, 2002.

Barton, Gregory Allen. "Introduction." *American Environmentalism*, ed. Gregory Allen Barton. San Diego, 2002.

Barton, Gregory Allen. "The Appeal of Orientalism." *British Scholar* 3/1, 2010.

Barton, Gregory Allen. "Environmentalism, Development and British Policy in the Middle East 1945–1965." *Journal of Imperial and Commonwealth History* 38/4, December, 2010.

Barton, Gregory Allen. "Albert Howard and the Decolonization of Science: From the Raj to Organic Farming." *Science and Empire: Knowledge and Networks of Science in the British Empire 1850–1970*, eds. Brett Bennett and Joseph Morgan Hodge. Basingstoke, 2011.

Barton, Gregory Allen. *Lord Palmerston and the Empire of Trade.* London, 2012.

Barton, Gregory Allen. *Informal Empire and the Rise of One World Culture.* Basingstoke, 2014.

Baumgartner, Judith. *Ernährungsreform- Antwort auf Industrialisierung und Ernährungswandel—Ernährungsreform als Teil der Lebensreformbewegung am Beispiel der Siedlung und des Unternehmens Eden seit 1893.* Frankfurt, 1992.

Bear, F. E. "Facts...and Fancies about Fertilizer." *Plant Food Journal,* April, 1947.

Beattie, James. "Book review: Environment and Empire." *New Zealand Journal of Asian Studies* 11/2, 2009.

Beinart, William. *The Rise of Conservation in South Africa: Settlers, Livestock and the Environment 1770–1950.* Oxford, 2003.

Beinart, William, and Lotte Hughes, eds. *Environment and Empire.* Oxford, 2007.

Bell, Anne Olivier, ed. The Diary of Virginia Woolf: 1915–1919, Vol. 1. London, 1977.

Bellich, James. *Replenishing the Earth. The Settler Revolution and the Rise of the Anglo-World, 1783–1939.* Oxford, 2009.

Bennett, Brett. *Plantations and Protected Areas: A Global History of Forest Management.* Cambridge, MA, 2015.

Benson, J., and G. Shaw, eds. *The Evolution of Retail Systems c. 1800–1914.* Leicester, 1992.

Berg, Auri C. "Reform in the Time of Stalin: Nikita Krushchev and the Fate of the Russian Peasantry." Ph.D. thesis, University of Toronto, 2012.

Berkhofer, Robert. *The White Man's Indian: Images of the American Indian From Columbus to the Present.* New York, 1978.

Best, Andrew, ed. "Introduction," in *Water Springing from the Ground: An Anthology of the Writings of Rolf Gardiner.* Dorset, 1972.

Birchall, Johnston. *The International Co-operative Movement.* Manchester, 1997.

Blackman, F. F., and G. L. C. Matthaei. "Experimental researches on vegetable assimilation and respiration. IV. A quantitative study of carbon-dioxide assimilation and leaf temperature in natural illumination." *Proceedings of the Royal Society* B76. London, 1905.

Bosazza, D. R. V. L. "Are the Deserts on the March?" *Veld Trust News,* December, 1949.

Bowles, John. *The Imperial Achievement: The Rise and Transformation of the British Empire.* Boston, 1975.

Boyd, James G. "In Search of Shambhala? Nicolas Roerich's 1934–5 Inner Mongolian Expedition." *Inner Asia* 14/2, 2012.

Brady, Nyle C. *The Nature and Properties of Soil.* New York, 1974.

Bramwell, Anna. *Blood and Soil: Walter Darre and Hitler's "Green Party."* Bourne End, 1985.

Briggs, Asa. *The History of Broadcasting in the United Kingdom.* Oxford, 1961.

Broadbent, Jeffrey. "Japan: A Foreword." *Forging Environmentalism: Justice, Livelihoods and Contested Environments,* ed. Joane R. Bauer. London, 2006.

Brodsky, Ira. *The History of Wireless: How Creative Minds Produced Technology for the Masses.* New York, 2008.

Brunt, L. P. *Municipal Composting Albert Howard Foundation of Organic Husbandry.* London, 1949.

Bryant, G. "J. I. Rodale: Pollution Prophet." *Penthouse* 2, 1971.

Burchard, Hank. "The Great Hunt for the Puny Potato: Despite High Prices, Ranks of Organic Food Buyers Swell." *Washington Post, Times Herald,* February 28, 1971.

Burnett, J., and D. Oddy. *The Origins and Development of Food Policies in Europe.* Leicester, 1994.

Burros, Marian. "A Tribute to Sidney Margolius." *Washington Post,* February 7, 1980.

Bury, J. B. *The Idea of Progress.* London, 1920.

Carson, Rachel. *Silent Spring.* New York, 1962.

Chalker-Scott, Linda. "The Science Behind Biodynamic Preparations: A Literature Review." *HortTechnology* 23/6, 2013.

Charlton, J. and M. Murphy eds. *The Health of Adult Britain 1841–1994 (I/II).* London, 2004.

Christophers, S. R. *Souvenir: The Indian Empire.* Calcutta, 1927.

Clark, Frederick Hugh. "Epileptoid attacks In Tachycardia." *British Medical Journal*, August 10, 1907.

Clayton, Paul, and Judith Rowbotham. "An unsuitable and degraded diet? Part one: public health lessons from the mid-Victorian working class diet." *Journal of the Royal Society of Medicine* 101, 2008.

Cobbett, William. *Rural Rides (Vol. I)*. London, 1832.

Colgrove, J. "The McKeown thesis: A Historical Controversy and its Enduring influence." *American Journal of Public Health* 92, 2002.

Collings, Gilbert H. *Commercial Fertilizers: Their Sources and Use*. Philadelphia, 1934.

Collis, John Stewart. *While Following the Plough*. London, 1946.

Collis, John Stewart. *Down to Earth*. London, 1947.

Conford, Philip. *The Origins of the Organic Movement*. Edinburgh, 2001.

Conford, Philip. *The Development of the Organic Network: Linking People and Themes, 1945–95*. Edinburgh, 2011.

Conford, Philip, and Patrick Holden. "The Soil Association." *Organic Farming: An International History*, ed. William Lockeretz. Oxfordshire, 2007.

Costanza, Robert, Lisa Graumlich, and William L. Steffen. *Sustainability or Collapse?: An Integrated History and Future of People on Earth*. Cambridge MA/London, 2007.

Cowan, Robin. "Pest Control." *The Oxford Encyclopedia of Economic History*, ed. Joel Mokyr. Oxford, 2005.

Craven, Avery O. *Soil Exhaustion as a Factor in the Agricultural History of Virginia and Maryland, 1606–1860*. Urbana, 1926.

Cromer, Evelyn Baring. *Modern Egypt*. New York, 1908.

Crook, Tim. *International Radio Journalism: History, Theory and Practice*. London, 1998.

Crosby, N. T. *Determination of Veterinary Residues in Food*. Cambridge, 1997.

Curzon, Lord. *Lord Curzon in India: Being a Selection from his Speeches as Viceroy & Governor-General of India, 1898–1905*, ed. Thomas Raleigh. London, 1906.

Dale, Tom, and Vernon G. Carter. *Topsoil and Civilization*. Oklahoma, 1955.

Danbom, David B. "Romantic Agrarianism in Twentieth-Century America." *Agricultural History* 65/4, Autumn, 1991.

Davis, Diana K. *Resurrecting the Granary of Rome: Environmental History and French Colonial Expansion in North Africa*. Athens, Ohio, 2007.

Davy, Humphry, and John Davy. "Consolations in Travel—Dialogue V—The Chemical Philosopher." *The Collected Works of Sir Humphry Davy* 9. London, 1840.

Diaz, L. F., M. de Bertoldi, W. Bidlingmaier, and E. Stentiford eds. *Compost Science and Technology*. London, 2007.

Dodson, B. "A Soil Conservation Safari: Hugh Bennett's 1944 Visit to South Africa." *Environment and History* 11, 2005.

Dragusanu, R., D. Giovannucci, and N. Nunn. "The Economics of Fair Trade." *Journal of Economic Perspectives* 28/3, 2014.

Egler, Frank. "Pesticides in our Ecosystem." *American Scientist* 52/1, March, 1964.

Eisenhower, David, and Julie Nixon Eisenhower. *Going Home to Glory: A Memoir of Life with Dwight David Eisenhower 1961–1969*. New York, 2010.

Engels, Jeremy. "The Two Faces of Cincinnatus: A Rhetorical Theory of the State of Exception." *Advances in the History of Rhetoric* 17/1, 2014.

Everest, A. E., and A. G. Perkin. *The Natural Organic Colouring Matters*. London 1918.

Folsom, Josiah C. "Review of *Labour in Agriculture: An International Survey*, by Louise E. Howard." *Journal of Farm Economics* 18/2, May, 1936.

Forclaz, Amalia Ribi. "A New Target for International Social Reform: The International Labour Organization and Working and Living Conditions in Agriculture in the Inter-War Years." *Contemporary European History* 20, 2011.

Fordham, Montague. *The Land and Life: A Survey of Problems of the Land.* London, 1942.

Francis, Daniel. *The Imaginary Indian: The Image of the Indian in Canadian Culture.* Vancouver BC, 1992.

Freyer, Bernhard, Jim Bingen, and Milena Klimek. "Ethics in the organic movement." *Re-thinking organic food and farming in a changing world*, ed. Bernhard Freyer Dordrecht, 2015.

Frezier, Anted, and Francois Frezier. *A Voyage to the South-Sea, and Along the Coasts of Chile and Peru, in the Years 1712, 1713, and 1714.* London, 1717.

Frost, Lionel. "The Correll Family and Technological Change in Australian Agriculture." *Agricultural History* 75/2, Spring, 2001.

Frye, Joshua J. *The Transnational Origin, Diffusion, and Transformation of "organic" Agriculture: A Study in Social Movement Framing and Outcomes.* Lafayette, OH, 2007.

Fujiwara, Tatsushi. *Nachisu Doitsu no yuki nogyo: "Shizen tono kyosei" ga unda "minzoku no zetsumetsu"* [Nazi Germany's Organic Farming: "The Extinction of Ethnicity" born of "Coexistence with Nature"]. Tokyo, 2005/2012.

Fukuoka, Masanobu. *The One-Straw Revolution.* Goa, 2014.

Galston, Arthur W. "The Organic Gardener and Anti-Intellectualism." *Natural History*, May, 1972.

Gardiner, Rolf. "Letter." *Organic Soil Association of South Africa.* Winter, 1957.

Gaynor, Andrea. *Harvest of the Suburbs: An Environmental History of Growing Food in Australian Cities.* Perth, 2006.

Gibbs, Anthony, and Sons. *Peruvian and Bolivian Guano: Its Nature, Properties, and Results.* London, 1843.

Grove, Richard. *Green Imperialism: Colonial Expansion, Tropical Island Edens and the Origins of Environmentalism, 1600–1860.* Cambridge, 1996.

Halevy, E. *History of the English People in the 19th Century (Vol. 3)*, trans. E. Watkin. London, 1961.

Hannam, John. *The Economy of Waste Manures: A Treatise on the Nature and Use of Neglected Fertilizers.* London, 1844.

Harrington, Anne. *Reenchanted Science: Holism in German Culture from Wilhelm II to Hitler.* Princeton, 1996.

Hay, Stephen N. "Rabindranath Tagore in America." *American Quarterly* 14/3, 1962.

Hays, Samuel P. *Explorations in Environmental History.* Pittsburgh, 1998.

Heckman, J. "A History of Organic Farming: Transitions from Sir Albert Howard's *War in the Soil* to USDA National Organic Program." *Renewable Agriculture and Food Systems* 21/3, 2005.

Hensl, Julius. *Bread from Stones: A New and Rational System of Land Fertilization and Physical Regeneration*, trans. anonymous. Unknown, 1894.

Henzell, Ted. *Australian Agriculture: The History and Challenges.* Victoria, 2007.

Hicks, Sir Stanton. "Food Production is Everybody's Business." *Organic Farming Digest* 1/6, July–September, 1947.

Higgs, Henry. *Physiocrats: Six Lectures on the French Economistes of the 18th Century.* London, 1897.

Hilgard, Eugene W. *Soils: Their Formation, Properties, Composition, and Relations to Climate and Plant Growth in the Humid and Arid Regions.* New York, 1906.

Hill, Cayce, and Hiroko Kubota. "Thirty-five Years of Japanese Teikei." *Sharing the Harvest: A Citizen's Guide to Community Supported Agriculture*, eds. Elizabeth Henderson and Robyn Van En. Vermont, 2007.

Hodge, Joseph M. "Science, Development, and Empire: The Colonial Advisory Council on Agriculture and Animal Health, 1929–43." *The Journal of Imperial and Commonwealth History* 30/1, January, 2002.

Hodge, Joseph M. *Triumph of the Expert: Agrarian Doctrines of Development and the Legacies of British Colonialism*. Athens, OH, 2007.

Hopkins, Anthony. *British Imperialism: Innovation and Expansion, 1688–1914*. Longman, 1993.

Hopkins, F. G. "Feeding experiments illustrating the importance of accessory factors in normal dietaries." *The Journal of Physiology* 44/5, 1912.

Houriet, Robert. "Review: *Getting Back Together* by Herbert A. Otto." *Saturday Review of Literature*, April, 1971.

Housman, A. E. "A Shropshire Lad." *Collected Poems of A. E. Housman*, ed. Michael Irwin. London, 1999.

Howard, Albert. "Fertilization and Cross Fertilization of the Hop." *The Hop and its Constituents: A Monograph on the Hop Plant*, ed. Alfred C. Chapman. London, 1905.

Howard, Albert. *Crop Production in India*. Oxford, 1924.

Howard, Albert. *Work Done by the Botanical Section, Agricultural Research Institute, Pusa, from May 1905 to January 1923*. Privately printed, 1924.

Howard, Albert. "Die Erzeugung von Humus nach der Indore-Mehode." *Der Tropenpflanzer: Zeitschrift für das Gesamtgebiet der Land und Forstwirtschaft warmer Länder* 39/2, February, 1935.

Howard, Albert. "The Manufacture of Humus by the Indore Process." *The West India Committee Circular*, April 23, 1936.

Howard, Albert. *Farming and Gardening for Health or Disease*. London, 1945.

Howard, Albert. "Review of *Organic and Mineral Fertilizers* by E. J. Salisbury." *Organic Farming Digest* 1/2, July, 1946.

Howard, Albert. "Activated and Digested Sewage Sludge in Agriculture & Horticulture." *Soil and Health* 2/1, 1947.

Howard, Albert. "The Animal as our Farming Partner." *Organic Gardening*, September, 1947.

Howard, Albert. *The Soil and Health: A Study of Organic Agriculture*. London, 1947.

Howard, Albert. "The Progress of Organic Agriculture in the U. S. A." *Organic Farming Magazine* 13/8, September, 1948.

Howard, Albert. *An Agricultural Testament*. Oxford, 1956.

Howard, Albert. *The Waste Products of Agriculture: Their Utilization as Humus*. Oxford, 1931.

Howard, Albert, and Gabrielle Howard. "The Varietal Characters of Indian Wheats." *Memoirs of the Department of Agriculture in India*. Calcutta, 1909.

Howard, Albert, and Gabrielle Howard. *Wheat in India: Its Production, Varieties and Improvement*. Calcutta, 1909.

Howard, Albert, and Gabrielle Howard. *Report of the Agricultural Research Institute and College, Pusa (including report of the imperial cotton specialist) 1907–09*. Calcutta, 1910.

Howard, Louise E. *Studies in Greek Tragedy*. Cambridge, 1918.

Howard, Louise E. *Labour in Agriculture: An International Survey*. Oxford, 1935.

Howard, Louise E. "The Birth of the Organic Farming Movement." *Organic Gardening Magazine* 13/8, September, 1948.

Howard, Louise E. "The Green Leaf: A Selection of Extracts from the Writings of the late Sir Albert Howard." *The Albert Howard Foundation of Organic Husbandry* 4, Undated (1948?).

Howard, Louise E. *Our Answer to the Land*. London, 1950.

Howard, Louise E. *Sir Albert Howard in India*. London, 1953.

Howard, Louise E. *Albert Howard in India and Earth's Green Carpet*. Cambridge, 2012.

Hume, Allan Octavian. *Agricultural Reform in India*. London, 1897.

Hunter, W. W. *The Life of the Earl of Mayo: Fourth Viceroy of India*. London, 1875.

Hutchinson, George Evelyn. "The Biogeochemistry of Vertebrate Excretion." *Bulletin of the American Museum of Natural History* 96, 1950.

Hutchinson, H. B., and E. H. Richards. "Artificial farmyard manure." *Journal of the Ministry of Agriculture* 28, 1921.

Ichiaku, Teruo. *Yuki noho: shizen junkan to yomigaeru seimei* [Organic Farming: Natural Circulation and Life that Revives], trans. J. I. Rodale. Tokyo, 1974.

Inden, Ronald. "Orientalist Constructions of India." *Modern Asian Studies* 20, 1986.

Isendahl, Christian, and Michael E. Smith. "Sustainable Agrarian Urbanism: The Low-density Cities of the Mayas and Aztecs." *Cities* 31, 2013.

Jackson, Carlton. *J. I. Rodale: Apostle of Non-conformity*. New York, 1974.

Jackson F. K., and Y. D. Wad. "The Sanitary Disposal and Agricultural Utilisation of Habitation Wastes by the Indore Process." *Institute of Plant Industry Indore, Central India* 1, 1934.

James Finlay & Company Limited. *James Finlay & Company Limited: Manufacturers and East India Merchants 1750–1950*. Glasgow, 1951.

Jie, Pan. "The Ethics and Business of Organic Food Production, Circulation and Consumption in Japan." Ph.D. thesis, The University of Hong Kong, 2014.

Johnson, Benjamin. *Wrekin College, 1880–1964: A Brief History*. Shrewsbury, 1965.

Johnson, Cuthbert W. *On Fertilizers*. London, 1839.

Johnson, Samuel W. *Essays on Peat, Muck and Commercial Manures*. Hartford, 1859.

Johnston, A. *The International Labour Organization: Its Work for Social and Economic Justice*. London, 1970.

Jones, Bertram B., and Frederick Owen. *Some Notes on the Scientific Aspects of Controlled Tipping*. Manchester, 1934.

Jones, Peter M. *Agricultural enlightenment: knowledge, technology, and nature, 1750–1840*. Oxford, 2016.

Jones, Rebecca. *Green Harvest: A History of Organic Farming and Gardening in Australia*. Collingwood, 2010.

Juan, Jorge, and Antonia de Ulloa. *A Voyage to South America*. New York, 1748/1978.

Kals, E., D. Schumacher, and L. Montada. "Emotional affinity toward nature as a motivational basis to protect nature." *Environment and Behavior* 31, 1999.

Kapsidelis, Tom. "Organic Farming is Accepted As Part of the Agricultural Mainstream." *Washington Post*, June 27, 1983.

Kelly, W. C. "Rodale Press and Organic Gardening." *HortTechnology* 2, 1992.

Kharin, N. *Vegetation Degradation in Central Asia Under the Impact of Human Activities*. Dordrecht, 2011.

King, Franklin H. *Farmers of Forty Centuries, or Permanent Agriculture in China, Korea and Japan*. Madison, 1911.

King, Franklin H. "Review of *Soils*, by Eugene W. Hilgard." *Science* 24, January, 1906.

Kipling, Rudyard. "In the Rukh." *The Jungle Book*, ed. W. W. Robinson. Oxford, 1987.

Kirchmann, Holger. "Biological dynamic farming—an occult form of alternative agriculture?" *Journal of Agricultural and Environmental Ethics* 7/2, 1994.

Kirkham, Ellinor. "Sir Albert Howard: Prophet and Champion of the Soil." *Organic Farming Magazine* 13/8, September, 1948.

Kohlmeyer, Fred W., and Floyd L. Herum. "Science and Engineering in Agriculture: A Historical Perspective." *Technology and Culture* 2/4, Autumn, 1961.

Könemann, Ewal. *Biologische Bodenkultur and Döngewirtschaft.* Tutzing, 1939.

Konrod, Kazumi. "The Alternative Food Movement in Japan: Challenges, Limits, and Resilience of the Teikei System." *Agriculture and Human Values* 32, 2015.

Kristiansen, Paul, Acram Taji, and John Reganold. *Organic Agriculture: A Global Perspective.* Canberra, 2006.

Kumar, Deepak. "Reconstructing India: Disunity in the Science and Technology for Development Discourse, 1900–1947." *Osiris* 15, 2000.

Large, E. C. *The Advance of the Fungi.* New York, 1962.

Lavelle, B. M. "The Complete Angler: Observations on the Rise of Peisistratos in Herodotos (1.59-64)." *The Classical Quarterly* 41/2, 1991.

Leopold, Aldo. *A Sand County Almanac: and Sketches Here and There.* New York, 1949.

Lewis, D. M. "Review of *Reconstruction by Way of the Soil* by G. T. Wrench." *Organic Farming Digest* 31, 1947.

Liebig, Justus von. *Organic Chemistry in its applications to Agriculture and Physiology.* Cambridge, 1841.

Liebig, Justus von. *Chemische Briefe.* Leipzig and Heidelberg, 1878.

Liu, Jung-Chao. "Fertilizer Supply and Grain Production in Communist China." *American Journal of Agricultural Economics* 47/4, 1965.

Livy. *The Early History of Rome, Books I–IV: The History of Rome from its Foundations*, trans. Aubrey De Selincourt. London, 2002.

Lockeretz, William. "Introduction." *Organic Farming: An International History*, ed. William Lockeretz. Oxfordshire, 2007.

Lockeretz William, ed. *Organic Farming: An International History.* Oxfordshire, 2007.

Loudon, John Claudius. *An Encyclopaedia of Agriculture.* London, 1825.

Loudon, John Claudius. *Encyclopaedia of Agriculture*, 5th Edition. London, 1844.

Lovejoy, Arthur O. "The Meaning of Romanticism for the Historian of Ideas." *Journal of the History of Ideas* 2/3, June, 1941.

Lucas, Adam. *Wind, Water, Work: Ancient Medieval Milling Technology.* Leiden, 2011.

Lunn, Eugene. "Cultural Populism and Egalitarian Democracy: Herder and Michelet in the Nineteenth Century." *Theory and Society* 15, 1986.

Lytle, Mark Hamilton. *The Gentle Subversive: Rachel Carson, Silent Spring, and the Rise of the Environmental Movement.* New York, 2007.

Macleod, Roy. "Scientific Advice for British India: Imperial Perceptions and Administrative Goals, 1898–1923." *Modern Asian Studies* 9/3, 1975.

Macleod, Roy. "Introduction." *Nature and Empire: Science and the Colonial Enterprise*, ed. Roy Macleod. Chicago, 2000.

Malone, Dumas, ed. *Correspondence Between Thomas Jefferson and Dupont de Nemours.* Boston and New York, 1930.

Manchester, Harold. "The Great Organic Gardening Myth." *Reader's Digest*, July, 1962.

Mann, Harold. *The Tea Soils of Assam and Tea Manuring.* Calcutta, 1901.

Maravanyika, Simeon. "Soil Conservation and the White Agrarian Environment in Colonial Zimbabwe c. 1908–1980." Ph.D. thesis, University of Pretoria, 2013.

Margolius, Sidney. "DDT is no Cure All." *Collier's Weekly*, November 17, 1945.

Margolius, Sidney. "Review *Unfit for Human Consumption*." *Washington Post*, December 9, 1971.

Margolius, Sidney. "Eating for Health: HEALTH FOODS—FACTS AND FAKES." *Washington Post*, April 25, 1974.

Marsh, George Perkins. *Man and Nature, Or, Physical Geography as Modified by Human Action*. Seattle, 2003.

Marshal, Peter. *The British Discovery of Hinduism in the Eighteenth Century*. Cambridge, 1970.

Martin, Ansgar. *Rassismus und Geschlichtsmetaphysik: Esoterischer Darwinismus und Freiheitsphilosophie bei Rudolf Steiner*. Frankfurt, 2012.

Martin-Leake, H. "Sir Albert Howard—An Appreciation." *Organic Farming Magazine* 13/8, September, 1948.

Martin-Leake, H. "How can we use our Sewage and our refuse?" *Albert Howard Foundation of Organic Husbandry* 2, 1949.

Martin-Leake, H., and Louise E. Howard. "Methane Gas from Farmyard Manure." *The Albert Howard Foundation of Organic Husbandry* 9, 1952.

Massingham, H. J. *English Downland*. London, 1936.

Massingham, H. J. *Tree of Life*. London, 1941.

Massingham, H. J. *English Countryman: A Study of the English Tradition*. London, 1942.

Massingham, H. J. *Wisdom of the Fields*. London, 1945.

Matthaei, Louise E. "The Place of Arbitration and Mediation in Ancient Systems of International Ethics." *The Classical Quarterly* 2/1, January, 1908.

Matthaei, Louise E. *Lover of Nations*. London, 1915.

Maverick, L. A. "Chinese Influences upon the Physiocrats." *Economic History* 3, February, 1938.

Maxwell-Lefroy, H. *Indian Insect Life: A Manual of the Insects of the Plains Tropical India*. Calcutta, 1909.

Maxwell-Lefroy, H. *List of Names Used in India for Common Insects*. Pusa, 1910.

Mayer, F. S., C. M. Frantz, E. Bruehlman-Senecal, and K. Dolliver. "Why is nature beneficial?: The role of connectedness to nature." *Environment and Behavior* 41, 2009.

Mayer, Jean. "The Nondefinition of 'Organic Foods.'" *Washington Post*, April 28, 1974.

McCarisson Robert. "Faulty Food in Relation to Gastro-Intestinal Disorder." *Journal of the American Medical Association* 78, January 7, 1922.

McCarisson Robert. "Nutrition and National Health." *British Medical Journal* I, 1936.

McDermott, Robert A. "Rudolf Steiner and Anthroposophy." *Modern Esoteric Spirituality*, eds. Antoine Faivre and Jacob Needleman. New York, 1992.

Mckeown, Thomas. "Reasons for the Decline in Mortality in England and Wales in the Nineteenth Century." *Population Studies* 16, 1962.

Metcalf, Thomas R. "Architecture and the Representation of Empire: India, 1860–1910." *Representations* 6, Spring, 1984.

Miles, Wyndham D. "Sir Humphrey Davie, the Prince of Agricultural Chemists." *Chymia* 7, 1961.

Moon, David. *The Russian Peasantry: The World the Peasants Made*. London and New York, 1999.

Moon, David. "The Environmental History of the Russian Steppes: Vasilii Dokuchaev and the Harvest Failure of 1891." *Transactions of the Royal Historical Society* 15, 2005.

Moon, David. *The Plough that Broke the Steppes: Agriculture and Environment on Russia's Grasslands, 1700–1914*. Oxford, 2013.

Moulton, E. "The Contributions of Allan O. Hume to the Scientific Advancement of Indian Ornithology." *Petronia: Fifty Years of Post-Independence Orthinology in India*, eds. J. C. Daniel and G. W. Ugra. New Delhi, 2003.

Mulgan, Aurelia George. "Agricultural Policy and Agricultural Policymaking: Perpetuating the Status Quo." *Japanese Governance: Beyond Japan Inc*, eds. Jennifer Amyx and Peter Drysdale. London and New York, 2002.

Müller, H. "Glaube und Technik." *Kulture und Politics*, 1949/50.

Müller, H. *Technik und Glaube: eine permanente Herausforderung.* Göttingen, 1971.

NA. "Medical Testament: Nutrition, Soil Fertility and the National Health: County Palatine of Chester: Local Medical and Panel Committee, 22 March, 1939." *British Medical Journal*, April 15, 1939.

Nakane, Chie. *Social aspects of Japan's Industrialization.* Honk Kong, 1981.

Needham, S. "Rothamsted Experimental Station." *Organic Farming Digest* 1/2, July, 1946.

Nesbit, John Collis. *History and Properties of the Different Varieties of Natural Guanos.* London, 1859.

Nichols, Edward L. "Science and the Practical Problems of the Future." *Science* NS 29/731, January 1, 1909.

Nicholson, Frederick Augustus. *Notes on Fisheries in Japan.* Madras, 1907.

Nicolson, N., ed. The Letters of Virginia Woolf: 1913–22, Vol. II. London, 1976.

Nipperdey, Thomas. *Réflexions sur l'histoire allemande, traduit de l'allemand par Claude Orsoni.* Paris, 1992.

Notehelfer, F. G. "Japan's First Pollution Incident." *Journal of Japanese Studies* 1/2, 1975.

O'Connel, Joseph T. "Gaudiya Vaisnava Symbolism of Deliverance from Evil." *Journal of the American Oriental Society* 93, 1973.

O'Sullivan, Robyn. *American Organic: A Cultural History of Farming, Gardening, Shopping and Eating.* Kansas City, 2015.

Padel S., and N. Mampkin. "The Development of Governmental Support for Organic Farming in Europe." *Organic Farming: An International History*, ed. W. Lockeretz. Oxfordshire, 2007.

Park, W. R. "The Progress of Agriculture." *The Farmer's Magazine* 32, 1867.

Paull, John. "The Lost History of Organic Farming in Australia." *Journal of Organic Systems* 3, 2008.

Paull, John. "From France to the World: The International Federation of Organic Agriculture Movements (IFOAM)." *Journal of Social Research & Policy* 2, December, 2010.

Paull, John. "Attending the First Organic Agriculture Course: Rudolf Steiner's Agricultural Course at Koberwitz, 1924." *European Journal of Social Sciences* 21/1, 2011.

Paull, John. "The Rachel Carson Letters and the Making of *Silent Spring*." *Sage Open*, July–September, 2013.

Pearce, Roy H. *The Savages of America: A Study of the Indian and the Idea of Civilization.* Baltimore, 1953.

Perkin, Harold J. *The Origins of Modern English Society, 1780–1880.* London, 1969.

Perkin, Harold J. *The Rise of Professional Society: England since 1880.* London, 1989.

Pfeiffer, Ehrenfried. *Bio-Dynamic Farming and Gardening: Soil Fertility, Renewal and Preservation*, trans. F. Heckel. New York, 1938.

Pinkett, Harold T. "The Soil Conservation Service and Farm Woodland Management, 1938–1945." *Agricultural History*, April 1, 1985.

Pollitts, Colonel. *Britain can Feed Herself.* London, 1942.

Porter, Dilwyn, and S. Wagg, eds. *Amateurism in British sport: it matters not who won or lost.* London, 2008.

Portsmouth, Earl of. *A Knot of Roots: An Autobiography.* London, 1965.

Post, John D. *The last great subsistence crisis in the Western World.* Baltimore, 1977.

Prasenjit. Duara. "The New Politics of Hinduism." *Wilson Quarterly* 15/3, 1991.

Preston, John F. "Lessons from the Farm Forestry Projects." *Journal of Forestry* 44, January, 1946.

Quinn, Patrick F. "Agrarianism and the Jeffersonian Philosophy." *Review of Politics* 2/1, January, 1940.

Rensburg C. J. J. van, and E. M. Palmer. *New World to Win*. Bloemfontein, 1946.

Risser, James, and George Anthan. "Why they love Earl Butz: Prosperous farmers see him as the greatest." *New York Times*, June 13, 1976.

Robertson, T. C. "All of Africa is Drying up." *Velt Trust News*, November, 1949.

Rodale, J. I. *Pay Dirt: Farming & Gardening with Composts*. New York, 1946.

Rodale, J. I. "Sir Albert Howard: A Tribute." *Organic Gardening Magazine* 13/8, September, 1948.

Rodale, J. I. *Organic Merry-Go-Round*. Emmaus, 1954.

Rodale, J. I. *The Healthy Hunzas*. Emmaus, 1955.

Rogers, Naomi. *An Alternative Path: The Making and Remaking of Hahnemann Medical College and Hospital of Philadelphia*. New Brunswick, 1998.

Ruffin, Edmund. *An Essay on Calcareous Manures*. Cambridge, 1832.

Russell, E. J. "Alfred Daniel Hall, 1864–1942." *Obituary Notices of Fellows of the Royal Society* 4, 1942–1944.

Russell, E. J. *A History of Agricultural Science in Great Britain: 1620–1954*. London, 1966.

Said, Edward. *Orientalism*. New York, 1979.

Sax, Boria. *Animals in the Third Reich: Pets, Scapegoats, and the Holocaust*. New York, 2000.

Saxon, Edgar J. *A Sense of Wonder*, ed. John Stewart Collis. London, ND.

Schmid, O. "Development of Standards for Organic Farming." *Organic Farming: An International History*, ed. W. Lockeretz. Oxfordshire, 2007.

Schumacher, E. F. *Small is Beautiful: A Study of Economics as if People Mattered*. London, 1973.

Scullard, H. H. *From the Gracchi to Nero: A History of Rome from 133 B.C. to A.D. 68*. London, 1963.

Shearer, E. "Notes on Agriculture in Japan." *Agricultural Journal of India* III, 1908.

Sheppard, J. T. "'Miss Matthaei on Tragedy.' Review of *Studies in Greek Tragedy* by Louise E. Matthaei." *The Classical Review* 33/3–4, May–June, 1919.

Sheppard, John H. *A Practical Treatise on the Use of Peruvian and Ichaboe African Guano: Cheapest Manure in the World*. London, 1844.

Sheppard, John H. *Anonymous Hints to Farmers on the Nature, Purchase and Application of Peruvian, Bolivian, and African Guano*. London, 1845.

Shippey, Tom. "Tolkien and the West Midlands: The Roots of Romance." *Lembas Extra*, 1995.

Shozo, Tanaka. *Tanaka Shozo senshu, Vol. 4*, ed. Anzai Kunio, Kano Masanao, Komatsu Hiroshi, Sakaya Junji, and Yui Masaomi. Tokyo, 1989.

Shuttleworth, D. W. G. "Past, Present and Future." *Veld Trust News*, July, 1945.

Simon, Eugene. *La Cité chinoise*. Paris, 1891.

Simpson, Lewis P. *The Dispossessed Garden: Pastoral and History in Southern Literature*. Athens, 1975.

Sinclair, Ward. "Seeds of Organic Farming Falling on Barren Ground These Days." *The Washington Post*, June 13, 1982.

Sinclair, Ward. "More Farmers Taking the Organic Route: Organic Farmers Must Plow Information Desert." *Washington Post*, April 3, 1983.

Slicher van Bath, B. H. *The Agrarian History of Western Europe, A. D. 500–1850*, trans. Olive Ordish. London, 1963.

Sly, F. G. "The Department of Agriculture in India." *Agricultural Journal of India* 1, 1906.

Smith, Sherry L. *The View from Officers' Row: Army Perceptions of Western Indians.* Tucson, 1990.

Smuts, J. C. *Holism and Evolution.* Cape Town, 1987.

Spiral, Archer, and L. Gleason. *History of Radio to 1926.* Washington DC, 1938.

Stapledon, R. G. *The Land Now and To-morrow.* London, 1935.

Stapledon, R. G. "The Green Hills." *Country Life* 79, 1936.

Staudenmaier, Peter. "Organic Farming in Nazi Germany: The Politics of Biodynamic Agriculture, 1933–1945." *Environmental History* 18, April, 2013.

Steiner, Rudolf. *Ueber die Wanderungen der Rassen.* Berlin, 1904.

Steiner, Rudolf. *Die geistigen Hintergründe des Ersten Weltkrieges.* Berlin, 1921.

Steiner, Rudolf. *The Education of the Child: Lectures on Education.* London, 1927.

Stolz, Robert. "Nature over Nation: Tanaka Shōzō's fundamental river law." *Japan Forum* 18/3, 2007.

Sturmey, S. G. "Owner-Farming in England and Wales, 1900–1950." *Essays in Agrarian History: Reprints edited for the British Agricultural History Society, Vol. II*, ed. E. E. Minchinton. Newton-Abbot, UK, 1968.

Sykes, F. "Milk and Soil Fertility." *Organic Farming Digest* 1/4, January, 1947.

Tanner, C. B., and R. W. Simonson, "Franklin Hiram King—Pioneer Scientist." *Soil Science Society of America Journal* 57/1, 1993.

Taylor, Renee. *Long Suppressed Hunza Health Secrets for Long Life and Happiness.* New York, 1964.

Thapar, Romila. "Imagined Religious Communities? Ancient History and the Modern Search for a Hindu Identity." *Modern Asian Studies* 23, 1989.

Thomas Jefferson. *Notes On Virginia.* New York, 1801.

Thompson, E. P. *The Making of the English Working Class.* London, 1963.

Thompson, F. M. L. "The Second Agricultural Revolution, 1815–1880." *Economic History Review* 21, April, 1968.

Throckmorton, R I. "Organic Farming—Bunk." *Reader's Digest*, October, 1952.

Trachtenberg Alan. *Shades of Hiawatha: Staging Indians, Making Americans, 1880–1930.* New York, 2004.

Tragardh, Lars. "Varieties of Volkish Ideologies." *Language and the Construction of Class Identities*, ed. Bo Strath. Gothenburg, 1990.

Treitel, Corinna. "Artificial or Biological? Nature, Fertilizer and the German Origins of Organic Agriculture." *New Perspectives on the History of Life Sciences and Agriculture*, eds. Denise Phillips and Sharon Kingsland. Geneva, 2015.

Truog, E. "Organics only?—Bunkum!" *The Land* 5, 1946.

Truog, E. "The Organic Gardening Myth." *Soil Survey Horizons* 4, 1963.

Uekötter, Frank. *The Greenest Nation? A New History of German Environmentalism.* Cambridge MA, 2014.

Uozumi, Michio. "Introduction." In Albert Howard, *Nogyo Seiten* [An Agricultural Testament], trans. Shigeru Yasuda. Tokyo, 2003.

Vardi, Liana. *Physiocrats and the World of the Enlightenment.* Cambridge, 2013.

Vasey, Daniel E. *An Ecological History of Agriculture: 10,000 BC–AD 10,000.* Ames, Iowa, 1992.

Veer, Peter van der. "Introduction." *Orientalism and the Postcolonial Predicament*, eds. Carol A. Breckenridge and Peter van der Veer. Philadelphia, 1993.

Vinning, J., M. S. Merrick, and E. A. Price. "The distinction between humans and nature: Human perceptions of connectedness to nature and elements of the natural and unnatural." *Human Ecology Review* 15, 2008.

Voelcker, John Augustus. *Report on the Improvement of Indian Agriculture.* London, 1893.

Vogt, Gunter. "The Origins of Organic Farming." *Organic Farming: An International History,* ed. William Lockeretz. Oxfordshire, 2007.

Wad, Yeshwant D. "The Work at Indore." *Organic Gardening Magazine* 13/8, September, 1948.

Waggaman, William H. *Phosphoric Acid, Phosphates, and Phosphatic Fertilizers.* New York, 1952.

Wallop, Gerard Vernon. *Alternative to Death.* London, 1943.

Ward, Marshall. "Coffee Leaf Disease: Second Report." *Ceylon Sessional Paper* 50, 1880.

Ward, Marshall. *Preliminary Report on the Enquiry into the Coffee-Leaf Disease in Supplement to the Ceylon Observer.* Colombo, Ceylon, 1880.

Warde, Paule. "The Invention of Sustainability." *Modern Intellectual History* 8/1, 2011.

Watson, E. Fairlie. "The Lessons of the East." *Organic Gardening Magazine* 13/8, September, 1948.

Watt, George. "Conditions of Wheat Growing in India." *Journal of the Royal Agricultural Society of England* 24, 1888.

Webber, Herbert J. *The water hyacinth, and its relation to navigation in Florida.* Washington, 1897.

Wells, H. G. *Love and Mr. Lewisham.* London, 1900.

Wells, H. G. *An Experiment in Autobiography.* Philadelphia, 1934.

Wheeler, Holmer J. *Manures and Fertilizers.* New York, 1914.

White, Gilbert. *The Natural History of Selborne.* Boston, 1975.

White, Harold. "Whiter Civilization." *Organic Farming Digest* 1/7, October–December, 1947.

Whitney, Milton, and F. K. Cameron. "The Chemistry of Soil as Related to Crop Production." *Forestry Quarterly* 2, 1903.

Whyte, R. O. "Soil Fertility and National Health." *Nature,* May 17, 1941.

Wiener, Joel H. *The Americanization of the British Press, 1830s–1914: Speed in the Age of Transatlantic Journalism.* Houndsmill, 2011.

William Beach Thomas, *The Yeoman's England.* London, 1934.

Williams, Michael. *The Making of the South Australian Landscape: A Study in the Historical Geography of Australia.* London, 1974.

Williams, Michael. "The Relations of Environmental History and Historical Geography." *Journal of Historical Geography* 20, January, 1994.

Wilson, E. O. "Biophilia and the Conservation Ethic." *The Biophilia Hypothesis,* eds. S. Kellert and E. O. Wilson. Washington DC, 1993.

Wilson, Sandra. "The 'New Paradise': Japanese Emigration to Manchuria in the 1930s and 1940s." *The International History Review* 17/2, 1995.

Wines, Richard A. *Fertilizer in America: From Waste Recycling to Resource Exploitation.* Philadelphia, 1985.

Wood, Barbara. *E. F. Schumacher: His Life and Thought.* New York, 1984.

Worster, Donald. *Nature's Economy: A History of Ecological Ideas.* Cambridge, 1985.

Wrench, G. T. *The Restoration of the Peasantries: with Especial Reference to that of India.* London, 1939.

Wynen, E., and S. Fritz, "NASAA and Organic Agriculture in Australia." *Organic Farming: An International History,* ed. W. Lockeretz. Oxfordshire, 2007.

Yao, K. K. *Fertilizers in China.* Washington DC, 1948.

Yates, Arthur. "A New Zealand Message." *Organic Farming Digest* 1/6, July–September, 1947.

ONLINE SOURCES

29th *Report of Science and Art Department* (1882): Reeks, *op. cit.* (ref. 7), p. 129. Available online at: http://www.british-history.ac.uk/survey-london/vol38/pp233-247#anchorn34 [accessed August 28, 2017].

American Medical Association, "The Medicine Men" [Film], circa 1950. Available online at: https://www.youtube.com/watch?v=3Aw9ucp2dMs [accessed 26 December, 2016].

Annuaire de la Société des Nations. *International Labour Organization.* Available online at: http://www.indiana.edu/~league/ilomembers.htm [accessed August 21, 2017].

Bergland, Robert. "Toward a National Food Policy" (September 9, 1977), The 38th Alfred M. Landon Lecture Series. Available online at: https://www.youtube.com/watch?v=qI0xGNqaLSo [accessed February 11, 2017].

Chalker-Scott, Linda. "The Myth of Biodynamic Agriculture." 2004. Available online at: https://puyallup.wsu.edu/wp-content/uploads/sites/403/2015/03/biodynamic-agriculture.pdf [accessed May 30, 2017].

Chevriot, Roland. "Creation of an International Federation" (ND). Available online at: http://infohub.ifoam.bio/sites/default/files/page/files/founding_letter.pdf [accessed May 30, 2017].

Duke, James A. Handbook of Energy Crops. Unpublished, 1983. Available online at: https://hort.purdue.edu/newcrop/duke_energy/Hymenaea_courbaril.html [accessed May 31, 2017].

Eden, Thomas. "Thomas Eton to Ronald Aylmer Fisher," University of Adelaide, March 1930–May 1934. Available online at: http://hdl.handle.net/2440/67664 [accessed June 16, 2016].

Garibay, Salvador V., and Roberto Ugas, "Organic Farming in Latin America and the Caribbean." *The World of Organic Agriculture—Statistics and Merging Trends*, eds. Helga Willer and Lukas Kilcher. Bonn, 2010. Available online at: http://orgprints.org/17931/1/garibay-ugas-2009-world-organic-agriculture.pdf [accessed February 11, 2017].

Gold, Mary V. "Organic Production/Organic Food: Information," June 2007. National Agricultural Library. Available online at: https://www.nal.usda.gov/afsic/organic-productionorganic-food-information-access-tools [accessed September 22, 2016].

"House of Commons Parliamentary Papers," ProQuest. Available online at: http://www.proquest.com/products-services/House-of-Commons-Parliamentary-Papers.html [accessed August 27, 2017].

Jiko-Kai. "What is the Jiko-Kai?" N.D. Available online at: http://www.jiko-kai.org/en/about.html [accessed December 10, 2016].

Laetsch, Watson M., Kevin Padian, and Roderic B. Park. "Biography of Thomas H. Jukes." Available online at: http://content.cdlib.org/view?docId=hb1r29n709&doc.view=content&chunk.id=div00029&toc.depth=1&brand=calisphere&anchor.id=0 [accessed December 27, 2016].

Mackethan, Lucinda H. "I'll take my Stand: The Relevance of the Agrarian Vision." *VQR* 56/4 (Autumn, 1980). Available online at: http://www.vqronline.org/essay/i%E2%80%99ll-take-my-stand-relevance-agrarian-vision [accessed January 24, 2017].

Madden, Patrick J. "The Early Years: the LISA, SARE, and ACE Programs." Available online at: https://www.google.com.au/url?sa=t&rct=j&q=&esrc=s&source=web&cd=2&ved=0ahUKEwi7svyg9Z3UAhXDUZQKHRDSBYEQFggsMAE&url=http%3A%2F%2Fwww.sare.org%2Fcontent%2Fdownload%2F50101%2F661407%2FThe_Early_Years_(Madden).pdf%3Finlinedownload%3D1&usg=AFQjCNF3zBQStYFZNsvtjDCB2mOS4lcklw [accessed June 2, 2017].

NA. "Booth, Frank S." *20th Century Japanese Dictionary of People*. Available online at: https://kotobank.jp/word/%E3%83%96%E3%83%BC%E3%82%B9-124755#E3.83.87.E3.82.B8.E3.82.BF.E3.83.AB.E7.89.88.20.E6.97.A5.E6.9C.AC.E4.BA.BA.E5.90.8D.E5.A4.A7.E8.BE.9E.E5.85.B8.2BPlus [accessed August 26, 2017].

NA. "Der ursprüngliche politische Kontext der Waldorf-Bewegung." March 1, 2011. Available online at: https://blog.psiram.com/2011/03/anthroposophie-dreigliederung-und-demokratie/ [accessed June 1, 2017].

NA. "Imperial College", Royal Institute of British Architects. Available at: https://web.archive.org/web/20121002170023/http://www.architecture.com/LibraryDrawingsAndPhotographs/Albertopolis/TheStoryOf/ImperialCollege/ImperialInstitute.aspx [accessed August 18, 2017].

NA. "J. Whiteley Tolson." *James Finlay & Co—Managers and Assistants Letter Books Index*, Volume 1–15. Available online at: http://www.gla.ac.uk/media/media_169147_en.pdf [accessed June 12, 2016].

NA. "Sanatogen," National Museum of American History. Available online at: http://americanhistory.si.edu/collections/search/object/nmah_714696 [accessed August 23, 2017].

NA. "The European Union's Ban on Hormone-Treated Meat," CRS Report for Congress. Available online at: http://congressionalresearch.com/RS20142/document.php?study=THE+EUROPEAN+UNIONS+BAN+ON+HORMONE-TREATED+MEAT [accessed May 30, 2017].

NA. "Broadbalk Winter Wheat Experiment," e-RA: the electronic Rothamsted Archive. Available online at: http://www.era.rothamsted.ac.uk/index.php?area=home&page=index&dataset=4 [accessed August 18, 2017].

NA. "Supplement," *The London Gazette* (June 19, 1914). Available online at: https://www.thegazette.co.uk/London/issue/28842/supplement/4879 [accessed May 31 2017].

Norris, Roland V. "The Work of the Tea Research Institute." *Tea Research Institute* (Thalawakele, 1949): 4. Available online at: http://tri.nsf.ac.lk/bitstream/handle/1/778/TQ-20_4.pdf?sequence=2&isAllowed=y [accessed June 16, 2016].

Oldfield, Sybil. "Howard, Louise Enrestine, Lady Howard (1880–1969)." *Oxford Dictionary of National Biography*. Oxford, 2004. Available online at: http://www.oxforddnb.com/index/101037576/Louise-Howard [accessed August 21, 2017].

Pritchard, Stephen. "At Home with the Organic Conductor." The Guardian (January 28, 2007). Available online at: http://www.theguardian.com/lifeandstyle/2007/jan/28/foodanddrink.features5 [accessed June 1, 2017].

Schwindenhammer, Sandra. "Global organic agriculture governance through standards: When inter-institutional policy-making oscillates between global harmonization and regional integration." Paper presented at the "International Conference on Public Policy," Milan, July 1–4, 2015. Available online at: http://docplayer.net/27895891-Sandra-schwindenhammer.html [accessed August 25, 2017].

Sinclair, H. M. "McCarrison, Sir Robert (1878–1960)." Oxford Dictionary of National Biography. Oxford, 2004. Available online at: http://www.oxforddnb.com/view/article/34678 [accessed August 21, 2017].

Statista. "Worldwide Sales of Organic Food from 1999 to 2015." ND. Available online at: https://www.statista.com/statistics/273090/worldwide-sales-of-organic-foods-since-1999/ [accessed August 25, 2017].

Staudenmaier, Peter. "Review of Rassismus und Geschechtsmetaphyik by Ansgar Martins." Waldorfblog (December 22, 2012). Available online at: https://waldorfblog.wordpress.com/2012/12/22/staudenmaier-rezension/ [accessed August 27, 2017].

Steinfeld, H., P. Gerber, T. Wasenaar, V. Castel, M. Rosales, and C. de Haan. Livestock's Long Shadow. Rome, 2014. Available online at: http://www.fao.org/docrep/010/a0701e/a0701e00.HTM [accessed April 29, 2014].

Tocklai Tea Research Institute. "Home." Available online at: http://www.tocklai.net/ [accessed June 10, 2016].

USDA Natural Resources Conservation Service, Plants Profile (2002). Available online: http://plants.usda.gov/cgi_bin/plant_profile.cgi?symbol=EICR [accessed August 21, 2017].

Whitehouse, Scott. "J. R. R. Tolkein in Staffordshire." Available online at: http://www.staffordshiregreatwar.com/wp-content/uploads/2014/10/Tolkien-Trail-Booklet1.pdf [accessed June 1, 2017].

Youngberg, Garth. "Garth Youngberg Interview Part 1" [video], June 17, 1991. Alternative Farming Information Center, National Agricultural Library, June 27, 2012. Available online at: https://www.youtube.com/watch?v=imBzVGzbEJY [accessed February 11, 2017].

Wilcox, Christie. "Are Lower Pesticide a Good Reason to Buy Organic? Probably Not." *Scientific American Blog*. September 24, 2012. Available online at: https://blogs.scientificamerican.com/science-sushi/pesticides-food-fears/ [accessed June 1, 2017].

Youngberg, Garth. "Garth Youngberg Interview Part 1" [video], June 17, 1991. Alternative Farming Information Center, National Agricultural Library, June 27, 2012. Available online at: https://www.youtube.com/watch?v=imBzVGzbEJY [accessed February 11, 2017].

Index

Abrams, M. H. 12n.31
Addison, Lord 132–3
Africa 2–3, 17, 99, 102, 104, 119, 121, 141,
    143, 146, 192, 195, 198, *see also* South
    Africa
African farmers 4, 130
Africans 132, 146
Afrikaans 142
agrarian
    activists 21
    advocates 21
    fashion 186
    ideals 20, 22, 25, 29, 176, 186
    ideas 30
    land reform 162
    movements 28
    norms 26
    theory 27
    values 28, 39, 185
    virtue 22
agrarianism 20–5, 29, 33
agricultural
    changes 4n.3
    colleges/schools 58, 140, 165
    conditions 63
    customs 81
    debt 187
    departments 92
    depression 27, 51
    development 62, 176
    disaster 17
    economy 160
    efficiency 104
    experiments 137n.71
    goods 21
    income 20
    industrial 33, 92, 187
    innovation 6
    interests 139
    labor/laborers 6, 59, 66, 98
    land 16, 22, 50, 63, 104, 135, 141, 167
    loans 122
    management 200
    markets 12, 102
    methods 11, 17, 45, 71, 75, 84, 92, 107,
        120–1, 123, 126, 134, 175, 189, 201
    output 129, 132, 165
    policies 18, 152, 159, 176, 189, 191
    practices 3, 15, 45, 71, 92, 114, 118–19,
        136, 171, 177
    prices 27, 178
    problems 7, 64

    production/productivity 5, 9, 11, 20, 27, 41,
        45–6, 65, 119, 122–3, 131, 135n.65, 135,
        141, 149, 176, 181
    reform 6
    research 8, 52, 57–8, 64, 103, 136–7,
        194, 199
    revolution 5–6, 8
    romanticism 45
    science 59, 63, 139–40, 181
    scientists 46, 53
    stations 8, 43, 52, 72
    themes 30
    theorists 9
    universities 8
    work/workers 29, 41
    writers 25
Agricultural Department (India) 70, 92
Agricultural Improvement Council 107
agriculturalists 16, 37, 64, 65n.14, 84, 101,
    164, 170
Agricultural Research Council 107
Agricultural Research Institute (Pusa),
    see Imperial Agricultural Research
    Institute (IARI)
agriculture 7, 9, 10n.27, 16, 18, 29–30, 33–40,
    42, 54, 59, 73–5, 77n.82, 78, 82, 85–6,
    88–90, 98–107, 111, 116, 118, 120, 124,
    126–7, 130, 146–9, 152–3, 160–1, 163,
    169, 171, 173, 181, 184, 188, 190–2,
    195, 198
    before the industrial age 3
    biodynamic 45
    conventional 202
    industrial 1, 3, 126, 166, 201–2
    methods 84
    modern 1
    organic 10
    organic-biological 126
    practices 84
    productivity 83
    reformers 83
    science 78, 83
    sustainable 1, 3–4, 189, 194
    traditional 200
    tropical 101
Agriculture Biologique 193
Alabama 153
Albert Howard Foundation of Organic
    Husbandry 146–7, 149, 150n.126
Albert Howard Society 50n.1, 51n.6
Albrecht, William 167
Alexander the Great 86

Alger, Horatio 169
Allen, G. K. 159
Allen, Robert C. 4n.2
Allentown 170
Alps 97
American
    cotton seeds 77
    culture 172
    depression 102
    efforts to address soil fertility 84
    entry into World War One 170
    fantasy of eastern culture 82
    farmers 186
    heroes 169
    Indians 85n.16, 86
    industrial ideal 28
    markets 196
    Midwest 84
    occupation of Japan 178
    Republic 14–15
    scientists 127
    South 28
    transcendentalist movement 14
American Association for the Advancement of
    Science 16, 185
Americanization 32
American Medical Association (AMA) 166
    The Medicine Men 165
Americans 85n.16, 140, 160, 169–70,
    see also North America, United States
Amish 6
ammonia 31, 42, 78, 91–2, 122, 128, 171
Anglo-Saxon
    countries 159
    farmers 22
    farming methods 50, 71
    industrial and cultural elites 168
animal
    disease 118
    feed 153
    husbandry 137
    life 25
    manure 8, 42, 44, 46, 74, 77–9, 111, 121,
        152, 176, 188–9
    parts 44
    power 32, 176
    residues 137
    stocks 5
    waste 9, 87, 108, 111, 115, 179
animals 3, 13, 25, 32, 37, 45, 50, 70, 113, 115,
    127, 129, 136, 138–9, 141–2, 144, 152–4,
    157, 161, 167–8, 171, 186–7, 194
Anthroposophical Society 40
anthroposophy 40–1, 43, 174
antibiotics 31, 179
anti-Semitism 26, 45, 159
Argentina 15, 31, 74
Ariyoshi, Sawako
    The Complex Contamination 180

Arizona 168
Arkansas 153
Arnon, Daniel I. 185
arrowroot 57–8
arsenic 9
Arthur Yates and Company 138
arts and crafts 21, 36
Aryans 43
ASEAN Standard for Organic Agriculture 195
Ashio Copper Mine Pollution Incident 177
Asia 2–3, 17n.42, 48, 80, 83, 102, 106n.52,
    118, 121–2, 146, 163, 192
    Central 4, 15, 87
    East 81, 87
    South 104
    South East 81
Asian
    farmers 4
    racial harmony 176
Asians 81
Asia Regional Organic Standards 195
Assam 104, 106, 107
Association of British Chemical
    Manufacturers 136
Association of Scientific and Clinical
    Medicine 113
Athens 21
Attlee, Clement 132
Attlee government 160
Auckland 138n.80
Audubon Society 153, 172–3
Austin 191–2
Australia 15, 17, 31, 72, 74, 106n.52, 120,
    125, 134–5, 141–3, 146, 152, 193–4,
    196, 198
    Select Committee on Wildlife
        Conservation 194
Australian
    farmers 135
    organic exports 194
    scene 134
    settlers 135n.65
Australian Organic Farming and Gardening
    Society 194
Australian Quarantine and Inspection
    Service 194
Austro-Hungarian Empire 40
Aztecs 4n.2

Babylon 157
bacteria 57, 74, 78, 104, 109, 118,
    126n.36, 140, 146, 148n.120, 150,
    see also microorganisms
Badenoch, A. G. 154
Bagot, A. D. G.
    Composting Tea Estate Wastes 111
Baldwin, W. S. 146
Balfour, Eve 116, 135n.64, 145, 157, 160,
    164–5, 189

*The Living Soil and the Haughley
  Experiment* 156
Balisera valley 105
Baltzer, Eduard 45–7
Baluchistan 72
bananas 58, 196
Bangladesh 105
Banks, Joseph 7
Barbados 54, 57–8, 77n.84, 137
barley 72, 181
Barnard, F. M. 26n.18
Barton, Gregory 20n.1, 25n.14
Basel 44
Bauer Chemical Company 133
Bayley, John 52–4
Beach Thomas, William 37
  The Yeoman's England 38
Bear, Firman E. 165
beef 31, 196
Beinart, William 15n.34, 85n.16, 141n.91
Belgian Empire 12
Bengal 69, 72–3, 82, 92, 106–7, 109, 115, 137
Bennett, Brett 199
Bennett, Hugh 144
Bentham, Jeremy 25
benzene hexachloride 9
Berg, Auri C. 152n.132
Bergland report 188–90, 192, 195
Bergland, Robert 186–7, 189
Bergland, Selma 187
beriberi 76
Berkeley 185
Bertrand, Anson R. 187
Besant, Annie 40
Beveridge, William 160
Bhutan 67, 109
Bicknell, Franklin 132–3
Biesele, John J. 175
Bihar 54, 64, 74, 92
biochemistry 136
biodiversity 13, 85n.15
biodynamic
  agriculture 42, 45
  attention to humus 127
  farmers 174
  farming 39, 41–2, 45, 161
  followers 44
  methods 42, 45, 182
  movement 42, 116, 126
biodynamics 20, 39–40, 44, 192
biological
  activity 85n.15, 127, 138
  agents 201
  agriculture 126
  community 16
  complexity 10
  cycles 85n.15
  despair 34
  factors 71

farming 20, 45–7, 127, 138
  laissez faire 70
  pest control 188
  research laboratory 44
biologists 110, 126, 155, 173, 181, 185
biology 13, 54, 110, 136, 138, 175, 189, 199
birds 1, 10, 114, 153, 171–2
Bishop's Castle 50, 51n.6, 197
Black Death 6
Black, Duncan 131
Blackheath 60–1, 148
Blackman, F. F. 57, 60
Blavatsky, Helena 40
Bledisloe, Viscount 150n.124
Block, John 189–90
blood 44
Bloomsbury 128
Bloomsbury group 96
Bogart, Humphrey 168
Bolshevik uprising 97
Bombay 59, 72, 99
Booth, Frank S. 177
Bosazza, D. R. V. L. 143
botanical
  courses 65
  exchange 70
  gardens 58
  stations 58
  survey 72
Botanical Survey of South Africa 130
botanists 5, 7, 11, 18, 58, 64–5, 73, 107, 130
botany 6, 54, 57, 69, 73, 99, 136
Botswana 141
Bould, Dr 150
Boyd Orr, Sir John 132, 140
Brabourne, Lord 106
Bradford, Lord 158
Bradshaw, Lord 156n.3
Brady, Nyle C. 10n.27
Brahmanism 81
Brazil 60, 106
  Ministry of Agriculture, Livestock and
    Food Supply 197
bread 34, 46, 74, 114, 116, 119, 130,
    160, 166
Britain 2, 5, 38, 130, 144, 152, 164
  Board of Agriculture 7, 11
  Board of Scientific Advice 62
  British Middle East Office 125
  Colonial Development and Welfare Act 137
  Colonial Office 56, 58, 108, 149
  Committee on Higher Agricultural
    Education 107
  Conservative Agricultural Committee 115
  Design of Farm Buildings Committee 107
  House of Commons 115–16, 153
  House of Lords 132
  Labour Party 163
  Ministry of Agriculture 115, 129, 139

Britain (*cont.*)
  Ministry of Food 133
  Ministry of Housing and Local
    Government 151
  National Coal Board 163
  National Health Insurance Act 113
  National Liberal Party 156
  Natural Resources Technical Committee 151
  Register of Organic Food Standards 164
  Soil Association 36–7, 115, 147, 156–8,
    160–2, 164, 192
British
  administration 60
  cabinet 63
  efforts to address soil fertility 84
  elites 59
  farmers 10n.27, 25, 142
  fascist economics 39
  fascist movements 59
  food 132
  foreign policy 133
  government 67, 107
  imperial holdings 146
  imperial officials 4, 90
  imperial power 64
  imperial world 43
  imperialists 15
  parliament 74, 132
  population 30–2, 148
  power 71
  preferential trade 199
  press 37
  romantic farm enthusiasts 28–9
  royals 3
  rule 14, 77n.83
  scientific networks 103
  scientists 62n.2, 127
  settlement colonies 2
  writers 30
British Association for the Advancement of
  Science 126n.36
British Basic Slag Companies 136
British Commonwealth 14, 140
British Dental Association 128
British Dominions 31, 144, 176, 198
British Empire 8, 33, 47, 54, 57, 62, 64, 68,
  70, 74, 76, 82, 103–4, 107, 116, 118,
  122, 125, 133–4, 135n.65, 137, 139–41,
  144, 148–9, 163, 182, 197–9
British Medical Association 113
British Union of Fascists 39
Brittany 61
Bromfield, Louis
  Early Autumn 168
  Pleasant Valley 168
  The Farm 167–8
Bruce, W. B. 105–6
Brunt, L. P.
  Municipal Composting 149

Buddhism 81, 89
Buddhist
  doctrine 181
  economics 161–3
  followers 3
  religiosity 181
  sources 87
Bülow, F. W. von 101
Bunyan, John
  Pilgrim's Progress 25
bureaucrats 3, 26, 64n.9, 75, 98–9, 107, 129,
  140, 144
Burma 161, 163
  Economic and Social Council 163
Burt, B. C. 77n.81
Burusho people 86
Bury, J. B. 24n.11
Bush, George 191
Butz, Earl 185–6

cacao 58
calcium 8
calcium carbonate 5
Calcutta 105–6, 108
Calicut 111
California 72, 188
California Organic Food Act 188
Cambridge University 54, 56–7, 95–6
Canada 74, 102, 119–20, 154, 193, 198
cancer 30, 44, 49, 86, 94, 172, 181, 184n.4
capitalism/capitalists 3, 20–1, 83, 85, 121, 134,
  138, 140, 160, 163–4
capitalist
  elites 160
  factory owners 21
  industry 139
  interests 140
  monocrop cultivation 137
  science 64, 134–5, 138, 140
  usury 71
Carlyle, Sir Robert 68
Carlyle, Thomas 20n.2, 26
Carnegie, Andrew 169
Carson, Rachel 134n.61, 140, 174
  Silent Spring 153, 166, 171–3, 180, 201
cartels 118, 120–2
Carter, Jimmy 187, 190n.21
Cartesian/Descartian
  eternal soul 162
  philosophy 13
cassava 72
Caterham 160
Catholic
  divines 25
  intellect 56
  magazine 128
Catholics 164, 180
cattle 4, 26, 41, 50, 78, 108, 111, 134, 139,
  153, 176, 186

Cavendish-Bentinck, Lord Henry 74n.75
Cavett, Dick 175
Central America 121, 195
certification 183, 185–6, 191–5
Ceylon 56, 70, 72, 104, 110–12
Chalker-Scott, Linda 42n.77
Chamberlain, Joseph 108
Charles, Prince 3, 140, 197
Chaucer, Geoffrey 2
Chekiang 122
chemical
　additives 153
　agriculture 166
　analyses 10–11, 12n.30, 16, 136
　authority 7
　cartels 120
　companies 34, 165, 172, 175, 179
　complexity 9
　composition 7, 16, 107
　elements 7
　farming 136
　fertilizer plants 123
　fertilizers 1, 8–9, 11–12, 16, 41, 59, 65n.14,
　　73, 78, 91, 99, 112, 118–24, 129, 135–7,
　　141, 150, 152, 165, 168, 171, 176–7,
　　180, 184, 187, 202–3
　fuels 178
　industries 46, 115, 119, 123
　manufacturers 121, 134
　manures 136–7
　mineral dope 18
　pesticides 41, 65, 70, 73, 112, 174, 176,
　　202–3
　spray 56
　theories 138
　treatments 126
　usage 191
　weed killers 172
chemicals 1, 10, 17, 34, 41, 47, 65, 70–1,
　76, 108, 112, 121–2, 129, 145, 153,
　157, 165–6, 173, 176, 178, 181,
　184, 188, 193
chemistry 6–8, 13, 136, 138
Cheshire Panel Committee 113, 116, 128
　Medical Testament 113–16, 118, 128
　Report on Garden Competition 124
Chevriot, Roland 192
Chicago 31, 63
Chile 47
Chilean nitrate producers 120
China 15, 17, 34, 83–4, 91, 119, 121–4,
　152, 195
　Communist bureaucracy 123
　Communist Party 122
　Cultural Revolution 123
　National Agricultural Research Bureau 122
Chinese
　agriculture 75, 152
　culture 83

　efforts 84
　methods 46
　peasants 46n.94, 79, 84, 152
Chisso chemical company 179
Christian
　community 127
　followers 3
　ideas 12–13
　lifestyle 126
　ruralism 126
　sentiment 89
　socialists 21
　tradition 1, 162
Christianity 81, 160
Cicero 22
Cincinnatus 22
Cistercian order 5
cities 4n.2, 5, 9, 12, 20–3, 28–9,
　37–8, 39n.63, 59, 84, 130, 146,
　148–9, 160, 163, 169, 179, 186,
　192, 203
class consciousness 25, 55
Clayton, Paul 31
Clements, Frederic 169, 173
climate 13, 15, 17, 62–3, 70, 121, 143,
　see also weather
closed circuit system 10n.27
Clouston, D. 71
clover 5, 153
coal 91, 119, 163
coal mines 92
coal tar 9
Cobbett, William 39
　Rural Rides 25–6
Codex Alimentarius Austriacus 193
coffee 44, 196
　blight 56–7
　growers 99
　plantations 56, 104
　plants 56–7
　rust 57
Colgrove, J. 31n.30
collectivism 21, 33
Collings, Gilbert H. 8n.19
colonial
　administration 107
　Africa 104
　architecture 64n.11
　concerns on desertification 17n.43
　development 108
　organization 154
　science 63n.7
　scientists 199
　world 43
colonies 2, 12, 46, 67, 105, 107, 131, 176,
　198–200
Columbia University 169
Commoner, Barry 175
communism 37, 186

communist
  bureaucracy 123
  countries 101n.30
  expansion 123
  revolution 160
  threat 29
communists 84, 159
Companion of the Indian Empire 67
compost 4, 18, 29, 43, 71–5, 78, 80, 91, 104,
    106, 109–12, 115, 118, 124n.29, 127–8,
    130–2, 146, 148n.118, 149–52, 160,
    194, 203
  wars 94, 155
composting 9, 11, 44, 47, 69, 75–8, 84,
    87–8, 91, 99, 104, 108–12, 115, 123,
    127, 129–31, 137, 144–52, 158, 176,
    198, 200
Conford, Philip 39–40, 41n.74, 42, 85n.16,
    90n.43, 164
Confucius 48
Connecticut research station 8
conservation movement 2, 15–16, 33, 49, 62,
    125n.31, 141, 144–5, 151, 155–6, 162,
    164, 168–9, 186, 200–1
consumer
  age 33
  base 174
  co-operatives 142, 178, 182
  demand 194–5
  habits 1–2, 32, 47, 80
  interest 182
  markets 3, 156, 175
  shoppers 184
  society 83
consumerism 21, 33, 145, 164
consumers 48, 120, 124, 131, 138, 169,
    177–9, 181–2, 184–5, 187–8, 191,
    193, 202–3
Continental System 26
Cook, Captain James 114
Coolidge, Calvin 167
Cooper, James Fennimore
  The Last of the Mohicans 86
copper 9, 44
copper chloride 44
copper salts 9
copper sulfate 93, 201
Corn Laws 6, 26–7
corporate
  enterprises 200
  farming 202
  farms 178, 186
  government 3
  growth 192
  institutions 3
  interests 92
  monopolies 178
  patronage 164
  retail chain 191

corporations 11, 21, 104–5, 120–1, 170,
    192, 198
Correll family 135
Costa Rica 125
cottage farms/industries 32, 51
cottagers 5
cottages 39, 67
cotton 70n.51, 77, 122
Coughlin, Father 170
counter-cultural
  movements 163, 194
  trends 165
Country Life Movement 168
Coventry, Bernard 66, 68, 70n.52, 72, 76
Craigmillar 151n.127
Crewe 113–15
Cromer, Lord 80
Crooks, Tim 32n.33
crystallization 43–4, 95
cultivation 3–4, 17, 27, 47, 67, 71–3, 90, 102,
    113, 132, 137, 173, 179, 188
cultural movements 1, 126, 163, 173, 194
Curzon, Lord 62–4, 75, 108, 139

Dalhousie, Lord 62
dams 143, 152
Dano system 151
Darjeeling 109
Darre, Richard Walther 45
Darwin, Charles 56
Davies, J. L. 150
Davy, Sir Humphry
  Elements of Agricultural Chemistry 7
DDT 9, 153, 171, 173–4, 184
death duties 11, 28
de Bary, Heinrich Anton 56
decentralization 35, 154
decolonization 85, 134, 146, 199–200
deforestation 4, 14–17, 33, 84, 141, 152, 156,
    161, 194, 201
Dehra Dun 63
Delany, James 172
Delhi 69, 76
democracy 23, 37–8, 43, 49
democratic
  governance 179
  government 140
  ideals 47
  institutions 3
  mob 22
Denmark 146, 193
desertification 17, 135, 141, 144, 157–8, 161,
    175, 201
deserts/dunes 14, 17, 33, 84, 136, 141–3,
    157–8
desiccation theory 14–15, 19, 33, 141, 143
disease 16, 19, 30, 31n.30, 46, 56–9, 65, 70,
    72, 74, 79, 91, 93, 104, 112, 114, 118,
    129, 133, 136–7, 140, 146, 153, 179

Disraeli, Benjamin 26
Dokuchaev, Vasilii 15
Dominican Republic 195
Dooars 106
Dornach 43
Dorset 18
Douglas, C. H. 39
Dravidians 79
drought 15, 131, 135, 142–3
Duke, James A. 106n.52
Dumbarton 151n.127
Dumfries 151
Duncan Brothers & Company 108
dung, *see* fertilizers
Düsseldorf 94
dust bowl 15, 84, 135, 141, 152, 167
Dutch 44
   Indonesia 180
   poldering 5

earthquakes 64, 75–6
East African Organic Products Standard 195
ecological
   approaches 11, 104
   associations 25
   basing of farming 187
   concerns 157, 168
   crises 192
   damage 107
   disaster 106
   entity 194
   ethic of organic farming 190
   ideas of organic farming 47
   ideas of recycling 9
   interconnectedness 200
   interdependence 156
   metaphors 13
   perspective 46
   principles 3, 167
   processes 1
   production 85n.15
   thinkers/thinking 35, 169
   wholeness 193
ecologists 18, 38, 173
ecology 3, 11–15, 19, 25, 34, 43, 80, 136, 138,
     145, 156
ecosystems 47, 126, 154, 193
Eden, Thomas 110
Edinburgh 154
Edinburgh Corporation 151
Egler, Frank 173
Egypt 17, 60, 80, 106n.52, 123, 158
Egyptian peasants 3
Eisenhower, Dwight D. 184n.4
Eliot, T. S.
   The Wasteland 96
Elizabethans 50
Emergency Economic Committee for
   Europe 123n.28

Emerson, Ralph Waldo 14, 82
Emmaus 170
empire foresters/forestry 11, 17, 72, 142, 198
Empire Marketing Board 107
England 2, 5, 8–9, 18, 20, 37–9, 50, 52, 60,
     65, 70–2, 76–7, 89, 91–2, 94, 100,
     112–14, 124, 129, 132–3, 136, 140, 146,
     148, 159–60, 163, 171, 197
   scientific revolution 6
Engledow, Frank 107
Engledow report 108
English
   chalk country 39
   countryside 26, 38
   cultural values 177
   farmers 5
   romantic farm literature 82
   rural romanticism 20
   settlers abroad 25
English Mistery 36
Enlightenment 24, 83
   doctrine of progress 1
   reforms 82
environmental
   action 32n.31
   activists 15, 82, 85, 124
   awareness 158
   concerns 41, 141, 148, 154, 187
   consciousness 49, 151–2, 155, 193,
     198, 201
   conservation 197
   contacts 147
   damage 84, 143
   degradation 132
   demands 194
   development 14
   disaster 17
   discourse 19
   ethics 25, 82
   focus 148
   groups 164
   history 15, 133, 173, 201
   ideas 145
   influence 201
   issues 147, 156–7
   movement 2, 5n.5, 14–15, 19, 49, 62, 85,
     134, 140–1, 145, 147, 151, 154–5, 156,
     158, 161–2, 164, 168–9, 175, 198–200
   pollution 187
   preservation 179
   progress 201
   reforms 154, 197
   solutions 106
   thinking/thought 23, 25, 157
   values 49, 81
   world view 152
environmentalism 15, 33, 50, 85, 145, 151,
     155, 164, 168, 197–8, 200–1
environmentalists 16, 177, 203

Erlich, Paul 175
erosion 4, 17, 62, 76, 83, 123, 131, 135, 141,
    143–4, 161, 167, 202
Eskimos 115
estrogen 153, 186
ethics 1–2, 82, 95, 134, 179, 202
Ethiopia 57
Eucalypt plantations 154n.143
eugenics 110, 159
Euro-Asia 3, 4n.2
Europe 2, 5, 12, 13n.32, 17, 20, 23, 29–30,
    36–7, 43, 45, 64, 71, 84, 95, 119, 121,
    125–7, 135–6, 154, 163, 170, 176, 183,
    192–6
European
    agriculture 4
    Christendom 36
    colonial world 43
    composting 84
    continent 14, 45
    countries 123n.28, 125, 146
    culture 19
    efforts to address soil fertility 84
    empires 163
    fascism 43, 59
    forests 24
    furniture 66
    gods and pagan culture 24
    history 41
    islanders 114
    markets 196
    peasant agriculture 75
    science and native art 64
    scientific literature 84
    states 102
European Commission 193
European Community 193
Europeans 24, 37, 86, 159
European Union 153, 192–4
Everest, A. E. 53

Fabian
    activists 97
    conference 160
famine 7, 45, 56, 68, 83, 123, 128, 133, 158
Farmers Bank 122
farmland 4–5, 18, 27, 50, 89, 134, 141,
    178–9, 190n.21, 196, 200
fascism 3, 26, 30, 35, 37, 43, 159, 163, 200
fascist
    economics 39
    ideals 132
    ideas 30
    movements 21, 59
    parties 101
    sympathies 134
    visions 121
fascists 84, 134, 157
Faulkner, E. H. 165

fermentation 2, 44, 78, 150
fertility 2–5, 7, 10n.27, 11, 16–18, 27–8,
    34–5, 41, 47, 63, 69, 71, 75, 83–4, 92,
    99, 112, 116, 121, 126, 135, 136n.68,
    141–2, 144–5, 150, 152, 160, 167, 169,
    175–9, 187, 196
fertilization 2, 9, 32, 41, 46, 52, 59, 78, 92,
    108, 120, 140
fertilizer
    companies/firms 10, 34, 92, 138
    industry 9, 136n.68
    plants 120–1, 123
Fertilizer Manufacturer's Association 136
fertilizers 10, 86, 93, 103, 105, 110, 120, 138,
    144, 147–8, 150, 167, 181, 194, 196, 203
    artificial/synthetic 9, 46–7, 73, 76, 84, 91–2,
        106, 108–12, 124, 126, 131, 135–6,
        188–9
    ashes 10, 108
    chemical 1, 8–9, 11–12, 16, 41, 59, 65n.14,
        73, 78, 91, 99, 112, 118–24, 129, 135–7,
        141, 150, 152, 165, 168, 171, 176–7,
        180, 184, 187, 202–3
    commercial 121
    distribution 122
    dung 3–5, 10, 52, 59, 78, 108, 111,
        148n.118, 176
    granulation 121
    guano 8–10, 11n.27
    importation 122
    inexpensive 79
    international trade 12
    manure/manuring 4–5, 7–8, 10–11, 32,
        41–4, 46, 52, 56, 59, 63, 69, 71, 73–5,
        77–9, 91, 108–9, 111, 116, 121–3, 126,
        131, 136–8, 147, 149, 152, 154, 176–7,
        181, 188–9, 194, 203
    mineral dope 11
    nitrate of soda 8
    nitrogen 7, 74, 92, 109, 119, 121, 123, 135
    nitrogen–phosphorus–potassium
        (NPK) 109, 122
    non-chemical 90
    pelleting 121
    phosphate rock 8, 10, 119, 123, 167
    potash 119
    poudrette 10
    Stone Meal 46
    superphosphates 8, 10, 138
    unnatural 165
films/radio 32–3, 35–6, 88, 133, 139, 157–8,
    165–6, *see also* lectures
Finland 193
Finlay Group (James Finlay and Co) 105
Fisher, Ronald Aylmer 110
Flanders 5
Flemming, Arthur 184n.4
Fletcher, Thomas Bainbrigge 70
floods 3, 14, 17, 142, 152, 158

Florida 106n.52, 153
fluoride/fluorine 154
Folsom, Josiah C. 101n.30
foot and mouth disease 153
Ford, Edward Onslow 60
Ford, Gerald 185
Forest Charter 62
forestry 11, 14–18, 36, 104, 141, 163, 167–8, 187, 198
forests 11, 15–17, 24, 26, 36, 47, 50, 63, 72, 128n.42, 154n.143, 186
France 6, 9, 102, 146, 192–3
    Inter-African Information Bureau for Soil Conservation and Land Utilization 154
Francé, Raoul 126
French
    colonial concerns 17n.43
    intellectuals (physiocrats) 23
    scientists 46, 56, 127
French Academy of Sciences 154
French Empire 12
French Enlightenment 83
French Revolution 23
Friends of the New Germany 159
Frost, Lionel 135
fruit 4, 31–2, 46, 50, 59, 70, 72, 104, 114, 147, 149, 161, 169, 174, 178
Fujiwara, Tatshushi 179n.108
Fukien 122
Fukuoka, Masanobu 182
    The One-Straw Revolution 181
fumigation 70
fungi 8–9, 18, 56–7, 78, 109–10, 140

Galaha Tea Estates Company 112
Galston, Arthur W. 165
Gandhi, Mohandas 48, 67, 82, 163
Ganges River 63–4, 91
gardeners 98, 112, 124, 146–7, 165, 169, 173, 182, 188, 200
Gardiner, Henry Balfour 36
Gardiner, Rolf 36–8, 142
genetics 6, 74, 107, 136, 194, 201
Geneva 94, 97, 99, 100
geologists 143
geology 39
Georgia (USA) 153
Georgians (England) 50
germ 34, 137, 185
German
    agricultural romanticism 45
    biological farming 20, 45
    colonies 105
    culture 36, 95
    heritage 95
    inflation 158
    language 60, 95
    nation 45
    national consciousness 45

newspapers 37
nutrition 46
recovery 158
scientists 7, 127, 136n.68
states 8
tropics 105
war guilt 158
German Empire 105
German Nitrogen Syndicate 120
Germany 5, 30, 35–7, 40, 43, 45–6, 60–1, 63, 68, 94–5, 119, 123n.28, 146, 153, 158–61, 164, 168, 176, 187
    British Control Commission 160
    Bunde 37
    Foods Act 153
    Jewish problem 158
    Lebensreform (Life Reform) 45–7, 126–7
    National Socialism/Socialists 30, 37, 45, 47, 84, 87, 159, 168, 176
    Naturschutz program 168
    Tripartite Pact 176
    Wandervogel youth movement 37
    wheat supply 47
Gilbert, Joseph Henry 8
Gilgit 86
globalization 81, 83, 85, 197
    of certification standards 195
    of farm markets 186
    of organic farming 156
    of the industrial Revolution 20
globalized world 12, 49, 186, 202
Global Organic Market Access Project 195
Glorious Revolution 6
Gloucestershire 50, 197
glycerophosphates 133
Gobi Desert 84
Goebbels, Joseph 37
Goetheanum research laboratory 44
Goethe, Johann 40
Gojo 180
Goyder, George 135n.66
Goyder's line 135
grain 3–4, 26, 45, 73, 79, 137, 152, 161, 174, 186, 190n.21
grape vines 8, 41, 56n.25
grass/grasslands 15, 17, 38, 132, 141, 167
grazing 4, 15, 38, 134, 141–2, 196
Great Barrier Reef 194
Great Chain of Being 12–13
Great Depression 29, 102
Greece 4, 14, 21–2, 193
Greek tragedy 60
green
    activists 3
    legislation 186
    manure/manuring 74, 122–3, 152, 188–9
greenhouse effect 194
Green Revolution 73, 76, 166
Griffiths, James 149, 150n.124

Guiana 70
Gurdjieff, George 161

Haeckel, Ernst 12, 43
Hahnemann Medical College 44
Hakkaido farming (cyclic farming) 176–7
Halevy, E. 25n.16
Hall, Daniel 58–9, 101
Harding, Warren D. 167
Harmer, Ruth
    Unfit for Human Consumption 184
Harmonized Organic Regulations 195
Harrison College 54, 57
Hawkesbury Agricultural College 138
health food 30, 33, 83, 141, 165, 171, 174,
    180, 182, 184–5, 188
heart disease 30, 133
Heckman, J. 165n.47
Heinz 31
Hemingway, Ernest 168
Hensl, Julius 46
herbal
    composting 44n.89
    preparations 31, 41–2
Herder, Johann von 26, 82–3
Herefordshire 50
Hesiod 22
Heversham 124
hexoestrol 153
Highgrove House 197
Hilgard, Eugene W. 12n.30
    Soils 11
Hilton, James
    Lost Horizon 87
Himalayas 63, 72, 86, 89
Hindi 67
    doctrine of the migration of the soul 87
    followers 3
    ideas of the sacredness of all life 14
    people 81
Hinduism 14, 77n.83, 81–2
Hippocrates 14
Hitler, Adolf 158–9
Hobbes, Thomas
    Leviathan 86
Hobson, John 97
    Imperialism: A Study 35
Hodge, Joseph 199
Hogarth Press 96, 99–100
Hokkaido 176
Hokkaido Cooperative Creamery
    Association 176
Holden, Patrick 164
holism 12–14, 19, 78, 80, 117, 173
Holmes, J. MacDonald 143
homeopathy 42, 44
Hoover, Herbert 159
Hopei 122
Hopkins, Frederick G. 114

Hopkins, Tony 198
hops 72, 115
hormones 153, 186
Houghton, John
    Collections on Husbandry and Trade 5
Housman, A. E. 51
    A Shropshire Lad 50
Howard, Albert 2, 6, 10, 17–20, 28–30, 39,
    42–4, 49–59, 61–80, 83, 85–95, 98–100,
    103–18, 121, 124–34, 136–7, 139–40,
    142, 144–50, 155, 157–8, 160–2, 165,
    167, 169–71, 174–5, 177–8, 180, 183,
    189–91, 195, 197–203
    An Agricultural Testament 75, 103, 117–18,
        128–9, 180
    Crop Production in India 91
    The Next Step 116
    The Waste Products of Agriculture 91, 100,
        102, 105, 124, 131, 149, 178, 191
    The Wheat of India 72–3
Howard, Anne 51
Howard family 51–2
Howard, Gabrielle (*née* Matthaei) 49, 52, 57,
    59–61, 63, 66–9, 73–4, 80, 85, 87–91,
    93–5, 97, 99, 114, 133
    The Wheat of India 72–3
Howard, Louise E. (*née* Matthaei) 2, 49, 51–2,
    56, 60–1, 67, 75, 77, 80, 85, 89–91,
    93–4, 96–9, 103, 106, 112, 117, 125,
    133, 145, 147–9, 150n.124, 151–5, 157,
    183, 190, 198–203
    Labour in Agriculture 100, 104, 124
    Our Answer to the Land 146
    Studies in Greek Tragedy 95, 101
    The Lover of Nations 95
    The Waste Products of Agriculture 102
Howard, Richard 51
Howard, William Henry 50n.1, 51
Hughes, Lotte 85n.16
Humboldt, Alexander von 7
Hume, Allan Octavian 63
humus 8, 11, 17–18, 41, 74, 77, 92, 108–9,
    126–7, 136n.68, 141
Hungary 72
hunter-gatherers 18, 86, 114, 139
Hunza 79, 86–7, 114–15
Hunza valley 86, 114
husbandry 8, 11, 137, 140, 146, 152
Hutchinson, C. M. 71
Hutchinson, George E. 10n.27
Hutchinson, H. B. 77–8, 203
Huxley, Thomas H. 54
hydraulics 6

immanence 13, 19
imperial
    conservationists 18
    government 137
    holdings 146, 198

masters of India 63
officials 4, 90
outposts 2
power 64
science 64, 133–5, 140, 199
science officers 73
scientists 72, 138
service in India 57
synthesis 64, 75
themes 60
world 43
Imperial Agricultural Bureaux 107
Imperial Agricultural Research Institute
     (IARI) 63–4, 67, 71–3, 75–6, 90, 108
Imperial Chemical Industries (ICI) 120,
     122, 136
Imperial College London 66
Imperial Forest School (India) 63
Imperial Institute 54
imperialism 85
imperialists 15, 80
Imperial Research Institute 62
India 4, 17, 43, 48, 52, 54, 57, 59, 61, 63–7,
     69–76, 79–80, 82, 86–95, 99, 104–9,
     111–15, 119, 121, 125, 128–9, 133–6,
     138, 148n.118, 149–50, 154n.143, 163,
     198, 201
Indian
   agriculture 9, 63, 71, 73, 106
   cattle dung 4
   colleges 65
   cotton seeds 77
   cultivators 99
   culture 67
   economy 74
   farmers 72, 93, 195
   farming 72
   forests 72
   government 63, 70, 77, 139
   heritage 62
   insects 66
   institutions 62
   peasants 71, 79, 87–92, 139
   plantations 34
   servants 67
   soils 71, 73n.67, 87, 92
   tobacco 72
   villages 71
   wheat 65, 72–4
Indiana 168
Indian Central Cotton Committee (ICCC) 76,
     77n.82, 92
Indian Cotton Cess Act 77n.82
Indian Department of Agriculture 63
Indian Empire 63–4, 68, 72–3, 82
Indian Medical Service 114
Indian National Congress 63
Indians 63–4, 66–7, 203
Indian Science Congress 69

Indian Tea Association 92, 108
India-wide Agricultural Education
     Committee 65
individualism 33n.35
Indonesia 180
Indore
   compost 18, 71, 74–5
   conference 94
   research station 72, 75, 99, 105, 108,
     128, 203
Indore Institute of Plant Industry 76–7
Indore Method/Indore Process 18, 29, 69, 71,
     77–80, 88–93, 98–9, 102–6, 109–13,
     115, 117–18, 121, 124–8, 130–2, 137,
     141, 144–7, 150–1, 155, 157, 169, 170,
     174, 183, 191, 200
Indus River 91
industrial
   age 3, 25–6, 134
   agriculture 1, 3, 33, 41, 92, 102, 123–4,
     126, 166, 177, 187, 189, 201–2
   base 29
   capitalism 134
   cartels 118
   change 198
   chemistry 136
   cities 20
   conditions 12
   conflict 130
   country 27
   culture 42
   development 176
   elites 168
   expansion 192
   farming 4, 7, 12, 27, 30, 101, 141, 149,
     152, 158, 181
   fertilizers 4, 109
   gases 194
   landscape 50
   machines 31
   market 175
   modernism 31
   plants 123, 160
   processes 119
   production 123, 200, 203
   progress 122–3
   schemes 161
   society 21, 200
   values 28
industrialism 20–1, 29, 33
industrialists 101, 169
industrialization 2, 20–1, 24, 28–9, 31–5,
     84–5, 102–3, 124, 160, 163–4, 179–80
Industrial Revolution 5–6, 12, 20, 25, 30,
     79, 155
infertility 9, 12, 42, 179
insecticides, *see* pesticides
insects 9, 18, 25, 46, 66, 70, 138, 153, 155,
     171–2, 179, 188

Institute of Public Cleansing 150
Institute of Sewage Purification 148
International Federation of Organic Agriculture
    Movements (IFOAM) 192–3, 195
International Institute of Agriculture 119
International Labour Organization (ILO)
    97–8, 100–1, 103
International Task Force on Harmonization and
    Equivalence in Organic Agriculture 195
Iowa 185
Ireland 56, 135n.65
Isendahl, Christian 4n.2
Islam 81
Italy 22, 30, 35, 99, 119, 146
    Tripartite Pact 176

Jackson, Carlton 170
Jamshedpur 92
Japan 2, 17, 48, 82n.6, 83, 119, 156, 176–82,
    187, 194–5
    Tripartite Pact 176
Japanese 123, 124n.29, 150n.124, 176–7
    agriculture 75
    farming 179
    fascists 84
    food supply 17
    government 177
    house 182
    literature 180
    National Diet 194
    occupation of Oceana 120
    officials 176
    prefectures 194n.39
    settlers in Manchuria 177
Japanese Empire 176
Japan Organic Agriculture Association
    (JOAA) 178n.96, 179–80
Java 70
Jeffersonian ideal 168
Jefferson, Thomas 23
Jenks, Jorian 157
Jersey 151
Jews 26, 46, 158–9, 170
Johannesburg 143
Johnson, G. A. 98
Jones, James 106
Jones, Peter M. 4n.3
Jones, Richard 51
Jorehaut Tea Company 106
journalism/journalists 25, 32n.33, 39, 96, 166
journals/magazines/newsletters/newspapers 6,
    32–3, 37, 49, 77n.84, 104–5, 113, 128,
    130, 132, 140, 145, 147–8, 152, 154,
    160, 174, 184, 190, 193
    Agricultural Journal of India 75
    Albert Howard News Sheet (*AHNS*) 147,
        150–5, 157
    *American Journal of Alternative
        Agriculture* 190n.19
American Scientist 173
Asashi Shimbun 180
Bebauet die Erde 47n.103, 126
British Medical Journal 113
Collier's 184
Farmer's Magazine 8
Farmer's Weekly 130
Forest and Conservation History 15n.35
Forest Quarterly 16
Grass Roots 194
Guild Gardener 139
Health Bulletin 169, 171–2
Health Digest 170
Healthy Life (*Health and Life*) 33
Hindustan Times 148n.118
International Review 96
Journal of Environmental History 15n.35
*Journal of the American Medical
    Association* 184
Journal of the Ministry of Agriculture 77
Journal of the Royal Horticultural Society 137
Kultur und Politik 126
Living Earth 164
Magazine for the Lay Apostle 128
Medical Press 132
Mother Earth 157, 164
Natural History 165
Nature 77, 185
New York Times 175
News-Letter on Compost 128, 145
Organic Farming Digest 134, 136, 139–40
Organic Gardening and Farming
    (*Organic Gardening*) 125, 128, 146–7,
        166, 170–1
*Organic Soil Association of Southern
    Africa* 141–5
Penthouse 174
Policies Studies Journal 189
Prevention 171–2, 189
Quarterly Journal of Agriculture 8
Reader's Digest 164–5
*Revista del Institutode Defensa del Café de
    Costa Rica* 125
Rural Affairs 8
Saturday Review of Literature 174
Soil and Health (*Health and the Soil*) 146–7
The Farmer 129
The Observer 160
The Times 104, 152, 160
*The Times Trade and Engineering
    Supplement* 73
Time 44, 166, 174
Tropical Planter 105
Vegetarian News 128
Veld Trust News 141
Washington Post 184–5, 190
Judaism 81
Jukes, Thomas H. 185
Junkers 6

Kaisar-i-Hind award 67–8, 114
Kansas State College 164
Karakorum Mountains 86
Karoo 141
Kashmir 72
Kent 58–9
Kentish farmers 59
Kenya 99, 104, 149
Kerr, Charles 156
Kerr, John 113
Keynesian analyses 161
Keynes, John Maynard 160
Keyserlingk, Count 40
Kharin, N. 4n.4
Khrushchev, Nikita 152
Kiangsu 122
King, Franklin H. 17n.42, 84
    Farmers of Forty Centuries 83, 91
Kinship in Husbandry 35–6, 39n.63
Kipling, Rudyard 82
    The Jungle Book 11
Kirchmann, Holger 41n.74
Kirkconnel 151
Kirkham, Ellinor 124–5
Klein, Maximilian 46
Könemann, Ewald 127
    Bodenkultur and Düngewirtschaft 126
Kongo Mountains 180
Koo, Wellington 124
Korea 17n.42, 186, 195
Kruger, Frederick 137n.71
Kumar, Deepar 62
Kurosawa, Torizō 176
    *National Policy on Strong Soil and Livestock
    Machine Agriculture* 177
Kwangtung 122
Kyoto University 180

Lake Geneva 97
Lake Ngami 143
lamb 31, 196
Latin America 57, 101n.30, 119, 121,
    192, 195
Laurino, Marcelo 197
Lawes, John B. 8, 136
Law of Return 9, 16, 65, 87, 128n.42,
    137, 202
League of Nations 14, 97–8
Leatherhead 150
Leather, John W. 9
lectures 7, 40–2, 54, 56–8, 60, 77n.84, 82,
    86n.19, 88, 104, 109, 114, 124, 128–9,
    138n.78, 198, *see also* films/radio
legumes 5, 188
Leopold, Aldo 168
    Sand Country Almanac 169
Liebig era 10–11, 136
Liebig, Justus von 7–8, 46n.94, 101,
    136n.68

*Organic Chemistry in its Application to
    Agriculture and Physiology* 7
Liebig system 138
life expectancy 30, 31n.30
lime 7, 10n.27
limes 58
Linlithgow, Lord 76, 114
linseed 74
Liu, Jung-Chao 123n.26
livestock 3, 179, 188, 191, 193
Livingstone, David 143
Livy 22
Lloyd George, David 113
Lockeretz, William 85n.16
Lohnis, Felix 126
London 26, 54–5, 59–60, 62, 67, 96–7, 132,
    154, 158
London University 58
London Vegetarian Society 128–9
Long, Huey 170
Long Island 173
Louisiana 153
Lovejoy, Arthur O. 12–13, 24
Lowe and Shawyer 108
Lucas, Adam 6n.8
Lymington, Viscount, *see* Wallop

Macarthur, Douglas 178
Macleod, Roy 63n.7
Madden, J. Patrick 1n.1
Madras 105, 112
Madupatty 110
magazines, *see* journals/magazines/newsletters/
    newspapers
Maine 188
Malaya 34
malnutrition/starvation 12, 113, 132, 186
Manchester 61, 146, 165
Manchester City Council 146
Manchuria 176–7
Manchurian war lords 84
Mann, Harold H. 108
manure/manuring, *see* fertilizers
Manyo poets 180
Mao Zedong 152
Maravanyika, Simeon 131
Margolius, Sidney 184
marling 5
Marsh, George Perkins
    Man and Nature 11
Martin-Leake, Hugh 90, 149, 154
Marxism 20–1, 161
Marxists 21, 83, 132
Marx, Karl 83, 159
mass media 21, 32, 120, 155, 162
Massingham, H. J. 35n.43
    English Downland 39
    The Wisdom of the Fields 39
Matthaei, Ernst 60

Matthaei family 60–1
Matthaei, Gabrielle, *see* Howard
Matthaei, Louise, *see* Howard
Matthaei, Marie 60, 68, 94
Maxwell-Lefroy, Harold 66
Mayas 4n.2
Mayo, Lord (Richard Bourke) 63
McCarrison, Robert 79, 83, 86, 113–15, 118,
    134, 135n.64, 138–9, 158–60
McKell, William John 134
McKeown, Thomas 31n.30
McKibbin, R. L. 143
meat 3, 31–2, 53, 114, 153, 166, 178, 188
mechanization 3, 32, 103, 123, 136, 176, 178
Mediterranean 17
Meiji, Emperor 176
Melbourne 194
Men of the Trees 163
methane 154
Mexico 76
microorganisms 3, 13, 57, 148n.120, 150–1,
    see also bacteria
Middle East 80, 107, 119, 125
Middle Eastern farmers 4
Midlothian County Council 151n.127
Miley, George 44
Millardet, Pierre Alexis 56n.25
Miller, Nancy Anne 77n.83
Milton, John
    Paradise Lost 12
Minamata disease 179
minerals 3, 11, 18, 74, 104, 149, 154, 167, 188
mining 8, 92, 137, 138n.80, 149, 154, 177
Minnesota Conservation Service 187
Minto, Lord 65
Mississippi 153
Mockern research station 8
modernism 29, 31, 37, 86, 194, 200
modernity 1, 71
modernization 5n.5, 83, 102–3, 107, 121, 163,
    178–9, 186
Mongols 4, 15, 84
Monsanto Company 165
Mont Blanc 97
Montealegre, Mariano 125
Moon, David 15nn.36–8
Mordialloc Creek 194
morphine 7
mortality 30–1
Mosely, Oswald 39
mountains 46, 86, 111, 114, 180
Mountbatten, Lord Louis 139
movies, *see* films/radio
Mowbray, J. M. 146
Müller, Hans 126–7
municipal
    composting 147–51, 200
    sewage/waste 121, 126–7, 130, 148
Murphy, Richard 173

Muslims 86
mycorrhizal process 18, 57, 75, 104, 106n.49,
    138, 150
mystical
    beliefs 157, 161
    connection to nature 39
    connection to the land 30
    East 82, 84
    formulations 40
    halo 81
    home 37
    ideas 43, 157, 161
    ingredients 127
    nationalism 45
    pantheism 162
    preparations 44
    protocols 41
    rites 42
    sense 34
    statement 19
    world 24
mysticism 19, 40, 42, 44, 80, 82, 85n.14, 89,
    116, 127, 147, 157
myths 2–3, 41, 80–1, 83–4, 86–7, 89, 91, 93,
    129, 161, 165, 185, 200

Nagoya 178
Nagrakata Club 109
Namibia 141
Napoleon III 83
Napoleon Bonaparte 26
Napoleonic
    occupation 82
    reforms 82
Napoleonic Wars 6, 26
National Farmers Union of England and
    Wales 153
nationalism 43, 45, 99n.25
natural processes 2, 9, 16, 85, 101, 155, 200
Nature et Progres 192
Nazis 132, 159
Needham, A. S. 136
neo-traditionalism 3, 36–7, 103–4, 113
Nesbit, John Collis 11n.27
Nestlé 31
Netherlands 146
New Delhi 148n.118
New Jersey 159
Newman, John Henry 20n.2
New Mexico 168
newsletters, *see* journals/magazines/newsletters/
    newspapers
New South Wales 134, 138
newspapers, *see* journals/magazines/newsletters/
    newspapers
New York 125, 169–70, 180
New Zealand 15, 17, 31, 120, 138, 143, 146,
    193, 198
    Humic Compost Club 125

Nichiro fishery company 177
Nichols, Edward L. 16
Nicholson, F. A. 75
nicotine 9
Nigeria 149, 198
Nile River 3
nitrates 8, 42, 47, 110, 119–20, 123, 186
nitrogen 5, 78, 92–3, 111, 119–20, 123,
    126n.36, 128, 135, 136n.68, 150
    fertilizers 7, 74, 92, 109, 119, 121, 123, 135
Nixon, Richard 185–6
noble savage 86
Nordic 24
Normans 50
Norris, Roland V. 110
North America 2, 15, 17, 23, 29, 43, 47–8, 74,
    102, 121, 125, 140, 146, 152, 160, 169,
    186, 191, 195–6, *see also* American,
    Americans, United States
North American Newspaper Alliance 184
North Carolina 153
nudism 34, 45
nutrients 3–4, 7–9, 11, 16, 18, 41–3, 63,
    65n.14, 69, 72–4, 79, 83, 87, 92, 115,
    118, 135, 141, 146, 150, 167, 176,
    188, 196
nutrition 10, 34, 41, 46–7, 71, 113, 115–16,
    126, 128, 132, 134, 136–9, 141, 144,
    150–1, 165, 167, 185, 193
nuts 58, 166
Nyasaland (Malawi) 36

occultism 39, 45
Ogg, William 136, 144
Ohio 165n.47, 168
oil 154, 163
oil seeds 72, 93
Olcott, Henry Steel 40
Oodlabari Tea Estate 108
opium 72
oranges 58
Order of the Indian Empire 68n.41
Oregon 188
organic
    certification 186, 193, 195
    chemistry 7
    compounds 7
    farming movement 1–2, 9, 13–14, 16–17,
        23, 28–30, 34, 37, 39, 45, 47, 49, 57, 76,
        78, 80, 83, 86–8, 100, 103–4, 115,
        117–18, 125, 127–8, 132–3, 136, 140,
        147, 151, 154–5, 158, 161, 163, 165,
        167, 169–73, 175, 182, 185, 187–8,
        191–2, 195, 197, 200–1, 203
    protocols 30, 44, 80, 85n.16, 86, 91, 144,
        157, 182, 193
organicism 26n.18
Organic Soil Association of Southern Africa
    (OSASA) 143–5

Organic Trade Association 191
organophosphates 9
orientalism 2, 76, 80–3, 163
Orissa 92
Orr, Sir John Boyd 132, 140
Osaka 178
Owen, Robert 20n.2
Oxford University 39, 158, 169
Oxford University Press 100, 105

Pacific 15, 125
Pacific Organic Standard 195
pagans 24, 37
Pakistan 86
Palmer, E. M. 125n.31
Panama 195
pantheism 24, 45, 162
parasites 56, 70
Paris 23, 155, 162, 168
Paris Peace Conference 101
Park Tea Estate 111
Pasteur Institute of India 114
Pasteur, Louis 154
Pathans 114
Patterson, Sir John 150n.124
Paull, John 134n.62, 173–4
Pearce, Roy H. 85n.16
Pearson, Alfred 135
peasantry/peasants 3, 15n.36, 20–2, 30, 41,
    46n.94, 48, 67, 71, 75, 79, 80, 82–93, 98,
    101–4, 116, 124, 126–7, 129, 139, 152,
    160–1, 163, 176, 200
Peisistratus 22
Pennsylvania 170
Perkin, Harold 24, 33n.35, 55
Persia 17, 142
pesticides 1, 8–9, 41, 56n.25, 65, 70–1, 73, 76,
    86, 91–3, 103, 105, 110, 112, 152–3,
    155, 165, 171–2, 174, 176, 180–1, 184,
    186–9, 196, 201–3
pests 9, 66, 70, 155, 188, 201
petroleum products 8
Pfeiffer, Ehrenfried 39, 43
    Bio-Dynamic Farming and Gardening 44
Phipps Laboratory 75
Phipps, Mr 63
phosphoric acid 123
phosphorous 8, 109, 135
physics 6, 13
physiocrats 23
Picton, Lionel J. 113, 115, 124, 128, 145,
    148n.120, 160
    Thoughts on Feeding 139
Pinchot, Gifford 168
Pinnell, L. G. 106
plants 3, 7–8, 11, 13, 16–18, 25, 37, 41, 56–7,
    59, 65n.14, 70, 93, 106, 108, 112, 115,
    120, 139, 141–2, 144, 150–1, 154, 161,
    171, 194, 198–200

poldering 5
Pole-Evans, Illtyd Buller 130
pollution 20, 34, 37, 154, 156–7, 172, 174–5,
    177, 179–81, 186–7, 200
Port Arthur 123
Portland, Duke of 11
Portsmouth, Earl of, *see* Wallop
Portugal 98
Portuguese Empire 12
Portuguese explorers 87
potash 50, 59, 110, 119–20, 123, 136, 150
potassium 8, 109, 135
potatoes 52, 56, 69, 114, 166, 185
Powderhall 151n.127
predators 70, 153
Prees Heath 159
pre-modern
    farming methods 173
    order 161
    society 162
    wisdom 80
Prevost, Isaac-Benedict 9
Price, Weston 139
propaganda 27, 35, 43, 95, 123n.26, 137, 203
Protestant
    churches 33
    divines 25
Prussia 6, 45
Pusa 54, 62–8, 70–7, 91, 108
Pusa 12 73–4
Pusa Institute 76

Quebec 119
Queensland 194
Quetta 72

radio, *see* films/radio
rain 3–5, 14–15, 17, 33, 62, 110–11, 141–3
rationalism 12n.31, 19
Ray, John 5
Rayner, Dr 106n.49, 139
Reagan, Ronald 189
realism 12, 19, 152
recycling 9, 14, 16, 46n.94, 65n.14, 115,
    127, 200
Red Gum 154n.143
reductionism 13
reforestation 142, 152
Reform Act 27
refrigeration 31, 180
reincarnation 43, 164
Rensburg, C. J. J. van 125n.31
reservoirs 152
Reynolds-Stephens, Sir William 61
Rhodes, Cecil 130
Rhodesia 99, 130–2, 146
    Natural Resources Act 129–30
    Natural Resources Board 131
ribbon development 38

rice 73, 122, 178–9, 181
Richards, E. H. 77–8, 203
Richards, Mary T. 173–4
Richards, Mr 109–10
Riddell, Walter A. 97, 101
Rimini 99–100
River Dee 34
rivers/streams 1, 3–4, 14, 16–17, 34, 63–4,
    106, 151–2
Robertson, T. C. 143
Rochdale Pioneers Cooperative 182
Rodale, Jerome I. 87n.22, 125, 128, 146, 157,
    165–75, 177–8, 189
    Organic Merry-Go-Round 175
    Pay Dirt 125, 171, 177, 180
Rodale Press 174, 187, 191–2
Rodale, Robert 192
Roerich Peace Pact 85n.14
Roman
    period 21
    populace 21
    Republic 22
    ruins 99
    senate 22
    society 4, 22
    writers 22
romantic
    farm enthusiasts 28–9, 40
    farm literature 9, 20, 25–6, 28–30, 33, 39,
        47–8, 71, 82–3, 86, 99, 103, 113, 117,
        159, 170, 194
Romantic Era 20n.2, 24
romanticism 2–3, 12–13, 19–21, 45, 47–8, 51,
    67, 80, 83–4, 89, 117, 127
Romantic Movement 11, 14, 24
Rome 4, 22, 37, 119, 158
Roosevelt, Franklin D. 84, 85n.14, 87, 119,
    158–9, 167
Roosevelt, Teddy 186
Rothamsted research station 8, 42, 52, 58–9,
    77–8, 92, 101, 105, 110, 136, 137n.71,
    138, 198, 202–3
Rothschild, Lord 133
Rousseau, Jean-Jacques 23, 86
Rowbotham, Judith 31
Royal Agricultural Society 9
Royal Asiatic Society of Bengal 67
Royal College of Physicians 114
Royal College of Science (RCS) 54–7
Royal Indian Engineering College 57
Royal Institute of International Affairs 101
Royal Society 5–6, 104
Royal Society of Arts 69, 154
Rubin, Louis 28
Rudolph, Walter 47n.103
rural
    areas 20, 28–9, 32, 47, 163, 170
    communities 122
    culture 36, 38

development 102–3, 163
economy 48, 163
existence 194
family doctors 113
homesteads 28
knowledge 33
life/living 3, 21, 24, 26, 29, 35, 37, 39, 71,
    84, 168, 176
merchants 36
order 25
reconstructionists 37
representation 101
romanticism 2, 20, 84
values 21, 32, 35, 39, 144, 198
villages 132
workers 99
ruralism 45, 126, 163
Rural Water Supply and Sewage Act 151
Ruskin, John 20n.2
Russell, E. John 8n.19
Russia 6, 15, 29, 36, 97, 123, 152, *see also*
    Soviet Union
Russian Empire 15
Rutgers University 165, 177

Sahara 142, 157
Said, Edward 81
Sale Frazer Company 177
Salisbury, D. J. 137
saltpeter 74
Sanatogen 133
Sandy, Cleve E. 152
São Paulo 197
Saracenic architecture 64
Sarah Lawrence College 180
Saxon, Edgar J. 33–4
Saxony 8
Scarborough 150–1
Scharff, J. W. 124, 150n.124
Schumacher, Edith 161
Schumacher, Ernst F. 158–4, 174–5
    Small is Beautiful 158, 160–3
Schwartz, Prof 143
Scotland 5–6, 38, 151
seaweed 5
secularization 12–13, 33
Seeley, Sir John
    The Expansion of England 198
sewage 4, 130, 146, 147n.118, 148–51, 200
Shambhala valley 87
Shamshernagar Tea Estate 109
Shanghai 84
Shangri-La 87, 127
Shantung 122
Shearer, E. 75
sheep 4–5, 152–3
Shintoism 81
Showra Denko chemical company 179
Shropshire 49–51, 59, 159, 197

Sicily 8
Sikhs 114–15
silt/silting 3, 106
Simon, Eugene 46
Singapore 124, 150n.124
slash and burn 4
Sly, F. G. 65
Smith, Michael E. 4n.2
Smith, Sherry L. 85n.16
Smuts, Jan C. 142, 173
    Holism and Evolution 14
Snow Brand Milk Products 176
socialism 3, 20–1, 55, 83, 160–1
Society of Chemical Industry 144
Soil and Health Foundation 167
soils 5, 7, 18, 41–2, 71–2, 92, 95, 119, 135,
    144–5, 167, 169, 196, 202
Solon 21
South Africa 14–15, 74, 99, 104, 120, 125,
    130, 141, 145–6, 152, 156, 192–3, 195,
    198–9
    Conservation Districts 144
    Department of Agriculture 144
    Drought Investigation Commission 141, 143
    Extension Areas 144
    Native Economic Commission 141
South African Association for the Advancement
    of Science 142
South Carolina 153
Southern Agrarianism 28–9, 38
South Pole 154
Soviet Union 35, 43, 84, 87, 119, 121, 152,
    176, 186, *see also* Russia
Spain 193
Spanish Empire 12
Spice Islands 34
Spock, Marjorie 173–4
spraying 152–3, 173
Springhead Ring 36
St Barbe Baker, Richard 33, 163
Staffordshire 50
Stalin, Joseph 15n.37, 21
Stanford University 175
Stapledon, Sir George 135n.64
    The Land: Now and To-morrow 38
Stebbing, E. P. 142
Steiner, Rudolf 39–45, 84, 116, 127, 147, 157,
    174, 181–2
Steppes 15–16
Stevens, Sir Harold 106
Stoughton, Prof 150
Strachey, Evelyn 132
straw 77–8, 151, 181, 194
Stroel, Kate 153
suburbs 20, 28, 33, 38–9, 67, 182
Suez 71, 123
sugar 7, 31–2, 34, 57–8, 70, 114, 129, 175
sulfur 8–9, 121
sulfuric acid 8, 10, 52

Surrey 150, 160
Swedish Biodynamic Association 192
Swiss Farmer's Movement for a Native Rural
	Culture 126
Switzerland 61, 102, 126–7, 187, 193
Sydney 134
Sykes, F. 137
Sylhet 105–6

Tagore, Rabindranath 82
Taiwan 122
Tanaka, Shōzō 177
Tansley, Arthur G. 169, 173
tariffs 102–3
Tarkington, Booth 168
Tata Iron and Steel Company 91–2
tea 34, 44, 52–3, 72, 97, 105, 114, 122, 137
	bushes/shrubs 18, 108, 111
	companies/corporations 105, 109
	estates 105, 108–12
	gardens 104
	growers 110
	industry 107–8
	plantations 18, 105, 110, 112, 137
	plants 18
	production 110
	roots 106
	traders 108
Tea Research Institute 110
teikei 179, 180, 182
Teller, Walter
	Roots in the Earth 168
Tennessee Valley Authority 8n.19
Texas 153, 175, 191–2
Theosophical Society 40
theosophy 40, 42–3, 84
Theravada system 81
Thompson, E. P. 25n.16
Thompson, F. M. L. 10n.27
Thoreau, Henry David 11, 14, 82
Throckmorton, R. I. 164–5
timber 15, 18, 62
tobacco 72, 74
Tocklai research station 105–9
Tocklai River 106
Tokyo 178–9, 182
Tolkien, J. R. R. 51
	The Hobbit 50
	The Lord of the Rings 50
transcendentalism 13–14, 82
transportation 20, 31–2, 119, 121–2
trees 11, 14, 16–18, 33, 36, 46, 70, 122, 134,
	141, 152
Treiterl, Corinna 46
Trinidad 58n.31, 150n.126
Tristan da Cunha 114
Truog, Emil 165
Tukojirao Holkar III, Maharaja 77
turnips 5

Uekötter, Frank 5n.5
Underwood 31
Union Club 158
United Nations (UN) 119, 122, 163, 195
	Conference on Trade and Development
		(UNCTAD) 195
	Food and Agricultural Organization
		(FAO) 103, 118–23, 132, 140, 152,
		187, 195
United Potash Company 136
United States 7, 15, 167, 173–4, 192
	Better Business Bureau 166
	Bureau of Soils 16, 83
	Conservation Reserve Program 190n.21
	Conservation Service 187
	Department of Agriculture (USDA) 8n.19,
		16, 83, 85n.15, 153, 155, 175, 185, 187–91
	Endangered Species Act 185
	Environmental Protection Agency 185
	Federal Reserve 170
	Food and Drug Act 172
	Food and Drug Administration 166
	Forest Service 168
	House Select Committee to Investigate the
		Use of Chemicals in Foods and
		Cosmetics 172
	Institute for Alternative Agriculture 190
	Internal Revenue Service 169
	National Agricultural Library 188
	National Environmental Protection Act 185
	National Organic Standards Board 85n.15
	National Organic Standards Program 191
	Organic Foods Production Act 191
	Senate 170
	Soil Conservation Service 144
	Study Team on Organic Farming 187
	United Farm Workers Organizing
		Committee 169
	see also American, Americans, North America
University College London 110
University of Berlin 36, 158
University of Bristol 150–1
University of California 185
University of Hawaii 180
University of Illinois 82
University of Kansas 169
University of Leipzig 126n.36
University of Missouri 167
University of Nanking 122
University of Paris 161–2
University of Reading 150–1
University of Strasbourg 56
University of Texas 175
University of Wisconsin 17n.42, 83, 165, 168
Untermöhlen, Karl 46
Uozumi, Michio 194
urban
	areas 4n.2, 9, 23, 32, 126, 178, 182
	composting 130

consumers 83, 182, 202
councils 146
culture 29
dwellers 25, 31
elite 21
environmentalists 203
environments 162
life/living 29, 32
planning 33
polities 101
poor 26
populations 6, 38
romanticism 47
society 20, 83
wastes 46, 84, 147, 149
Urbana 82
urbanization 20, 29, 32–3, 121

vaccines 153
Vaillant, François le 142
vegetable matter 77–8, 87, 104, 111, 115, 132, 147, 149–50
vegetables 4, 31–2, 44, 50, 53, 70, 76, 79, 114, 147, 149, 160–1, 166, 169, 174, 178–9
vegetarianism 45, 127
Versailles 192
Versailles Treaty 97, 101, 158
Victoria (Australia) 194
Victorian age 14, 30, 31n.29–30
Victorian Department of Agriculture 135
Victorians 31, 50
Victoria, Queen 60, 67–8
Victor Immanuel, King 119
Vietnam 186
Virgil
    Eclogues 22
    Georgics 4
vitalism 7, 13, 31, 34, 76, 114, 165–6
Voelcker, Augustus 63

Wad, Yeshwant D. 92, 149
    The Waste Products of Agriculture 91, 100, 102, 105, 124, 131, 149, 178, 191
Waggaman, William H. 8n.19
Waldorf School 40
Wales 38, 107, 115, 153
Wallace, D. 190n.19
Wallace Foundation 190n.19
Wallace, G. 190n.19
Wallace, Henry A. 84, 85n.14, 167
Waller, Robert 157
Wallop, Gerard Vernon (Earl of Portsmouth, Viscount Lymington) 35–6, 43, 135n.64
    Alternative to Death 34, 137
Ward, H. Marshall 56–7, 130–1
Warde, Paule 4n.2
Waring, P. Alston
    Roots in the Earth 168

Warren, Robert Penn
    I'll Take My Stand 28–9
Warwickshire 50
Washington 169
Washington University 175
water 1, 5, 14–16, 34, 42, 44, 46, 76, 82, 106, 109–11, 114, 119, 141, 143, 151, 153–4, 156, 179–80, 186, 200, 202
water hyacinth 106, 148
Watson, E. F. 115
weather 11, 14, 27, 53, 167, *see also* climate
Webb, Beatrice 97
Webb, Sydney 97
Weimar Republic 43, 47
Wellington College 52, 54
Wells, H. G. 55–6
    Love and Mr. Lewisham 54
West Indies 34, 57, 70, 125, 137
    Imperial College of Tropical Agriculture 58n.31, 150n.126
    Imperial Department of Agriculture 57, 58, 77n.84
    West Indian Agricultural College 58n.31
    West Indian Royal Commission 58
wheat 4, 9, 15, 34, 42, 47, 65, 72–4, 76, 84, 91, 107, 114, 122, 128, 130, 135, 137, 166, 185, 187
White, Gilbert 39
    Natural History of Selborne 25, 37
White, H. F. 134
Whitman, Walt 14
whole foods 33, 153
Whole Foods 191–2
Wilderness Society 168
wildlife 145, 153, 156–7, 168–9, 171–2, 175, 194, 200, 202
Williams, Michael 135
William the Conqueror 22
Wilson, R. G. M. 115
Wisconsin 169
Wodicks, Virgil O. 185
Wood, Barbara 158
Woolf, Leonard 96
Woolfolk Chemical Works 165
Woolf, Virginia 96–7
Woolton, Lord 132
Wordsworth, William 26
World Bank 103
World Trade Organization 97n.21
World War One 3, 9, 35, 37, 47, 53, 61, 82, 107, 128, 135, 158, 170
World War Two 2, 9, 28, 35–6, 45, 60, 107n.53, 118–20, 126–7, 134–5, 140, 142, 150, 154, 156, 163, 168, 176, 180, 182, 194, 199, 201
Worster, Donald 25n.14
Wrekin 50, 53
Wrench, G. T. 83, 86–7, 134, 135n.64
    Reconstruction by Way of the Soil 138

Wye 58–9
Wye College 58–9, 101
Wylie, J. C. 150

Yale University 165
  Beinecke Rare Book and Manuscript
    Library 173
Yanase, Giryo 180
  Revolution for Organic Farming 181
Yates, Arthur 138
Yellow River 17, 152

yeomen 6, 27–8, 55
  farmers 6, 22, 25, 28, 162
  independence 2, 113
  lifestyle 51
  tradition of farming 27
Yokohama 177, 181
Youngberg, Garth 188–90, 202
Young Farmer's Coalition 116
youth movements 37, 45

Zen Buddhism 81